Paradoxes of Time Travel

D0732904

Ryan Wasserman is Professor of Philosophy at Western Washington University. He is the co-editor of *Metametaphysics* (OUP 2009) and the author of various papers in metaphysics, ethics, and the philosophy of language.

Praise for *Paradoxes of Time Travel*

'Besides being fascinating and extremely readable, this commendable volume is currently unique. No other full-length philosophy book about time travel exists, despite decades of time travel fiction, science and philosophy. There are some astonishing finds herein, which even specialists will find new but henceforth essential.... The book is very wel-organized and should shape its chosen field for years hence.... The whole volume can be recommended without reservation to students and professionals alike.'

Alasdair Richmond, Analysis

'Wasserman's book fills a gap in the academic literature on time travel.... as far as I know, this is the first book length work devoted to the topic of time travel by a metaphysician homed in on the most important metaphysical issues. Wasserman addresses these issues while still managing to include pertinent scientific discussion and enjoyable time-travel snippets from science fiction. The book is well organized and is suitable for good undergraduate metaphysics students, for philosophy graduate students, and for professional philosophers. It reads like a sophisticated and excellent textbook even though it includes many novel ideas.'

John W. Carroll, Notre Dame Philosophical Reviews

Paradoxes of
Time Travel

Ryan Wasserman

OXFORD
UNIVERSITY PRESS

OXFORD
UNIVERSITY PRESS

Great Clarendon Street, Oxford, OX2 6DP,
United Kingdom

Oxford University Press is a department of the University of Oxford.
It furthers the University's objective of excellence in research, scholarship,
and education by publishing worldwide. Oxford is a registered trade mark of
Oxford University Press in the UK and in certain other countries

© Ryan Wasserman 2018

The moral rights of the author have been asserted

First published 2018
First published in paperback 2020

Published in the United States of America by Oxford University Press
198 Madison Avenue, New York, NY 10016, United States of America

British Library Cataloguing in Publication Data
Data available

Library of Congress Cataloging in Publication Data
Data available

ISBN 978-0-19-879333-5 (Hbk.)
ISBN 978-0-19-886520-9 (Pbk.)

To Ben and Zoë
May you always be filled with wonder

Contents

Preface

One cannot help but wonder.

—H. G. Wells, *The Time Machine*

In the fall of 2005, I taught my very first introductory philosophy course. That course included a unit on freedom and determinism and I decided to conclude that section by spending a day on the grandfather paradox. That meeting ended up being so much fun that I added two extra days on the topic the next time I taught the class. Among other things, we discussed David Lewis's definition of time travel, Robert Heinlein's tales of causal loops, and Doc Brown's explanation of branching timelines from the *Back to the Future* movies. Student feedback on these topics was so positive that I eventually expanded the material into an entire course on time travel. The notes from that course went on to provide the basis of the book that you now hold.

This book retains many features of my original classroom lectures. I have tried my best to introduce all of the topics in an entertaining way, and to provide as much background material as is required. I have also included many of the examples and illustrations that have proven helpful in class. My hope is that the resulting work is accessible to all students of philosophy, and that teachers will find the text useful in their own philosophy courses. I would like to thank all of the students who have discussed these topics with me over the years—your feedback has helped me to improve this work in many different ways. I am especially grateful to three current students: Trevan Strean, who helped with the illustrations, Dee Payton, who worked on the index, and Sean Nalty, who did proofreading. I would also like to thank Western Washington University for providing me with a teaching sabbatical and research support.

Another prominent feature of this book is its heavy use of examples from the science fiction genre. As will become clear, almost all of the philosophical issues raised by time travel have their roots in science fiction, and I have done my best to trace out the history of these ideas. I have been greatly aided in this task by Paul J. Nahin's excellent book *Time Machines: Time Travel in Physics, Metaphysics, and Science Fiction*, and Michael Main's comprehensive website <http://www.storypilot.com/>. Both of these works have provided me with endless examples and inspiration. I am also very grateful to the library staff at Western Washington University who helped me track down some truly obscure publications. My hope is that this research will help make this book of interest to science fiction fans, as well as philosophers.

Still, the main audience for this book will be professional philosophers—especially those with research interests in contemporary analytic metaphysics. Philosophers in this area will already be aware of some of the important issues raised by time travel—issues having to do with the nature of time, freedom, causation, and identity. However, philosophers in this area also know that, until this point, there has been no comprehensive study of these topics. That is the primary goal of this book—to survey, systematize, and expand upon the philosophical literature on time travel. I would like to thank all of the philosophers who have helped me in this task by providing comments on earlier drafts of this work. This includes Thomas Hall, Dan Howard-Snyder, Frances Howard-Snyder, Hud Hudson, David Manley, Ned Markosian, Gerald Marsch, Tim Maudlin, Jeff Russell, Michelle Saint, Neal Tognazzini, James Van Cleve, and two anonymous readers for Oxford University Press. I would also like to thank Andreas Riemann, who proofread the material on special relativity, and Jonathan Bennett and Steffi Lewis, who provided me with unpublished materials relating to David Lewis's work on time travel. Finally, I gratefully acknowledge Springer, Wiley, Oxford University Press, Cambridge University Press, and Hud Hudson for giving me permission to include portions of the following works in this book: "Van Inwagen on Time Travel and Changing the Past," in Dean Zimmerman, ed., *Oxford Studies in Metaphysics, Volume 5* (Oxford: Oxford University Press, 2010); "Personal Identity, Indeterminacy, and Obligation," in Georg Gasser and Matthias Stefan, eds., *Personal Identity: Simple or Complex?* (Cambridge: Cambridge University Press, 2013); "Theories of Persistence," *Philosophical Studies*, 173 (2016): 243–50; and "Vagueness and the Laws of Metaphysics," *Philosophy and Phenomenological Research*, 95 (2017): 66–89.

Lastly, and most importantly, I would like to thank my family—Christine, Ben, and Zoë. You have been a constant source of encouragement, support, and perspective throughout this process. I couldn't have done it without you.

1

Introduction

"It's against reason," said Filby.

"What reason?" said the Time Traveller.

—H. G. Wells, *The Time Machine*

In the spring of 1927, Hugo Gernsback published a version of *The Time Machine* in his fledgling science fiction magazine, *Amazing Stories*.[1] The story was an immediate hit with readers, and generated a steady stream of letters.[2] Some of these responses were filled with praise, while others took a more critical tone. Reader Jackson Beck, for example, complained that there was "something amiss" in *The Time Machine*, for "How could one travel to the future in a machine when the beings of the future have not yet materialized?" (Gernsback 1927: 412). Another reader, identified as "T.J.D." from Cleveland, wrote in with a much longer list of complaints:

How about this "Time Machine"? Let's suppose our inventor starts a "Time voyage" backward to about A.D. 1900, at which time he was a schoolboy... [Suppose] he stops the machine, gets out and attends the graduating exercises of the class of 1900 of which he was a member. Will there be another "he" on the stage[?] Of course, because he *did* graduate in 1900. Interesting thought. Should he go up and shake hands with this "alter ego"[?] Will there be two physically distinct but characteristically identical persons? Alas! No! He can't go up and shake hands with himself because you see this voyage back through time only duplicates actual past conditions and in 1900 this stranger "other he" did not appear suddenly in quaint ultra-new fashions and congratulate the graduate. How could they both be wearing the same watch they got from Aunt Lucy on their seventh birthday, the same watch in two different places at the same time[?] Boy! Page Einstein!... [Also] The journey backward must cease on the year of his birth. If he could pass *that* year it would certainly be an effect going before a cause...

---

[1] Launched in 1926, *Amazing Stories* is widely recognized as the first science fiction magazine. Gernsback, who founded the publication, is often cited as one of the fathers of science fiction.

[2] *The Time Machine* deserves credit for sparking the popular fascination with time travel, but it was not the first publication on the topic (*contra* Calvert 2002: 2, Gleick 2016: 5, and many others). Published in 1895, Wells's novella was preceded by at least twenty other time travel stories, including Samuel Madden's *Memoirs of the Twentieth Century* (1733), Edward Page Mitchell's "The Clock that Went Backwards" (1881), and Wells's own 1888 story "The Chronic Argonauts" (reprinted in Wells 2009). Indeed, the concept of time travel arguably goes back to ancient tales like the Hindu story of King Kakudmi, the Chinese legend of Ranka, and the Japanese tale of Urashima Taro. For an excellent overview of the pre-Wellsian literature, see Main (2008).

[Finally] Suppose for instance in the graduating exercise above, the inventor should decide to shoot his former self, the graduate[;] he couldn't do it because if he did the inventor would have been cut off before he began to invent and he would never have gotten around to making the voyage, thus rendering it impossible for him to be there taking a shot at himself, so that as a matter of fact he *would* be there and *could* take a shot—help, help, I'm on a vicious circle merry-go-round!   (1927: 410)

Gernsback would go on to publish many more letters on the topic of time travel,[3] but these first few examples are particularly noteworthy since they represent some of the very first publications on the paradoxes of time travel.[4] These paradoxes would prove to be a favorite topic in early science fiction forums,[5] and would go on to be the source of much debate in physics, philosophy, and popular culture.[6] Among other things, it has been argued that the paradoxes of time travel have important implications for how we think about time, tense, ontology, causation, chance, counterfactuals, laws of nature, explanation, freedom, fatalism, moral responsibility, persistence, change, and mereology. These are just a few of the topics to be addressed in this book.

In this chapter, we will clarify the concept of time travel (sections 1 and 2), introduce the main question of the book (section 3), and preview the paradoxes to come (section 4).

1. Time Travel

Time travel obviously involves traveling to other times. But what exactly does this mean? Talk of "travel" suggests a kind of movement, but movement is a matter of being

---

[3] The early relationship between science fiction writers and readers was a symbiotic one—new stories would generate objections from readers and those objections would often lead to new ideas for stories. One of the best examples of this is Mort Weisinger's "Thompson's Time Traveling Theory" (1944) in which a science fiction author, frustrated by the skeptical response to his time travel stories, builds a working time machine in order to prove its possibility to his readers. (As the author tells his editor: "*I'm going into the past and kill my grandfather!* Then we'll see just how hot you and your readers are!")

[4] The very first discussion of a time travel paradox I am aware of is in Enrique Gaspar's *The Time Ship: A Chrononautical Journey* (originally published in 1887). In Gaspar's story, two "time trekkers" set out for the past and, along the way, discuss the possible implications of their journey:

> "Since we are bound for yesterday and will arrive in the past bearing the experience of History, wouldn't we be able to change the human condition by avoiding the catastrophes that have caused so much turmoil in society?"
> ... "Not in in the slightest. We may be present to witness facts consummated in preceding centuries, but we may never undo their existence. To put it more clearly: we may unwrap time, but we don't know how to nullify it. If today is a consequence of yesterday and we are living examples of the present, we cannot, unless we destroy ourselves, wipe out a cause of which we are its actual effects."   (1887/2012: 59)

This, of course, is a variation on the famous grandfather paradox, which we will discuss in more detail below.

  Credit for the first academic discussion of time travel should probably go to Walter B. Pitkin for his paper "Time and Pure Activity" (1914). Among other things, Pitkin discusses a version of the time discrepancy paradox (section 1 of this chapter) and the double-occupancy problem (Chapter 2, section 2).

[5] The first such forum was the "Discussions" section of *Amazing Stories*. That magazine went bankrupt in 1929, but the discussion continued in Gernsback's next publication—*Science Wonder Stories*—in the "Reader Speaks" section.

[6] For an excellent overview of these debates, see Nahin (1999).

in different *places* at different times. So what could it mean to move about *in time*? One might think that movement in time involves being in different *times* at different times, but this seems like nonsense—what could it mean to say that something exists "in different times at different times"?[7]

Consider a specific example. Suppose a time traveler enters her time machine, turns some dials, and then, a minute later, arrives one hundred years in the past. This seems to involve a direct contradiction, since it seems to involve two events—the time traveler's departure and arrival—being separated by unequal amounts of time (namely, one minute and one hundred years).

The same worry also arises in cases of future time travel. Here is how the science fiction author Milton Kaletsky puts the problem:

As for traveling into the future, suppose the traveler to journey at some rate such as one year per hour, i.e., he travels for one hour...and finds himself one year in the future...This is sheer nonsense. A year cannot elapse in one hour for the simple reason that an hour is **defined** as less than a year. A fraction and the whole cannot be equal; a year and an hour cannot elapse in the same interval of time because they are **different** intervals of time, by **definition**...Hence...time traveling into the future is impossible.   (1935: 173)[8]

What these examples seem to show is that time travel (in either direction) requires a discrepancy between *time* and *time*. Since this is contradictory, the very concept of time travel is incoherent. This is what Dennis Holt (1981) calls the *time discrepancy paradox*.[9]

The time discrepancy paradox has led some philosophers to dismiss the possibility of time travel altogether.[10] But those philosophers are in the minority. The more popular response, due to David Lewis, is to draw a distinction between two different kinds of time:

How can it be that the same two events, [the time traveler's] departure and his arrival, are separated by two unequal amounts of time?...I reply by distinguishing time itself, *external time*

---

[7] A similar line of questioning is pressed by Smart (1963).

[8] Kaletsky (1911–1988) was an early science fiction author who published under the names 'Milton Kaletzky', 'Dane Milton', and, my personal favorite, 'Omnia'. He was also an active figure in the early science fiction forums, publishing letters in *Wonder Stories*, *Amazing Stories*, and *Astonishing Stories*.

[9] One of the most famous examples of the time discrepancy paradox can be found in the epilogue of *The Time Machine*, in which the book's narrator speculates about the "current" whereabouts of the Time Traveller:

> It may be that he swept back into the past, and fell among the blood-drinking, hairy savages of the Age of Unpolished Stone; into the abysses of the Cretaceous Sea; or among the grotesque saurians, the huge reptilian brutes of the Jurassic times. He may even now—if I may use the phrase—be wandering on some plesiosaurus-haunted Oolitic coral reef, or beside the lonely saline lakes of the Triassic Age.   (Wells 2009: 71)

The tension in this passage comes from the suggestion that the Time Traveller is *now* doing something in the *past*. Other famous examples of the time discrepancy paradox can be found in *Doctor Who* (see the exchange between the Doctor and Sally Sparrow in the episode "Blink"), *Lost* (see the exchange between Miles and Hurley in the episode "Whatever Happened, Happened"), and *Back to the Future* (see the exchange between Doc and Marty when Marty first arrives in the past).

[10] See, for example, Christensen (1976), Grey (1999: 57–8), Holt (1981), and Pitkin (1943: 523). For other statements of this worry, see Dretske (1962: 97–8), Harrison (1971: 3), Niven (1971), Smart (1963: 239), and Williams (1951: 463).

as I shall also call it, from the *personal time* of a particular time traveler: roughly, that which is measured by his wristwatch. His journey takes an hour of his personal time, let us say; his wristwatch reads an hour later at arrival than at departure. But the arrival is more than an hour after the departure in external time, if he travels toward the future; or the arrival is before the departure in external time (or less than an hour after), if he travels toward the past. (1976: 146)[11]

As Lewis notes, the distinction between personal time and external time seems to provide a simple solution to the time discrepancy paradox. The departure and arrival are separated by one amount of personal time and a different amount of external time. This is a discrepancy, but not a contradiction, since personal time and external time are two different things.

To further illustrate the idea, imagine a case in which a time traveler—Doctor Who, let's say—is born at t_3, enters the TARDIS time machine at t_6, and travels back to t_1. (See Figure 1.1.)

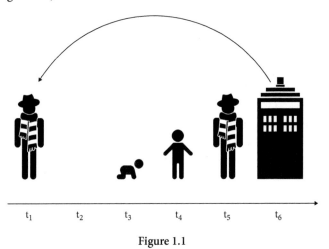

t_1 t_2 t_3 t_4 t_5 t_6

Figure 1.1

According to the Objective World Historian, the first event in this series is the Doctor's appearance at t_1. After that comes the birth, the stages of childhood, the experiences of adulthood, and, finally, the trip back in time. This is the ordering of those events, according to external time. According to the Doctor, these events take place in a different order—the birth, for example, comes before the appearance in the past. This is the ordering of those events—the very same events—according to his personal time. This last point deserves special emphasis. Personal time, for Lewis, is not a separate dimension filled with its own collection of events. Rather, it is an alternative assignment of coordinates to ordinary temporal events—an assignment that corresponds, in some way, to the experiences of a particular individual.

---

[11] Lewis also mentions a second solution to the time discrepancy paradox that involves two-dimensional time. We discuss this model in Chapter 3 of this book.

Note that this correspondence does not simply concern the *ordering* of those events—personal time also provides a metric that allows for comparisons of temporal distance. For example, the assignment of coordinates to the Doctor's stages should reflect the fact that the distance between his t_6-stage and his t_1-stage is much less than the distance between his t_3-stage and his t_5-stage. This aspect of personal time also allows for an additional kind of discrepancy with external time. For example, the Doctor's departure and arrival might be separated by forty years of external time, but only a few seconds of personal time.

Note also that personal time does not need to be limited to events going on inside the time traveler's mind or body. As Lewis notes, we can also "extend the assignment of personal time outwards from the time traveler's stages to the surrounding events" (1976: 147). Suppose, for example, that the Doctor's companion, Leela, is sleeping when the TARDIS takes off at t_6 and that she awakens when they arrive at t_1. In that case, the Doctor might very well count the awakening as coming after the nap since (i) the nap is simultaneous with his t_6-stage, (ii) the awakening is simultaneous with his t_1-stage, and (iii) his t_1-stage comes after his t_6-stage according to his personal time.

However, this kind of "extension" leads to a potential problem.[12] Consider, for example, the inventor that T.J.D. mentions in his letter to *Amazing Stories*. That inventor goes back in time to visit his graduating ceremony—a ceremony that he has already experienced once as a child. Since he is about to experience that event again, it will have to make a second appearance in his personal history. But that means that a single event—the graduation ceremony—will be both before and after itself according to his personal time. So, it seems as if we are still stuck with a kind of temporal discrepancy.

Fortunately, this kind of discrepancy does not seem all that paradoxical. To say that this event occurs after itself according to the inventor's "extended" personal time is just to say that (i) it is simultaneous with one stage of the inventor, (ii) it is simultaneous with another stage of the inventor, and (iii) the second stage of the inventor comes after the first, according to his personal time. And all of those conditions are met, owing to the unusual fact that the inventor has two stages present at the same point in external time. What *would* be strange is if time—*real time*—allowed for a single event to occur both before and after itself. This would be strange because we normally think of external time as being linear. But if we want to allow for self-visitation (of the sort described by T.J.D.) and we want to "extend" personal time (in the way suggested by Lewis), we will have to have a much more open view about its structure. Unlike external time, personal time can run in reverse, repeat itself, and generally get tied up into all sorts of knots. This might be part of what Doctor Who had in mind when he described time as a "big ball of wibbly-wobbly, timey-wimey stuff" (*Doctor Who*, Season 29, Episode 10).

---

[12] Thanks to Andrew Law for helping me get clearer on this point.

The distinction between personal time and external time allows us to make sense of temporal discrepancies, but it also suggests a natural account of time travel. For someone to travel in time is for there to be a discrepancy between external time and that individual's personal time. That is, *time travel occurs only if, and in that case because, there is a discrepancy between external and personal time.* This is the standard definition of time travel in the philosophical literature.[13]

The standard definition of time travel is plausible, but the accompanying definition of personal time is not. Lewis initially defines personal time in terms of "wristwatch" time—that is, time as measured on a watch. The problem is that, on this characterization, a discrepancy between personal time and external time is neither necessary nor sufficient for time travel—it is not *necessary* since people can always travel without watches, and it is not *sufficient* since watches can always malfunction.[14]

One natural response to these worries is to move to an idealized version of the wristwatch definition. For example, one might say that personal time is what would be measured if the relevant person *were* wearing an *accurate* watch. That would avoid both of the problems just raised, but it would also create problems of its own. For one thing, an "accurate" clock is presumably defined as a clock that would correctly track personal time.[15] But, in that case, the proposed definition would be immediately circular (personal time is what an accurate watch would measure and an accurate watch is one that would correctly measure personal time).[16]

Lewis's response is to replace his original definition of personal time with the following "functional" alternative:

[P]ersonal time...is that which occupies a certain role in the pattern of events that comprise the time traveler's life. If you take the stages of a common person, they manifest certain regularities with respect to external time...Memories accumulate. Food digests. Hair grows. Wristwatch hands move. If you take the stages of a time traveler instead, they do not manifest the common regularities with respect to external time. But there is one way to assign coordinates to the time traveler's stages, and one way only (apart from the arbitrary choice of a zero point), so that the regularities that hold with respect to this assignment match those that commonly hold with respect to external time...The assignment of coordinates that yields this match is the time

---

[13] Versions of the standard definition are endorsed by Arntzenius (2006), Decker (2013: 181), Devlin (2001: 33–4), Dowe (2000: 441–2), Eaton (2010: 76–7), Everett and Roman (2012: 12), Fulmer (1983: 31–2), Horwich (1987: 114), Hunter (2004), Keller and Nelson (2001: 334), Kutach (2013: 301–2), Ney (2000: 312–13), Perszyk and Smith (2001), Richmond (2008: 39), Sider (2001), and others. The main alternative in the literature is to define time travel in terms of closed timeline curves in general relativity—see, for example, Malament (1984: 91).

[14] As Lewis puts it, "my own wristwatch often disagrees with external time, yet I am no time traveler" (1976: 146).

[15] An alternative is to characterize both clock accuracy and personal time in terms of the invariant interval of special relativity. We will return to this idea in Chapter 2, section 5.

[16] Also, counterfactual definitions never work. Suppose, for example, that the Doctor is traveling in the TARDIS and that he has developed an unusual phobia of time traveling while wearing watches. So, if he *were* wearing a watch at this time, he would immediately stop the TARDIS. In that case, there would no longer be any discrepancy between external time and personal time (as currently defined). So, the definition would incorrectly entail that the Doctor is not currently time traveling.

traveler's personal time. It isn't really time, but it plays the role in his life that time plays in the life of a common person. It's enough like time so that we can—with due caution—transplant our temporal vocabulary to it in discussing his affairs.   (1976: 146)

So, the revised proposal is that personal time is an assignment of coordinates to person-stages that preserves the regularities we ordinarily see in people.[17] For example, in Figure 1.1, the Doctor's t_5-stage should be assigned a later coordinate than the t_4-stage since older-looking stages typically come after younger-looking stages. Or suppose that the Doctor has just finished a snack when he enters the time machine at t_6. In that case, he will still be digesting corresponding bits of food when he emerges from the time machine at t_1. This is part of the explanation for why the t_1-stage comes after the t_6-stage in his personal time—digesting regularly comes after eating in the life of a normal human being. And this reversal of ordering is part of what makes the Doctor a time traveler.

Unfortunately, there is an obvious problem with the revised definition: It only applies to persons! In order to provide an adequate definition of time travel, we have to be able to generalize the notion of "personal time" so that it applies to plants, animals, and other kinds of objects. However, this generalization turns out to be difficult. To make the problem vivid, imagine a world filled with nothing but unchanging elementary particles—electrons, let's say. Now imagine picking out one of those electrons, and assigning coordinates to its stages in accordance with external time (Figure 1.2).

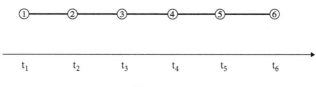

Figure 1.2

Here is the problem. If electrons do not undergo any intrinsic change, then there will be many other ways of assigning coordinates to the electron's stages so that "the regularities that hold with respect to those assignments match those that commonly hold with respect to external time." The most obvious option is to simply reverse the ordering indicated in Figure 1.2, so that the t_1-stage is labeled '6', the t_2-stage is labeled '5', and so on. If we track the electron's career according to this assignment, we will still see the same patterns that are observed with other electrons—for example, the electron will still move continuously, and its charge will still remain constant—but this would obviously not be enough to make the electron a time traveler.

In order to broaden our account of personal time, we must move beyond the functional definition. Ideally, what we would like to find is a perfectly general relation that

---

[17] We will say more about "person-stages" in Chapters 2 and 6; for now, we can simply think of stages as parts of a person's life.

could provide an order and metric for any object, whether it be a person, a particle, or a time machine.

The most obvious candidate for this job is *causation*, since it is generally agreed that identity over time requires causal dependence.[18] For example, it is often said that a person at one time can only be identical to a person at another time if there is an appropriate causal connection between the relevant mental states. What counts as an "appropriate" causal connection is a difficult question, as is the question of which states, exactly, must stand in that relation.[19] We will not enter into those debates here. Rather, we will assume that there are answers to these questions and that the specified causal relation will order the stages of a given object in the way required. We will then say that an object's personal time is the assignment of coordinates to its stages that matches the coordinates given by the underlying causal relation. In the case of non-time-travelers, this assignment will correspond to the one given by external time; in the case of time travelers, it will not. Time travel thus amounts to a discrepancy between time—*real* time—and the kind of causal relations that make for identity over time.

2. …And Not

Now that we have said what time travel *is*, we should also say a few words about what it is *not*.

First, traveling across time zones is obviously not an example of time travel.[20] If someone flies from New York to Los Angeles, she may set her watch back three hours, but she does not travel back three hours. Rather, she simply travels to a city that assigns a different number to the current moment (the number dictated by Pacific Standard Time). To think that one could travel through time by changing the numbers on a watch would be like thinking that one could speed up a car by renumbering its speedometer.[21]

---

[18] See, for example, Armstrong (1980), Lewis (1983), and Perry (1976: 69–70).

[19] For an introduction to these issues, see Zimmerman (1997).

[20] This seeming truism is sometimes disputed—see, for example, Hunter (2016: 14). For criticism of this idea, see Dowden (2009: 48–9), Nahin (2011: 14–15), and Smith (2013: section 1). A related mistake is the idea that one could travel through time by circling the earth faster than the sun. Believe it or not, this suggestion actually forms the basis of the H. S. MacKaye story *The Panchronicon*. As one character in the story explains it:

> What is it makes the days go by—ain't it the daily revolution of the sun?…[So] Ef a feller was to whirl clear round the world an' cut all the meridians in the same direction as the sun, an' he made the whole trip around jest as quick as the sun did—time wouldn't change a mite fer him…[And] ef a feller'll jest take a grip on the North Pole an' go whirlin' round it, he'll be cuttin' meridians as fast as a hay-chopper? Won't he see the sun getting' left behind an' whirlin' the other way from what it does in nature? An' ef the sun goes the other way round, ain't it sure to unwind all the time thet it's ben a-rollin' up? (1904: 14–16)

This theory goes wrong at the very first step in assuming that the revolution of the sun is what makes time pass. But this does not stop the characters in the story from successfully using this method to travel back in time.

[21] Fans of Spinal Tap will recognize this as instance of "the Nigel Tufnel fallacy."

Second, remembering past events is clearly not enough for time travel. Some psychologists do refer to memory as "mental time travel,"[22] but this kind of talk is metaphorical. Memory only "transports" us into the past in the way that *Star Wars* transports us to a galaxy far, far away.

Similarly, having visions of the past or future is not enough for time travel. Consider, for example, the case of Ebenezer Scrooge. Some have cited Scrooge's encounter with the Ghost of Christmas Past as an early example of backward time travel.[23] Others demur.[24] Who is correct? That depends on the details of the case. If Scrooge's thoughts and sensations are literally taking place in the past, then there would indeed be a discrepancy between his personal time and external time. If, on the other hand, Scrooge is simply having a vision, then the relevant experiences may be *of* the past, but they are not taking place *in* the past. In that case, Scrooge would not count as a genuine time traveler.[25]

Fourth, it might seem obvious that going to sleep is not enough to make one a time traveler.[26] However, some have suggested that this depends upon the length of the nap.[27] Consider, for example, the case of Rip Van Winkle, who is said to have fallen asleep for twenty years. If Van Winkle is completely unconscious while he sleeps, his experiences will be internally indiscernible from those of a time traveler who disappears from one time and reappears twenty years later. From both of their perspectives, the "next" thing that happens is not really the next thing that happens. So, one might think that both cases involve discrepancies between personal and external time. However, there is at least one important difference between Van Winkle and the "jumpy" time traveler—Van Winkle's body is present throughout the entire period, and it is natural to think that the causal processes going on in his body are what preserves his identity during that time (i.e., they help explain why the person who wakes up after the slumber is the same person as the one who went to sleep). Moreover, these processes seem to be going at something like a normal rate since Van Winkle's body shows the typical signs of aging when he awakens (for example, in the story we are told

---

[22] See, for example, Murray (2003), Stocker (2012), and Suddendorf and Corballis (1997). Clegg (2011: 1–2) seems to suggest that memory involves genuine travel to the past.

[23] See, for example, Jones and Ormrod (2015: 14), Kaku (2009: 218), and Rickman (2004: 370).

[24] See, for example, Bigelow (2001: 78), Main (2008), and Nahin (1999: 9).

[25] There is arguably evidence for both of these readings in the text. On one hand, Scrooge and the Ghost certainly seem to interact with past objects—they are said to be "walking along the road" and Scrooge is "conscious of a thousand odours floating on the air" (Dickens 1843/1908: 38). On the other hand, the Ghost says that the objects of Scrooge's perception "are but shadows of the things that have been," suggesting that Scrooge is not really experiencing the past (Dickens 1843/1908: 39). On the *other* hand, we are also told that (old) Scrooge gets a pimple when he revisits the days of his youth. So it's not exactly clear what's going on.

[26] Smith (2013: section 1).

[27] See, for example, Booker and Thomas (2009: 15), Gleick (2016: 30–1), Hunter (2016: 8), Karcher (1985: 32), and Mellor (1998: 124). Kutach (2013: 302) says that whether or not Rip Van Winkle counts as a time traveler is a matter of interpretation.

that his joints are sore and his beard has grown).[28] If all of this is correct, then there doesn't seem to be any mismatch between external time and the causal relations that make for identity in this case.[29,30]

But now consider an example of suspended animation. In the *Captain America* story, Steve Rogers crashes an aircraft in the Arctic during the closing days of World War II. Rogers is then encased in ice and preserved in a state of suspended animation for nearly seventy years.[31] When he is thawed out, Rogers shows no sign of aging, and soon returns to normal superhero activity. Here is the problem. Unlike Rip Van Winkle, all of Captain America's bodily processes are stopped while he sleeps. So, for example, if Rogers had a light snack before his final mission, that food will not digest at all during the intervening years. But then (to quote Lewis), there is only "one way to assign coordinates to [Captain America's stages] ... so that the regularities that hold with respect to this assignment match those that commonly hold with respect to external time." This assignment will require us to give the very same coordinate to each stage during the period of suspended animation, and to resume the standard numbering once Rogers awakens. This is the only assignment on which his bodily processes will "match" those that commonly hold with respect to external time. However, this assignment will obviously give us a discrepancy between personal time and external time. For example, the process of digesting his last meal will take approximately seven hours of Rogers's personal time and seventy years of external time. On Lewis's definition, that kind of discrepancy is all it takes to make someone a time traveler.[32]

---

[28] Of course, there is *something* unusual about these causal processes, since they are being sustained in the absence of food and water. But the important point is that the causal order of the body's stages matches the one given by external time.

[29] Here it may be helpful to compare the case of Rip Van Winkle to the case of a watch that is taken completely apart and then reassembled. Presumably, there is no watch when all the pieces have been taken apart, so there is a sense in which this object "jumps" forward in time—it exists for a while, then it goes out of existence, and then it comes back again. However, the watch at the end of this process is only identical to the watch at the beginning because of the continued existence of the parts. Moreover, there are no causal abnormalities in the lives of the parts, so there is no discrepancy in the underlying identity-making relations. Depending on one's view of persons, one might think that there is no person present while Van Winkle's body is hibernating. Still, the basic parts of the body are all there, and those parts—like the watch's parts—do not exhibit the kind of causal abnormalities that are characteristic of time travel.

[30] For a very different explanation of why Rip Van Winkle is not a time traveler, see Read (2012: 139–40).

[31] This is the movie version of the story. In the comics, Rogers is frozen for less than twenty years.

[32] A similar point can be made using a different comic character. Consider the case of the Flash, whose superpower is to move at incredibly high speeds. While it is not entirely clear in the comics, we can suppose that all of the Flash's biological processes speed up when he uses his power—from our perspective, his hair grows faster, his food digests quicker, and his thoughts occur more rapidly. Of course, we can also imagine that, from the Flash's perspective, things are reversed—as he sees it, his mental and physical processes continue as normal, while everyone around him slows down. This kind of case poses a potential problem for Lewis's definition, since the Flash is not typically portrayed as a time traveler. (Actually, the Flash *is* portrayed as a time traveler, but only when he uses his powers in a special way—see, for example, his use of the "Cosmic Treadmill" in *The Flash* no. 125.)

The problem, of course, is that cases of suspended animation are not normally considered cases of time travel.[33] This suggests that something is wrong with Lewis's definition.

In response, it may be helpful to compare the case of suspended animation to a different kind of example. In *The Time Machine*, Wells describes the maiden voyage of his Time Traveller as follows:

I drew a breath, set my teeth, gripped the starting lever with both hands, and went off with a thud. The laboratory got hazy and went dark. Mrs Watchett came in and walked, apparently without seeing me, towards the garden door. I suppose it took her a minute or so to traverse the place, but to me she seemed to shoot across the room like a rocket. I pressed the lever over to its extreme position. The night came like the turning out of a lamp, and in another moment came to-morrow. The laboratory grew faint and hazy, then fainter and ever fainter. To-morrow night came black, then day again, night again, day again, faster and faster still...   (2009: 17)

The key feature of this case is that it involves *continuous* travel into the future. Unlike some time travelers, Wells's character does not disappear when his machine is turned on. Rather, he simply stays where he is, while everything around him speeds up. At least, that's how things seem to him. But we could just as well view things from the opposite perspective—when the time machine is turned on, everything in the time machine slows down, while ordinary life continues as normal. Indeed, if we think about things from this perspective, Wells's Time Traveller does not seem all that different from someone in a cryogenic freezing device. This can be brought out by considering the following addendum to *The Time Machine*, in which Stephen Law imagines a visit to the Time Traveller's lab:

The housekeeper led me through a door into an amazing Victorian laboratory filled with experimental equipment. But the most astonishing thing of all was that there, sat in the saddle of his glittering brass, ivory, and crystal machine, *was the time traveller himself.*

"I thought you were off travelling in time!" I gasped. There was no reply from the time traveller. In fact, he remained strangely motionless.

"He can't hear you," explained Mrs Watchett.

"But you said he was travelling in time?" I said.

"He is," replied Mrs Watchett...

I was beginning to understand. The time traveller's machine had merely slowed him right down. His heart beat once a minute. His brain activity had been reduced to a crawl. Just as, from his perspective, we seemed to be whizzing about like gnats, from our perspective he appeared frozen like a statue.

"And now it's me that has to dust him every week," continued Mrs Watchett...   (2008: 47–8)

Law takes some liberties with Wells's story, since the original Time Traveller was invisible while he was using his machine. Still, we can imagine things as Law describes them

---

[33] In the literature, this case is more controversial. For example, Smith (2013: section 1) claims that suspended animation is not time travel, whereas Everett and Roman (2012: 60–1) argue it is.

and, when we do, the case of the Time Traveller does not seem all that different from that of Captain America—in both cases, the relevant individuals are (more or less) "frozen" in time.

There are at least three different reactions one might have to this analogy. First, one might think that the Time Traveller is obviously a time traveler, and the Time Traveller is relevantly similar to the person who undergoes suspended animation. So, one might conclude that the person who undergoes suspended animation is a time traveler after all. If that's correct, then the case of Captain America does not present a problem for Lewis's definition.

A second reaction is to run this same argument in reverse: The person who undergoes suspended animation is clearly *not* a time traveler, and that person is relevantly similar to Wells's character. So, despite his name, the Time Traveller is not really a time traveler. (Indeed, if one thinks of things from Mrs Watchett's perspective, this conclusion may seem correct even if one does not draw an explicit analogy to the case of suspended animation.)

One way to make this idea fit with the general approach of the previous section would be to modify Lewis's earlier definitions. Previously, we said that personal time provides both an order and a metric, and that time travel occurs whenever there is a discrepancy in either of these things. However, we could restrict this definition so that only discrepancies of *order* give rise to genuine time travel. This definition would still classify Doctor Who as a time traveler, since he experiences things in a different order than the Objective World Historian (Figure 1.1). The same thing is true for Wells's character when he travels backward in time.[34] But the Traveller's trip to the future would not count as a case of time travel, since it would not disrupt the ordinary order of events. Once again, the Time Traveller and the Objective Historian do not disagree about which events happen in what order—they simply disagree about how long those different events take.

A third reaction is to think that there must be some relevant difference between these cases that explains why one is an example of time travel and the other is not. But what could it be?

One obvious difference between these cases is that the Time Traveller is awake throughout his journey and Captain America is not. But this distinction does not seem to matter. If the Time Traveller is knocked unconscious for the duration of his trip, he will still (intuitively) count as a time traveler when he awakens in the future.

A second difference between these cases is that suspended animation literally *suspends* the bodily processes, whereas Wellsian time travel merely *slows them down*. This is a genuine difference, but it's not clear if it's relevant. Suppose, for example, that Rogers's body aged a little bit while he was encased in ice. That still wouldn't seem like enough to make him a time traveler. Or suppose that the Time Traveller was temporally

---

[34] The same thing is also true for the "jumpy" individual who disappears from one moment and reappears years later.

frozen while traveling in his time machine. In that case, his bodily processes would be suspended, but he would still (intuitively) count as a time traveler.

A third idea is less obvious, but more promising. This idea is suggested by David Lewis himself:

> I'm not sure about cryogenic procedures. They slow down different processes to different degrees, and the rates of the fundamental atomic processes...are unchanged. So it's not clear to me that if we take a functional analysis of personal time...we get a discrepancy between personal and external time.[35]

Lewis's suggestion is that freezing—at least the kind of freezing associated with cryopreservation—does not slow down subatomic processes in the same way that it slows down biological processes. If this is right, then we might be able to distinguish between Captain America and the Time Traveller by restricting our attention to the former kinds of processes. We could, for example, say that time travel consists in a discrepancy between personal time and external time *at the fundamental physical level*, where only the Time Traveller experiences that kind of discrepancy.

There is much more that could be said on this topic, but the good news is that we do not need to settle the issue now. For one thing, cases of continuous travel to the future are comparatively rare in the philosophical literature. This is unsurprising, since the most puzzling cases of time travel are those involving causal reversals and causal gaps. Since these kinds of cases are the focus of this book—and since they will clearly count as "time travel" on any reasonable definition—we can safely set aside the more controversial cases for now.[36]

3. Possibility

The central question to be addressed in this book is whether or not time travel is possible. However, there are many different kinds of possibility, and thus many different things that this question might mean.[37]

First, there is the notion of *logical* possibility. To say that something is possible in the logical sense is to say that it is compatible with all the laws of logic.[38] It is possible, in this sense, for some cats to be dogs, since the statement *some cats are dogs* does not, by

---

[35] This is taken from an unpublished letter to Jonathan Bennett, dated March 29, 1977.

[36] We will return to some of these cases at the end of Chapter 2 when we discuss the theory of special relativity.

[37] According to one popular view, all questions about possibility are questions about compatibility—to ask whether or not something is possible is to ask whether or not it is compatible *with the relevant facts*, where which facts are relevant can vary from context to context (Lewis 1976; Kratzer 1977). This is one way of understanding the claim that there are different "kinds" of possibility. Whether or not this view is correct is a matter of debate (Fine 2002). But it is at the very least a helpful heuristic for our purposes here.

[38] This is what is sometimes called the "narrow" sense of logical possibility. Some writers use the term "logically possible" or "broadly logically possible" to pick out what we will call "metaphysical possibility" (see later in this section).

itself, violate any laws of logic. However, it is not logically possible for some cats to be non-cats, since that statement implies a contradiction in first-order logic.

Is time travel logically possible? The answer, pretty clearly, is *yes*. To say that time travel is logically possible is to say that the statement *time travel occurs* is consistent with all the laws of logic. And that is clearly the case since *time travel occurs* is an atomic statement and all atomic statements are consistent with the laws of logic. This is a trivial point, and is therefore uninteresting—the debate over time travel is not a debate over logical possibility.

Second, there is the notion of *technological* possibility. To say that something is technologically possible is to say that it is compatible with all the facts about our current technology (along with the laws which govern that technology). It is possible, in this sense, to send a person to Madagascar or the moon, but not to Alpha Centauri.

Is time travel technologically possible? That depends. In the case of backward time travel, the answer is almost certainly *no*. Some scientists have suggested that the Large Hadron Collider—the world's largest particle accelerator—could be used to create Higgs singlets, which could then be used to send a signal back in time.[39] But even the most optimistic physicists take this to be a "long shot."[40] However, most physicists have a very different attitude when it comes to forward time travel. Indeed, most physicists claim that forward time travel is not only technologically possible, but that it has already occurred. This claim is based on the theory of special relativity, which says that the elapsed time between events depends on the motion of an observer. So, if two observers are moving relative to each other, the result will be a temporal discrepancy. For example, if an astronaut takes an atomic clock with her into space, she will find that, upon her return, her clock will have ticked off less time than those of her friends on Earth. For this reason, it is sometimes said that all astronauts are time travelers from the recent past.[41] Whether or not this is the *right* thing to say is another matter. We will return to this issue when we discuss the theory of special relativity in Chapter 2, section 5.

A third question is whether time travel is *physically* possible. To say that something is possible in the physical sense is to say that it is compatible with all the laws of physics (whether or not we have the technology to take advantage of that possibility).[42] It is possible, in this sense, for something to travel at the speed of light, but not for something to accelerate beyond that point.[43]

---

[39] See, for example, the interview with physicists Thomas Weiler and Chui Man Ho in Salisbury (2011).

[40] Weiler, quoted in Salisbury (2011).

[41] See, for example, Kaku (2009: 219). Cf. Davies (2001: Chapter 1).

[42] One can also define a stricter notion of physical possibility on which it corresponds to compatibility with the laws of physics, logic, and metaphysics (see fn. 43). My choice of terminology is for presentational purposes only.

[43] Physical possibility is sometimes equated with *theoretical* possibility, but this terminology can be misleading. For one thing, there are many theories besides physical ones (including philosophical theories) and consistency with those other theories will not entail consistency with the physical laws. Second, and more importantly, theoretical possibility is often understood in terms of consistency with our *current*

Is time travel possible in this sense? Once again, many physicists take Einstein to have shown that travel to the future is physically possible, but the more interesting question is whether the laws of physics allow for travel to the past. Some physicists have certainly resisted this possibility. Stephen Hawking, for example, famously suggested what he called "the chronology protection conjecture": *The laws of physics prevent the appearance of closed timelike curves* (1992: 610). But most physicists take this conjecture to be mistaken. Indeed, most physicists take general relativity to allow for backward time travel in a variety of different scenarios—for example those involving wormholes (Thorne 1995), cosmic strings (Gott 1991), or infinite universes filled with rotating dust (Gödel 1949).[44] We will look at some of these examples when we discuss the theory of general relativity in Chapter 2, section 6.

A fourth and final question is whether time travel is *metaphysically* possible. This is the central question to be addressed in this book. However, this question requires clarification, since it is not always clear what it means to say that something is metaphysically possible.

One suggestion is to think of metaphysical possibility in terms of *metaphysical laws*—to say that something is metaphysically possible is to say that it is compatible with the laws of metaphysics (just as logical possibility is compatibility with the laws of logic and physical possibility is compatibility with the laws of physics).[45] Of course, this definition relies on the concept of a metaphysical law, and that concept might seem somewhat mysterious. But the following analogy might be helpful.

A law of nature is a suitably general generalization about *what causes what*.[46] The "what"s at issue are natural phenomena (hence, laws of *nature*), and the causation at issue is roughly what Aristotle called "efficient" causation (the primary source of change or rest). To illustrate, consider Newton's first law of motion: Objects at rest will stay at rest, and objects in motion will stay in motion, unless acted upon by a force. This way of stating the law does not explicitly mention causation—it is simply a generalization about motion and forces: For any object x, x will undergo a change in motion only if it is acted upon by a force. But Newton obviously had more than this in mind, since he aimed to provide a theory of motion, and a mere generalization does not constitute a theory. Ordinary generalizations only *report* patterns, whereas theories are supposed to *explain* patterns. For example, the preceding generalization says that there is a force for every change in motion—whenever you have one, you have the other. But it doesn't

---

physical theories, but our current theories might very well be mistaken (in which case theoretical possibility would not be equivalent to physical possibility).

[44] See Everett and Roman (2012), Gott (2001), and Toomey (2007) for surveys of these and other scenarios.

[45] On this conception of metaphysical possibility, see Rosen (2006) and Schaffer (2009: 56).

[46] The requirement for suitable generality is important—a true generalization about what causes what *in my office* is not general enough to count as a genuine law of nature (though it may follow from a genuine law).

say anything about *why* this pattern prevails, which is exactly what a theory of motion should do. Theories are, by their nature, explanatory.[47]

Of course, the explanation in this case is obvious. Newton's idea wasn't just that things change their motion *when* they are acted upon by forces—his idea is that things change their motion *because* they are acted upon by forces. That is, for any object *x*, *x* will undergo a change in motion only if, *and in that case because*, it is acted upon by a force. Crucially, the "because" in this claim expresses the relation of *causal explanation*, so the law implies that changes in motion are caused by applications of force. That is what makes Newton's claim a theory, and that is what his theory has in common with the true laws of nature—these principles explain natural phenomena by identifying the causes of those phenomena.

Something similar is true in the case of metaphysics. The laws in this case are suitably general generalizations about *what grounds what*.[48] The "what" in this case includes *everything* (hence, the generality of metaphysics) and the grounding at issue is something like a mixture of Aristotle's material and formal causes ("that out of which," together with "the account of what-it-is-to-be").[49]

Grounding is a non-causal generative relation that imposes a hierarchical structure on reality.[50] For example, it's often said that the existence and features of a whole are grounded in the existence and features of its parts.[51] If this is correct, then the existence and features of the whole can be explained by referring to the existence and features of its parts (including the various relations that hold between those parts). In this way, grounding provides for metaphysical explanations in much the same way that causation provides for casual explanations.[52]

Much has been written about grounding and metaphysical explanation in recent years.[53] However, as Jonathan Schaffer points out, these ideas have been at the heart of philosophy since the very beginning:

Plato brings the notion of natural priority to prominence in the *Euthyphro* dilemma, asking: "Is what is holy holy because the gods approve it, or do they approve it because it is holy?" Many of us teach this dilemma to our first year students. They get it. Priority then resurfaces in the

---

[47] Here it is important to distinguish between a theory *of X* and a theory *about X*. A theory of *X* is an explanation of why *X* exists or why it has the features that it does. A theory about *X* is simply a speculative claim about *X*. The second kind of theory, unlike the first, does not need to be explanatory. See Wasserman (2016).

[48] I borrow this phrase from Schaffer (2009).

[49] It is unclear whether contemporary talk of grounding can be adequately translated into Aristotelian terminology (Correia and Schnieder 2012: 2). But the parallel to formal and material explanations is at least suggestive.

[50] Grounding is sometimes referred to as a "determination" relation, but this way of speaking is controversial. See Wasserman (forthcoming a).

[51] For a challenge to this claim, see Schaffer (2009). For more on metaphysical laws, see Wilsch (2015).

[52] The relata of the grounding relation are a matter of some debate. See, for example, Cameron (2008), Rosen (2010), and Schaffer (2009). In this book, we will most often speak of grounding as a relation between facts.

[53] See, for example, Correia (2005), Correia and Schnieder (2012), and Schaffer (2009).

metaphor of the cave in *Republic*, where the form of the good is compared to the sun, and declared ultimately prior: "the objects of knowledge not only receive from the presence of the good their being known, but their very existence and essence is derived to them from it,..." Aristotle then codifies the notion of priority in nature, characterizes substances as ultimately prior, and conceives of metaphysics as the study of such substances.   (2009: 375)

Like Schaffer, I assume that we have an intuitive notion of grounding. I also assume that, if we understand this concept, we grasp the idea of a metaphysical law. Once again, a metaphysical law is simply a suitably general generalization about what grounds what. We can illustrate this idea with Schaffer's initial example. In the *Euthyphro*, Socrates's goal is to understand what makes pious acts pious. His friend suggests that pious acts are those that are loved by the gods. This way of stating the account takes the form of a universal generalization—Euthyphro's claim is that, for any x, x is pious if and only if x is loved by the gods. What Socrates's question brings out is that this generalization fails as an account of piety, since it fails to provide an explanation. The generalization simply reports a pattern—wherever there is piety, there is divine love (and vice versa). But there are at least two explanations for this pattern. It could be that things are pious because they are loved by the gods, or it could be that gods love pious things because those things are pious. Only the former claim would constitute a theory of piety, so Euthyphro's proposal should be put in these terms: For any x, x is pious only if, *and in that case because*, x is loved by the gods (where this "because" expresses the relationship of metaphysical explanation).[54] This claim would constitute a genuine theory of piety and, given its generality, it would be a candidate for a law of metaphysics (a law about the nature of piety).

Unfortunately, many philosophers often ignore the *Euthyphro* lesson, and frame their theories in terms of material biconditionals, or necessary and sufficient conditions.[55] When we teach normative ethics, for example, we often say that act utilitarianism is the view that actions are morally permissible if and only if they maximize utility. But this is wrong. This biconditional may be true. It may even hold of necessity. But a necessarily true biconditional is not a theory of moral permission. For this reason, act utilitarianism should be formulated as the view that an act is permissible only if, *and in that case because*, it maximizes utility (where this "because," again, picks out the relation of metaphysical explanation). This theory might entail various modal claims, of course, but those claims are not themselves theories.[56]

What goes for ethics also goes for metaphysics. Theories of causation, or freedom, or personal identity are not simply lists of necessary and sufficient conditions. They are theories about what grounds what. If these theories are sufficiently general, then they are candidates to be laws. And if those candidates are correct, then they *are* laws. It is

---

[54] "Because" is clearly stronger than "if" in one respect: It might be true that A, *if B* even if the fact that A is not explained by the fact that B. But it might also be weaker in another respect: The fact that B might explain the fact that A even if A does not logically imply B. See, again, Wasserman (forthcoming a).

[55] See, for example, Wasserman (2004a: 694), Wasserman (2004b: 75), and Wasserman (2011: 426).

[56] For further discussion and additional examples, see Wasserman (2016).

these laws—the laws of metaphysics—that determine what is possible, metaphysically speaking.[57]

We now have a better understanding of the question with which we began. To ask whether time travel is possible is to ask whether discrepancies between personal and external time are consistent with the laws of metaphysics—laws, for example, about the nature of causation, freedom, and identity. This understanding of our question also suggests a natural strategy for determining an answer. In order to settle whether or not time travel is possible, we will first have to survey some of the relevant metaphysical theories. Once we have done that, we will be in a better position to determine whether or not those theories allow for the possibility of time travel. That is the plan for this book.[58]

4. Paradoxes

At this point, we have said a bit about what time travel is, what it is not, and what it would mean to say that it is possible. But why would someone say that time travel is *im*possible? After all, many people *do* say that. John Bigelow, for example, claims that, "Time travel stories … are essentially incoherent" (2001: 57). William Grey complains that, "The very idea of time travel is bizarre" (1999: 68).[59] And D. H. Mellor says that "time travel" is either a "misnomer" (1998: 125) or "*necessarily* impossible" (1998: 128). In each of these cases, the claim is not about the contingent laws of nature or our current technological capacities. Rather, the claim is that time travel is incompatible with the basic laws of metaphysics. Why think that? In a word: Paradoxes.

---

[57] For more on this conception of metaphysics, see Wasserman (forthcoming a).

[58] It is sometimes suggested that the set of physically possible worlds is a subset of the metaphysically possible worlds. In that case, one might worry that the question of whether or not time travel is metaphysically possible is already settled. After all, most physicists agree that time travel is compatible with the laws of physics, and whatever is physically possible must be metaphysically possible as well.

In some cases, this worry is just a matter of terminology (see fn. 42). But in other cases it seems to be based on a general skepticism about metaphysics: Metaphysicians have no business telling physicists what is or is not possible. If the laws of physics say that time travel is possible, then it *is* possible (in any reasonable sense of the word).

This worry raises methodological concerns that we cannot fully address here. But we will note that this kind of worry is not really about metaphysics—it is about all of philosophy. After all, the laws of physics do not conflict with consequentialist views in ethics, or causal theories of reference, or reliabilist theories of epistemic justification. So, all of these things are physically possible (in our sense of the term). If physical possibility entailed metaphysical possibility, it would follow that all of these views (as well as all their competitors) are metaphysical possible. But then, given the kind of skepticism espoused above, philosophers would have no business trying to provide philosophical objections to any of these views. So, unless we are willing to give up on all of ethics, epistemology, and the philosophy of language, we should be open to the possibility of philosophical contributions on the topic of time travel as well.

[59] More carefully, Grey says that the idea of time travel is bizarre *given a certain view about the nature of time* (what he calls the "Heraclitean" view). However, he goes on to say that time travel has "intolerable consequences" even if we set this view aside (Grey 1999: 70).

There are many different examples of time travel paradoxes, but most of them fall into one of four basic categories. All four of these categories can be illustrated using examples from the start of this chapter.

First, there are the *temporal paradoxes*. Consider, for example, the initial question posed by Jackson Beck in his letter to *Amazing Stories*: "How could one travel to the future…when the beings of the future have not yet materialized?" This question presupposes a certain view on the nature of time—namely, that the future has not yet "materialized." If this view were correct, then Beck would seem right—one cannot travel to the future if there is no future to travel *to*.

Many philosophers have pointed out that the same argument could be made against backward time travel, given certain views about the nature of time. For example, many philosophers have claimed that the present time is the only time that truly exists. According to this view—the *presentist* view—there are no past or future moments, in which case one could not travel in either direction. As William Grey puts it:

A fundamental requirement for the possibility of time travel is the existence of the destination of the journey. That is, a journey into the past or the future would have to presuppose that the past or future were somehow real…Travel…on this view would be ruled out because there is simply nowhere to go. (1999: 56–7)

We will address this argument and other paradoxes of time in Chapter 2 of this book.

The second set of puzzles is comprised of *the paradoxes of freedom*. Consider, for example, the inventor introduced in T.J.D.'s letter to *Amazing Stories*. That inventor creates a time machine, travels back to his childhood graduation, and attempts to shoot his former self. As T.J.D. notes, it seems obvious that the inventor *can* kill his younger self, since he has the means, motive, and opportunity. But it also seems obvious that he *cannot* kill his younger self, since that act would be literally self-defeating—if the inventor were to kill his younger self then his younger self would not grow up to invent a time machine, in which case he would not be able to travel back in time and kill his younger self. The upshot is that, if time travel were possible, one both could and could not kill one's younger self. Since this is contradictory, time travel is reduced to absurdity.

T.J.D.'s argument is an instance of *the retrosuicide paradox*, which is a close relative of *the grandfather paradox*—the most famous paradox of time travel. Many versions of the grandfather paradox have been discussed in the philosophical literature, but the most enduring example is due to David Lewis:

Consider Tim. He detests his grandfather, whose success in the munitions trade built the family fortune that paid for Tim's time machine. Tim would like nothing so much as to kill Grandfather, but alas he is too late. Grandfather died in his bed in 1957, while Tim was a young boy. But when Tim has built his time machine and traveled to 1920, suddenly he realizes that he is not too late after all. He buys a rifle; he spends long hours in target practice; he shadows Grandfather to learn the route of his daily walk to the munitions works; he rents a room along the route; and there he lurks, one winter day in 1921, rifle loaded, hate in his heart, as Grandfather walks closer, closer… (1976: 149)

As Lewis notes, there seem to be good reasons for thinking that Tim *can* kill Grandfather.

He has what it takes. Conditions are perfect in every way: the best rifle money could buy, Grandfather an easy target only twenty yards away, not a breeze, door securely locked against intruders. Tim a good shot to begin with and now at the peak of training, and so on. What's to stop him? The forces of logic will not stay his hand! No powerful chaperone stands by to defend the past from interference... In short, Tim is as much able to kill Grandfather as anyone ever is to kill anyone. (1976: 149)

But, as Lewis goes on to point out, there seem to be equally good reasons for thinking that Tim *cannot* kill Grandfather:

Grandfather lived, so to kill him would be to change the past. But the events of a past moment... cannot change. Either the events of 1921 timelessly do include Tim's killing of Grandfather, or else they timelessly don't... It is logically impossible that Tim should change the past by killing Grandfather in 1921. So Tim cannot kill Grandfather. (1976: 150)

The upshot, it seems, is that time travel implies the contradiction that Tim both can and cannot kill Grandfather.[60] We will discuss this argument and other paradoxes of freedom in Chapters 3 and 4 of this book.

The third set of time travel puzzles includes the various *causal paradoxes*. For example, in his *Amazing* letter, T.J.D. points out that time travel would allow one to journey back to before one's own birth. But this, he claims, is impossible, since it would require "an effect going before a cause." This argument assumes a particular view about causation—namely, that it is impossible for causation to run in reverse. If this view were correct, then all travel to the past would be impossible, since all backward travel would require at least one effect (the arrival) to precede its cause (the departure).

There are several reasons for being skeptical about backward causation, but one of the most common complaints is that causal reversals would allow for *causal loops*—that is, a series of events in which each event is a cause of its successor, and where the last event in the series is also a cause of the first. These kinds of loops are a popular plot device in many science fiction stories,[61] but they are also a point of contention in many

---

[60] Science fiction authors often try to avoid this contradiction by introducing a group of individuals who are charged with protecting the past—see, for example, the Chad Oliver story "A Star Above It" (1955), the Poul Anderson book *The Guardians of Time* (1981), and the Jean-Claude Van Damme movie *Timecop* (1994). These kinds of contrivances are fine for fictional purposes, but they do not solve the philosophical problem. After all, if time travel is possible, then it is presumably possible to travel back in time to when there aren't any timecops around. And, in that case, it doesn't seem like there would be anything to stop you from killing your own grandfather.

[61] See, for example, Bolton (1931), Bridge (1931), and Cloukey (1929). In Cloukey's story ("Paradox"), a time traveler to the future brings back instructions on how to build a time machine so that his younger self can be sent into the future (to bring back instructions on how to build a time machine). In Bolton's story ("The Time Hoaxers"), a woman travels one hundred years into the past because she finds an old newspaper story that describes her arrival in the past. In Bridge's story ("Via the Time Accelerator"), a nervous pilot decides to go through with a trip to the future because he sees himself safely return in his time machine. As the pilot later explains:

philosophical debates. As David Lewis notes, these loops are particularly puzzling when they involve the transmission of information:

Recall the time traveler [who visited his younger self]. He talked to himself about time travel, and in the course of the conversation his older self told his younger self how to build a time machine. That information was available in no other way. His older self knew how because his younger self had been told and the information had been preserved by the causal processes that constitute recording, storage, and retrieval of memory traces. His younger self knew, after the conversation, because his older self had known and the information had been preserved by the causal processes that constitute telling. But where did the information come from in the first place? Why did the whole affair happen? There is simply no answer. The parts of the loop are explicable, the whole of it is not. Strange!   (1976: 149)

One problem with Lewis's loop is that it seems to involve "self-caused" events that bring themselves into existence. For example, the conversation between the time traveler and his younger self is a cause of the time machine being built, and the time machine being built is a cause of the conversation. So, the conversation seems to be a cause of itself. This is an example of what is sometimes called the *bootstrapping paradox*.[62] A second problem with this loop is that it seems to involve something coming from nothing. As Lewis points out, the parts of the loop might be individually explicable, but the entirety of the loop is not. In other words, it seems as if the loop comes out of nowhere. This is what we might call the ex nihilo *paradox*. We will discuss these and other paradoxes of causation in Chapter 5.

The final set of puzzles includes the *paradoxes of identity*. Consider again the case of T.J.D.'s inventor, who takes his watch back to a time at which it already exists. This results in a material object being in two different places at the same time—something that T.J.D., at least, finds hard to believe ("Boy! Page Einstein!"). This kind of worry seems to presuppose a certain view about identity[63]—namely, that the same thing can't be in two places at once. If this principle were correct, then the "self-visitation" featured in this kind of story would be straightforwardly impossible.

More recently, it has been suggested that self-visitation would violate an even more basic principle of identity—namely, the principle that nothing can differ from itself. Nicholas J. J. Smith puts the worry as follows:

[One] traditional objection to time travel is this: the time traveler has grey hair when they begin their journey in 2014 and when they end it in 1984; but in 1984 they had black hair; therefore

---

That decided me... I had seen myself return from my time-trip *before* I had started it; had I *not* seen that return, I would *not* have commenced that strange journey, and so could *not* have returned in order to induce me to decide that I *would* make the journey! (Bridge 1931: 916)

See also the references in Nahin (1999: 304–19).

[62] For science fiction examples of the bootstrapping paradox, see Dee (1954), Gerrold (1973), and Heinlein (1959).

[63] Or at least it assumes a particular view that can be *formulated* in terms of identity. As David Lewis (1986a: 192–3) points out, many puzzles that seem to be about identity are really puzzles about something else.

the same individual both does and does not have black hair in 1984; this violates Leibniz's Law (the principle that if one thing is identical with another then any property possessed by the one is also possessed by the other); therefore time travel is impossible.   (1998: 157)

We will discuss this problem and other issues that arise for self-visitation in Chapter 6.[64]

. . .

As this brief survey suggests, the paradoxes of time travel take a variety of different forms, but they all share the same conclusion—namely, that time travel is (metaphysically) impossible. So, in order to determine whether time travel is possible, we must determine whether or not these arguments are sound. That is the goal of this book.

---

[64] There is at least one family of "paradoxes" left out of our survey—what we might call the "epistemic" paradoxes of time travel. The most famous member of this family is the "Where are they?" argument, which was first given by D. L. Cumming in a letter to *Amazing Stories* (April 1928):

> I believe the best proof that time-traveling will never be attained is the absence of travelers now. The future beings do not come back to this era, for we do not see them; and as no one has seen or talked with any, it means that this ambition will never be realized. If they recede in time at all, they will come back indefinitely, and we would see them. What better proof would one need?

Other versions of this argument have been given by Clarke (1962), Fulmer (1980), Hawking (1994), and Reinganum (1986), among others. However, I do not consider this kind of argument to be a genuine paradox since it does not give us any reason to think that time travel is *impossible*—at best, it gives us a reason to think that time travel won't be *actual*.

For more on the "Where are they?" argument, see Toomey (2007: Chapter 11). For a very different kind of epistemic paradox, see Sorenson (1987) and the discussion in Dyke (2005) and Richmond (2010a). For yet another kind of epistemic paradox, see Dummett (1964) and the discussion in Garrett (2014a) and Roache (2015).

2

Temporal Paradoxes

Only time will tell.

—Proverb of unknown origin

The Time Machine opens with a dinner party at the house of an unnamed time traveler. Among the guests are a psychologist, a medical man, and a provincial mayor, all of whom are treated to a lengthy lecture on a "recondite matter":

'Scientific people,' proceeded the Time Traveller...'know very well that Time is only a kind of Space. Here is a popular scientific diagram, a weather record. This line I trace with my finger shows the movement of the barometer. Yesterday it was so high, yesterday night it fell, then this morning it rose again, and so gently upward to here. Surely the mercury did not trace this line in any of the dimensions of Space generally recognized? But certainly it traced such a line, and that line, therefore, we must conclude was along *the Time-Dimension*.'

'But,' said the Medical Man, staring hard at a coal in the fire, 'if Time is really only a fourth dimension of Space, why is it, and why has it always been, regarded as something different?'

'...the great difficulty is this,' interrupted the Psychologist. 'You can move about in all directions of Space, but you cannot move about in Time.'

'That [replied the Time Traveller] is the germ of my great discovery.'   (Wells 2009: 5)

In this passage, Wells's time traveler suggests that he was led to his discovery of time travel by rethinking his views on time. According to his new, "scientific" way of thinking, time is nothing more than a dimension of space. Since we can move back and forth along the spatial dimensions, he reasoned that we should be able to do the same thing in time. Something similar was true of Wells himself.[1] During the Victorian England of his youth, there was a popular fascination with higher-order dimensions.[2] Some people thought of these dimensions in spatial terms,[3] while others speculated that they

---

[1] For further details, see the very helpful preface to Nahin (2011).

[2] This interest was largely due to the writings of mathematicians like Simon Newcomb and Charles Hinton. Wells himself probably heard about the fourth dimension from Simon Newcomb's address to the New York Mathematical Society in 1893. This lecture was published in *Nature* in 1894, and is referenced in *The Time Machine* (which was published in 1895). For an overview of Victorian views on the fourth dimension, see Henderson (1983).

[3] The spatial interpretation was suggested by Edwin A. Abbott's novella, *Flatland* (1884).

were spiritual in nature.[4] But Wells was gripped by the idea that *time* was the fourth dimension, and it was this thought that led to his speculations on time travel.

Some have claimed that Wells's view of time is required to make sense of time travel.[5] After all, if times were not like places, it would not make any sense to talk about "traveling" to them. Whether or not this is right is a matter of some debate,[6] but this much is clear: In order to properly evaluate the prospects for traveling in time, we must first have a better understanding of time itself.[7]

1. Two Debates in the Philosophy of Time

Philosophical debates about the nature of time are as old as philosophy itself. These debates can be helpfully organized around two related topics: the ontology of time and the reality of tense.[8] We will address each of these topics in turn.

1.1 The ontology of time

The first debate about time concerns the existence of the past and the future. Some philosophers, known as *eternalists*, claim that past and future times are just as real as other places.[9] For example, we all think that the North Pole and the South Pole exist, even though they don't exist *here*. In the same way, the eternalist claims that yesterday and tomorrow both exist, even though they don't exist *now*. What goes for past and future times also goes for non-present objects, people, and events. For example, the eternalist claims that our ancient ancestors and future descendants all exist and are just as real as the people around us, even though none of those people exist right now.

Eternalists often illustrate their view by depicting the physical universe as a four-dimensional manifold (or "block universe"[10]) in which time is treated just like a spatial dimension. (See Figure 2.1.)[11]

---

[4] The spiritualist interpretation was suggested by German astronomer Johann Carl Friederich Zöllner. For an introduction to his views, see Rucker (1984: Chapter 5).

[5] See, for example, Bigelow (2001), Godfrey-Smith (1980), and Grey (1999).

[6] See, for example, Dowe (2000), Keller and Nelson (2001), and Licon (2011).

[7] This point was first made by Enrique Gaspar in his early time travel novel *El Anacronópete*: "But in order to explain how to turn back time, it is first necessary for us to know what time consists of" (1887/2012: 10).

[8] There are, of course, many other debates about time (including, for example, the debate between substantivalists and relationists). But these two debates are the ones that are most relevant to the topic of time travel. (Various debates about the structure of time are also important; some of these debates will be introduced later in this chapter.)

[9] Eternalism is defended by many philosophers, including Lewis (1976), Quine (1950), and Russell (1914).

[10] This description goes back at least to F. H. Bradley (1893: Chapter II, section 13).

[11] Eternalism is sometimes *equated* with the view that reality consists of a "block universe," but this is probably misleading since one could believe in the reality of past and future entities without thinking that reality has anything like the structure of a block. See fn. 12 and, especially, sections 5 and 6 of this chapter.

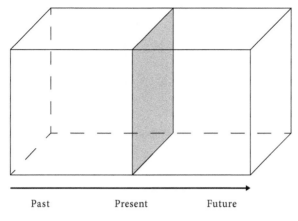

Past   Present   Future

Figure 2.1[12]

This is the picture of time suggested by Wells. It is also the view suggested—with some adjustments[13]—by contemporary physics. We will discuss the implications of this view for the possibility of time travel in section 2 of this chapter.

A very different picture of time is suggested by *the presentist*, who thinks that only the current moment is real. There are various ways of understanding this view, but the most common one is eliminativist: When the presentist says that the past and future are *unreal*, she means that they are *non-existent*. The same thing is true for people, objects, and events—everything that exists, exists now.[14] Pictorially, the presentist can be thought of as shrinking the eternalist's block to a single slice of time. (See Figure 2.2 on the next page.)

---

[12] This figure is limited in several important ways. First, the drawing represents the universe as having only two spatial dimensions (corresponding to the height and depth of the block). Second, the drawing represents the universe as having both a beginning and an end, whereas time might be infinite in at least one direction. Finally, the drawing also limits the block in all spatial directions, whereas space might be infinite in extent.

[13] See sections 5 and 6 of this chapter.

[14] Three points of clarification. First, some presentists wish to distinguish between past objects and *merely* past objects. I am a past object, it is sometimes said, since I existed in the past, whereas Abraham Lincoln is a *merely* past object, since he exists *only* in the past. Those presentists should understand my talk of past objects to be about merely past objects. Second, some presentists suggest that we can identify "past times" with presently existing entities—e.g., maximally consistent conjunctions of statements that express a truth when prefixed by an appropriate past-tense operator. These "times" are "past" in the sense that they used to express truths. But they are not *genuinely* past entities—they are not on a par with Abraham Lincoln—since those statements still exist. When I say that presentists do not believe in past (or future) times, I mean that they do not believe in any times with the genuine, irreducible property of *being past* (or *being yet to come*)—whatever exists has the property of *being present*. Finally, some presentists may wish to claim that there are some things which exist, but do not exist *now*—God, for example, is sometimes said to exist outside of time, in which case he would not have the property of *being present*. For this reason, it may be best to keep to a purely negative characterization of presentism—namely, the characterization according to which there are no (genuine, merely) past or future entities.

Present

Figure 2.2

The presentist picture is controversial,[15] but the guiding idea is attractive: *The past no longer exists and the future is yet to be.* Whether or not this idea can be squared with the possibility of time travel is something we will return to in section 3 of this chapter.

A third and final view about the ontology of time holds that past and present times exist, but future ones do not. On this view, the present time is conceived of as the leading edge of a "growing block"—a universe in which new slices are continually being added to the existing four-dimensional manifold.[16] (See Figure 2.3.)

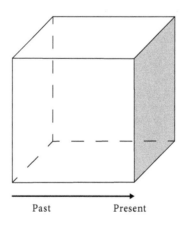

Past   Present

Figure 2.3

[15] For example, it has been argued that the view is unable to account for cross-time relations (Sider 2001: 25–34), that it posits ungrounded truths about the past and future (Lewis 1992: 219), and that it is inconsistent with the teachings of special relativity (Putnam 1962). For a discussion of these and other issues, see Bourne (2006).

[16] See Adams (1986: 322), Broad (1923), and Forrest (2005). Tooley (1997) is often cited as a defender of the growing block theory, but it is unclear whether his view fits the above characterization. On this point, see Zimmerman (2005: 404, fn. 10).

This "growing block theory" is often criticized as an untenable middle ground between eternalism and presentism. But the view is based on a very natural idea—namely, that *the future, unlike the past, is open*.[17] We will discuss the implications of this view for time travel in section 4 of this chapter.

1.2 The reality of tense

A second debate in the philosophy of time concerns the status of tensed facts.[18] Following McTaggart (1908), philosophers refer to these as *A-facts*.[19] Examples include the following:

> The sun rose.
> The sun is rising.
> The sun will rise again.

Each of these statements can be thought of as attributing a property to the sun. These properties—*having risen*, *rising*, and *being such that it will rise again*—are examples of *A-properties*. The characteristic feature of these properties (and the corresponding facts) is that they change over time.[20] The sun was rising this morning, for example, but it is not doing so now. And tomorrow's sunrise will soon change from being *future* to being *present*. Indeed, tomorrow's sunrise is *constantly* becoming less and less future, so the A-facts are continually changing.

Things are very different when it comes to *B-facts*. For example:

> The American Revolution was earlier than the French Revolution.
> The French Revolution was simultaneous with the Haitian Revolution.[21]
> The Chinese Revolution was later than the French Revolution.

These facts all concern the temporal relations between different events. These relations—*earlier than*, *simultaneous with*, and *later than*—are called *B-relations*. Crucially, these relations do not change with the passage of time.[22] This is clearest if we picture these

---

[17] This is the picture of time suggested by John Connor in *Terminator 2*: "The future's not set. There's no fate but what we make for ourselves." However, Connor later takes this back at the beginning of *Terminator 3*: "The future has not been written. There is no fate but what we make for ourselves. I wish I could believe that."

This idea that the future is open can also be used to motivate a "branching" picture of time on which there exist many possible futures. See, for example, McCall (1994). McCall's view is related to (but distinct from) the branching timeline theory that we will discuss in Chapter 3.

[18] Facts are not linguistic entities, so the phrase "tensed facts" is something of a misnomer. However, the characteristic feature of these facts (discussed below) is that they can change over time in much the way that tensed sentences can change their truth-values over time. For this reason, it is natural to extend "tense" talk to facts (and also to properties and statements).

[19] McTaggart focused on what he called "the A-series," but the "A" terminology naturally extends to talk about statements, properties, and facts.

[20] In fact, it is sometimes said that the passage of time consists in the alteration of these A-properties.

[21] More carefully, *a large part* of the French Revolution was simultaneous with *a large part* of the Haitian Revolution.

[22] Or, at least, they do not change *because* of the passage of time. Whether or not they can be changed by time travelers is a matter we will return to in Chapter 3.

events from the perspective of eternalism: On that view, the location of all the world's events—past, present, and future—are fixed within the four-dimensional spacetime manifold.[23] So, while the French Revolution may have changed from being *present* to being *past*, it did not (and cannot) change from being *after* the American Revolution to being *before*. In this sense, the B-facts are eternal.

Given the distinction between A-facts and B-facts, we can ask how these two kinds of facts relate. In particular, we can ask whether one kind of fact is reducible to the other. Of course, there are many different things one might mean by "reducible," but it is natural to understand this question in terms of *grounding*: Is it the case that one set of temporal facts can be grounded in the other? According to *the B-theorist*, the answer is *yes*—all the facts about what *was*, *is*, or *will be* the case can be grounded in facts about temporal relations. In other words, all A-facts are grounded in B-facts.[24]

There are many different ways that this reduction might go, but it is natural to think that a past-tensed fact—like the fact that the sun *was* rising—is grounded in the fact that the corresponding event—the sunrise—was going on earlier than some other salient event (like the typing of this sentence). Similarly, the sun *is* rising only if, and in that case because, there is a sunrise that is *simultaneous* with some salient event, and the sun *will* rise again only if, and in that case because, there is a sunrise that is *later* than that event. In this way, facts about what *was*, *is*, or *will* be the case are grounded in facts about the temporal relations between events.[25]

B-theorists often try to motivate their view by drawing an analogy to space. For example, it is natural to think that the sun is rising *in the east* only if, and in that case because, the sunrise is located *to the east of* some salient event (like the typing of this sentence). The same thing is true for claims about what is going on to the west, north, or south. All these things are a matter of perspective, in the sense that they depend of how things relate, spatially, to a given observer. For the B-theorist, the same thing is true in the case of time—claims about what is past, present, or future are all a matter of perspective. The idea that there is an objective, non-relational fact about what is "present," for example, is no more plausible than the idea that there is an objective, non-relational fact about where "here" really is.

According to *the A-theory*, this analogy is deeply mistaken.[26] What's going on *here* may be a matter of what's going on around *me*, but what's happening *now* is not a matter of how things relate to me, or to you, or to anything else. In other words, at least

---

[23] Things are less clear if we think of the issue from the perspective of the growing block theory. After all, that theory says that new things are constantly coming into existence, and each of these entities will obviously enter into new relations to previously existing events. In this sense, *what B-relations there are* will change. However, the growing block theorist will presumably want to say that these B-relations, *once established*, are unchanging.

[24] B-theorists include Mellor (1998), Smart (1949), and Williams (1951).

[25] See Mellor (1998: Chapters 2 and 3) for a much more detailed discussion of the B-theory.

[26] A-theorists include Gale (1968), Prior (1968), and Smith (1993).

some A-facts are objective, irreducible features of the world. Reality, in this sense, is irreducibly "tensed."[27]

The debate over tensed facts is closely related to the issue of temporal ontology. This is most obvious in the case of the B-theory. That theory directly quantifies over past and future events, so it clearly requires the truth of eternalism.[28] The presentist, in contrast, denies the existence of past and future entities, so she cannot ground tensed facts in the temporal relations involving those things. For this reason, presentism implies the A-theory.

The relationship between tense and the growing block theory is more complicated. Obviously, the growing block theorist accepts the existence of past and present entities, so he can (if he wishes) accept the B-theoretic treatment of past-tensed facts. On the other hand, the growing block theorist does not believe in future entities, so he cannot provide a B-theoretic ground for future-tensed facts. One option for the B-theorist is to simply say that there are no future-tensed facts to ground. Indeed, one might think that the lack of future-tensed facts is what constitutes the "openness" of the future.[29]

In the end, however, the growing block theory of time cannot be squared with the B-theory of tense. The sticking point concerns the "growing" part of the growing block theory.[30] To say that the block is "growing" is to say that *it used to include fewer things*. This is supposed to be part of what distinguishes the growing block universe from a duplicate, eternalist universe that just so happens to end *now*. However, the B-theorist can only understand this claim in relational terms—namely, as the claim that fewer things were present at some past time than there are now. This claim may or may not be true, but, either way, it will not distinguish the growing block theorist from the eternalist—after all, both parties agree about how many objects are present right now, and about how many things are present at each point in the past. So, in order for the growing block theorist to distinguish his view from that of the eternalist, he will have to say something like the following: There used to be fewer things *when past times were present*—that is, when past times had the irreducible A-property of *being*

---

[27] Note that the A-theorist could go one step further and say that all facts about temporal relations are grounded, in some way, in facts about what *was*, *is*, or *will be* the case. Consider, for example, the fact that the French Revolution and the Haitian Revolution were going on at the same time. The A-theorist might say that this relational fact is grounded in the following non-relational fact: There is some unit n such that the French Revolution and the Haitian Revolution were both going on n units ago. If this strategy could be successfully generalized, we would have a theory on which B-facts are grounded in A-facts, rather than the other way around. (Whether or not this strategy *could* be successfully generalized is not a question we will address here.)

[28] More carefully, it requires an eternalist ontology *on the assumption that there are some past- and future-tensed facts*. Note that the reverse does not hold: One can consistently believe in past and future times without thinking that all tensed facts are reducible. This combination of views is suggested (but not endorsed) by Broad (1923: 59–60); for a more recent defense, see Smith (1993).

[29] For an alternative approach to "open future" talk, see Barnes and Cameron (2009).

[30] Here I follow Sider (2001: 21–5).

present. This would successfully distinguish the growing block theory from the eternalist view, but only at the cost of accepting the A-theory of tense.[31]

2. Eternalism and Time Travel

Having surveyed some of the main views in the philosophy of time, we are now in a position to explore the implications of those views for the topic of time travel. We begin, in this section, with the doctrine of eternalism.

The eternalist picture of time travel is often associated with David Lewis. He describes this view as follows:

The world—the time traveler's world, or ours—is a four-dimensional manifold of events...A time traveler, like anyone else, is a streak through the manifold of space-time, a whole composed of stages located at various times and places. But he is not a streak like other streaks. If he travels toward the past he is a zig-zag streak, doubling back on himself. If he travels toward the future, he is a stretched-out streak. And if he travels either way instantaneously, so that there are no intermediate stages between the stage that departs and the stage that arrives and his journey has zero duration, then he is a broken streak.   (1976: 146)

This passage begins with the assumption of eternalism—the view that past, present, and future are equally real. It adds to this the assumption that objects persist through time by having different "stages" at different times, in the same way that objects extend through space by having different parts in different places.[32] On this combination of views, persisting objects can be thought of as spacetime streaks or "worms" that stretch throughout the block universe. For example, Figure 2.4 depicts a simple particle that is stationary from t_1 to t_3 and then moves continuously upward from t_3 to t_5, before returning to rest.

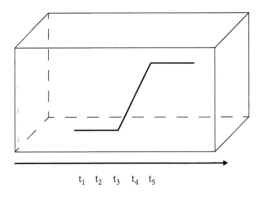

t_1 t_2 t_3 t_4 t_5

Figure 2.4

---

[31] For a more detailed discussion on the relation between tense and the growing block theory, see Tooley (1997) and Sider (2001: 21–5).
[32] We discuss this view of persistence in much more detail in Chapter 6.

Each point on this line represents a momentary stage of the particle. When we take all of those points together, we get a "worldline" that tracks that particle's position over time.

For the eternalist, time traveling objects can also be depicted as spacetime streaks, with the only difference being in the shape that those streaks take. In Lewis's terminology, they will either be "zigzagged," "broken," or "stretched out."

First, consider a simple particle that starts off at rest, and then travels back in time while moving upward in space. When that object eventually resumes its normal journey toward the future, its worldline will have formed the shape of a backwards "Z." (See Figure 2.5.)

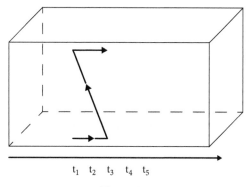

Figure 2.5

This is what Lewis has in mind when he talks about a "zigzag" streak.

Second, consider a particle that "jumps" directly back in time, in the way that Marty McFly does in the *Back to the Future* movies. If that particle also moves *up* when it jumps, it might look just like the Figure 2.5 particle, but without the intermediate stages. (See Figure 2.6.)

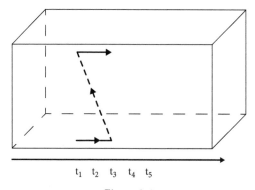

Figure 2.6

In this figure, the dotted line indicates a direct causal connection between the last stage of the particle before it departs and first stage of the particle when it arrives. This connection is "direct" in the sense that it does not run through any intermediate stages. That is why Lewis refers to this kind of time traveler as a "broken" spacetime streak.

Finally, recall the discussion of Wells's Time Traveller from Chapter 1. That was a case of continuous forward time travel, which is very different from the kind of discontinuous backward time travel depicted in Figure 2.6. Indeed, if we were to illustrate that kind of case with a single particle in the block universe, it might look just like Figure 2.4. The only difference would be in the numbers assigned to the different points along the particle's worldline. For example, in Figure 2.4, there is only one unit of external time separating the t_3-stage of the particle from the t_4-stage. However, if this is a case of forward time travel, one unit of personal time might correspond to hundreds of units of external time. This is what Lewis has in mind when he describes this kind of time traveler as "stretched out"—the actual time between its stages will be longer than the personal time between those stages.

The eternalist picture of time travel is simple and straightforward. Indeed, traveling through time, on this picture, is not that different from traveling through space—the only real difference has to do with the angle of the relevant worldline.[33] However, there is at least one potential problem for the eternalist view. This problem has to do with the "zigzag" model of continuous backward time travel. Here is how William Grey puts the worry:

One difficulty for zig-zag aggregates, not widely remarked upon, is what may be called the double-occupancy problem. [Let us suppose that] Tim...stepped into the time machine on 1 January 2000, adjusted the dial, and precisely at noon set off into the past. For the observers outside it seems that the machine simply vanishes when Tim presses the button. But how can the 'movement' into the past possibly get started? We know that at times later than noon there is no machine present, since it has disappeared into the past. But what of the moments just before noon? At those times there seem to be not one but *two* machines—one going backwards and the other forwards—each apparently occupying (or attempting to occupy) the same location! That is, it seems that as the machine sets out into the past it will collide with itself...the Tim-at-noon stage has earlier and later stages at the same space-time location.   (1999: 61–2)

The implicit premise in Grey's argument is that double-occupancy is impossible—two objects (or two stages of the same object) cannot exist in the same place at the same time.[34] Hence, travel to the past cannot get started, since the earlier stages of a potential time traveler will invariably block the way.

---

[33] Of course, the difference in angles indicates that there are at least some differences between the cases. Most obviously, the acute angle in Figure 2.5 generates backward-pointing arrows, which are supposed to indicate the presence of reverse causal dependence. This is very different from the case of Figure 2.4, in which the direction of causation matches the direction of time. Still, if the eternalist view is correct, time travel and spatial travel have many important features in common.

[34] The puzzles of material constitution have led some philosophers to reject this thesis—see, for example, Baker (2000), Fine (2003), and Wiggins (1968). However, these philosophers are only interested in allowing for co-located objects when those objects are *constitutionally related*—as, for example, when a lump of clay

Grey's objection is particularly vivid in the case of Wellsian time travel, since Wells (2009: 11) makes it clear that his time machine stays in the exact same place as it moves back and forth in time.[35] But, in that case, backward time travel would require the machine to retrace its very own worldline, which would require it to have two different stages in the same place at the same time. Since two things cannot be in the same place at the same time, backward time travel is prohibited. This is *the double-occupancy paradox*.[36]

The obvious reply to this argument is to part ways with Wells and say that time travel to the past requires a corresponding movement in space. This is the reply recommended by Phil Dowe:

> How does a particle run around in time without getting in its own way? Answer: same way that two particles collide, i.e., by being in motion…[F]or a time machine to travel back in time on the method envisaged by Grey, it could be moving across a field, and we should also see its reverse alter self moving towards it…and as the switch is hit the two collide, apparently annihilating both. Thus the time machine avoids colliding with itself.   (2000: 445–6)

The situation described by Dowe is like the one depicted in Figure 2.5. To the uninformed observer, this will look like a case of two particles coming together and being destroyed upon contact. But what is really going on (as indicated by the arrows) is a single particle turning around and going backward in time. It is this upward movement that allows the particle to get around its earlier self. That, one might think, is the whole point of the "zig" in the zigzag model of time travel.

Unfortunately, this response underestimates the force of Grey's objection. To illustrate, it will be helpful to consider the case of a solid line segment that tries to travel back in a one-dimensional space. (See Figure 2.7.)

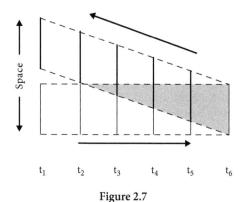

Figure 2.7

comes to constitute a clay statue. Those who are attracted to this "constitution view" are therefore encouraged to qualify the relevant principle as follows: Two objects cannot exist in the same place at the same time *without being constitutionally related*. (In Chapter 6, we will see that even this qualified principle can be challenged.)

[35] Talk of "same place" should be understood in relational terms—the Time Traveller's machine stays in the same place, relative to his laboratory, the surface of the Earth, etc.

[36] This objection to Wellsian time travel has been endorsed by many, including Cook (1982: 52), Edwards (1995: 21), Harrison (1971: 13–5), Nahin (1999: 23–5), and Pitkin (1914: 524–5).

In this diagram, the narrower vertical lines (in the lower series) represent the one-dimensional bar as it passes from t_1 to t_6. At t_6, the bar begins to move upward in space and backward in time (this being indicated by the diagonal series of bold vertical lines). The shaded region indicates the area of spatiotemporal overlap that results.[37]

The important feature of this case is that the dimensionality of the line matches the dimensionality of the space in which it is embedded. Hence, the line can move up or it can move down, but it cannot move *around* its former self (not, at least, if it moves continuously). Thus, any attempt at backward time travel will result in either spatial coincidence or self-collision. Either way, we seem to have run into trouble.

The same argument can be extended to a two-dimensional object in a two-dimensional space, or a three-dimensional object in a three-dimensional space. For example, Wells's own story—which features a three-dimensional object continuously moving into the past of a three-dimensional world—would seem to be impossible, since his machine would inevitably be blocked by its former self. The same point also applies to Lewis's model of time travel, since he clearly intends his picture to apply to three-dimensional objects in a world of three spatial dimensions. In this respect his model fails. At best, Lewis has provided a coherent picture of how one- and two-dimensional objects might travel back to the past.

Many authors have discussed the double-occupancy problem, and many different replies have been put forward.[38] For example, one could defend the coherence of a Wells-type story by insisting that co-location is metaphysically possible. This seems to have been the option that Wells himself recommended. In his story, the Time Traveller sets out for the future in his time machine and, as the years flash by, he begins to reflect upon the dangers of stopping:

The peculiar risk lay in the possibility of my finding some substance in the space which I, or the machine, occupied. So long as I travelled at a high velocity through time, this scarcely mattered; I was, so to speak, attenuated—was slipping like a vapour through the interstices of intervening substances! But to come to a stop involved the jamming of myself, molecule by molecule, into whatever lay in my way; meant bringing my atoms into such intimate contact with those of the obstacle that a profound chemical reaction—possibly a far-reaching explosion—would result, and blow myself and my apparatus out of all possible dimensions—into the Unknown.   (2009: 18)[39]

Wells's description is entertaining, but it is also problematic. For one thing, it is not at all clear what it would mean to say that someone "traveled at a high velocity through time"

---

[37] Although the diagram may not be clear, the description of the case implies that there is no time at which the time traveling line overlaps its earlier self in its entirety. Rather, the line partially overlaps its earlier self at every moment between t_2 and t_6, where this overlap involves the complete overlap of distinct spatial parts of the corresponding line-stages. For example, at t_4 the bottom half of the upper line-stage overlaps with the top half of the earlier line-stage.

[38] See, for example, Bernstein (2015), Carroll (2008a), Dowe (2000: 445–6), and Le Poidevin (2005).

[39] See also the exchange between the Time Traveller, the Psychologist, and the Provincial Mayor on p. 11 of the text.

(as opposed to traveling at a high velocity through space).[40] Moreover, it is unclear how moving at a high velocity would help with double-occupancy—after all, interpenetrating matter seems incredible, no matter how fast one is moving. In any case, this response has few modern defenders, since the possibility of co-location is at least as controversial as the possibility of time travel itself.[41]

A second option is to give up on the coherence of Wells's story, while still insisting that backward time travel is possible. There are at least five different ways of developing this idea.

First, if one continues to think of the world as having only three spatial dimensions (in addition to the one temporal dimension), one could still allow for zero-, one-, or two-dimensional objects to travel back in time. As we have already seen, such objects can easily get around their earlier selves, provided that they are embedded in a higher-order space.

Alternatively, one could make room for three-dimensional time travelers by introducing a fourth spatial dimension. In that case, Wells's Time Traveller would be free to move into the past, provided that he also moves in a direction perpendicular to height, length, and depth. Such a traveler would be like the flatland inhabitant who cuts in front of a line by moving up and over his two-dimensional plane-mates.[42]

Third, one could move even further away from the traditional view of time by allowing for the kinds of closed timelike curves discussed in general relativity. For example, one might allow an object to move continuously into its (local) future, enter into a wormhole, and then emerge into its (local) past. This kind of backward time travel would avoid double-occupancy, since it would eliminate any "turnaround."[43]

Fourth, one could allow for three-dimensional objects to move back and forth in a (flat) three-dimensional world by giving up on the requirement of spatiotemporal continuity. As Lewis notes, it is possible to picture a case of discontinuous time travel in which a particle disappears at one time and reappears at another without any stages between. (See Figure 2.6.) The same approach can be applied in the case of the time traveling line segment. (See Figure 2.8 on the next page.)

In this case the line segment remains motionless from t_1 to t_6. At that point, it jumps back to a different location at t_1 (with the curved arrow indicating the relevant causal connection). From there, the line continues on toward the future (as indicated by the bold vertical line at the top). Since there are no intermediate stages in this case, there is no worry about collision or co-location. In this way, discontinuous time travel avoids the double-occupancy paradox.

---

[40] However, see Le Poidevin (2005: 339–41) for some interesting suggestions.

[41] For more on the matter of interpenetrating matter, see the exchange between Cortes (1976), Barnette (1978), Ginsberg (1981), and Teller (1983).

[42] Abbott (1884). Relatedly, Grey (1999: 61) and Le Poidevin (2005: 340–3) suggest that one could avoid the double-occupancy paradox by introducing a second temporal dimension.

[43] We will discuss this idea in more detail in section 6 of this chapter.

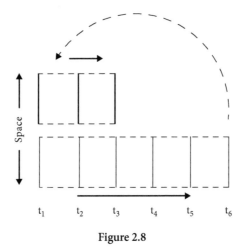

Figure 2.8

The most common objection to this solution concerns the problem of identity over time.[44] One way of making this worry vivid is by imagining a case of a miraculous appearance.[45] Suppose, for example, that an ordinary line segment is sitting motionless at t_1. At that exact moment, a second line segment (which just so happens to look like the first) pops into existence out of nowhere, just a little bit to the north. Sometime later (at t_6) the original line segment pops out of existence for no reason whatsoever. To an outside observer, this kind of case would look exactly like the example depicted in Figure 2.8. However, this would not be a case of time travel—it would simply be a case of two unrelated lines. The challenge, of course, is to say what the relevant difference is between the two cases.

The natural response is to point to causation. In the case of time travel, the line segment that appears at t_1 depends, in the right sort of way, on the segment that disappears at t_6. Some, however, reject this response since it requires unmediated causal action at a distance. This is very different from the kind of causal interactions we normally see on a day-to-day basis. Typically, when one thing exerts a causal influence on another, it does so by coming into contact with that second object, or by being connected to the second object through a chain of different objects, each of which comes into contact with another (in the way that one domino might exert a causal influence on another by tipping over a series of dominoes in between them). Obviously, there is nothing like this going on in the case of discontinuous time travel. The t_6-stage in Figure 2.8, for example, exerts a causal influence on the upper t_1-stage, even though there is no contact or connection between the two. This kind of causation is unusual, to say the least.[46]

---

[44] See Lewis (1976: 147) and Grey (1999: 147).   [45] See Dowe (2000: 445).

[46] Einstein famously refers to this kind of causation as "spooky action at a distance." Similarly, Le Poidevin (2005: 334) calls it "radical" and Edwards (1995: 21) deems it "magical." However, as is often pointed out, cases of quantum entanglement provide some reason for thinking that this kind of causation is not only possible, but actual. (For an introduction to these issues, see Berkovitz 2007.)

We will have much more to say about the topic of causation in Chapter 5. For now, we should note that there is one last way to solve the paradox without resorting to discontinuous time travel. This solution is suggested by Robin Le Poidevin:[47]

We run into the problem of overlap…because we have assumed that the entire machine starts to travel backwards at [once]. An alternative suggestion is that…only part of the machine will have disappeared into the past. The remaining part is still travelling forwards through time in the normal way and advancing on d [a specific point in space]. For us (non-time-travelling) onlookers, the time machine, as we might put it, behaves like the Cheshire Cat: it slowly disappears from sight. Under these circumstances there is no double-occupancy problem.   (2005: 344–5)

This description of the case is somewhat cryptic, but we can understand the proposal by considering a variant on our earlier example. (Figure 2.9.)

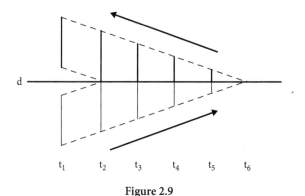

Figure 2.9

In this case, a one-dimensional line is moving upwards in space as it goes forward in time from t_1 to t_2. (This is indicated, once again, by the vertical lines on the bottom half of the diagram.) At t_2, the end of the line reaches point d, which we can think of as a "point of destruction". As the bottom portion of the line continues moving upward, the top parts are continuously destroyed, so that no part of the line moves beyond d. By t_6, the one-dimensional line has shrunk to a zero-dimensional point. And, as a zero-dimensional object in a one-dimensional space, that object is then free to "reverse" its temporal direction without colliding with its former self. Imagine that it does. As the object travels back in time it gradually grows in length (indicated by the bold verticals lines above d). By t_2, the line has completely re-grown and, by t_1, it has completely separated from its earlier self.[48] Crucially, the line does all of this without coinciding with any of its earlier stages. Hence, we have a one-dimensional object in a (flat) one-dimensional space that travels continuously to the past while avoiding any

---

[47] Le Poidevin credits this idea to Dowe (2000).

[48] This is how we should describe the case, given that we know it to be a case of time travel. To the uninformed observer, the case will look like one in which two sticks come together, and gradually annihilate each other, until both sticks are permanently destroyed.

double-occupancy. Moreover, it is easy to extend this treatment to a two-dimensional time traveler (that shrinks to a line-segment and then re-grows) or a three-dimensional time traveler (that shrinks to a slice and then re-grows). In other words, we seem to have a perfectly general solution to the double-occupancy paradox.

However, Le Poidevin mentions a potential worry for this solution:

In a nutshell...the problem is this: how can something continue to exist if there are...times when only a spatial part of it does so? As Figure [2.9] shows...the spatial extent of the time machine in existence at any one time gradually diminishes until it disappears altogether. We might be able to tolerate the disappearance of a small part of the machine, and concede that the machine itself is still in existence. But when half or more of it is gone, we would be much less willing to do so. For some impossible-to-specify period before the last part of the machine disappears, the machine itself is no longer in existence... [Hence] the object has a discontinuous existence: It goes out of existence and then comes back.   (2005: 345–6)

Le Poidevin calls this "the Cheshire Cat problem" after the character in *Alice's Adventures in Wonderland* who shrinks to a smile before disappearing altogether. The problem is supposed to be the following. If we imagine Wells's three-dimensional time traveler gradually shrinking to a two-dimensional slice, we are not really imagining *the time traveler* shrinking to a two-dimensional slice—after all, a human being cannot survive that kind of process. Similarly, the line in Figure 2.9 cannot shrink to a point (and then re-grow), since a point is not enough for a line. Since the line does not exist throughout the process, we do not have a case of continuous time travel.

Perhaps Le Poidevin is right. This depends on what, exactly, we mean by "continuous" time travel. But the important point is that, in this case, the first and final stages of the time-traveling line are connected by a continuous series of intervening stages (even if some of those stages are not *line*-stages). Because of this, we do not need to appeal to unmediated causal action at a distance in order to link the first stage to the last. That was what Le Poidevin found objectionable about the earlier model of discontinuous time travel, and that worry does not apply in the current case.[49]

In summary: We have seen that, for the eternalist, time travelers are not all that different from the ordinary objects around us. *All* persisting objects can be thought of as streaks through spacetime, with time travelers being distinguished by one of three characteristic shapes ("stretched," "broken," or "zigzagged"). We have also seen that the zigzag model can avoid the paradox of double-occupancy by either adding dimensions (or curvature) to spacetime, or by subtracting dimensions from time travelers in the manner described by Le Poidevin.

3. Presentism and Time Travel

On the eternalist view, other times are like other places. Since we can travel to other places, it is natural for the eternalist to think that we can—at least in theory—travel to

---

[49] Le Poidevin (2005: 346).

other times. For the presentist, it is tempting to run this argument in reverse: We can only travel to other times if those times are like other places. But, on the presentist view, other times are *not* like other places. So, on the presentist view, time travel is impossible.

Something like this line of thought has convinced many people that presentism and time travel are incompatible.[50] This section investigates several versions of this argument, and finds them all wanting.

3.1 *The no destination argument*

The most common version of the incompatibility argument is the *no destination objection*.[51] Simon Keller and Michael Nelson put this line of reasoning as follows:

On the presentist model, the past and future do not exist, so there is nowhere for the time traveler to go. Traveling to Portland is possible, because Portland is right there waiting for you. But traveling to the Land of Oz is impossible, because there is no such place. Traveling to the past or future is more like traveling to the Land of Oz, if presentism is true . . . So presentism implies the impossibility of time travel.   (2001: 334–5)

We will formulate this argument as follows:

   (P1) If presentism is true, then there are no past or future times.
   (P2) It is impossible to travel to things that do not exist.
   (P3) If it is impossible to travel to past or future times, then time travel is impossible.
   (C)   If presentism is true, then time travel is impossible.

This line of thinking is initially plausible, but ultimately unsound. To see why, consider the following argument:[52]

On the presentist model, the past does not exist, so there is nothing for the historian to study. Studying Portland is possible, because Portland is right there waiting for you. But studying the Land of Oz is impossible, because there is no such place. Studying the past is more like studying the Land of Oz, if presentism is true . . . So presentism implies the impossibility of historians.

This line of thinking is obviously unsound—no one thinks that presentism is incompatible with the study of history. But this line of thinking is exactly analogous to the no destination argument. So, something is wrong with that objection.

To begin, we should note that, while the presentist denies the existence of past times, she does not deny the existence of past-tensed *facts*. For example, the presentist does not believe that yesterday exists, but she is happy to say that the sun rose yesterday. Similarly, the presentist does not believe that George Washington exists, but she is happy to say

---

   [50] See, for example, Bigelow (2001), Eldridge-Smith (2007: 173), and Grey (1999: 56).
   [51] Versions of this objection have been endorsed by Edwards (1995: 12), Eldridge-Smith (2007), Goff (2010: 68), Grey (1999: 56–7), Hanley (1997: 201), Le Poidevin (2003: 171), and Perszyk and Smith (2001). For replies to this objection, see Carroll (2008a), Carroll et al. (2014: Chapter 3), Keller and Nelson (2001), and Monton (2003).
   [52] This analogy is due to Carroll (2008a).

that George Washington was the first president of the United States. These examples may seem problematic. After all, the fact that George Washington was president seems to be a fact about George Washington—it seems to involve George Washington having the past-tensed property of *having been president*. But, on the presentist view, this is impossible. There is no such person, so he cannot have that property.

The presentist typically responds to this worry by drawing an analogy. Suppose someone believes that Sherlock Holmes is the world's greatest detective. One *might* think that this is equivalent to saying that Sherlock Holmes has a certain property— namely, the property of *being believed by someone to be the world's greatest detective*. But many philosophers would take this to be a mistake. According to them, there is no Sherlock Holmes, so he does not have any properties at all (including the property of *being believed by someone to be the world's greatest detective*). In that case, we might find it much more natural to represent this fact as follows:

It is believed to be the case that (Sherlock Holmes is the world's greatest detective).

Here, the phrase "It is believed to be the case that" functions as a sentential operator— that is, a phrase that attaches to one sentence in order to form another. Crucially, this operator is taken to be "ontologically innocent" in the sense that the resulting sentence could be true, even if there is no Sherlock Holmes. In other words, there can still be facts about what people believe, even if the subjects of those beliefs do not exist.

The presentist says the same thing about past-tensed facts. For example, to say that Washington was the first president is not to say that Washington *exists* and that he has the property of *being the first president*. Rather, it is to say the following:

It was the case that (George Washington is the United States' first president).

Here, the phrase "It was the case that" (often abbreviated as "WAS") functions as a sentential operator and, like the belief operator, is taken to be ontologically innocent. In other words, the relevant sentence can be true, even though George Washington no longer exists. More generally, the presentist claims that there can still be facts about what *was* the case for various objects, even if those objects no longer exist.

To return to the topic of history: The presentist will presumably say that, strictly speaking, history is not the study of past times (since there are no such things). Rather, it is the study of presently existing objects in an attempt to learn past-tensed truths. Suppose, for example, that George Washington's favorite color was blue. And suppose that that Zoë is about to learn this past-tensed fact by reading an old journal that she has discovered. In that case, we can say that Zoë is going to "learn about the past," even though the past no longer exists. In this sense, the doctrine of presentism is perfectly compatible with the study of history.

By analogy, the presentist will presumably want to reject the third premise of the no destination argument and say that, strictly speaking, time travel does not require traveling to past or future times (since there are no such things). Rather, it involves interacting with presently existing objects in order to establish certain past- and future-tensed facts. Suppose, for example, that Wells's Time Traveller once sat by a lonely lake during the Triassic Age. And suppose that this past-tensed fact is explained, in part, by the fact that the Time Traveller is about to set his time machine to the year 200,000,000 BCE. In that case, we can say that the Time Traveller is about to "travel to the past," even though the past no longer exists. In this sense, the doctrine of presentism is perfectly compatible with the possibility of time travel.

There is a second way in which the analogy to history helps to undermine the argument for incompatibility.[53] To begin, consider the following claim:

It is impossible to study things that do not exist.

This claim is ambiguous, owing to the scope of the modal operator. To see this, consider the following pair of open sentences:

It is impossible to (study x if x does not exist).
(It is impossible to study x) if x does not exist.

Obviously, the first sentence will express a truth, no matter what one substitutes for 'x'. There is no possible scenario in which someone studies something that does not exist *in that scenario*. However, this possibility is not required by the second sentence. Presumably, there are many things that do not actually exist, but which are studied in some other possible scenarios (scenarios in which those things *do* exist). Indeed, there are many things that *were* studied in the past, even though those things no longer exist. The crucial point is that it *was* the case those things existed *when* they were being studied.

Now consider the analogous claim from the no destination argument:

(P2) It is impossible to travel to things that do not exist.

And consider the following pair of open sentences:

It is impossible to (travel to x if x does not exist).
(It is impossible to travel to x) if x does not exist.

As in the previous case, the first sentence will express a truth no matter what one substitutes for 'x'. There is no possible scenario in which someone travels to a time or place that does not exist *in that scenario*. But, of course, there were many places that were traveled to in the past, and which no longer exist. Presumably, the same thing could be true for times. For example, the Triassic Age is no longer present. So, according to the presentist, it no longer exists. But the presentist could still say that it was the case that: The Time Traveller appeared in the Triassic Age. The crucial point, once again, is that it *was* the case that that time existed *when* the Time Traveller visited.

The more general point, of course, is that traveling to the past is in many ways analogous to studying the past. Since it is generally agreed that presentism is compatible with studying the past, we should also think that it is compatible—one way or another—with time travel.

---

[53] See Rea (2014: 79–80).

3.2 The definitional argument

The no destination argument is unsuccessful, but it does raise an important question—namely: What, exactly, does time travel amount to for the presentist?

The answer to this question is not immediately obvious. In fact, one might try to turn this question into an argument against presentist time travel: According to Lewis, time travel requires there to be a discrepancy between external time and personal time (where external time is the order and metric provided by time itself, and personal time is the order and metric provided by the relevant causal relation). But in order for there to be a discrepancy of this sort, there would have to be at least *two* different stages of an object, standing in different temporal relations (for example, one stage being *earlier than* the other according to external time and *later than* the other according to personal time). This, however, is inconsistent with presentism, for the presentist will say that there is typically only *one* stage for each object—namely, the one that presently exists.[54] A single stage cannot be subject to different temporal orderings; nor can it be separated from itself by different temporal distances. Hence, presentism is incompatible with Lewis's version of time travel.

We will refer to this argument as the *definitional argument* for incompatibility, since it is based on the standard Lewisian definition of time travel.

It should come as little surprise that Lewis's definition raises a problem for the presentist. After all, Lewis is an eternalist and his account is framed in eternalist terms. The challenge for the presentist, then, is to reformulate Lewis's account in a way that fits with her own theory of time.

This situation is not peculiar to time travel. Consider, for example, Lewis's counterfactual theory of causation.[55] According to Lewis, causation is fundamentally a relation between particular events. In its simplest form: event *c* is a cause of event *e* only if, and in that case because, *c* and *e* are distinct events and, if *c* had not occurred, then *e* would not have occurred. Suppose this is correct, and that there are no cases of instantaneous causation (i.e., it is never the case that a cause is simultaneous with its effect). In that case, the presentist who accepts Lewis's account will have to say that there is no causation at all, since there will never be any *c* and *e* that exist at the same time and that satisfy Lewis's definition.

Of course, this argument does not force the presentist to give up on the counterfactual approach to causation. Rather, it simply shows that the presentist will have to translate Lewis's idea into her own terminology. One strategy for doing this is to take causation to be a relation between presently existing facts, rather than temporally separated events. For example, the eternalist might say that Monday's match-strike caused Tuesday's forest fire. The presentist, on the other hand, can say that there was a forest fire on Tuesday because there was a match-strike on Monday—that is, the fact that there was a forest fire on Tuesday is causally explained by the fact that there was a

---

[54]   One potential exception to this rule is the case of self-visitation, which we discuss in Chapter 6.
[55]   Lewis (1986b). We will discuss this view in more detail in Chapter 5, section 6.

match-strike on Monday. The presentist can then go on to say that this causal fact obtains in virtue of the counterfactual dependence between the relevant facts—if the one hadn't obtained, then neither would the other.

This way of thinking about causation also suggests a new way of thinking about personal time, and thus a new way of characterizing time travel.[56]

Let's begin with a simple example. Imagine a case of discontinuous backward travel, in which a particle begins its career at t_4, persists until t_5, and then "jumps" back to t_1 (where it persists for one additional unit of time). An eternalist might picture this case as in Figure 2.10.

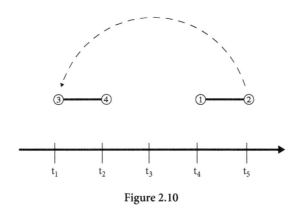

Figure 2.10

On this way of thinking about the case, the external facts would include the following:

③ is earlier than ④.
① is later than ④.
There are three units of time between ④ and ②.

Meanwhile, the personal facts would include the following:

③ is earlier than ④.
④ is later than ①.
There is one unit of time between ④ and ②.[57]

Recall that, on our interpretation of Lewis's proposal, personal time is an assignment of coordinates to the stages of an object that corresponds to the causal order and metric for those stages. Hence, to say that ④ is later than ①, for example, is to say that ④ is causally dependent on stage ①, in the right sort of way (the sort of way that makes for identity over time).

---

[56] For closely related ideas, see Sider (1999), Keller and Nelson (2001), and Sider (2005).

[57] Again, this assumes that the "jump" from t_5 to t_1 is instantaneous, so that the distance between ② and ③ is zero (according to the particle's personal time).

Presentists, of course, will have a very different account of what the facts are in this case. Suppose, for example, that t_4 is present. Since stage ④ does not exist at t_4, the presentist will say that it does not exist *period*. Hence, it is not, strictly speaking, true that ① is later than ④ (according to the external ordering). For the presentist, this fact gets replaced with the following pair of truths.

> ① exists and ④ does not.
> WAS(④ existed and ① did not).

The same point applies in the case of metric operators. For example, it is not, strictly speaking, true there are three units of time separating ④ and ②. If t_4 is the present time, then neither of these stages exist, in which case they cannot stand in any temporal relations. However, the presentist can replace this fact with the following (assuming, again, that t_4 is present):

> ① exists.
> $\text{WILL}_{\text{1-UNIT-HENCE}}$(② exists).
> $\text{WAS}_{\text{2-UNITS-AGO}}$(④ existed).[58]

The first two facts capture the idea that that ② exists one unit after ①; the last two facts capture the idea that ④ exists two units before ①. Taken together, these facts provide a sense in which there are three temporal units between ④ and ②.

The presentist can also make a related move in the case of personal time, although this move is a bit more complicated.

Let's begin with the eternalist's suggestion that stage ④ comes after ①, according to the particle's personal time:

> ④ is later than ①.

The presentist does not think that stage ④ exists (when t_4 is present), so she cannot say that ④ comes after ①. However, she can say both of the following things:

> ① exists and ④ does not.
> WILL-FOR-P(④ exists and ① does not).

Here, the one-place operator 'WILL-FOR-P' is to be read as 'It will be the case for P that'. We will refer to this as a *personal tense operator* for the particle (P) in our example. Other personal tense operators (for P) include WAS-FOR-P and the various metric operators—$\text{WILL-FOR-P}_{\text{2-UNITS-HENCE}}$, $\text{WAS-FOR-P}_{\text{3-UNITS-AGO}}$, etc. All of these operators are reducible to ordinary tense operators and causal facts, in much the same way that Lewis's personal time is reducible to external time and causal facts. For Lewis, *it will be the case that ϕ*, according to my personal time, if and only if there is some time t such that (i) ϕ holds at t and (ii) my current stage has an appropriate causal successor at t. Since

---

[58] Here, "$\text{WILL}_{\text{n-UNITS-HENCE}}$" is to be read as "It will be the case n units hence that" and "$\text{WAS}_{\text{n-UNITS-AGO}}$" is to be read as "It was the case n units ago that."

the presentist cannot quantify over non-present times, she cannot accept (i) and (ii) as they stand. But she can replace these conditions with appropriate presentist transla- tions. Roughly, the idea is that there are two ways for these two conditions to be satis- fied: either (i) it *will be* the case that φ and I will have an appropriate causal successor at that time or (ii) it *was* the case that φ and I had an appropriate causal successor at that time. More carefully, for any object O:

> WILL-FOR-O(φ) only if, and in that case because:
> (i) WILL(φ and O has an appropriate causal successor), or
> (ii) WAS(φ and O had an appropriate causal successor).

Now: What does it mean, exactly, to say that it will be the case that O has "an appropri- ate causal successor"? That will depend, in part, on one's theory of identity over time. But Lewis's basic idea is that, for two stages to be co-stages of an ordinary object, the existence and features of the one must depend upon the existence and features of the other (in the right sort of way). Once again, the presentist does not believe in past or future stages; nor does she believe in cross-time causal relations between stages. So she cannot say exactly what Lewis says about causal successors. But the presentist does believe in various tensed facts; moreover, she believes that some of these facts provide a causal explanation for others. So, for example, the presentist can say that I will have an appropriate causal successor at some future time if and only if (i) it will be the case that there is a person-stage with such-and-such features and (ii) that future-tensed fact obtains because my current stage exists and has the features that it does. Similarly, to have an appropriate successor at an earlier time is for it to be the case that (i) it was the case that there was a person-stage with such-and-such features and (ii) that past- tensed fact obtains because of facts about my present person-stage. More generally, and more formally:

> WILL-FOR-O(φ) only if, and in that case because, O exists and has features F_1–F_n, and:
> (i) WILL(there is some y such that y has features G_1–G_n, and φ) because O exists and has features F_1–F_n, or
> (ii) WAS(there is some y such that y has features G_1–G_n, and φ) because O exists and has features F_1–F_n.

Parallel truth-conditions can be given for the past-tense personal operator, as well as the metric variants thereof.

The specifics of the preceding account are important, but it is also important not to get lost in the details. The key point to keep in mind is that, for the eternalist, personal time is ultimately a function of what things are like at different times, and how those things are causally related. If presentism is to be *at all* plausible, then it must allow for *some* way of understanding these kinds of claims. That is, the presentist must be able to capture facts about the past and the future as well as facts about how the past, present, and future are causally related. But, once she has done this, she will have an analysis of personal time. And once she has *that*, she will have her own definition of time travel: *time travel amounts to a discrepancy between tensed facts and personal-tensed facts.* For example, in the case of our earlier particle, we have:

NOT: WILL(④ exists).

and

WILL-FOR-P(④ exists).

In other words: stage ④ won't exist in the external future, but it will exist in P's personal future. According to the presentist, this kind of discrepancy is definitive of time travel.[59]

3.3 The annihilation argument

In the previous section, we saw how the standard definition of time travel can be translated into presentist-friendly terminology. However, some have suggested that this translation is inadequate, and that presentist "time travel" does not really deserve the name. Here is one way of putting this worry, due to Ted Sider:[60]

[A]ccording to presentism...personal time does *not* "play the role that time plays in the life of a common person". This remark of Lewis's is no throwaway; it is crucial to the status of Lewisian time travel as genuine travel...A presentist can use the words: "gazing at the dinosaur is in the future in my personal time". But if personal time bears little similarity to external time then "personal time" is merely an invented quantity, and is misleadingly named at that. That I will view a dinosaur in my personal future amounts merely to the fact that I once viewed a dinosaur, and moreover that this is caused by my entry into a time machine. Since this fact bears little resemblance to the facts that constitute a normal person's genuine future, I could not enter the time machine with anticipation and excitement at the thought of seeing a dinosaur, for it is not true that I am about to see a dinosaur, nor is the truth much like being about to see a dinosaur. If anything, I should feel fear at the thought of being annihilated by a device misleadingly called a "time machine". The device causes it to be the case that I once viewed a dinosaur, but does not make it the case in any real sense that I will view dinosaurs.   (2005: 332–3)

---

[59]   More than one reader has raised the following kind of concern: The presentist may be able to recognize past- and future-tensed facts, as well as causal facts, but she cannot recognize time travel because she does not believe that anything actually *moves* in time. In order for something to really move back and forth in time, there must be other times to move to. In reply, it may be helpful to consider the spatial analogy again. The standard theory of spatial motion is the at-at theory: For any x, x moves only if, and in that case because, x is at different places at different times. Since presentists do not believe in different times, the combination of this theory and presentism implies that nothing actually moves. Since this is absurd, the presentist will want to move to a modified version of the at-at theory. Very roughly: For any x, x moves only if, and in that case because, [WAS(x is in one place) and x is in a different place] or [x is in one place and WILL(x is in a different place)]. In other words, the presentist will say that some things really are moving about in space—it's just that this movement is a matter of there being certain tensed truths (which are grounded in the right kind of causal truths). The presentist will say the exact same thing about "movement" in time.

[60]   A very similar worry is raised by Goff (2010) and Hales (2010). See also the exchange between Licon (2011, 2012, 2013), Hales (2011), and Hall (2014).

Sider's objection seems to be this. According to the presentist, a time traveler's personal future (when he travels to the past) consists in three different kinds of facts:

(i)   past-tensed facts (e.g. the fact that Ted saw a dinosaur),
(ii) present or future-tensed facts (e.g. the fact that Ted is going to turn on his time machine), and
(iii) causal facts (e.g. the fact that Ted saw a dinosaur because he is going to turn on his time machine).

On the other hand, a non-time-traveler's external future simply consists in *future-tensed* facts. That's it. So, for the presentist, there's a big difference between the facts that make up one's personal future and the ones that make up one's external future (at least in the case of backward time travel). But in that case, it is no longer appropriate to use temporal language when describing personal time.[61] It would no longer be appropriate, for example, to say that Ted "will" see a dinosaur "after" he turns on his time machine. Strictly speaking, Ted will no longer be doing *anything* after that, since he will no longer be in existence.

This last way of putting the objection is particularly seductive. Imagine, for the moment, that you are a presentist and that you are sitting in Wells's time machine with the coordinates set for a one-way trip to the past. Should you turn on the machine? Of course not! After all, the past does not exist, and will never exist again. So, if you push the button, *you* will never exist again. On this way of looking at things, a "one-way trip to the past" sounds a lot like a one-way ticket to the grave.[62]

However, this way of looking at things is misleading, since the exact same thing is true for the eternalist. Suppose, once again, that you are about to start the time machine with the coordinates set for the past. Lewis, like the presentist, will then say that *you are about to be annihilated*. After all, there is an annihilation of you that occurs a little later than that assertion. Moreover, Lewis will agree with the presentist in saying that *you will never exist again*. After all, you do not exist at any times that are externally later than the time machine's disappearance. You *do* exist in the distant past, of course, by virtue of having person-stages at those earlier times. And those person-stages *do* follow after

---

[61] Here it may be helpful to recall Lewis's original explanation of personal time:

[T]here is one way to assign coordinates to the time traveler's stages...so that the regularities that hold with respect to this assignment match those that commonly hold with respect to external time...The assignment of coordinates that yields this match is the time traveler's personal time. *It isn't really time, but it plays the role in his life that time plays in the life of a common person. It's enough like time so that we can—with due caution—transplant our temporal vocabulary to it in discussing his affairs.* (1976: 146, emphasis added)

[62] This is how Hales (2010: 357) puts the worry. He writes:

Permanent "time traveling into the past,"...is merely death. Consider H. G. Wells's time traveler. Wells writes, "he may even now—if I may use the phrase—be wandering on some plesiosaurus-haunted Oolitic coral reef, or beside the lonely saline lakes of the Triassic Age." For a presentist, that is not an apt description of the situation. The time machine may have caused it to be the case that the traveler was wandering on some plesiosaurus-haunted Oolitic coral reef [but]...the traveler is no longer in the objective present and therefore no longer exists.

See also Goff (2010: 68).

your current stage, according to your personal time. But the key point is that they do not exist after your current stage according to *external* time—that is, *time itself.* Since external time is *real* time, you will not really be viewing any dinosaurs in the future.[63]

Of course, Lewis wants to insist that there is a legitimate sense in which you "will be" seeing a dinosaur in your future. That sense amounts to this:

(i)   You have a person-stage at the current time,
(ii) there is a person-stage viewing a dinosaur at an earlier time, and
(iii) the earlier stage depends, in the right sort of way, on the current one.

Crucially, these facts mirror the facts that obtain in ordinary, non-time-traveling cases. Suppose, for example that you decide to visit the local zoo, rather than the distant past. And suppose that you will, in the external sense, see a zebra at the zoo. That fact about the (real) future amounts to the following:

(i)   You have a person-stage at the current time,
(ii) there is a person-stage viewing a zebra at a later time, and
(iii) the later stage depends, in the right sort of way, on the current one.

Given this symmetry, Lewis claims that we can transplant our temporal vocabulary to the time travel case and say that *you will be seeing a dinosaur.*

You may agree with Lewis on this, or you may not. But the important point is that the presentist is no worse off than the eternalist in this regard. According to her, you will not really be seeing any dinosaurs if you start up the time machine. But the presentist will point out that all of the following facts do obtain:

(i)   You exist and have features F_1–F_n,
(ii) WAS(someone with features G_1–G_n viewed a dinosaur), and
(iii) WAS(someone with features G_1–G_n viewed a dinosaur) because you exist and have features F_1–F_n.

In other words, the fact that there was a dinosaur sighting depends, in the right sort of way, on the fact that you exist and have the features that you do (and also that you will do certain things in the external future, like turning on the time machine). That is what makes it true that you will see a dinosaur, according to your personal future. Moreover, these facts are analogous to the facts that obtain if you end up traveling to the zoo, rather than the past. In that case, it is true that you will see a zebra. And that truth consists in the following facts:

(i)   You exist and have features F_1–F_n,
(ii) WILL(someone with features G_1–G_n views a zebra), and
(iii) WILL(someone with features G_1–G_n views a zebra) because you exist and have features F_1–F_n.

---

[63] At one point, Hales suggests that eternalist time travel does not result in suicide since the person who enters the time machine will still exist at past times, even if he or she is no longer present. However, this would imply that it is impossible for *anyone* to commit suicide, if eternalism is correct (since every existing person will always exist at some time or other). Clearly, that is not the right result.

The only difference between the two cases is the tense operator being used (and the kind of animal being viewed). This exactly parallels the eternalist's account, where the only difference between the two cases is the temporal relation at issue.

If all of this is correct, then Sider's mistake is claiming that, on the presentist's account, "my external future ... does not concern causation at all, and [only] concerns *future-tensed* statements" (2005: 332). On the current proposal, one's external future *does* concern future-tensed facts, but it also concerns how some of those facts depend on the present, causally speaking. In this respect, the normal person's external future is just like the personal future of those who travel in time.[64]

4. The Growing Block and Time Travel

According to the growing block theory, past and present times exist, but future ones do not. The universe can therefore be depicted as a truncated version of the eternalist's block, with the present time constituting the very edge of being. (See Figure 2.3.)

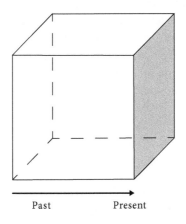

Past   Present

Figure 2.3

This picture is sometimes motivated by a felt asymmetry between the past and future—namely, the feeling that the past is *fixed* and the future is *open*. The growing block theory seems to fit this feeling well. After all, this theory accepts the existence of past and present entities, and it is natural to think that past-tensed facts are grounded in—and thus fixed by—facts about these objects.[65] By the same token, it is natural to think that future-tensed facts are ungrounded—and thus left open—since there are no future entities.[66]

---

[64] A related point is made by Daniels (2012).

[65] Here, it is important to set aside non-temporal sources of indeterminacy. Perhaps facts about heaps and other vague objects are not "fixed" in the relevant sense. But this will be the same for both past and future heaps. The interesting feature of the current view is the postulated asymmetry of indeterminacy.

[66] This view of future-tensed truths is not forced upon the growing block theorist. Such a theorist could deny the existence of the future, while insisting that there are future-tensed truths (Briggs and Forbes 2012).

This "open future" view raises several interesting questions about time travel. In particular, some have questioned whether this version of the growing block theory can accommodate time travelers from the future.[67] To see why, let's begin with the following story, as told by Matthew Slater:

> As Tim rifles through newspapers from the '20s (a favorite pastime), a faded photo catches his eye: it seems to be of Tim himself. How could that be? Tim was born in 1966; the photo dates to 1921. The resemblance is striking but imperfect: Tim has more hair and fewer wrinkles. After ruling out obvious explanations, he considers an unlikely alternative. The mystery man was seen stepping out of a sort of cabinet said to have appeared out of nowhere. Perhaps, Tim thinks, the photo is a photo of *me*! Perhaps I was caught stepping out of a *time machine* in 1921. But Tim's excitement at the prospects of time travel (all he might do) gives way to a vague unease: if that was *me* back in 1921, am I not *fated* to travel through time?   (2005: 363)

Here's the problem.[68] According to the open future view, the past and present are fixed, in the sense that past- and present-tensed statements are either determinately true or determinately false.[69] So, for example, it is either determinately true that Tim is the person in the photo ("Tim*") or determinately the case that he is not. But, if Tim is determinately Tim*, then he must (determinately) travel in time at some point in the future, for that is the only way to establish the requisite causal link between Tim and Tim*. Similarly, if Tim is determinately *not* Tim*, then it must already be determinate that he will *not* travel in time (in such a way that the relevant causal link would be established). Thus: It is already determinate that Tim will travel in time or determinate that he won't. Either way, we have a determinate, contingent, future-tensed truth. This violates the "open future" part of the open future view.

To put the argument the other way around: According to the open future view, it is now indeterminate whether Tim will one day travel to the past. That is:

(P1) ∇(Tim will travel to the past) & ∇(Tim will not travel to the past)

(where "∇" is to be read as "It is not determinately the case that"). But if it is not determinate that Tim will travel, then it is not determinate that Tim is Tim*:

(P2) ∇(Tim will travel to the past) → ∇(Tim = Tim*)

And if it's not determinate that Tim won't travel, it is not determinate that Tim is not Tim*.

(P3) ∇(Tim will not travel to the past) → ∇(Tim ≠ Tim*)

Or he could say that all contingent future-tensed statements are false (Todd 2016). There are other options. However, we will focus on this version of the growing block theory, since it raises the most interesting challenge to time travel. (See Torre 2011 for an overview of "open future" views.)

[67]   See Miller (2005, 2008) and Slater (2005), as well as the responses from Daniels (2012) and Martínez (2011). For a slightly different argument, see Dwyer (1978: 36).

[68]   My way of putting the worry does not exactly match Slater's. His argument is partly put in terms of fatalism, and I wish to ignore that issue for now.

[69]   Keep in mind that we are setting aside other, non-temporal sources of indeterminacy.

Finally, from these premises we can deduce:

(C) $\nabla(\text{Tim} = \text{Tim}^\star)$ & $\nabla(\text{Tim} \neq \text{Tim}^\star)$

In other words, it is indeterminate whether or not Tim and Tim* are identical. The upshot, says Slater, is that "indeterminism about the future seeps back into the past" (2005: 362). The problem, of course, is that this conclusion is inconsistent with the "fixed past" part of the open future view. In other words, this view turns out to be inconsistent with the possibility of time travel. This is *the indeterminacy paradox* for the growing block theorist.

One potential response to this paradox is to simply accept the conclusion and say that the openness of the future implies some indeterminacy in the past. But that is a cost to the view, since it requires a revision of the original position. Moreover, this particular kind of indeterminacy—*the indeterminacy of identity*—is often thought to be especially problematic.[70]

But perhaps there is a way to understand Slater's example that will not commit us to this conclusion. To begin, let's consider a different kind of case. Imagine a machine that can make very subtle changes to your body (including your brain) and can therefore make equally small changes to your psychology.[71] There are approximately fifty trillion cells in the human body, so let's imagine that the machine has a keypad that allows us to enter any number from zero to fifty trillion. If we enter '0' and you enter the machine, nothing will happen—you will emerge from the machine in almost exactly the same state that you entered. If we enter the number '1', however, the machine will destroy a randomly selected cell from your body and replace it with a new cell—or perhaps several cells—which qualitatively duplicate the corresponding part in the body of Albert Einstein (circa 1950). If we enter the number '2', the machine will replace two cells, if we enter '3' it will replace three, etc. Now suppose that we place Frank into the matter replacement machine and enter the number '20,000,000,000,000'. In that case, the man who emerges from the machine will be, so to speak, 60 percent Frank and 40 percent Einstein. The question is: What should we say about this Frank–Einstein creature? Is he Frank? Or is he not?

Let's consider these questions from the perspective of the person who believes that objects persist through time by having different stages or "temporal parts" at different times. On this picture, there are distinct person-stages—PS1, PS2, etc.—for each time in our story. There is also the sum of all the pre-machine person-stages—call it 'A'—and the sum of all the post-machine stages—call it 'B'. Finally, there is the sum of all the person-stages from beginning to end—A+B. (See Figure 2.11 on the next page.)

Crucially, there is no indeterminacy when it comes to the individual stages in this picture—PS1 is determinately identical to PS1, PS2 is determinately identical to PS2, and so on. What *is* indeterminate is whether there is enough continuity between all of these

---

[70] The standard argument against indeterminate identity is due to Evans (1978). For discussion, see Williamson (1994: Chapter 9).

[71] This case is taken from Wasserman (2013).

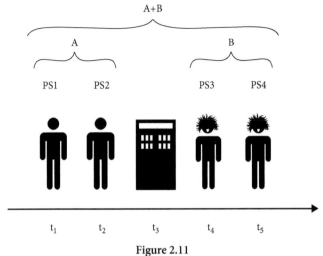

Figure 2.11

stages—and, in particular, between PS2 and PS3—so that the stages compose a single person. As a result, it is indeterminate whether the proper name 'Frank' refers to the sum of pre-machine stages (A), or the sum of all the stages taken together (A + B). In this sense, there is indeterminacy of reference, but there is no indeterminacy of identity.

The growing block theorist could say the same thing about Slater's case. (See Figure 2.12.)

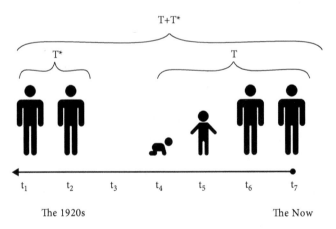

Figure 2.12

In this figure, there are three salient objects—the sum of Tim's recent stages (T), the sum of person-stages from the 1920s (T*), and the sum of all those stages taken together (T+T*). There is no indeterminacy in any of these objects. Rather, it is indeterminate whether the right kinds of connections will hold between Tim's current stage (at t_7) and those that existed in the 1920s. As a result, it is now indeterminate whether

'Tim' refers to T or to the sum $T + T^*$. Similarly, it is indeterminate whether the name 'Tim*' refers to the larger sum of stages, or whether it just refers to the collection of stages from the 1920s (T^*).

On this way of looking at things, one could accept Slater's earlier conclusion:

(C) $\nabla(\text{Tim} = \text{Tim}^*) \ \& \ \nabla(\text{Tim} \neq \text{Tim}^*)$

Moreover, one could do this without saying that the identity relation is itself indeterminate. Once again, the only indeterminacy is in what the relevant names refer to.

However, once we view Slater's story from this perspective, it seems that we should not even say this much.

We have assumed throughout this chapter that identity over time requires a special causal connection. Hence, we should only say that 'Tim' refers to the sum of all the person-stages ($T + T^*$) if there is an appropriate causal connection between Tim's current stage (at t_7) and those from the 1920s. But, by hypothesis, Tim has not yet time traveled. So, there is no causal connection running from the present stage to the past (at least not yet). Moreover, all of this is a determinate matter. So it is currently determinate that 'Tim' does *not* refer to the sum of all the stages in question. Rather, 'Tim' refers determinately to T (the sum of recent person-stages) and 'Tim*' refers determinately to T^* (the sum of person-stages from the 1920s). Since T is determinately distinct from T^*, Tim is determinately different from Tim*. Hence, we should deny both the second and third premises from Slater's argument:

(P2) $\nabla(\text{Tim will travel to the past}) \rightarrow \nabla(\text{Tim} = \text{Tim}^*)$
(P3) $\nabla(\text{Tim will not travel to the past}) \rightarrow \nabla(\text{Tim} \neq \text{Tim}^*)$

On this view, it is currently unsettled whether or not Tim will travel to the past. But it is nonetheless determinate that Tim and Tim* are distinct … at least for now.

Of course, things might change. Suppose that time marches on and the growing block grows. It is now t_8 and, at that time, Tim is twiddling some knobs in a time machine. (See Figure 2.13 on the next page.)

Suppose further that Tim's twiddling determinately establishes an appropriate causal connection between the t_8-stage and the t_1-stage (indicated by the dashed line in the diagram). In that case, it is now determinately the case that Tim is the man from the photograph. In other words, Tim is determinately identical to Tim*.

This conclusion may seem to contradict our earlier assertion. At t_7, we said that (1) was determinately false:

(1) $\text{Tim} = \text{Tim}^*$.

Now, at t_8, we say that it is determinately true. Is that not contradictory?

No. Not on the growing block theory. For, on that theory, facts can change as time passes. The most obvious examples are A-facts like:

(2) t_7 is past.

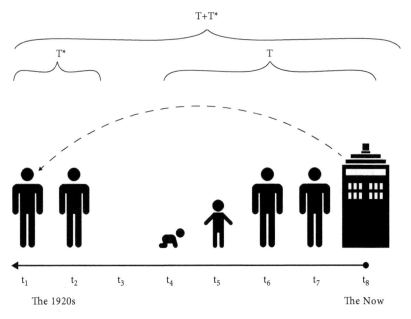

Figure 2.13

At t_7, this statement was false; now (at t_8) it is true. That is because, on the growing block theory, objects and times can change with respect to their A-properties (properties like *being present* and *being past*).

But, interestingly, the same point applies to facts involving B-relations (relations like *being simultaneous with* or *being earlier than*). Take, for example, statement (3):

(3)   The American Revolution was earlier than the French Revolution.

This is now true, but it was not always so. When 1700 was present, for example, neither of these revolutions had occurred. So, on the growing block theory, neither of those events existed. Hence, it was not true then that the first was earlier than the second. (3) has thus changed from being determinately false to being determinately true.

The same thing is true for B-statements about cross-time causal relations. For example, it is now true that the American Revolution was caused, in part, by British taxation. However, this was not the case when 1700 was present, since neither of those events existed at that point (and so did not stand in any causal relations).

The exact same thing is true for Tim and his stages. When t_7 was present, it was determinately false that:

(4)   Tim's t_7-stage is causally related to the person-stage at t_1.

But now, at t_8, that statement is determinately true. That is why (1) has changed from being determinately false to being determinately true.

Of course, it is a little strange to think that past-tensed facts can change in this way from being determinately false to being determinately true. But that is because we normally think of the past as being independent of the future. If we are committed to the open future view of time, and we take the possibility of backward causation seriously, then this is exactly the kind of result we should expect.

5. Special Relativity and Time Travel

Our presentations of the traditional views on time have presupposed certain views about the structure of the world. For example, in presenting the B-theory of time, we assumed that there were objective B-relations like *being earlier than*, *being simultaneous with*, and *being later than*. And in presenting the growing block and presentist views we assumed that there were A-properties like *being past*, *being present*, and *being future* (as well as the metric versions thereof). Those properties were taken to provide the world with its temporal structure by exhaustively dividing its contents into objective temporal categories.

The idea that *time orders all things* is a familiar part of our ordinary conceptual scheme. However, this way of thinking about time seems to be inconsistent with our best physical theories, including Einstein's theory of relativity.[72] In challenging our traditional assumptions about time, Einstein also provided a new way of thinking about time travel. This section discusses the implications of special relativity for time travel, and addresses one famous paradox associated with that view.[73]

Throughout this chapter, we have been working with the kinds of spacetime diagrams that are familiar from philosophy texts. Recall, for example, Figure 2.1.

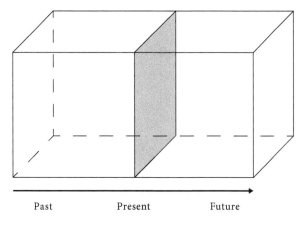

Past   Present   Future

Figure 2.1

[72] Whether or not this appearance is accurate is a matter of some debate. This debate turns, in part, on how we think about the content of scientific theories. For example, it is well known that the theory of special relativity does not say that there is a privileged reference frame. If this theory is correct, and we think of this theory as a *complete* account of spacetime's structure, then we should conclude that there is no privileged present. However, if we think of this theory as being silent of which it does not speak, then it would be perfectly compatible with that theory to believe in a privileged present. For further discussion of these issues, see Hawley (2006), Monton (2006), Sklar (1981), Tooley (1997), and Zimmerman (2011).

[73] There are many excellent discussions on relativity and its implications for time travel. For popular introductions, see Davies (2001), Everett and Roman (2012), Gott (2001), Pickover (1998), and Toomey (2007). For more philosophically oriented introductions, see Arntzenius and Maudlin (2010), Earman (1995), and Earman, Smeenk, and Wüthrich (2009).

In this figure, the length of the block was supposed to correspond to the temporal dimension, while the height and "depth" were supposed to correspond to two of the three spatial dimensions.

When philosophers introduce these kinds of diagrams, they are quick to point out certain imperfections. For example, when we introduced this figure in section 1, we noted that it incorrectly represents space as having only two dimensions.[74] But, if modern physics is correct, there are much bigger problems with this picture.

First, Figure 2.1 highlights a certain moment of time—"the present"—where this moment is naturally taken to include all and only the events that are simultaneous with (say) the typing of this sentence. This moment is especially important to the presentist (who takes the present to encompass all of reality) and the growing block theorist (who takes the present to be the edge of all becoming). But even the eternalist will usually grant that there are objective facts about what is simultaneous with what.

According to Einstein, this last claim is mistaken. In the theory of special relativity, there is no such thing as objective simultaneity. Instead, there is only simultaneity *relative to a given frame of reference*. For example, the events represented by the "present" slice in Figure 2.1 might be all of the events that are present, relative to one observer, at a particular point in spacetime. However, a second observer passing through one of those points at a different velocity will identify a different set of events as being present. (See Figure 2.14.)

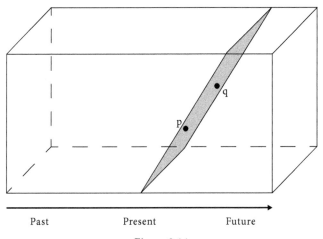

Figure 2.14

The observer in this case will take the two designated events (p and q) to be occurring at the same time—both events will be present, relative to this observer's frame of reference. However, the observer from Figure 2.1 will judge both of these events to be in the future, and for one to be occurring later than the other. Crucially, the disagreement

---

[74] See fn. 12.

between these two observers is not the result of some miscalculation or illusion. Rather, this is a case of *faultless disagreement*—*q* really is present relative to one frame of reference and non-present relative to the other. Moreover, on the standard interpretation of relativity, there are no further (frame-independent) facts on which these parties disagree. That is because, on the standard interpretation, there are no further facts about what is "really" present.

A second problem with the traditional picture of the block universe is that it suggests all spacetime events can be exhaustively divided up according to their A-properties—every event is either past, present, or future. Similarly, this way of depicting reality suggests that any two spacetime events will stand in one of the familiar B-relations—Figure 2.1, for example, is supposed to represent *all* spacetime events, and it is supposed to convey the fact that every event on the right side of the block stands in the *later than* relation to every event on the left.

According to modern physicists, these aspects of our image are also mistaken. There is *a sense* (to be explained) in which we can say that some events are past, present, or future, but there are also events that fall outside of these categories. So too, there is *a sense* in which we can say that some events are earlier than, later than, or simultaneous with others, but there are also some events that do not stand in any of these B-relations.

We can get a better understanding of this point by comparing the preceding pictures with the kind of figures that are typically found in physics texts. (See Figure 2.15.)

This spacetime diagram is centered on a certain spacetime point—point *p*. This point can be thought of as the location of a certain spacetime event—namely, a momentary

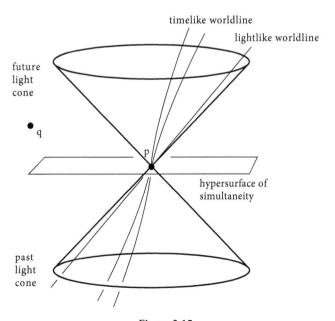

Figure 2.15

flash of light. As this flash spreads out in a two-dimensional space, it creates larger and larger rings of light. When all of these rings are taken together, they form an upward-opening cone, which we will refer to as the *future light cone* of *p*. In the other direction, we can consider all of the spacetime points such that, were momentary flashes of light to take place at those points, the resulting light beams would eventually pass through point *p*. These points, taken together, form a downward-opening cone, which we will refer to as the *past light cone* of *p*. If we assume that all objects travel slower than light, then the points falling within the future light cone represent all of the possible points that an object might pass through after leaving point *p*. Similarly, the points in the past light cone represent all of the points an object might have passed through on its way to point *p*. So, if we draw a line passing from the past light cone, through point *p*, and into the future light cone, we get a *timelike worldline*—that is, a line corresponding to the possible career of some point-sized object. These can be contrasted with *lightlike worldlines*, which represent the paths taken by light. Finally, all points falling outside of the light cone structure are said to be *spacelike separated* from *p*. This exhausts the fundamental features of the standard spacetime diagram.

Crucially, this structure leaves out the familiar B-relations that we have been taking for granted. However, there are two different ways of bringing these relations back into the picture. First, it is natural to think of all the points in *p*'s future light cone as being *later than p*, and to think of all the points in its past light cone as being *earlier than p*. This exhausts the list of objective B-facts depicted by our diagram. However, there are also some *frame dependent* B-facts in our picture. First, for any particle passing through point *p*, there will be a corresponding *hypersurface of simultaneity*—roughly, a collection of (possible) spacetime events that, from the particle's perspective, are occurring at the same time it passes through *p*. For each point on the hyperspace of simultaneity, there will be a corresponding past and future light cone. We can then say that every point falling within one of these future light cones will be later than *p*, and that every point falling within one of the past light cones will be earlier than *p*. However, these facts only hold *relative to a particular frame of reference*, and that frame will vary depending on the object's state of motion. For example, the hypersurface depicted in Figure 2.15 is the hypersurface for *one* possible particle passing through point *p* and, relative to *that* particle's frame of reference, point *q* would be in the future. However, a different particle passing through the same point at a different speed would have a different hypersurface associated with it and, relative to *that* way of slicing up the manifold, *q* might be simultaneous with *p* or even in the past. Hence, there are no objective facts about how these points relate—*p* and *q* may stand in B-relations relative to certain frames of reference but, objectively speaking, *p* is not earlier than, later than, or simultaneous with *q*. This is just one of the ways in which special relativity requires us to rethink our traditional conception of time.

The theory of time suggested by relativity is important for a number of different reasons. One reason is that it suggests a new way of thinking about time travel. In order to understand this picture, we must first introduce the idea of the *invariant interval*. In order to introduce this idea, it will be helpful to begin with the more familiar concept of *Cartesian distance*. In a two-dimensional Cartesian plane each point is associated with a pair of coordinates, (x,y), and the distance between any two points, (x_1,y_1) and (x_2,y_2), can be calculated using the Pythagorean theorem:

$$(\Delta r)^2 = (\Delta x)^2 + (\Delta y)^2$$

(where $\Delta x = x_2 - x_1$ and $\Delta y = y_2 - y_1$). For example, if the coordinates are $(0,0)$ and $(5,5)$, then the distance between the relevant points can be calculated by taking the square root of each side and solving for Δr:

$$\Delta r = \sqrt{5^2 + 5^2}$$

$$\Delta r = \sqrt{25 + 25}$$

$$\Delta r = \sqrt{50}$$

$$\Delta r \approx 7.07$$

Similar calculations can be done for Cartesian systems with more than two dimensions. For example, the distance between two points in a four-dimensional Cartesian space can be calculated using the following equation:

$$(\Delta r)^2 = (\Delta x)^2 + (\Delta y)^2 + (\Delta z)^2 + (\Delta w)^2$$

The spacetime of relativity—*Minkowski spacetime*—is also four-dimensional, which means that each point can be uniquely characterized by four different coordinates. These coordinates—*the Lorentz coordinates*—are traditionally labeled t, x, y, and z.[75] The distance between any two points in Minkowski spacetime is then given by the following equation:[76]

$$(\Delta s)^2 = (\Delta x)^2 + (\Delta y)^2 + (\Delta z)^2 - (\Delta t)^2$$

(where c is a constant fixed by the speed of light). The distance (or quantity) determined by this equation is referred to as the *invariant interval* (or *interval*, for short).[77]

The Minkowski interval is in some ways analogous to Cartesian distance, but there are also some important differences between the two. For one thing, the interval is typically identified with the square of the difference $((\Delta s)^2)$ rather that the difference itself (Δs). More importantly, Cartesian distance is always positive (or zero, if we include the distance between each point and itself). The interval, in contrast, can be either positive, negative, or zero.[78] In fact, in Minkowski spacetime, it is possible for two *distinct* points

---

[75] It is tempting to think of the 't' as standing for some kind of objective time, but this would be a mistake. After all, every spacetime point has a t-coordinate—even those that fall outside of a point's light cone—and we have already said that there are no objective temporal relations between spacelike separated points.

[76] Here I follow the standard presentation that one finds in most physics textbooks. For a different approach to this topic, see Maudlin (2012).

[77] It is also called "the space-time interval," "the relativistic interval," and, in the case of timelike world-lines, "the proper time interval."

[78] This is one of the reasons that is usually given for identifying the interval with $(\Delta s)^2$, rather than Δs—if the right side of the equation is negative and we want to solve for Δs, we will end up with the square root of a negative number (i.e. an imaginary number).

to be at zero "distance" from each other. For example, if we plug the coordinates (0,0,0,0) and (c,0,0,1) into the interval equation, we get:

$$(\Delta s)^2 = c^2 + 0^2 + 0^2 - (c1)^2$$
$$(\Delta s)^2 = c^2 + 0 + 0 - c^2$$
$$(\Delta s)^2 = 0$$

In fact, for any point p in Minkowski spacetime, there will be an infinite number of distinct points that are at zero interval from p. As it turns out, these are exactly the points that lie on the future and past light cones of p. This is important for a number of different reasons. One reason is this. In special relativity, it is assumed that accurate clocks measure the invariant interval (this is what is sometimes called the "clock hypothesis"). In other words, the elapsed time measured by an accurate clock that moves between two events will be proportional to the interval traveled between those events. Since the interval between any two points on a lightlike worldline will be 0, an accurate clock traveling at the speed of light would not record any temporal passage. This point is related to the somewhat misleading (but still very popular) claim that time "slows down" as one approaches the speed of light.

In order to put this idea more carefully, it will be helpful to focus on a specific case. So, suppose there are two twins—Alice and Bob—who start off at rest with respect to each other on the surface of the Earth. Bob then boards a rocket ship, which begins to move with respect to the Earth (and Alice). From Alice's perspective, she remains at rest, while Bob blasts off along the x-axis at a constant velocity of v. Since change of position is a product of velocity and time, and since Bob does not move along the y-axis or z-axis, Alice will calculate Bob's separation from the point of origin as follows:

$$(\Delta s)^2 = (v\Delta t)^2 + 0^2 + 0^2 - (c\Delta t)^2$$
$$(\Delta s)^2 = (v\Delta t)^2 - (c\Delta t)^2$$

As Bob sees it, however, he is simply sitting at rest in his rocket, while the world moves quickly away from him. Accordingly, he will calculate the interval as follows:[79]

$$(\Delta s)^2 = 0^2 + 0^2 + 0^2 - (c\Delta t')^2$$
$$(\Delta s)^2 = -(c\Delta t')^2$$

Now, since the interval is invariant, we know that all observers will agree about the value of $(\Delta s)^2$. So, we can substitute the right-hand side of Bob's equation into the left-hand side of Alice's:

$$-(c\Delta t')^2 = (v\Delta t)^2 - (c\Delta t)^2$$

This, in turn, is equivalent to:

$$\Delta t = \frac{\Delta t'}{\sqrt{1 - \dfrac{v^2}{c^2}}}$$

---

[79] Note that we use t' in this case rather than t since Bob and Alice are using different coordinate systems.

This way of putting the equation can then be used to calculate the so-called time dilation effect of special relativity. To make things concrete, suppose that Bob is, from Alice's perspective, traveling at 80 percent the speed of light ($v = .8c$). And suppose that Bob's clocks have recorded 1 hour of elapsed time since he left home ($\Delta t' = 1$). Plugging those numbers into the above equation gives us:

$$\Delta t = \frac{1}{\sqrt{1-\dfrac{.8c^2}{c^2}}} = \frac{1}{\sqrt{1-.64}} = \frac{1}{\sqrt{.36}} = \frac{1}{.6} = 1\frac{2}{3}$$

What this means is that, from Alice's perspective, Bob has been gone for $1\frac{2}{3}$ hours, or 100 minutes. Since Bob's clock will only show an hour as having passed, Bob's clock will appear to be running slowly from Alice's perspective.

It is this phenomenon that is often said to allow for time travel in Minkowski spacetime. To see why, let's continue our story. Suppose that, from Alice's perspective, Bob continues his journey for 5 years until he reaches a star 4 light years away ($5 \times .8c$). At that point, he quickly turns around and returns home at the same speed. (For simplicity, let's suppose the "turnaround" is instantaneous, so that Bob is traveling at the same speed for the entire duration). In that case, 10 years will have ticked off of Alice's clock when the twins are finally reunited. Figure 2.16 shows how things will look from Alice's perspective.[80]

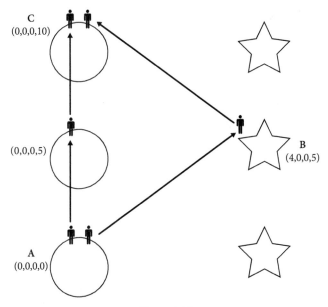

Figure 2.16

---

[80] This figure is adapted from Carroll (2008b) and Maudlin (2012: 78).

However, things will be very different for Bob. If we want to calculate how much time has elapsed on his clock, we can use the following equation:[81]

$$10 = \frac{\Delta t'}{\sqrt{1 - \frac{.8c^2}{c^2}}}$$

Solving for $\Delta t'$:

$$\Delta t' = 10\sqrt{1 - \frac{.8c^2}{c^2}} = 10\sqrt{1 - .64} = 10\sqrt{.36} = 10 \times .6 = 6$$

In other words, only 6 years will have ticked off of Bob's clock when the twins are reunited. Crucially, this does not just apply to Bob's wristwatch, but to his "biological" clock as well. When Bob emerges from the rocket, Alice will find that he has fewer grey hairs than her, fewer wrinkles, and so on. In this respect, Bob is analogous to Wells's original Time Traveller. The Time Traveller, it will be recalled, got into his machine, turned it on, and when he came to a stop, found that everyone he had left behind had aged much more than him. Indeed, in Wells's story, all of the Time Traveller's friends are dead and gone by the time he completes his journey. Bob's case is not as drastic as that, but the basic story is the same: Bob gets into his machine, turns it on, and, when he comes to a stop, he finds that everyone he left behind has aged more than him. For this reason, many are inclined to call Bob a time traveler from the past.[82]

Time dilation may provide an opportunity for travel to the future, but it also gives rise to one of the most famous worries about relativity—the so-called twin paradox.[83] We have, of course, just noted one odd feature of the twin scenario—Bob ages less than Alice just because he takes a ride on a rocket. That's strange. Of course, this phenomenon has been empirically verified many times.[84] But that does not make it any less weird.

A second oddity about this scenario is that there seems to be a puzzling asymmetry. Earlier, we said that, during his journey, Bob's clock will seem to be running slow from Alice's perspective. This last qualification is important. When we say that Bob's clock is running slow, we are only saying something about the measurements *made in Alice's frame of reference*. From Bob's perspective, things will be completely reversed. Given his coordinate system, Alice will be moving away from him along the *x*-axis (in the opposite direction) at a constant velocity of .8*c*. So, if Bob watches an hour tick off on his clock, we can calculate the change he will see on Alice's clock as follows:

---

[81] Note that $\Delta t'$ is the elapsed time for the person who is moving at velocity v, relative to this frame of reference. Since Alice is at rest in her own frame, we need to put a 10 on the left side and then solve for $\Delta t'$.

[82] See, for example, Carroll (2008b), Davies (2001: Chapter 1), and Kaku (2009: 219). Whether or not this is the right thing to say about these cases is something we will return to in the next section.

[83] My analysis of the twin paradox is heavily indebted to Maudlin (2012).

[84] For example, in 1971 Hafele and Keating famously placed a cesium beam clock aboard an airplane traveling eastward around the world. Upon its return, the traveling clock was compared with its stay-at-home twin, and was found to have recorded 59 fewer nanoseconds—almost the exact value predicted by relativity theory. Similar results have been observed by using radioactive particles, rather than clocks. For further discussion of these cases, see Gott (2001: 36), Greene (2004: 449), and Pickover (1998: 119–21).

$$\Delta t' = \sqrt{1 - \frac{.8c^2}{c^2}} = \sqrt{1 - .64} = \sqrt{.36} = .6$$

In other words, only .6 hours, or 36 minutes, will have ticked off of Alice's clock, according to Bob. Thus, Alice's clock will appear to be running slow relative to Bob's frame of reference, just as his clock appears to be running slow relative to hers. But, in that case, shouldn't Bob expect Alice to be younger than him when he returns to Earth? And shouldn't Alice still expect herself to be older? Do we not then have a logical contradiction?[85]

No. There is no contradiction in this case, but there is some disagreement about how the paradox is to be resolved. The standard response to the twin case is to focus on the issue of acceleration. Here is how Richard Feynman puts the point:

> This is called a "paradox" only by people who believe that the principle of relativity means that *all motion* is relative...But in order for [the twins] to come back together and make the comparison, [Bob] must either stop at the end of the trip and make a comparison of clocks, or, more simply, he has to come back, and the one who comes back must be the man who was moving, and he knows this, because he had to turn around. When he turned around, all kinds of unusual things happened in his space-ship—the rockets went off, things jammed up against one wall, and so on—while [Alice] felt nothing.
>
> So the way to state the rule is to say that *the man who has felt the accelerations*, who has seen things fall against the walls, and so on, is the one who would be the younger; that is the difference between them in an "absolute" sense, and it is certainly correct.
>
> (Feynman, Leighton, and Sands 1975: 16)

Feynman is correct that acceleration is an objective matter in relativity. Unlike motion and rest, there is an objective difference between accelerated and non-accelerated (inertial) frames. This difference shows up in spacetime diagrams as a distinction between straight and curved worldlines. Here is why this is important. Earlier we suggested that, since all motion is relative, Bob could legitimately think of himself as staying at rest (relative to the rocket), while Alice zooms away. This way of thinking is depicted in Figure 2.17.

But this picture is objectively incorrect, since it represents Bob as being in an inertial frame of reference throughout the entire episode. In order to correctly illustrate our example, Alice's worldline must be straight and Bob's must be bent. So, for example, we could picture things as shown in Figure 2.18 on the next page.

On this way of construing the situation, Bob starts off at rest (relative to the rocket) while Alice moves away. Then, when Bob gets to B, he accelerates in order to catch up with Alice. This is a perfectly legitimate way for Bob to tell the story. The important point is that this story, unlike the one told by Figure 2.17, correctly captures an objective difference between the twins.

However, it is unclear whether these observations fully resolve the puzzle. For one thing, as Tim Maudlin (2012: 81–3) points out, it is possible to generate a twin paradox

---

[85] Cf. Resnick (1968: 201).

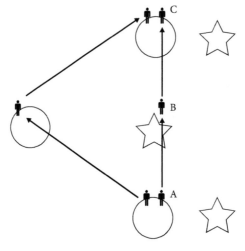

Figure 2.17

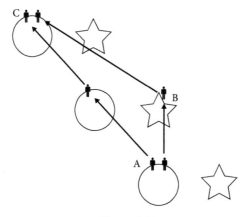

Figure 2.18

in which *both* twins undergo acceleration.[86] So, one cannot fully resolve the paradox by pointing out that (in our version of the case) only one of the twins does so. More importantly, it is unclear how the difference in acceleration is supposed to explain the relevant differences between the twins.[87] To fully resolve the paradox, it is not enough to merely identify *some* difference between the two. Ideally, what we want to do is identify an asymmetry that would explain, for example, *why Alice has more grey hairs than Bob*. On the face of it, the asymmetry in acceleration does not do this.

---

[86] Imagine, for example, that Alice blasts off after Bob, quickly changes her mind, and returns to wait on Earth. This would create a small "bump" on her worldline, but she would still be older when he returns.

[87] This is pointed out by Maudlin (2012: 83).

Fortunately, there is such an explanation. Given the interval equation, and given the details of the case, it will follow that Alice experiences more proper time elapse between the departure and the reunion of the twins—that is, the interval for her worldline from A to C will be greater than that of Bob's. This, again, is an objective matter that both twins will agree on. Second, there is the clock hypothesis from earlier. This was the assumption that accurate clocks always measure the interval. This point applies not just to wristwatches, but to biological clocks as well. Putting these two things together, we have a complete explanation of the twin phenomenon: There is an objective difference between the intervals along the worldlines, and "longer" worldlines mean more grey hairs. That is why Alice and Bob look different upon their eventual reunion.

6. General Relativity and Time Travel

General relativity is an extension of special relativity that provides an account of gravity in terms of spacetime structure. As it turns out, this structure also provides a new way of thinking about travel to the past.

In order to appreciate the difference between Minkowski spacetime and the spacetime of general relativity, it will be helpful to begin with the difference between Euclidean and non-Euclidean geometry. These geometries are often distinguished by way of the parallel postulate—in a Euclidean space, locally parallel lines cannot intersect; in a non-Euclidean space, they can. Consider, for example, the geometry of the surface of a sphere. (See Figure 2.19.)

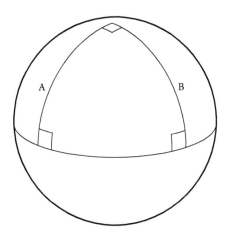

Figure 2.19

In this diagram, the lines A and B both intersect a third line at right angles. In this sense, A and B are parallel to each other. However, these lines are very different from parallel lines in a Euclidean space, since A and B also form a right angle at the top of the sphere. A second difference between Euclidean and non-Euclidean geometry has to do with the triangle sum theorem. In a Euclidean space, the interior angles of a triangle always sum to 180°; in a non-Euclidean space, this is not true (in our diagram, for example, the sum of the interior angles is 270°). A third and final difference between Euclidean and non-Euclidean geometry is that, in a Euclidean space, a straight line goes on forever, without ever meeting itself. In a non-Euclidean space, it is possible for a straight line to pass by itself, intersect with itself, or even "meet" its own end. For example, on the surface of a sphere, it is natural to identify "straight" lines with great circles;[88] all of these lines eventually meet themselves.

Something similar can be true of worldlines in the spacetime of general relativity. To begin, imagine "rolling up" a flat region of Minkowski spacetime. (See Figure 2.20.)

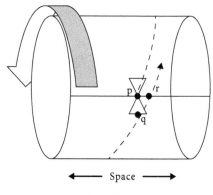

Figure 2.20

This spacetime can be "foliated" in the sense that, given a past and future light cone centered on some point p, we can exhaustively divide the spacetime up into distinct "time-slices" (i.e. mutually exclusive and exhaustive sets of events where all of the events in a set can be thought of as occurring simultaneously). The crucial difference is that, in this case, all of these time-slices will be both earlier and later than themselves. Consider, for example, the hypersurface of simultaneity running through point p. A timelike worldline running through that hypersurface will eventually circle back around and intersect with that slice again (as denoted by the dotted line). If that line leads to p, we will have what physicists call a "closed timelike curve"—that is, a path that would allow a persisting object to meet its earlier self.[89]

Of course, Figure 2.20 is not a realistic picture of the actual universe. But there are other, more realistic models that also incorporate closed timelike curves. One popular approach, associated with physicist Kip Thorne, does this by introducing "wormholes" into the picture.[90] (See Figure 2.21.[91])

---

[88] That is, circles which divide the sphere into two equal hemispheres.

[89] Whether or not this should count as a case of "time travel" is controversial. See below for more details. See also Weingard (1979: 331) and Richmond (2013: 239–41).

[90] For discussion of wormholes as devices for time travel, see Al-Khalili (1999), Visser (1995), and, especially, Thorne (1995).

[91] This image is adapted from Arntzenius (2006).

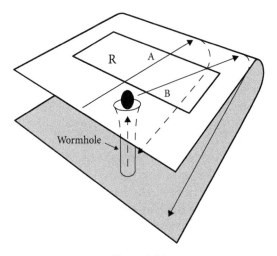

Figure 2.21

In this model, one bends a flat region of Minkowski spacetime, and then completes the curve by adding a wormhole shortcut. The image indicates how such a shortcut would allow an object to pass by its earlier self. Such an object might start out along path A, enter the lower mouth of the wormhole, and then exit along path B. Importantly, at each point along this path, the object's worldline extends into the future light cone of that point. In this sense, the object is always moving into its "local" future. But, given the structure of spacetime, it will eventually end up in its past—that is, it will eventually fall within the past light cone of its previous position.[92]

The question is whether this kind of case is a genuine example of time travel. There is at least one reason for thinking not. In fact, there is at least one reason for thinking that *none* of the cases considered in this section and the last are genuine examples of time travel.[93] This worry stems from the definition of "time travel" given in Chapter 1. Following Lewis (1976), we said that time travel consists in a discrepancy between external time and personal time. *External time* was understood as an assignment of coordinates to events that would be given by an Objective World Historian, whereas *personal time* was understood as an assignment of coordinates that would track the causal relation that makes for identity over time (for a specific individual). The problem is that this definition has no application in a relativistic world. Given the relativity of simultaneity, there is no global assignment of coordinates that would be given by an Objective World Historian. In other words, there is no such thing as external time. But, if there is no external time, then there cannot be any discrepancy between external time and personal time. Hence, there cannot be any time travel.

---

[92] See Everett and Roman (2012), Gott (2001), and Toomey (2007) for surveys of other ways in which closed timelike curves could be produced.

[93] Versions of this worry have been raised by Arntzenius (2006: 602), Carroll (2008b), Daniels (2014a), Smeenk and Wüthrich (2011: 580), and Smith (2013: section 1).

To illustrate this worry, recall the twin case from the previous section (Figure 2.16). It is tempting to think of this as a case in which ten years "really" pass on Earth, but where the traveling twin (Bob) only experiences six. That is why it is tempting to think of that twin as a time traveler. But this way of thinking about the case is mistaken. There is no good sense in which ten years "really" elapse between the departure and arrival. We can only say that ten years pass *along Alice's path* (and that six years pass along Bob's). Since there are no objective, path-independent facts about how much time elapses, there cannot be any discrepancy between external time and personal time. Of course, there is a discrepancy between the twins' clocks upon their reunion, but this does not reflect a discrepancy between personal time and external time. Rather, it reflects a discrepancy between the worldlines of the two individuals. Crucially, there is no discrepancy for either twin when it comes to his or her personal time and the interval measured by his or her watch.[94] So, there is no time travel along either path.

Of course, one could try to avoid this conclusion by adjusting Lewis's definition. For example, Daniels (2014a: 339) suggests that (future) time travel occurs whenever there is time dilation. This would allow us to say that the traveling twin is a time traveler, but it would also require us to say that the stay-at-home twin is a time traveler (recall that Alice's clock initially runs slow from Bob's perspective, just as his clock runs slow from her perspective). Indeed, as Daniels notes, this definition would require us to say that just about *everyone* is a time traveler. But this does not seem any more plausible than the conclusion we are trying to avoid (namely, that *no one* is a time traveler). Daniels tries to mitigate the oddity of his conclusion by pointing out that most cases of "time travel" (in his sense) are not "philosophically interesting" (in the sense that they do not give rise to the kinds of paradoxes we normally associate with time travel). That, he suggests, is why we do not normally call someone like Neil Armstrong a "time traveler" (2014a: 340). That might be correct, but it seems like the same kind of strategy could be employed in the opposite direction. For example, we could say that, strictly speaking, no one is a time traveler, since there is no such thing as objective time. However, there are some possible cases that give rise to the kinds of paradoxes we normally associate with time travel. That is why we are tempted to call those cases "time travel." Neil Armstrong's case is not like that, which is why we don't normally think of him in those terms.

In any case, the situation is slightly different when it comes to the kind of time travel countenanced by general relativity.[95] General relativity, like special relativity, lacks a global notion of objective time. In this sense, there is no external time in general relativity. But general relativity, like special relativity, does include the objective structure provided by the light cones, including the distinction between past and future light

---

[94] In fact, this kind of discrepancy is impossible in relativity. For this reason, it is natural to identify personal time with proper time—that is, the interval along the worldline.

[95] My analysis of this case is heavily indebted to Arntzenius (2006).

cones. This distinction may not be relevant in the case of forward time travel, but it does help to make sense of backward time travel.

To see why, consider Figure 2.20 once more. The horizontal line in this figure represents the hypersurface of simultaneity associated with some frame of reference. Relative to this frame, p is later than q and simultaneous with r. Of course, since p and r are spacelike separated, there will also be some frames of reference in which p is earlier than r and some in which it is later. However, the same is not true for p and q. Since q is in the past light cone of p, it should come out as (locally) earlier than p on all coherent ways of dividing this portion of the world into time-slices. In this sense, q is objectively earlier than p. If we refer to this objective ordering as "light cone time," we can say that, in relativistic worlds, time travel consists in a discrepancy between light-cone time and personal time. And that is exactly what we have in this case. If we let the dotted line represent the path of a persisting object, we can say that q is earlier than p in light-cone time, but later than p in the object's personal time.[96] In this sense, that path represents the journey of a genuine time traveler.

Unfortunately, this characterization of backward time travel cannot be directly translated to the case of wormholes. The problem is that spacetimes with this structure are not temporally orientable in the way that "rolled" spacetimes are. (To see this, just imagine drawing a time-slice that meets the mouth of the wormhole, and ask yourself how the line should be extended from that point onward.) Since wormhole spacetimes cannot be coherently divided into time-slices, one cannot characterize "objective" temporal facts as those that hold on all such divisions. So, one cannot have a discrepancy between objective and personal time. Fortunately, as Frank Arntzenius points out (2006: 603–4), there is a natural fix in this case. Rather than trying to divide the entire spacetime into slices, we can restrict our attention to the flat region of Minkowski spacetime labeled 'R' (in Figure 2.21). We can then suppose that there is some point p on path A and some point q on path B such that (i) p and q both fall within region R and (ii) q is in the past light cone of p. In that case, q should count as earlier than p on every way of dividing R up into time-slices. In this sense, we can say that q is objectively earlier than p. And, given this, we can say that an object tracing the path from p to q would count as a genuine time traveler.

---

[96] Of course, given the shape of this spacetime, there is a sense in which p can be thought of as coming later than q in the object's personal time. Since the spacetime is "rolled," the object can look forward to seeing point p, even though it can also recall having been there before. The crucial point is that there is an asymmetric causal dependence of the q-stage (of the object) on the p-stage. It is in this sense that the p-stage comes first, according to the object's personal time.

3

Paradoxes of Freedom I

All is now secure and fast,
Not the gods can shake the Past.

—Ralph Waldo Emerson, "The Past"

In December of 1929, Hugo Gernsback published an early time travel story by Henry Kirkham in his science fiction magazine, *Science Wonder Stories*. Along with the story, Gernsback offered the following challenge to his readers:

In presenting this story to our readers, we do so with an idea of bringing on a discussion as to time traveling in general. The question in brief is as follows...Suppose I can travel back into time, let me say 200 years; and I visit the homestead of my great great great grandfather, and am able to take part in the life of this time. I am thus enabled to shoot him, while he is still a young man and as yet unarmed. From this it will be noted that I could have prevented my own birth; because the line of propagation would have ceased right there. Consequently, it would seem that the idea of time traveling into a past where the time traveler can freely participate in activities of a former age, becomes an absurdity.[1]

This is the oldest and most familiar argument against time travel: If backward time travel were possible, then you would be able to travel back in time and kill your paternal grandfather (or your great-great-great-grandfather).[2] Moreover, you would be able to do this before your father was ever conceived. But, in that case, your father would not be born, in which case *you* would not be born. And in that case you would not be able to travel back in time to kill your grandfather. Hence, if time travel were possible,

---

[1] This is the first clear statement of the grandfather paradox that I am aware of, but it is unlikely that Gernsback deserves credit for its discovery. Similar puzzles had already been raised by Gernsback's own readers as early as 1927 (recall the *Amazing* letter from Chapter 1). In fact, these puzzles go back at least to Gaspar (1887/2012).

[2] Note that this premise involves an implicit assumption: If backward time travel were possible, then it would be possible to travel to *a particular* time and place in the past (namely, the time and place at which your grandfather is a child). However, this assumption seems uncontroversial since it would seem mysterious—or perhaps *arbitrary*—if the laws of metaphysics permitted travel to some past events and not others.

you both could and could not kill your grandfather before your father was conceived. Since this result is contradictory, time travel must be impossible.[3]

The grandfather paradox is one of several puzzles about what time travelers can and cannot do. These "paradoxes of freedom" are among the most famous arguments against time travel, and have been discussed by many philosophers, scientists, and science fiction authors. They are also among the most important puzzles of time travel, since they raise significant questions about time, fate, and moral responsibility.[4] These paradoxes are the subject of this chapter and the next.

1. Stories of Self-Defeat

The first thing to note about the grandfather paradox is that it's not really about *grand-fathers*. The same problem arises with the retrokilling of any ancestor,[5] including one's mother,[6] grandmother,[7] or great-great-great-...grandmother.[8] In fact, the very same

---

[3] Stated in this way, the grandfather paradox seems to take the following form (where '>' denotes the counterfactual connective): A>B, B>C, C>~B ∴ A>(B&~B) ∴ ~A. This formulation seems to require the transitivity of the counterfactual connective: A>B, B>C ∴ A>C. And that suggests a problem, since the standard view is that transitivity fails—see Bennett (2003: 159–61), Lewis (1973: 12–13), and Stalnaker (1968: 107).

Two points should be made in response. First, it is not at all clear that the counterfactual connective is non-transitive—see Wright (1983: 139–40), Wright (1984), and, especially, Brogaard and Salerno (2007). Second, it is not obvious that the grandfather paradox assumes transitivity. As Jonathan Bennett (2003: 298–301) notes, when we make a speech of the form A>B, B>C, ∴ A>C, we often have in mind something like the following: A>B, A&B>C ∴ A>C. The latter form of reasoning is uncontroversial and we can easily restate the grandfather paradox in these terms: If you were to go back in time and kill your grandfather, your father would not be born. And if you were to go back in time and kill your grandfather, and your father was not born, you would not be born. So, if you were to go back in time and kill your grandfather, you would not be born.

[4] For example, many philosophers take it for granted that "ought" implies "can." If that is correct, then a time traveler's inability to perform certain actions would absolve him of any responsibility to perform those actions. For further discussion of time travel and moral responsibility, see Cohen (2015).

[5] The ancestor in question does not need to be biological. In *Terminator 2*, for example, we can think of the Cyberdyne Corporation as the grandfather, Skynet as the father, and the T-800 as the son. If the Terminator robot were to destroy the Cyberdyne Corporation (or, at least, the relevant research being done by that corporation), then Skynet would not be created, in which case the Terminator would not exist. It is also possible to have cases that mix biological and technological lines of ancestry. For example, if the Terminator had successfully killed Sarah Connor in the first *Terminator* movie, then Sarah would not have given birth to John Connor, and he would not have gone on to become the leader of the human resistance in the future. But, if John would not have gone on to lead the resistance, the Terminator would not have been sent back in time to kill his mother (the purpose of that mission being to prevent Connor's rise to power).

[6] The "matricide paradox" is mentioned by Davies (2001: 95), Nahin (1999: 48), and others.

[7] See Season 1, Episode 5 of *Continuum*: "A Test of Time."

[8] P. S. Miller takes the paradox back multiple generations in his story "Staus Quondam". When his protagonist arrives in the fifth century BCE, he realizes he must take great care since:

> Ninety-five generations back you'd have more grandfathers than there are people on Earth, or stars in the Galaxy! You're knit to everyone...You as much as take a poke at anyone and the odds are you won't even get to be a twinkle in your daddy's eye.

problem arises in the case of a time traveler who goes back in time to kill his younger self.[9] After all, if I were to travel back in time and kill my younger self, then I would never grow up. And, in that case, I would not be able to go back in time and kill my younger self. This version of the puzzle is known, alternatively, as the *autofanticide paradox*,[10] the *autoinfanticide paradox*,[11] and the *retrosuicide paradox*.[12]

Most variations on the grandfather paradox involve murder, but one needn't commit a crime in order to get into trouble. In fact, saving a life can be just as problematic. Consider, for example, the case of *Back to the Future III*. In that movie, Marty learns through historical records that his friend, Doc Brown, was shot and killed in 1885. Fortunately, Marty is able to travel back in time and save his life.[13]

Here's the problem. If Doc Brown didn't die in 1885, then the record of his death would not be present in 1955. And if the record of his death were not present in 1955, Marty would not have traveled back to 1885, in which case he would not have prevented Doc Brown's death.[14] In this case, Doc Brown's death is the "grandfather," Marty's discovery of the historical records is the "father," and his trip to the past is the "son." If the son were to "kill" the grandfather, there would be no father, and hence no son... in which case the son would not be able to kill the grandfather.

Each of the foregoing cases involves a *self-defeating act*—an act such that, if it were performed, it would not be. Self-defeating acts are obviously impossible, since the performance of such an act would imply a contradiction. Yet time travel seems to make such acts possible. This suggests the following line of argument against backward time travel:

(P1)   If backward time travel were possible, it would be possible to perform a self-defeating act.[15]

(P2)   It is impossible to perform a self-defeating act.[16]

(C)   Backward time travel is impossible.

Charles Dye takes the paradox back even further in his story "Time Goes to Now". His time traveler accidentally kills a crucial hominine from our evolutionary history and, in the process, destroys all of humankind.

[9] For examples of this kind of case, see Gold (1953), Grigoriev (1968), and the letter by T.J.D. from the start of Chapter 1.

[10] Horwich (1987: 116).

[11] Horacek (2005), Kiourti (2008: 343), Sider (2012: 115), and Smith (1998: 157).

[12] Vranas (2009).

[13] Thus ignoring Doc's own warning not to risk "further disruptions of the space-time continuum."

[14] In which case the record *would* be present, in which case Marty *would* go back to the Old West and save Doc Brown, in which case...

[15] Strictly speaking, the premise should say that, if backward time travel were possible, *then it would be possible that* it is possible to perform a self-defeating act. Or, to put it another way: If time travel were possible, then there is a *possible world* in which someone *can* perform a self-defeating act. However, if we assume that *possibly possible* implies *possible*, we can stick with the simpler premise. See Vranas (2009: 523).

[16] More carefully, it is not possible that someone can perform a self-defeating act.

This is the general challenge raised by the grandfather paradox, the retrosuicide paradox, and the *Back to the Future III* story. We will refer to it as *the paradox of self-defeat*.

The first premise of this paradox is typically motivated by describing a particular case of past-visitation, and inviting the reader to agree with the relevant possibility claim. For example, as first considered in Chapter 1, section 4, David Lewis begins his discussion of the grandfather paradox by telling the following story:

> Consider Tim. He detests his grandfather, whose success in the munitions trade built the family fortune that paid for Tim's time machine. Tim would like nothing so much as to kill Grandfather, but alas he is too late. Grandfather died in his bed in 1957, while Tim was a young boy. But when Tim has built his time machine and traveled to 1920, suddenly he realizes that he is not too late after all. He buys a rifle; he spends long hours in target practice; he shadows Grandfather to learn the route of his daily walk to the munitions works; he rents a room along the route; and there he lurks, one winter day in 1921, rifle loaded, hate in his heart, as Grandfather walks closer, closer... (1976: 149)

Lewis then invites us to agree that Tim can kill Grandfather, in the scenario described. After all,

> He has what it takes. Conditions are perfect in every way: the best rifle money could buy, Grandfather an easy target only twenty yards away, not a breeze, door securely locked against intruders. Tim is a good shot to begin with and is now at the peak of training, and so on.
> (1976: 149)

In short, Tim has everything that one could hope for in a potential murderer. He has the skill, the means, and the opportunity. He has the desire and resolve. As Lewis puts it, "Tim is as much able to kill Grandfather as anyone ever is to kill anyone" (1976: 149). But if Tim could kill Grandfather, then Tim could perform a self-defeating act. So, if backward time travel were possible, it would be possible to perform a self-defeating act.

This is one way of motivating (P1), but Lewis also mentions a second:

> Suppose that down the street another sniper, Tom, lurks waiting for another victim, Grandfather's partner. Tom is not a time traveler, but otherwise he is just like Tim: same make of rifle, same murderous intent, same everything. We can even suppose that Tom, like Tim, believes himself to be a time traveler. Someone has gone to a lot of trouble to deceive Tom into thinking so. There's no doubt that Tom can kill his victim; and Tim has everything going for him that Tom does. [So] By any ordinary standards of ability, Tim can kill Grandfather.
> (1976: 149–50)[17]

Lewis's argument in this passage proceeds by analogy. Tom can kill Grandfather's partner, and the case of Tom and Partner is analogous to the case of Tim and Grandfather, so Tim can kill Grandfather as well. Hence, the possibility of backward time travel implies the possibility of self-defeating acts.[18]

---

[17] Gorovitz (1964) gives a related argument against backward causation. We will discuss this argument briefly in Chapter 5, section 1.

[18] Lewis's argument is based on the principle that relevantly similar people can do relevantly similar things. For more on this principle in the context of time travel, see Wasserman (2017).

The rationale for (P2) is more straightforward. If A is a self-defeating act, then the following is true by definition:

If A were performed, then it is not the case that A would be performed.

Moreover, it is a truth of counterfactual logic that:

If A were performed, then A would be performed.

From these two statements we can infer:

If A were performed, then: A would be performed and it is not the case that A would be performed.[19]

Since it is impossible for a contradiction to be true, it is impossible for A to be performed. So, it is impossible for there to be a self-defeating act.[20]

Note that this line of reasoning is consistent with the claim that it is metaphysically possible to kill one's grandfather before one's father is conceived. After all, there are presumably possible worlds in which that action would not be self-defeating. Suppose, for example, that there are some worlds in which humans can be resurrected from the dead. And suppose that, in one of those worlds, your grandfather is being watched over by a guardian angel who would quickly bring him back to life, were he ever to be killed. In that case, there would be no paradox in killing your own grandfather.[21]

The important point is that this kind of case does nothing to defeat the paradox of self-defeat. There might be *some* cases in which retro-grampatricide would not be self-defeating, but there are many cases in which it *would*. So, we can stipulate that Tim's case is a case like this. But Tim would still seem to have the ability to kill his grandfather in his scenario, for the reasons given above. So, once again, backward time travel would seem to be impossible.

2. Rewriting History

Self-defeating acts fall within a broader category of actions that involve past-alteration. A past-altering act is an act that would make the past different from how it actually is.[22] Every self-defeating act would be an act of past-alteration,[23] but not all acts of

---

[19] Here I assume the validity of A>B, A>C ∴ A>(B&C).

[20] We will consider a more general argument for the second premise in the following section.

[21] MacBeath (1982: 411) mentions another possibility: Your grandfather could be a time traveler himself. In that case, your (teenage) grandfather could travel to the future, sire your father, and then return to a time before your father is conceived. You could then return to that time and kill your grandfather, without creating a paradox.

[22] To say that an action is past-altering in this sense is *not* to say that it would make the actual past different from how it (actually) is. Rather, a past-altering act is one that would make *the past in the world where the action is performed* different from the past in this world (where the action is not performed). On this distinction, see Vranas (2005).

[23] For example, if I were to commit retrosuicide, then I would *not* commit retrosuicide (because I would not be around to do so). But it is also the case that, if I were to commit retrosuicide, then I wouldn't live to

past-alteration would be self-defeating. For example, if time travel were possible, then I could travel back to the time of the Civil War and prevent the Gettysburg Address. That would be an example of past-alteration, since it would result in the past being different from how it actually is. But there is no reason to think this act would be self-defeating, since it would not kill my grandfather, or thwart my future birth, or undermine itself in any other (obvious) way.[24]

Of course, most of us don't want to retroactively kill our grandparents or prevent the Gettysburg Address. But everyone would like to change the past in some way or other. Indeed, the power to change the past is one of the most enticing features of time travel:

> Oh, if you could but travel in time, just think what you could do. You could provide advance warning and prevent the assassination of Abraham Lincoln or the bombing of Pearl Harbor. You could prevent Caligula or Hitler or Pol Pot from ever being born. You could bring back a cure for the Black Death and prevent the decimation of Europe. You could play the stock market and become richer than Bill Gates... (Goddu 2003: 16)

The possibilities seem endless!

And yet the possibilities also seem impossible. After all, *these events have already occurred*—Abraham Lincoln *was* assassinated, Pearl Harbor *was* bombed—and no one can undo what has already been done. As John Hospers puts it:

> This is an unchangeable fact: *you can't change the past.* That is the crucial point: the past is what has happened, and you can't make what *has* happened *not* have happened. Not all the king's horses or all the king's men could make what has happened not have happened, for this is a logical impossibility. (1967: 177)

Most philosophers agree with Hospers's pessimistic assessment. Paul Horwich, for example, claims that past-alteration is "logically impossible" (1975: 436). Gilbert Fulmer says it is "logically incoherent" (1983: 33). And Anthony Flew calls it "radically absurd" (1954: 57).[25,26]

---

see my tenth birthday. Since I did (actually) live to see my tenth birthday, retrosuicide would result in the past being different from how it actually is. Hence, it would be both self-defeating and past-altering. The same applies to all other self-defeating acts.

[24] Of course, there might be some worlds where this act would turn out to be self-defeating, owing to the so-called "butterfly effect." But presumably there are many worlds in which it would not.

[25] For similar dismissals, see Brier (1973: 361), Casati and Varzi (2001: 582), Cook (1982: 49), Craig (1988: 147), Davies (2011: 26), Dummett (1954: 34–5), Dwyer (1975: 347; 1977), Earman (1972: 232), Gorovitz (1964: 367), Hanley (1997: 205), Harrison (1971: 7), MacBeath (1982: 423), Nahin (1999: 181), Ney (2000: 315), Niven (1971: 113), Pierce (2011: 49–50), Putnam (1962: 669), Richmond (2010b: 16), Smart (1963: 241), and Swinburne (1966: 343). One exception to this pattern is the eleventh-century philosopher Peter Damian. Damian apparently held that God's omnipotence gave him the power to nullify past events. For a discussion of this view, see McArthur and Slattery (1974) and Remnant (1978).

[26] There is at least one kind of past-alteration that is unproblematic. Take, for example, the Boston Red Sox's 1908 World Series victory. Prior to 2004, that victory had the property of *being the most recent Red Sox world championship*. After 2004, it did not. So, there is *a sense* in which that past event changed. However, this is *not* the kind of change that people have in mind when they are thinking about time travel. For more on this point, and on different senses of changing the past, see Ni (1992).

If this is correct, then we have another argument against the possibility of time travel. We will refer to it as the *altered past paradox.*[27]

(P1) If backward time travel were possible, it would be possible to change the past.

(P2) It is impossible to change the past.

(C) Backward time travel is impossible.

This argument is obviously related to the paradox of self-defeat. Both arguments claim that time travelers would have certain abilities. Both claim that those abilities are impossible. And both conclude that backward time travel cannot be done. In fact, some philosophers have claimed that the paradox of self-defeat is nothing more than an "especially vivid" illustration of the problem with past-alteration.[28] Whether or not this is the case is a matter we will return to in the next chapter.

The first premise of the altered past paradox says that backward time travel would allow for past-alteration. This seems intuitively plausible, but we can illustrate with an example. Let *t* be a time at which no time travelers exist. Now suppose that time travel is possible and that you have a time machine at your disposal. Set the dial for *t*, and put your finger on the starter. Suppose that the button is in working order and that you are free to move your finger. Can you push the button? Of course! But if you were to press that button, you would be transported back to *t*, and we have already assumed that *t* is a time at which no time travelers are (actually) present. So, the pressing of the button would be an act of past-alteration. Hence, the ability to travel in time would provide the power to change the past.[29]

The rationale for (P2) is equally straightforward, but in this case there are two different arguments to consider.

First, there is the argument from non-contradiction.[30] In order to change the past, one would have to (i) make something that happened not have happened, or (ii) make something happen that did not. But neither of these options seems possible. If Lincoln was assassinated, for example, I cannot make it the case that he was *not* assassinated—that would be an obvious contradiction. Since contradictions cannot be true, the past cannot be changed.[31]

---

[27] This argument is sometimes referred to as the "bilking paradox"—see, for example, Horwich (1987: 120). However, this name is also used for a slightly different argument about past-alteration—see, for example, Flew (1954: 57). We will discuss this other argument in Chapter 5, section 1.

[28] The quote is from Sider (2002: 115), but similar suggestions have been made by Decker (2013: 188), Lewis (1976: 150), Lockwood (2005: 164), Nahin (1999: 260), Smith (1998: 157), and others. For exceptions to the rule, see Brown (1992), Maudlin (1990: 304), and Vihvelin (1996).

[29] Recall from Chapter 1 that we cannot avoid this argument by positing a "Time Patrol Agency" whose job is to prevent time travelers from meddling with the past. That might explain why *some* time travelers are unable to change the past, but since it is possible to have time travel without timecops, that explanation would be incomplete.

[30] See Hospers (1967).

[31] This way of stating the argument suppresses an important premise—namely, that whatever was the case will always have been the case. (Thanks to James Van Cleve for pointing this out.) We will return to this premise in section 5 of this chapter.

Note that this argument against *changing* the past does not undermine the possibility of *affecting* the past.[32] To affect the past is to have a causal influence on the past, and one could have this kind of influence without changing the past.[33] Suppose, once again, that time travel is possible, that you have access to a time machine, and that you set the controls for some past time, *t*. Suppose further that you in fact push the button—at time *t**, let's say—and are transported back to *t*. This does not imply any contradiction, since we have not (in this example) stipulated that *t* was a time at which no time travelers were present. If you do in fact press the button at *t**, then it is true at that time that at least one time traveler *was* present at *t*—namely, you. In this case, your pressing the button at *t** causes it to be the case that you were present at *t*. But it does not *change* the past, since (we can assume) it was always the case that you were present at that time.[34]

The second argument for (P2) is the argument from the nature of change.[35] According to the B-theory of time, change consists in variation across the temporal dimension—for a person, object, or event to change is for it to have different properties at different times.[36] But in order for an entity to have different properties at different times, it must *exist* at different times. And while an object can exist at different times (and an event can occur at different times), the same cannot be said for *times themselves*—times do not exist at times any more than places exist at places. So, times cannot change.[37]

The same point applies to past events. Take, for example, Lincoln's assassination, which occurred on April 15, 1865. The actual shooting only took a few seconds, but it still consisted of very many momentary events corresponding to each of the instants

---

[32] This point is made by Brier (1973: 363), Dwyer (1975), and Horwich (1975: 435–7), among others. The distinction between changing and affecting the past is challenged by Flew (1973); for a response to his argument, see Dwyer (1978: 30–1).

[33] The same point applies to future events as well.

[34] Several science fiction stories play with the distinction between changing and affecting the past. For example, in Isaac Asimov's "The Red Queen's Race" (1949), a physics professor sends a Greek translation of a chemistry book back to the ancient world (killing himself in the process). When people learn about what happened, they fear that the book will change the past, and that the ripple effects will obliterate their future ("like the pebble that starts the avalanche"). However, a colleague from the philosophy department points out that these worries are misplaced—if the physicist *did* send the book back, then it was *always* the case that textbook was sent back. Hence, his actions would not have *changed* the past—they would simply be a part of the casual explanation for how the past got to be the way it was. (As the philosopher points out, this would also explain the sudden appearance of atomic theory in the days of Leucippus and Democritus.)

[35] See Lewis (1976: 145–6).

[36] See Chapter 2 for more on the B-theory. See Chapter 6 for more on change.

[37] Here is how Lewis puts the point:

> If change is qualitative difference between temporal parts of something, then what doesn't have temporal parts can't change. For instance, numbers can't change; nor can the events of any moment of time, since they cannot be subdivided into dissimilar temporal parts...Could a time traveler change the past? It seems not: the events of a past moment could no more change than numbers. (1976: 146–8)

Lewis states the objection in terms of temporal parts, but that is not required—the important point is that, for something to change, it would have to have different properties at different times.

during the attack. Those momentary events cannot change, since they do not exist at—and thus cannot have different properties at—different times. But in order to delay or prevent the assassination, I would have to change all of those individual events, by making them occur later than they actually did, or by preventing them altogether. Since those events cannot be changed, the assassination cannot be prevented. And what goes for Lincoln's assassination goes for every past event—changing *any* event would require changing momentary events, and momentary events cannot be changed. Hence, past events cannot be altered.

Time travel stories often obscure this issue by implicitly suggesting that a single event can occur multiple times, and thus differ from one occasion to the next.[38] Consider, for example, the case of *Back to the Future* (*BttF*). Early in the movie, Marty McFly watches helplessly as his friend, Doc Brown, is shot and killed by terrorists. Marty is able to escape from the terrorists in his time machine and inadvertently ends up thirty years in the past. There, he manages to warn Doc of what awaits him in the future. When Marty returns to his own time, he witnesses the same shooting again—but *this time around* Doc is wearing a bulletproof vest because of Marty's warning. In this way, Marty is able to change the past and save his friend's life.

The movie is terrific, but the story is misleading, since it suggests that the same shooting occurs twice, with only the first shooting being fatal. This element of the story is confused. There is only one Doc, one time, and one shooting. As a time traveler, Marty is able to *witness* that event twice—once at the beginning of the movie, and once at the end—but to think that the second viewing corresponds to a second occurrence of the event is to commit what Nicholas J. J. Smith calls "the second time around fallacy" (1997: 365).[39] There is only *one* occurrence of the shooting, and that occurrence either results in death, or does not. A coherent movie cannot have it both ways.

Or can it?

3. The Branches of Time

According to Martin Gardner, "There is only one good way" to solve the paradoxes of freedom "and science-fiction scribblers have been using it for more than half a century."

The basic idea is as simple as it is fantastic. Persons can travel to the future of their universe, with no complications, but the moment they enter the past, the universe splits into two parallel worlds, each with its own time track. Along one track rolls the world as if no looping had occurred. Along the other track spins the newly created universe, its history permanently altered...

---

[38] Philosophers sometimes make the same mistake—see, e.g., Hospers (1967: 177).
[39] See also Dyke (2005) and Smith (1998: 156).

It is easy to see that in such a metacosmos of branching time paths, it is not possible to generate paradox...if [for example] you go back and murder yourself in your crib, the universe obligingly splits. Universe 1 goes on as before, with you vanishing from it when you grow up and make the trip back...In Universe 2 with you and the dead baby it rolls on. You are not annihilated by your deed, because now you are an alien from Universe 1 living in Universe 2.

(1987: 7–8)

This response to the paradoxes of freedom is an old one, dating back to at least 1935.[40] It is also very popular, having been embraced by both scientists[41] and science fiction authors.[42] In this section, we clarify some details of the theory (3.1) and then consider three objections (3.2–3.4).

3.1 The branching timeline model

Time is often depicted as a line extending infinitely in each direction. (See Figure 3.1.)

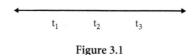

$$t_1 \qquad t_2 \qquad t_3$$

Figure 3.1

This model is natural, since the mathematical structure of the line matches the traditional conception of time in many respects. Like a line, time has no beginning or end. Like a line, time is composed of unextended points (or moments). And, like the points of a line in a coordinate system, the moments of time are subject to an ordering under the *earlier than* relation that is strict,[43] total,[44] and continuous.[45]

According to the branching timeline theorist, we should modify this model by giving up on the requirement of totality. (See Figure 3.2 on the next page.)

On this picture, time is still composed of unextended moments, like t_1, t_2, t_3, and t_{2*}. Moreover, the set of all moments is still subject to a strict, continuous ordering under the *earlier than* relation. But this ordering is only partial, since there are some

---

[40] See the David R. Daniels story "The Branches of Time." This view is often associated with Jorge Luis Borges' story "The Garden of Forking Paths," although that story was not published until 1941. It is sometimes suggested that Edward Everett Hale's story *Hands Off* (1895) is the first time travel story to use alternative histories, but it is unclear whether this story is about a time traveler or someone who is instead located "outside" of time.

[41] A variation on this picture—the "multiverse" model of time travel—is endorsed by Deutsch (1991, 1997) and Deutsch and Lockwood (1994); it is also cited approvingly by Greene (2004) and many others. For criticism of the multiverse model of time travel, see Abbruzzese (2001), Arntzenius and Maudlin (2010), Effingham (2012), Everett (2004), and Everett and Roman (2012: 155–7).

[42] Nahin (1999: 294–303) provides an extensive list of fictional references. Interestingly, few philosophers seem to take these proposals very seriously. Lewis (1976: 145), for example, only acknowledges the idea in order to set it aside. The same is true of Smith (1997: 365), van Inwagen (2010: 6, fn. 6), and others.

[43] That is, an ordering that is irreflexive, asymmetric, and transitive.

[44] That is, for any two distinct moments, either the first is earlier than the second or the second is earlier than the first.

[45] That is, it has the structure of the real numbers on the number line.

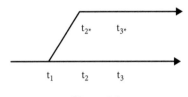

Figure 3.2

members of that set—like t_2 and t_{2*}—such that (i) t_2 is not earlier than t_{2*}, (ii) t_{2*} is not earlier than t_2, and (iii) $t_2 \neq t_{2*}$.[46] As a result, the branching timeline theorist gives up on the following principle, which is a theorem of the standard model:

> *Connectedness*: For any times t_1, t_2, and t_3, if t_2 and t_3 are both later than t_1, then either (i) t_2 is earlier than t_3, (ii) t_3 is earlier than t_2, or (iii) $t_2 = t_3$.

In other words, the branching timeline theorist claims that it is possible for two times to be temporally related to a third, without being temporally related to each other.[47] That is the distinctive feature of the branching timeline model.

To illustrate the utility of the model, recall the central elements of the *Back to the Future* story: Doc Brown is shot (①) and dies (②) in 1985. Marty then travels back to 1955 (③) and, after arriving (④), warns Doc Brown of the upcoming attack (⑤). Marty then goes back to the future (⑥), where he again sees Doc Brown shot (⑦). But, this time around, Doc survives the shooting (⑧) because of Marty's warning. On the branching timeline model, we can depict this sequence of events as follows. (See Figure 3.3.)

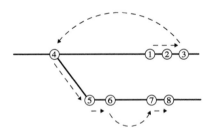

Figure 3.3

---

[46] Some philosophers take this result to be metaphysically—or even conceptually—impossible. See, for example, Prior (1967: 198–9).

[47] There is one way of thinking about this model on which these times—times like t_2 and t_{2*}—are temporally related. The key would be to give up on the assumption that, for any times, t_x and t_y, t_x is simultaneous with t_y only if $t_x = t_y$. One could then say that t_2 and t_{2*} are simultaneous with each other while also being distinct. This would require us to give up on some intuitive principles about temporal relations, but that is probably to be expected when dealing with the branching model. In any case, we will proceed on the assumption that times on separate branches do not stand in any of the standard temporal relations to each other.

(In this picture, the numbers correspond to the relevant events, the pointed lines indicate the flow of Marty's personal time, and arched lines indicate discontinuous jumps from one time to another.)

Here is how this model is supposed to help answer the anti-change arguments from the previous section.

First, the model avoids the argument from non-contradiction, since it provides two different versions of 1985—one in which Doc Brown is killed and one in which he is not. But there is no single time (or single version of the same time) at which he is both killed and not. So there is no contradiction.

Here is a second way to make the same point. Earlier, we said that, in order to change the past, one would have to either (i) make something that happened not have happened, or (ii) make something happen that did not. Those options both sound contradictory, but the branching timeline model provides a consistent reading of each. Take, for example, the death of Doc Brown (②). As Marty is departing 1985 in his time machine (③), he can truthfully say that *that event happened*, since (②) is externally earlier than (③). Moreover, at the end of the movie (after ⑧), Marty can truthfully say that *he prevented that event from happening*, since (i) his warning (⑤) saved Doc's life (⑧), and (ii) both of those events are externally earlier than the utterance in question.

In fact, there is even a sense in which Marty can, at the end of the movie, say that *he made something that happened not happen*. That sense is this: There is an event—namely, the death of Doc—that is personally earlier, but not externally earlier, than his end-of-the-movie utterance. Thus, Marty made something that happened (in his personal past) not happen (in his external past). Of course, Marty does *not* make it the case that something both happened (in the external past) and did not (in the external past). That *would* be contradictory. But, according to the branching timeline theorist, that kind of contradiction is not required for past-alteration.[48]

Second, the branching timeline model seems to avoid the second anti-change argument that was based on the nature of change. According to that argument, change requires variation across time, in which case instantaneous events—like the momentary stages of Doc Brown's death—cannot be changed. And, in that case, it was argued that Marty cannot change the fact that Doc died.

In response, the branching timeline theorist can grant that momentary entities cannot change along a *single* timeline, since they have no extension along that dimension. However, he can point out that there *is* variation across *multiple* timelines. Marty is sad in the original 1985, for example, and happy in the alternative branch. Doc is blood-stained at one time (on one branch) and unmarked at another (on a different branch). If these kinds of variation are sufficient for change, then the metaphysical argument against past-alteration is also unsound.[49]

---

[48] We examine this claim in more detail in section 3.3.

[49] Again, we examine this claim in more detail in section 3.3.

In sum, the branching timeline theorist claims that the branching timeline model allows us to block both of the standard arguments for the second premise of the past-alteration paradox.

The branching timeline theorist also has an answer to the paradox of self-defeat. Here is that argument once again:

(P1) If backward time travel were possible, it would be possible to perform a self-defeating act.

(P2) It is impossible to perform a self-defeating act.

(C) Backward time travel impossible.

Recall that the reasoning behind (P1) consisted of two claims. First, time travel would allow you to commit retrogrampatricide. Second, retrogrampatricide would be self-defeating since, if you were to kill your grandfather, you would not be born, in which case you would *not* kill your grandfather. Hence, time travel would allow you to perform a self-defeating act.

The branching timeline theorist rejects the second step in this line of reasoning—time travel *would* allow one to go back in time and kill one's infant grandfather, but that act would *not* be self-defeating, since it is not the case that, if you were to do it, then you wouldn't. This point can be illustrated with the case of Tim and Grandfather. In Lewis's story, Grandfather was born (①) and not killed (②). Hence, Father was born (③); hence, Tim was born (④). (See Figure 3.4.)

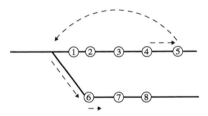

Figure 3.4

Now suppose that Tim travels back to 1920 (⑤), enters into an alternative branch, and kills Grandfather (⑥). In that case, Father would not be born (⑦), in which case Tim would not be born (⑧). That is, Tim would not be born *on the alternative timeline*. But this would not change the fact that Tim was born on the original timeline. And as long as Tim would still be born somewhere or somewhen, there is no puzzle about how he got there to commit the crime.[50] Hence, the branching timeline theorist will reject

---

[50] Of course, it *would* be self-defeating for Tim to kill Grandfather *on the original timeline*, but that is not a problem, since the branching timeline does not provide for that possibility.

the first premise of the self-defeat paradox. Once again, the upshot is that there is no threat to the possibility of time travel.

Or so it seems.

3.2 The inconsistency objection

According to the branching timeline theorist, the proposed model avoids the logical problem of past-alteration by dividing contradictory elements into distinct temporal branches. Doc is killed in 1985 and not killed in 1985-A, but there is no single point at which he is both killed and not. Similarly, it will be true in 2015 that Doc *was* killed and it is true in 2015-A that he *was not*, but there is no single point at which it is true that he was both killed and not. In this way, the branching timeline model avoids both present and past-tensed contradictions.

But what about future-tensed contradictions?

On the standard semantics, tensed metric operators are given the following truth-conditions:

(W)   *It will be the case in n units that P* is true at *t* if and only if there is some time *t** such that *t** is *n* units later than *t* and P is true at *t**.

In addition, standard tense logic implies the following equivalence:

(E)   It will be the case in *n* units that not-P if and only if it is not the case that it will be the case in *n* units that P.

Together, these principles imply a contradiction in the scenario described above. Let *t* be a time in 1885, precisely one hundred years before Doc's death (①). (See Figure 3.5.)

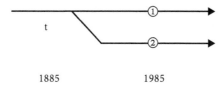

Figure 3.5

From (W), it follows that (1) is true at *t*:

(1)   It will be the case in one hundred years that Doc is killed.

Moreover, since Doc is not killed in 1985-A, and since 1985-A is one hundred years later than 1885, it follows that (2) is true at *t*:

(2)   It will be the case in one hundred years that Doc is not killed.

And, given (E), (2) implies that (3) is true at *t*:

(3)   It will not be the case in one hundred years that Doc is killed.

Yet (1) and (3) cannot both be true at *t*, for that would be a contradiction.

There are several potential replies to this problem.

One idea would be to repeat the standard branching strategy for avoiding contradiction: Replace the single 1885 in which Doc will and won't be killed with two 1885s—one in which he will be killed (①) and one in which he won't (②). (See Figure 3.6.)

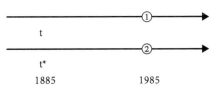

Figure 3.6

This solution is simple and consistent. The problem is that this is no longer a branching timeline model, since there is no longer any shared trunk on the timeline. In fact, one might argue that this is no longer a model of time travel at all, but is instead a picture of moving between parallel universes.[51]

A second option would be to reject one of the two principles with which we began. For example, one could replace (W) with:

> (W*)   *It will be the case in n units that P* is true at *t* if and only if there is some time *t** such that *t** is *n* units later than *t* and, for every such time, P is true at *t**.

Given (W*), it will *not* be true in 1885 that Doc will be killed in one hundred years (since he will not be killed on all the branches). It is also not true that Doc will *not* be killed in one hundred years (since he will not survive on all the branches).

This move would avoid contradiction, but it would only do so by leaving a truth-value gap. Given rule (E), neither (1) nor its negation will be true at time *t*. This may or may not be a tolerable result.

A third option would be to deny (E). This move may seem natural. After all, the fact that there are non-beautiful cities in the world does not imply that there are no beautiful cities. In the same way, the fact that there is a future in which Doc is not killed does not mean that there are no futures in which he is. On the branching timeline model, there could be many different futures, some with killings and some without.

A fourth and final option is to posit ambiguity.[52] In particular, one might replace the standard future-tensed operator (*It will be the case that,* along with its metric variants) with quantifiers over paths and path-specific operators. *It will be the case along all paths that P in n units* is true at time *t* if and only if P holds at all times *n* units after *t* and *it will be the case along some path that P in n units* is true at *t* if and only if P holds at some time *n* units after *t*. On the "universal" reading of our principles, (E) will be true, but (W) be

---

[51] For more on the distinction between time travel and universe hopping, see section 3.4.

[52] This is the option endorsed by computation tree logics. See, for example, Reynolds (2001).

false. On the "existential" reading, (W) will be true, but (E) will be false. But there is no single reading on which both principles will be true, so there is no non-equivocal argument against the view.

3.3 The immutability objection

A second objection to the branching timeline model is that it does not provide for genuine past-alteration. Perhaps time has a branching structure. Perhaps time travel allows one to access alternative branches. And perhaps this access provides one with the ability to bring about alternative events. But, the complaint goes, the ability to bring about alternative events on other branches is not enough to change the past. Hence, the branching timeline model does not allow for true past-alteration.

There are at least two different ways of developing this worry for the branching timeline model. To illustrate, consider again the branching interpretation of the *BttF* story in Figure 3.3 and consider a time between ② (Doc's death) and ③ (Marty's departure). At that time, it is true that

(1)   Doc died.

Moreover, the branching timeline theorist claims that, at that time,

(2)   Marty can save Doc.

Hence, the branching timeline theorist concludes that, at that time,

(3)   Marty can change the past.

The opponent of the branching timeline model might object to this line of reasoning in one of two ways: She could either deny (2) or reject the inference to (3). We will consider each of these options in turn.[53]

First, according to the branching timeline theorist, different branches of time are composed of different temporal intervals. For example, the "original" branch in *BttF* includes 1985 (but not 1985-A), while the "alternative" branch includes 1985-A (but not 1985). One might worry that the same point applies to the *occupants* of those branches as well. For example, the alternative branch in *BttF* might include an "alternative version" of Doc Brown, but Doc and "Doc-A" are no more identical than are 1985 and 1985-A. Thus, if the branching theory is correct, Marty may be able to travel to the A-branch and prevent Doc-A from dying, but that is not the same thing as being able to save *Doc*, which is what (2) asserts.[54]

The same point applies to the case of Tim and Grandfather. If the branching theory is correct, then Tim might be able to travel to an alternative branch and kill Alternative Grandfather, but that is not the same as being able to kill *Grandfather*, which is what

---

[53] The first form of the objection is suggested by Lewis (1976: 135), Le Poidevin (2005: 340–1), and Smith (1997: 365–6). For discussion, see Goddu (2011).

[54] My statement of the objection parallels that of Smith (1997).

Tim longs to do. As Nikk Effingham puts it, Tim "may as well have stayed at home and just created a simulacrum of [his] grandfather to kill instead" (2012: 376–7).[55]

Whether or not this objection succeeds depends, in part, on the relationship between Doc and Doc-A. To see this, consider a case of *personal fission* in which a single person seems to survive as two distinct individuals.[56] To make matters simple, imagine a race of intelligent amoeba-like creatures that occasionally undergo binary fission. (See Figure 3.7.)

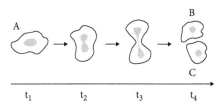

Figure 3.7

Suppose further that the consciousness of these creatures is housed in their nuclei, and that the process of splitting does not interrupt their mental lives in any way. Finally, suppose that unbroken psychological continuity is sufficient for personal identity.[57] In that case, we appear to have a puzzle. For, given the continuity between A and B, we can infer:

(4) A = B.

And given the continuity between A and C, we can infer:

(5) A = C.

But given the reflexivity and transitivity of identity, we can deduce:

(6) B = C.

Yet this seems clearly mistaken, since B and C exist in different places, have different spheres of consciousness, and might go on to live very different lives.

There are, of course, many different replies to this puzzle. Some reject (or modify) the standard psychological criterion of personal identity, and thus reject (4) or (5) (or both).[58] Others reject these identifications by interpreting the names 'A', 'B', and 'C' as labels for instantaneous person-stages that do not persist from one moment to the next.[59] Others simply endorse the argument, and accept the surprising conclusion that B = C.[60]

[55] Effingham does not himself endorse this objection.

[56] On fission, see Lewis (1983), Parfit (1971), and Perry (1976).   [57] Lewis (1976).

[58] See, for example, Shoemaker's contribution to Shoemaker and Swinburne (1984).

[59] See, for example, Lewis (1976). On the temporal parts picture, persons are identified with cross-time sums of momentary person-stages and cases of personal fission are taken to be analogous to cases in which two different roads share an initial road-segment. Again, we discuss this view in more detail in Chapter 6.

[60] See, for example, Ehring (1987).

We will not discuss all of these ideas here, but we will note that the same issues arise in the case of branching timelines, since branching also results in personal fission. Prior to the branch (in 1955) there seems to be a single person present (Doc-PreBranch). After the branch (in 1985 and 1985-A) there seem to be two people present (Doc and Doc-Alternative). However, given the psychological criterion of personal identity (and assuming that branching does not interrupt continuity), we can deduce both (7) and (8):

(7)   Doc-PB = Doc.

(8)   Doc-PB = Doc-A.

And from (7) and (8) we can infer (9):

(9)   Doc = Doc-A.

As before, there are various ways of resisting this argument, but one option is to simply accept the conclusion and say that the original Doc and the alternative Doc are one and the same.[61] On this way of looking at things, branching results in fission and fission results in bi-location, with the result that a single person—like Doc Brown—can be wholly present in two different branches. On this way of looking at things, the argument against (2) quickly falls apart. After all, we already granted that, on the branching model, Marty can save Doc-A. And, according to the current proposal, Doc-A is Doc. So, given the branching model and the proposed theory of fission, it follows that Marty can in fact save Doc Brown.

So far, so good.

The problem, however, is that Marty doesn't just want to save Doc Brown when he travels to the past. What Marty wants to do is prevent a very specific event from occurring—namely, *the 1985 death of Doc Brown* (event ② in Figure 3.3). Marty wants to prevent *that very event* (which he witnessed) from happening. But that cannot happen. Of course, Marty *does* prevent a death on the alternative branch, but preventing a 1985-A death is not the same thing as preventing the 1985 death, which is what Marty wanted to do.[62] From the "God's eye view," Doc Brown is still there in 1985, suffering and dying in the Twin Pines parking lot.

This is the second way of pressing the immutability objection to the branching timeline model. According to this version of the objection, (1) and (2) are true, but they do not imply (3). That is, Doc *did* die, and Marty *did* save him, but Marty did *not* change the past. In order to do *that*, Marty would have had to change the past in his original timeline.

---

[61] Wright (2006).

[62] Here it is important to note that events are arguably individuated, in part, by the time of their occurrence (Kim 1976). If Doc is shot in 1955 and in 1985, then those are different shootings, since they occur at different times. The same point applies to times on different branches. If Doc were killed in both 1985 and 1985-A, then those would be different killings (even if they involved the same, bi-located person). Hence, if Marty prevents Doc from being killed in 1985-A, that does not suffice for preventing the original event.

Interestingly, this way of putting the objection goes back to the earliest appearances of the branching model. For example, the David R. Daniels story "The Branches of Time" (1935) tells the tale of one James H. Bell, an explorer who repeatedly travels back in time to improve human history. In the course of his adventures, Bell encounters a visitor from the future, who explains the branching structure of reality to him. As a result, Bell quickly despairs of his project:

> I did have an idea...to go back to make past ages more livable. Terrible things happened in history, you know. But it isn't any use. Think, for instance, of the martyrs and the things they suffered. I could go back and save them those wrongs. And yet all the time they would still have known their unhappiness and their agony, because in this world-line those things happened. At the end, it's all unchangeable...   (1935: 303)

As Daniels's protagonist sees it, bringing about alternative histories (on alternate time-lines) does not count as changing the past, since it does not alter the original line. Hence, the branching timeline model does not allow for genuine past-alteration.

Here is an analogy to help make the point. Suppose that I want to change my coffee-stained shirt. There are two very different things this might mean. First, I might want to take off the original shirt and put on a new, clean shirt. Second, I might want to alter the original shirt by removing its stain. These are obviously two different things.[63]

In the case of Marty McFly, it is clear that he longs for the second kind of change—he wants to remove the stain of Doc Brown's blood from the tapestry of human history. But, on the branching timeline model, Marty is only able to bring about the first kind of change—he is only able to exchange one branch for another.[64]

This may be disappointing for Marty, but it doesn't seem like a worry for the branching timeline theorist. As originally conceived, the theory was intended as a model of both time travel and past-alteration. Thus, the branching timeline theorist traditionally accepts the first premise of the past-alteration paradox while denying the second:

(P1)   If backward time travel were possible, it would be possible to change the past.

(P2)   It is impossible to change the past.

But those who are moved by the current objection can simply flip the script. Time travel *is* possible, and traveling to an alternative branch *does* allow one to bring about alternative events, but bringing about those events does *not* amount to changing the past. So, the possibility of time travel does not imply the possibility of past-alteration. In short, bringing about cross-branch variation is either sufficient for changing the past or not. If it is, the branching timeline theorist will reject (P2). If not, the branching

---

[63] Ni (1992: 352–3).

[64] Here is a slightly different way of making the same point. Imagine a world of multiple universes that are spatiotemporally disconnected from each other. Imagine further that God creates a bi-located sphere that exists, wholly present, in each of two different universes. In Universe 1, the sphere exists for a single instant and is red; in Universe 2 it exists for a moment and is green. Such a sphere would possess different colors at different times (in different universes), but that is not enough for change. The same thing seems true for Doc Brown.

timeline theorist will deny (P1). Either way, the branching theorist will conclude that the argument is unsound.

3.4 The irrelevance objection

In 3.2 we encountered the problem of future-tensed contradictions, and we noted that, if one responds to this problem by replacing branching timelines with parallel universes, it is no longer plausible to think of Marty McFly as a time traveler. But the same objection can be raised against the original model, in which parallel branches share a common trunk. This way of putting the objection raises a more serious problem for the branching timeline theory.

To begin, consider the original illustration of Marty's adventure (Figure 3.3). This figure suggests that Marty first travels back in time before entering onto the alternative branch. This is what makes this seem like a genuine case of time travel. But this suggestion is mistaken. Remember: Marty was not present in the original 1955, which is part of the explanation for Doc Brown's death (in the original 1985). So, when Marty heads back to change the past, his arrival must itself constitute a change in the past. And, once again, the branching timeline model tells us that this kind of change always involves variation across different branches. In other words, we need two different moments in 1955—an original moment in which Marty is absent, and an alternative version in which he appears.

To illustrate, let t (in Figure 3.8) be the moment of branching—that is, the last moment in 1955 that is shared by both timelines. Since t is in the past, relative to the original 1985, Marty does not appear at that moment. When *does* he appear? That depends. One possibility is that there is some time t^{**} on the alternative branch such that Marty exists at t^{**}, but does not exist at any earlier time. On the second option, Marty does not exist at t, but he does exist at all times immediately after t on the alternative branch. For simplicity, we will go with the first alternative. (See Figure 3.8.)

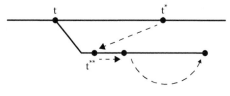

Figure 3.8

Figure 3.8 is a more accurate representation of Marty's adventures than is Figure 3.3. However, it seems clear that this picture does not represent a true case of time travel. After all, in order to travel to the past *from* t^*, one would have to travel to the past *of* t^*—that is, one would have to travel to a time that is earlier than t^*. But Marty does *not* do this since t^{**} is not earlier.

To underscore the point, imagine a different kind of story involving two parallel universes—one of which matches Marty's original timeline and one of which matches the alternative path from t^{**} onward. (See Figure 3.9.)

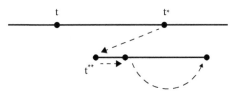

Figure 3.9

Once again, trips to parallel universes are not journeys in time, so this would not be a case of time travel. But this case is *exactly* like the previous case, insofar as Marty is concerned. In neither case does Marty travel to an earlier time. In both cases, Marty's time of departure stands in no temporal relation to the time of his arrival. So, Marty does not travel to the past in either scenario.[65]

I conclude that the branching timeline model turns out to be a theory of parallel universe travel, rather than time travel. As such, the model has no relevance to the current paradoxes.[66]

4. Traveling in Hypertime

We have seen that the branching timeline model faces a variety of challenges. But a related view—the *hypertime view*—offers a more promising alternative.[67] This section explains the alternative model (4.1), argues for its advantages (4.2), and discusses some potential objections (4.3).

4.1 The hypertime model

In 1971, Alex and Phyllis Eisenstein published their first science fiction story—a short piece titled "The Trouble with the Past." That story tells the tale of an inventor named James Thomas, who travels back in time from the year 2314 with the intention of making a permanent settlement in the past (circa 1870). But when his "time-cage" arrives, Thomas is met with a deafening crash.

---

[65] This kind of worry has been raised by many people, including Arntzenius and Maudlin (2010: section 9), Kutach (2013: 303), and Rucker (1984: 173). Dainton (2001: 1160) also mentions the worry, but takes it to be a terminological issue.

[66] Interestingly, the standard definition of time travel—Lewis's definition—seems to count this as a case of time travel, since there is a clear discrepancy between external time and personal time. (See Chapter 1, section 1.) Perhaps this shows that we need to add another condition to Lewis's definition: Time travel occurs only if (i) there is a discrepancy between personal and external time, and (ii) all of the relevant events are temporally related to each other.

[67] The exact relation between these views is a matter of some debate. Forrest (2010), for example, suggests that the hypertime view is just a restatement of the branching view.

Startled, James Thomas turned. He stared at the time-cages massed in front of him—two of them inextricably enmeshed, several connected to each other like links on a chain, and one off to the side by itself. He stared at eight duplicates of himself who, with their machines, had all materialized in 1870 within a few minutes of his own appearance.   (1971: 52)

Thomas is understandably confused until one of his counterparts steps forward with an explanation:

We assume that time passes in a manner analogous to the stringing of an infinite number of beads. Each bead is the instant of Now when it is last on the chain. Beads are continually being added, and each one is only the Now until another is placed after it…It can also be likened to the process of knitting. No matter how many stitches are knitted, there is only one last stitch, only one Now. And like a person knitting (or the stringer of beads), in order to travel back in time, to make some previous stitch or bead the Now, we must unravel all the stitches that come after it, remove from the string all the beads that follow it until the selected bauble (or stitch) lies exposed as the top one of the line. Gentlemen, by choosing a Now in 1870, we have unraveled time. By coming to rest, we allow time to reknit itself naturally, but it does not necessarily weave the same pattern as before.   (1971: 53)

The counterpart's description of time recalls the growing block theory, which we introduced in Chapter 2. On that view, the past and present exist, but the future does not. Moreover, the existing block is continuously growing, as more and more times are being added. This is what the counterpart has in mind when he likens time to a string of beads with new beads being continually added. One way to understand this idea is to imagine that the universe has two different time dimensions—time and hypertime. The "growth" of the block can then be understood as temporal expansion along the hypertime dimension.[68] (See Figure 3.10.)

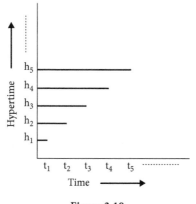

Figure 3.10

[68] Similar suggestions have been made for other versions of the A-theory. Broad (1938: 278), for example, argues that a second time dimension is required in order to make sense of "the moving spotlight view" (i.e. the view that combines eternalism and the A-theory). And Smart (1949) argues that an infinite number of time dimensions are required in order to make sense of any view on which time "passes." For further discussion of multi-dimensional time, see MacBeath (1993), Meiland, (1974), Thomson (1965: 20–7), Wilkerson (1973, 1979), and Zemach (1968). See also the readings in Part I of Bars and Terning (2010).

In this figure, the x-axis represents one dimension of time, which we can think of as "normal" time. The y-axis represents a second temporal dimension, which we can call "hypertime". Each of the horizontal lines represents the growing block universe, relative to a given hypermoment. We can then understand the claim that the block "grows" as the claim that it gets bigger and bigger as one moves along the hypertime dimension.

In the ordinary case, time is assumed to pass at a constant rate of one instant per hyperinstant, so that the four-dimensional universe adds a single slice for each instant of hypertime. However, on the Eisenstein theory this growth can be reversed by the process of backward time travel. When someone travels into the past, the fabric of history is unwound, and slices of the four-dimensional manifold are erased. This process may be gradual or it may be immediate, but, either way, it results in a temporary shrinking of the block. So, if the Eisensteins' theory is correct, their story can be illustrated as in Figure 3.11.

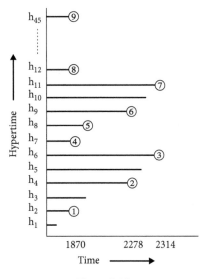

Figure 3.11

In this diagram, the growing block begins growing normally. At hypertime h_2, the leading edge of the block is in 1870 and, at that moment, James Thomas is not present (①). The block then continues growing through 2278 (when Thomas is born—②) up until 2314 (when Thomas's time machine is built—③). Thus, at hypertime h_6, the growing block has a substantial past that includes moments from 1870, 2314, and all of the years between. However, Thomas then turns on his machine and the block quickly shrinks, so that—at hypertime h_7—it includes moments from 1870, but not 2314 (or any of the years between). Moreover, this 1870 differs from the h_2 1870 in that James Thomas is now present (④). From that hyper-point on, the block resumes its normal rate of growth, building through the early 1900s (when Thomas dies—⑤), to the 2200s (when Thomas is born again—⑥), and up until 2314 (when Thomas again turns on his machine—⑦). At that hyper-point, the block shrinks again, so that the leading edge is once more a moment from 1870. But *this* 1870 now includes *two* versions of James Thomas (⑧)—one from the h_6 2314 and one from the h_{11} 2314. This process then repeats seven more times, until—in the h_{45} version of 1870—a startled James Thomas is left staring at eight bewildered duplicates (⑨).

We will refer to this picture of time travel as the *hypertime model*. Like the growing block model, it allows for new times to come into existence from one hypertime to the next. But unlike the standard model, it also allows for old times to go out of existence. It is this kind of change that helps to avoid the paradox of past-alteration.

Earlier, we objected to the *Back to the Future* story on the grounds of inconsistency. In the beginning of the movie, Doc is killed and, in the end, he is saved. Hence Doc is both killed and not—a clear contradiction.

The hypertime model avoids this inconsistency by allowing Doc to have different properties at the same time, relative to different hypertimes. (See Figure 3.12.)

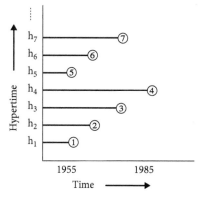

Figure 3.12

In this diagram, Marty is not initially present in 1955 (①), so Doc is not warned (②), so Doc is initially killed (③). Marty then takes off in his time machine (④), arrives in 1955 (⑤), and warns Doc (⑥). The result is that Doc is saved in the end (⑦). In other words, Doc is killed in 1985, relative to one hypertime (h_3) but not relative to another (h_7). Crucially, there is no time at which Doc is both killed and not killed, relative to the same hypertime. Hence, Marty is able to change the past and save Doc Brown without any contradiction.

The same is true for Tim and his efforts to kill Grandfather. According to the hypertime theorist, Tim's universe initially develops in a perfectly unremarkable way, with Grandfather (①), Father (③), and Tim (④) all being born. Then, at some point in the 1970s (the 1970s relative to h_7) Tim turns on his machine (⑤) and the previous fifty years disappear. (See Figure 3.13.) Time then marches on and—this time around—Tim kills Grandfather (⑦).

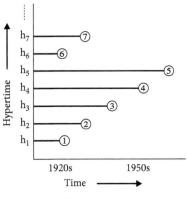

Figure 3.13

As in the previous case, the story is free from contradiction. The year 1921 has a property at one hypertime—it is murder-free at h_3 (②)—and lacks it at another—it is not murder-free at h_7 (⑦). But there is no single hypertime according to which 1921 both does and does not include the murder of Grandfather. So, there is no contradiction. Moreover, there is no mystery about how Tim managed to pull off the crime. If Tim kills Grandfather in 1921 (relative to h_7), then he will not be born, relative to later hypertimes. But that will not change the fact that Tim was born, relative to some earlier hypertimes. Nothing will change the fact that Tim was born in the 1950s-relative-to-h_4. So there is no threat of self-defeat if Tim goes on to kill Grandfather at some other time, relative to a later hypertime.

4.2 Three advantages to the hypertime model

The hypertime model of past-alteration has been defended, in one form or another, by Jack Meiland (1974), Geoffrey Goddu (2003), and Peter van Inwagen (2010). In fact, this model is more popular among philosophers than the branching timeline theory. One reason for this is that the hypertime model is able to avoid some of the objections facing the former view.

The first objection to the branching timeline theory was the problem of future-tensed contradictions (the inconsistency objection). According to the branching model, all cases of past-alteration involve an event—e—and three times—t_1, t_2, and t_3—such that (i) e occurs at t_2, (ii) e does not occur at t_3, and (iii) t_2 and t_3 are each later than t_1. Given the standard semantics for tensed statements, this situation generates an immediate contradiction at t_1.

The hypertime model avoids this objection, since it doesn't require this kind of situation. As the earlier diagrams suggest, the set of all times is subject to a strict, total, and continuous ordering, relative to each hypertime. Thus, there are no branching temporal structures. Thus, there is no threat of future-tensed contradictions.

The second objection to the branching theory was that it did not provide for genuine past-alteration (the immutability objection). First, it was argued that the model does not allow one to interact with past people (or objects), since time travel takes one to an alternative timeline populated by numerically distinct individuals. Second, it was argued that even if one *could* interact with past people and bring about alternative histories, that would not be enough to change the past—times on different branches are analogous to times in disconnected universes, so variation across them is not enough for change.

The hypertime model avoids both versions of this objection. First, we normally think of persons and other objects as having three or four dimensions—they are extended in the three spatial dimensions and persist through time. But, on the hypertime model, individuals can instead be thought of as five-dimensional objects, extending through three spatial dimensions and along two temporal axes. On this picture, objects persist through both time and hypertime. Just as a single person can be present at two different times, a person can be present at two different hypertimes. For example, Tim's Grandfather exists at hypertimes h_3 and h_7 (Figure 3.13). Thus, when Tim travels back to the 1920s of h_7 and kills Grandfather, he is really killing *Grandfather* (and not just a duplicate from another dimension).

Second, hypertime is supposed to be a genuine dimension, which, like time, has an objective ordering. Variation across hypertime thus counts as change, in the same way that variation across time counts as change.[69] So, for example, when Doc is killed in the h_3 1985 and then saved in the h_7 1985, this is a genuine case of change. Of course, Marty does not make it the case that Doc was not killed in the h_3 version of 1985, so he does not change the hyper-past. But that is not a criticism of the theory, since it is only intended as a model of past-alteration.

The final worry for the branching theory was that it was a model of parallel universe travel, rather than time travel (the irrelevance objection). The worry was that, when Marty travels from 1985 to 1955-A, he does not travel to a past time.

Once again, the hypertime model seems to avoid this objection. On this model, we can think of '1955' as picking out the sum of the 1955 points from each of the individual hypertimes. So, when Marty travels back to the h_5 part of *1955*, he is really going back to 1955 (rather than some alternative version).[70] Of course, Marty does

---

[69] Baron (2017) dismisses this kind of change as nothing more than a "shift in perspective" (section 4.2). As he sees it, the main promise of the hypertime model is to give us a sense in which time travelers can "overwrite" the past by removing certain events from the universe (where "the universe" apparently includes all of time and hypertime). But it's unclear why the hypertime model should be understood in that way. After all, variation across time (relative to a given hypertime) certainly seems like a genuine kind of change. And that is analogous to variation across hypertime (relative to a given time). So, variation across hypertime (relative to a given time) also seems like a genuine kind of change.

[70] On this way of thinking about things, Marty visits 1955 in the same way that a tourist visits California by traveling to Los Angeles—that is, he visits 1955 by visiting *a part* of 1955.

not go back to the h_1 part of 1955, so he does not travel backward in hypertime. But that is not a criticism of the theory, since it is only intended as a model of backward time travel.[71]

In sum, the hypertime model avoids all the problems facing the branching timeline theory. Most importantly, the current view allows for genuine travel to the past, as well as genuine past-alteration.

4.3 Three objections to the hypertime model

The hypertime model may have some advantages over the branching theory, but there are still some potential worries. Here, we will briefly mention three objections and show how these worries can be answered by modifying the view in various ways.[72]

The first worry for the hypertime model is that it is guilty of false advertising. One of the most salient features of the model—perhaps *the most* salient feature—is that it involves the obliteration of many entities from the past and present. Because of this, some might be tempted to say that "time machines," on this account, are really nothing more than annihilation machines.[73] Even those who do not find this worry persuasive may still find this feature disappointing. It would be a bit of a let-down, to say the least, if going back in time required one to kill billions of people.

Fortunately, the annihilation element of the hypertime model turns out to be inessential. To illustrate, consider the two-dimensional model of time travel suggested by Jack Meiland. (See Figure 3.14.)

Meiland explains his diagram as follows:

The moments labeled t_1 to t_7 on the diagonal line are present moments. The line $P_1-t_1 \ldots$ represents the past when t_1 is the present moment. That is, P_1 is the past at (or with respect to) the present moment t_1. Similarly, P_2 is the past with respect to t_2. The dotted vertical lines indicate the positions of moments in the past. For example, the intersection of P_3 with vertical line Pt_1 is the position of the moment t_1 in the past with respect to $t_3 \ldots$ (1974: 159)

[71] Smith (2015) raises a potential worry for this response. According to him, the hypertime theorist owes us an explanation of why the h_3 1985 is the same time as the h_7 1985. Moreover, this explanation must explain how things at the h_7 version of 1985 depend, in the right sort of way, on what is going on at the h_3 version. However, Smith objects that "this sort of causal dependence and sufficiency across hypertime is incompatible with normal causality over normal time—with how [the h_7 1985] is depending on how [the h_7 1984] is and how [the h_7 1984] is sufficing for how [the h_7 1985] is" (2015: section 6). In response, the hypertime theorist will presumably grant that how things are in 1985-relative-to-h_7 depends on how things are in 1984-relative-to-h_7. However, how things are in 1984-relative-to-h_7 will also depend, in part, on what happens in 1985-relative-to-h_3. (For example, the fact that Doc is killed in the h_3 version of 1985 is part of the explanation for why he has a note of warning in the h_7 version of 1984; and *that* is part of the explanation for why he is wearing a bulletproof vest in the h_7 version of 1985.)

[72] Portions of this section are based on Hudson and Wasserman (2010).

[73] Hudson and Wasserman (2010) argue that this temptation should be resisted. But they also raise a puzzling—and potentially worrisome—question. Suppose that uncountably many would-be time travelers all set their dials to different times in the past (such that no time is left unselected) and all put their machines into motion at the exact same moment. Question: *What happens hyper-next?*

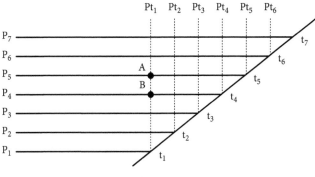

Figure 3.14

He then explains how his two-dimensional diagram can be used to consistently model a case of past-alteration:

Consider the present moment t_4 in Figure [3.14]. P_4 is the past associated with t_4. Now, suppose that t_1 is the time of the Great Exhibition (1851, that is). So the point in Figure [3.14] labeled 'B' is the time of the Great Exhibition in t_4's past. Suppose further that Harrison is not at B. But between t_4 and t_5, someone invents a time machine which Harrison enters at t_5 and travels to the Great Exhibition. If time travel into the past takes no time (that is, is instantaneous), then Harrison will arrive at the point labeled 'A'. Thus, the proposition 'Harrison was not at the Great Exhibition' is true at t_4 and false at t_5.   (1974: 159–60)

Although Meiland does not use the terms 'hypertime' or 'growing block' in his explanation, we can easily retell his story in our terms. In particular, we can take P_1, P_2, etc. to be various hypertimes, and we can take t_1, t_2, etc. to correspond to the leading edge of the block as it expands from one hypertime to the next. Moreover, we can continue to understand time travel as relocation within the growing block, and we can continue to understand past-alteration as variation in past times with respect to different hypertimes. The only difference in the Meiland model is that we drop the assumption that relocation in the growing block requires the annihilation of past and present objects. Rather than shrinking and re-growing, the block simply continues to grow in the normal fashion, with an altered past. Hence, it is possible to have a hypertime model of past-alteration that does not involve time-annihilation.

A second worry for the hypertime model is that—as currently configured—it requires a commitment to the growing block theory, and many take this to be the most implausible theory of time.[74] A related worry is this: Many of the most familiar time travel stories involve changing the past,[75] but other time travel stories tell the same kind of tale in the opposite direction—the future was one way, then the time traveler did his

[74] For some of the reasons why, see Merricks (2006).
[75] See, for example, *Back to the Future I* and *III*.

or her thing, and now the future is somehow different.[76] However, if there are no merely future objects or events (as the growing block theory tells us) and every episode of time-travel-with-change involves the annihilation and eventual replacement of some objects or events (as the hypertime theory tells us), then it is impossible to travel to the future and change what will be.

In response to these concerns, Hudson and Wasserman (2010) argue that the growing block component of the hypertime model is also inessential, and that eliminating this component allows us to make sense of time travel with future-alteration. If they are correct, then we can answer both of the preceding worries at once.

It will be recalled from Chapter 2 that one of the most popular pictures of time is the one recommended by the eternalist. The eternalist block differs from the growing block in that it contains future objects, events, and times. In addition, most of those who accept the eternalist ontology also endorse the B-theory of tense and therefore deny the passage of time (which is a central feature of the growing block view). But this combination of views is not compulsory, since one can be both an eternalist and an A-theorist. One way to do that is to embed an eternalist block in a hypertemporal dimension. (See Figure 3.15.)

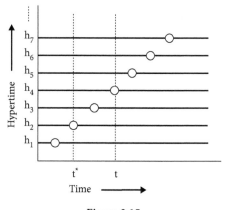

Figure 3.15

Each line in this diagram represents the complete four-dimensional block, relative to each hypertime. At each hypertime, a single slice of the four-dimensional block has the property of *being present* (as denoted by the dot) and the present marker moves forward at a constant rate through hypertime. As the marker moves, objects, events, and times change from being future, to being present, to being past. But beyond these shifting A-properties, the block does not normally change along the hypertime dimension. In particular, no new objects, events, or times come into (or go out of) existence as we move toward the hyperfuture. Moreover, none of these entities normally change their non-A-properties from one hypertime to the next...not unless there happen to be some time travelers about.

---

[76] See, for example, *Back to the Future II*.

Let t (in Figure 3.15) be the moment at which Marty's time-traveling DeLorean hits 88 mph and let t^* be a few seconds before. Furthermore, suppose that t^* is present at hypertime h_2 and that, relative to h_2, the past of t does not include any time travelers. In particular, Marty does not exist in the h_2 1955, so Doc is not warned about the shooting, so he is not wearing a bulletproof vest, so...Doc is dead. But when the Now moves onto t (at h_4, let's say) and Marty hits 88 mph, the past of t (and of t^*) is changed. In particular, Marty exists in the h_4 1955, where he successfully warns Doc of the future attack. As a result, Doc wears a bulletproof vest (in the h_4 version of t^*) and survives being shot (in the h_4 version of t). In this way, Marty is able to make the block morph, without any shrinking or growing. So, one can endorse the hypertime model of past-alteration without being committed to the growing block picture of reality.[77,78]

Note that the current version of the view also allows for time travel to the future, as well as future-alteration. For example, let t^* be a time in 1985, and suppose that, when t^* is present (at h_2), it is the case that Marty's future son will get into big trouble in 2015.[79] Suppose further that, when t^* is past and t is present (at h_4), Marty hits 88 mph in his DeLorean and heads to the future to prevent his son's predicament. Suppose finally that Marty will be successful so that, from h_4 onward, it will *not* be the case at t (or at t^*) that Marty's future son will get into big trouble in 2015. As in the previous case, this story involves variation in an eternalist block along the hypertime dimension. Assuming that this kind of variation suffices for change, we now have an account of future-alteration that exactly mirrors the case of past-alteration.

A third and final worry for the hypertime model is that it requires a commitment to hypertime. This is a commitment that many people find hard to accept. Richard Swinburne, for example, says that the one-dimensionality of time is as a matter of "logical necessity" (1968: 209). John Lucas likewise insists that "time must...only have one dimension" (1999: 9). And even those who think that hypertime is a coherent idea still take it to be a "cumbersome ontological posit casting shadows on the very idea of past-changing" (Loss 2015: 3–4). For these reasons, it would be nice if there were a model of past-alteration that did not require multiple temporal dimensions. Fortunately, there is.

5. The A-Model of Past-Alteration

To begin, we should note there is a sense in which all A-theorists believe in past-alteration. After all, things are always changing from being present to being past, so the past is continuously adding new things. In this sense, at least, the past is continually changing.

---

[77] This account of past alternation is perfectly consistent, but it does raise a pressing question: Why do things change when t becomes present? We will return this point at the end of this chapter.

[78] Bernstein (2017) suggests a slightly different way of combining these views. On her account, Marty does not simply relocate himself in the block when he travels back in time. He also takes the objective present back with him to the past. (Imagine the "moving spotlight" in Figure 3.15 jumping back when Marty hits 88 mph.)

[79] See *Back to the Future II*.

To illustrate and expand on this point, suppose that the A-theorist accepts an eternalist view of time. In that case, she might depict current reality as in Figure 3.16 (with the highlighted slice indicating that 2016 has the irreducible A-property of *being present*).

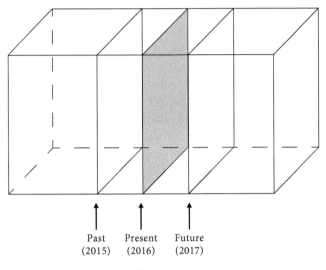

| Past | Present | Future |
| (2015) | (2016) | (2017) |

Figure 3.16

However, the A-theorist will emphasize that this picture is only accurate for a moment, since the A-facts are constantly changing. 2016, for example, is present but will soon be past. Given this fact, the A-theorist will soon have to redraw her figure as in Figure 3.17.

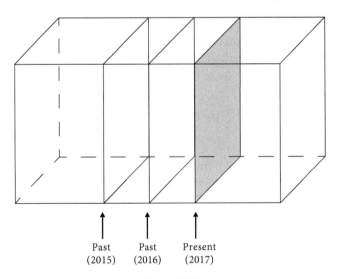

| Past | Past | Present |
| (2015) | (2016) | (2017) |

Figure 3.17

Of course, the A-theorist could combine all of these figures into a single diagram by redrawing them as timelines and embedding them in a second temporal dimension. This is the picture of reality suggested by the eternalist-hypertime model (Figure 3.15). But this picture is not forced upon the A-theorist. In fact, she is probably better off without it. Rather than trying to reduce the passage of time to variation in A-properties across hypertime, the A-theorist should simply take some A-facts as basic—the world *is* one way, and it *will be* different in the future, but these facts are not reducible to relational facts about what things are like at different hypertimes.

Now, the A-theorist typically assumes that A-properties are the only things that change with the passage of time. In particular, the past only changes insofar as (i) it adds new times, events, and objects, and (ii) past times, events, and objects recede further and further into the past (e.g. they change from *being one day past*, to *being two days past*, etc.).

But this assumption is not essential. It is consistent with the eternalist-A-theory to think that all sorts of things change with the passage of time. This includes the kinds of changes we would expect to find in the typical time travel story.

To illustrate this idea, let's return to the case of Marty McFly, and let's suppose it is currently 1955. In that case, the imagined A-theorist will say the following:

- Marty McFly is not present.
- Doc Brown will die thirty years hence.
- Marty McFly will time-travel thirty years hence.

However, in fifteen years, these facts will have changed. In particular, when 1970 is present, the relevant facts would include the following:

- Marty McFly was not present fifteen years ago.
- Doc Brown will die fifteen years hence.
- Marty McFly will time travel fifteen years hence.

Finally, let's suppose that it is now 1985. Doc has just been shot, and Marty has *just* hit 88 mph in his time machine. At this moment, all of the following facts hold:

- Marty McFly has just traveled in time.
- Marty McFly was present thirty years ago.
- Doc Brown is not dying (because of Marty McFly's earlier warning).

In other words, the past has now changed. Whereas it was the case that Marty was not present in 1955 (and hence did not warn Doc of the future shooting), it is now the case that he was (and that he did).

The same point can be put pictorially. When 1955 is present, the eternalist block would look like Figure 3.18 on the next page.

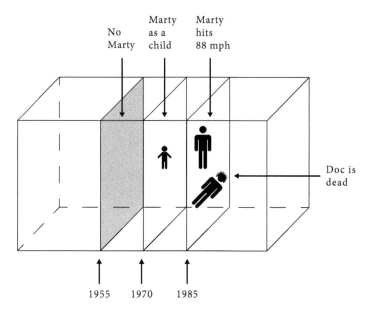

Figure 3.18

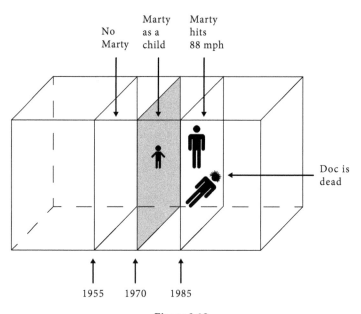

Figure 3.19

When 1970 is present, the block would look like Figure 3.19.

Finally, when 1985 is present and Marty hits 88 mph, the block would look like Figure 3.20.

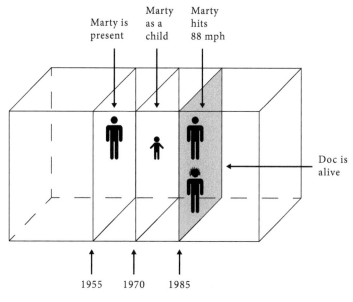

Figure 3.20

As before, the A-theorist *could* understand this kind of past-alteration as variation in the past across a second temporal dimension. She could, for example, take these different sets of facts as corresponding to the eternalist block, relative to different hypertimes. But she could also understand past-alteration in terms of irreducible A-properties. For example, she could say that Marty McFly did not exist in the past when one time is present (i.e. when one time has the irreducible A-property of *being present*) and does exist in the past when a different time is present. That is all there is to past-alteration on the A-model. There are no hypertimes. There are no temporal branches. Things simply change with the passage of time.

The A-model raises several immediate concerns. The first has to do with consistency. To begin, note that each of the preceding sets of facts is internally consistent. For example, none of the sets says that Marty both is and is not present at a certain time, or that Doc both will and will not be killed. However, one might worry that these sets create inconsistencies when taken together. One way of making this worry more precise is by invoking the following principle, which is an axiom in the minimal temporal logic, $\mathbf{K_t}$:

(GP) $\phi \rightarrow GP\phi$[80]

Here, 'G' and 'P' are Arthur Prior's temporal operators for 'It will always be the case that' and 'It has at some time been the case that'.[81] So, what (GP) says is that whatever *is* the

---

[80] See Goranko and Galton (2015) and Rescher and Urquhart (1971).   [81] See Prior (1957).

case will always *have been* the case. This, however, conflicts with the basic idea behind the A-model of past-alteration. On this view, the fact that there are no time travelers around today does not imply that it will always be the case that there were no time travelers around today (since time travelers might travel back to today at some point in the future).

The same problem arises with other principles of temporal logic. Consider, for example, the following:

$$\text{WAS}_{n\text{-UNITS-AGO}} \left(\text{WAS}_{m\text{-UNITS-AGO}} \, \varphi \right) \rightarrow \text{WAS}_{n+m\text{-UNITS-AGO}} \, \varphi$$

This principle says that, if it was the case n units ago that φ was true m ago, then φ was true $n + m$ units ago. For example, if it was true one year ago that event e occurred one year before *that*, then it is now true that e occurred two years ago. This, again, would conflict with the A-model of past-alteration. Suppose, for example, that it is 1985 and that Marty has just hit 88 mph in his time machine. In that case, it is now true that Marty was around thirty years ago (in 1955). However, that was not true fifteen years ago. That is, when 1970 was present, it was not the case that Marty was around in 1955. That is because, when that time was present, Marty had not yet traveled back.

These kinds of examples can be multiplied, but the general point is clear: The A-model of past-alteration violates the standard principles of temporal logic. The question is whether this is an objection to the A-model and, if so, how damaging that objection is. This question touches on larger issues of philosophical methodology, but there is at least one reason to be skeptical about this kind of objection: Standard temporal logic begins with the assumption that the past cannot change. (GP), for example, is treated as an axiom in $\mathbf{K}_t$, so it cannot provide an *independent* reason to reject that possibility. Of course, there might be good reasons to assume that the past cannot change, in which case there would be good reasons to reject the A-model. But appealing to temporal logic alone cannot settle this issue. Interestingly, this view about the role of temporal logic is the one put forward by its own founder, A. N. Prior:

> The logician must be rather like a lawyer...in the sense that he is there to give the metaphys- ician, perhaps even the physicist, the tense logic that he wants, provided that it be consistent. He must tell his client what the consequences of a given choice will be...and what alternatives are open to him; but I doubt whether he can, qua logician, do more.   (1967: 59)

Of course, the A-theorist might end up disliking some of the consequences of this model, in which case she might end up rejecting that view. But Prior's point is that this kind of decision is not forced upon one by logic alone.

A second worry for the A-model is more serious. This worry takes the form of an explanatory challenge. According to the A-model, it only becomes true that Marty McFly was present in 1955 after he hits 88 mph in his time machine (in 1985). At first, this might seem unremarkable. After all, the reason Marty appears in 1955 is that he traveled in time, and he didn't travel in time until he hit 88 mph (in 1985). However, on the eternalist version of the A-model, things are not so simple. After all, on the eternalist view, past and future events exist and are just as real as current events. So, the event of Marty's hitting 88 mph exists when 1955 is present (though that event is not yet present itself). From this it seems to follow that, when 1955 is present, it is true that Marty will travel back to that time. But this seems to leave us with a puzzle. After all, if it is true that Marty will travel back to that time, one would expect him to be there, when that time is present. But, according to the A-model, that is not the case. Of course, Marty's departure from 1985 is not *present* in 1955, but it is hard to see how this fact could explain Marty's absence.

Here is a slightly different way of making the same point. When the event of Marty's hitting 88 mph changes from *being future* to *being present*, another change takes place: 1955 changes from not including Marty to including Marty. The question is: What explains this correlation? What we want to say, of course, is that the past changed *because* Marty hit 88 mph. That is why the two things go together. But the event of his hitting 88 mph existed all along. So the question is: Why did it only affect the past *when it became present*? After all, the only things that changed were its A-properties. So, this would seem to indicate that the property of *being present* is what explains the correlation—that the event in question only gets its "causal oomph" when the Now shines upon it. But this seems ridiculous. After all, on the eternalist view, there are all sorts of future facts, and many of these facts are causally explained by others. For example, when 1955 is present, it is a fact that Oswald will fire a gun eight years hence. It is also true that Kennedy will die eight years hence. Moreover, it is true that Kennedy will die eight years hence *because* Oswald will fire his gun. But, in that case, we don't have to wait for 1963 to become present in order for the 1963-events to have their effects—whatever "oomph" they have, they have right now (speaking, again, from the perspective of 1955). But, in that case, we should expect the same thing to be true of Marty's departure from 1985. In other words, we should already expect the past to be altered.

Note that this worry also arises for the eternalist version of the hypertime model that we discussed in the previous section. On that view, there are some hypertimes relative to which Marty is not present in 1955, despite the fact that he will hit 88 mph in his time machine in 1985 (relative to that same hypertime). There are other hypertimes relative to which Marty *is* present in 1955 (and where he also hits 88 mph in his time machine in 1985). The question then naturally arises: Why the change? After all, the only other relevant change in the block is that Marty's hitting 88 mph goes from *being future* to *being present*. But again: It is unclear why this change would generate a corresponding change in the past as we move from one hypertime to the next.

One option at this point for the defender of the A-model would be to give up on the eternalist ontology and to go back to the growing block view. In that case, she would seem to have a better explanation of what is going on in the case of past-alteration. When 1955 is present, there are no future events. In particular, there is no event of Marty hitting 88 mph in his time machine. So, there is no reason to think that it is true, in 1955, that Marty will travel back to that time. But, in that case, there is no reason to expect Marty to be present at that time. When 1985 becomes present, however, things will have changed. And we seem to have a natural explanation for *why* they have changed. When Marty hits 88 mph, this is not simply a case of an existing event changing from *being future* to *being past*. Rather, it is a case of a brand new event coming into existence. And it is not implausible to think that this new event will have new effects. In particular, it is not implausible to think that this event will make it the case that Marty was present in 1955.

Of course, many people will consider this move a cost, since the growing block view is relatively unpopular. In fact, some people will say the same thing about a more basic assumption behind this model: *Every version of the A-model presupposes the A-theory of time*. This is the case whether that theory is coupled with the ontology of eternalism, presentism, or the growing block theory. Of course, whether or not one takes this to be a cost will depend on what one thinks of the A-theory. But many people are skeptical of this view, and that skepticism will transfer to the A-model of past-alteration. For those people, the central question of this chapter will remain unanswered: What are we to say about the paradoxes of freedom? In the next chapter, we consider a very different response to that question.

4

Paradoxes of Freedom II

I am a double person; a riddle...
I can and I cannot.

—Rev. John Newton, Letter to D. West, Esq.

In "The Paradoxes of Time Travel," David Lewis suggests a solution to the paradoxes of freedom that does not involve branching timelines, additional temporal dimensions, or any other controversial views about the nature of time. In fact, Lewis suggests all of these paradoxes arise from confusion over one little word:

To say that something can happen means that its happening is compossible with certain facts. Which facts? That is determined, but sometimes not determined well enough, by context... What I can do, relative to one set of facts, I cannot do, relative to another, more inclusive, set. Whenever the context leaves it open which facts are to count as relevant, it is possible to equivocate...

[For example] Tim's killing Grandfather that day in 1921 is compossible with a fairly rich set of facts: the facts about his rifle, his skill and training... and so on... But his killing Grandfather is not compossible with another, more inclusive set of facts. [For example] There is the simple fact that Grandfather was not killed... You can reasonably choose the narrower delineation, and say that he can; or the wider delineation, and say that he can't. But choose. What you mustn't do is waver, say in the same breath that he both can and can't, and then claim that this contradiction proves that time travel is impossible. (1976: 150–1)[1]

---

[1] For earlier suggestions along the same lines, see Horwich (1975: 435–7), Thom (1975), and, especially, Fitzgerald (1970, and 1974: 539–40). In fact, Fitzgerald's suggestion is worth quoting in full, since his ideas have gone largely unnoticed:

We have a contradiction here only if both of the descriptions, with quasi-modal "can" and "cannot" taken in the same sense, must apply to the situation.

But this is not so. Just ask yourself: *which* single sense of "can" is such that it and its negation must both apply to the case? Is not the case exactly analogous to an ordinary one in which a man believes that he can shoot either of two men in front of him, since [he] has the means and skill required and nothing is preventing him (at least ostensibly), whereas another person says that the first man cannot shoot either, because his brain states causally determine that he will decide not to shoot? No one suggests that this sort of situation

In this passage, Lewis suggests a *semantic* solution to the grandfather paradox. On his view, there is a sense in which Tim *can* kill Grandfather and a sense in which he *can't*. But there is no sense in which he both can *and* can't, so there is no contradiction.[2] Moreover, what goes for Tim would also go for Marty McFly, and for any other person who would seek to change the past. For this reason, Lewis concludes that the paradoxes of freedom fail to undermine the possibility of backward time travel.

Lewis's solution has proven very popular, having been endorsed, in one form or another, by Brown (1992: 435–6), Dainton (2001: 117), Dowe (2000: 448–51), Eldridge-Smith (2007: 184), Fitzgerald (1974: 539–40), Hanley (1997: 209–10), Kiourti (2008), MacBeath (1982: 411), Perszyk and Smith (2001), Richmond (2003: 299–300), Sider (1997b: 143), Smith (1997: 366), Thom (1975: 214–16), and others. Indeed, Lewis's response is so popular that it is often called "the standard reply" to the paradoxes of freedom.[3] The goal of this chapter is to clarify, motivate, and evaluate this response.[4]

1. On Lewis's Way Out

The basic idea behind Lewis's response is simple, but several points need to be clarified. This section provides a more detailed explanation of Lewis's solution.

1.1 Clarifications

Lewis begins with the claim that 'can' is equivocal. This is not quite right. Lewis's intended view is that 'can' is *context-sensitive*.[5] To appreciate the difference between these claims, consider the following pair of arguments.

> Frances put her money in a bank.
> A bank is a body of land along a river or lake.
> So, Frances put her money in a body of land along a river or lake.

> That is Hud. [pointing to a human]
> That is the cookie monster. [pointing to a muppet]
> So, Hud is the cookie monster.

---

involves any logical impossibility...Both descriptions (*can* and *cannot*) may apply together, since different senses of "can" are involved.   (1974: 539–40)

(Fitzgerald's paper contains many other interesting ideas as well—see, for example, fn. 57 and fn. 76 of this chapter.)

[2] Here it may be helpful to recall our formal statement of the paradox of past-alteration:

(P1)   If backward time travel were possible, it would be possible to change the past.
(P2)   It is impossible to change the past.
(C)   Backward time travel is impossible.

The branching timeline theorist and the morphing block theorist accept (P1) and reject (P2). Lewis's response is to accept (P2) and reject (P1).

[3] See, for example, Arntzenius (2006: 601), Vihvelin (2011a), and Vranas (2009: 520).

[4] Maier (2010) provides a good starting point for those who wish to locate Lewis's views within the broader philosophical literature on abilities and freedom.

[5] Lewis clarifies this point in his (1979).

The first argument is guilty of equivocation, since it turns on the ambiguity of 'bank'. The second argument is also unsound, but it is not guilty of equivocation, since 'that' has a single set meaning (on at least one meaning of "meaning"). Following Kaplan (1989), we can think of this term as denoting the most relevant entity in any given context. Since different things are relevant in different contexts, the denotation of 'that' will vary, but the *function* associated with the term will remain constant. In this sense, 'that' is context-sensitive, but unambiguous.

Context-sensitivity is most obvious in the case of demonstratives and indexicals (like 'that', 'there', 'here', and 'I'). But many other terms are context-sensitive in the same way. Quantifiers like 'many', 'some', and 'all' are common examples. Consider:

(1)   All of the beers are in the fridge.

An assertion of (1) will not normally say that all beers everywhere are in the fridge. Rather, it will communicate that all of the *relevant* beers—perhaps all of the *nearby* beers, or all of the *available* beers—are in the fridge. There are various ways of understanding this kind of quantifier restriction.[6] For simplicity, we will assume that determiner phrases (like 'all' and 'some') combine with formulas (like 'nearby(x)' or 'beer(x)') to form restricted quantifiers, which can then combine with open formulas (like 'x is in the fridge') to form statements. Thus, if the context specifies that the relevant beers are the *nearby* beers, we can represent the proposition expressed by (1), relative to that context, as follows:

(1*)   [all x: nearby beer(x)] x is in the fridge.

This says, in effect, that the set of nearby beers is a subset of the things in the refrigerator.

If modal claims are understood in terms of quantification over possible worlds (or situations[7]), then the context-sensitivity of the quantifiers will transfer to our modal terms. That is exactly what we find. As Lewis notes, the sentence 'I can speak Finnish' can express a truth relative to some contexts, and a falsehood relative to others, even if the time and speaker are held fixed. Here is one way of understanding this phenomenon. First, we treat Lewis's assertion as a possibility claim:

(2)   Possibly, David Lewis speaks Finnish.

Second, we analyze possibility in terms of existential quantification over possible worlds:

(2*)   [some x: world(x)] David Lewis speaks Finnish in x.

Finally, we assume that context typically restricts the domain of quantification to a subset of all possible worlds. One way in which context does this is by providing what Kratzer (1977) calls a *modal base*. Formally, the modal base is a function from one world (a world considered as actual) to a set of other worlds (the worlds in the domain

---

[6] Westerståhl (2005) is a good place to start on quantifiers. My notation most closely resembles that of Neale (1990).

[7] As in Barwise and Perry (1983).

of quantification).[8] Informally, we can think of a modal base as a set of propositions in view of which the modal claim is made. For example, if one is talking about what is physically possible, then the modal base will consist of the actual laws of nature. If the claim is about what is epistemically possible, then the modal base might be the body of one's evidence or knowledge. In each of these cases, the modal base restricts the relevant quantifiers by limiting the domain to those worlds at which the corresponding propositions hold.[9]

When it comes to claims about what is *humanly* possible—that is, claims about what certain people can or cannot do—the modal base will typically include (i) a complete description of the laws of nature, and (ii) a more-or-less complete description of the agent's intrinsic properties[10] and environment.[11] The more detailed the description, the more realistic the base will be, and the smaller the domain of quantification. So, in most ordinary contexts, an assertion of (2) would express something like the following:

(2**)   [some x: realistic-world(x)] David Lewis speaks Finnish in x.

Let's suppose that the restriction to realistic worlds would limit us to cases in which Lewis had all of the same mental features, including his actual lack of knowledge when it came to speaking Finnish. In that case, we would not be left with any worlds in which he speaks Finnish. His assertion—"I can speak Finnish"—would therefore express a falsehood, relative to those contexts.

In other contexts, however, our quantifiers are less restrictive. Suppose, for example, we are in a physiology class, and we are comparing the structure of the human mouth to that of an ape. Relative to that context, (2) might express something like the following:

(2***)   [some x: physiologically-realistic-world(x)] David Lewis speaks Finnish in x.

Here, a "physiologically-realistic-world" is a world in which Lewis has his actual physiological properties, but may differ in other respects. (2***) is true, since there are some possible worlds in which Lewis's jaws, lips, tongue, etc. have their actual physiological features and where Lewis successfully speaks Finnish. These are worlds at which

---

[8] This is a simplification in various respects. See Kratzer (2012) for all the details.

[9] This is what Lewis has in mind when he says that 'can'-claims are always claims about "compossibility". In the current framework, compossibility amounts to compatibility with the propositions that constitute the modal base.

[10] To be more precise: We typically hold fixed *all* of the intrinsic, non-mental properties of the agent and *some* subset of the intrinsic, mental properties. For example, Michael Stocker (1971: 311) considers the case of an agent who is "physically" able to reach into a cesspool for her wallet, but is "psychologically" unable. In some contexts we would not hold the relevant psychological fact fixed; in that context, it would be true that the agent can reach into the cesspool. In other contexts we *would* hold it fixed; in those contexts it would be true that the agent cannot. (Note that we rarely ever keep the relevant desires fixed, for in ordinary contexts we can almost always say "I can, but I don't want to.")

[11] This statement is imprecise in various respects. See fn. 10 and the following two examples.

Lewis has the proper training—and thus the relevant mental features—for speaking that language.[12]

As a second illustration, we can modify an old example from J. L. Austin.[13] Imagine that Ingrid is a classically trained pianist who has been locked up in a piano-less cell. And consider the question of whether or not Ingrid can play piano. For many of us, this question invites ambivalence—we are equally happy saying that Ingrid *can* play piano (since she has the relevant training) and that she *can't* (since there are no pianos around). On the Lewis–Kratzer framework, we can explain this uncertainty as follows. In some contexts, the question is whether or not Ingrid can play piano *in view of her current situation*. In those contexts, we hold fixed all of the environmental facts, including the fact that she is behind bars with no access to a piano. As a result, (3) would express something like (3*):

(3)   Ingrid can play piano.

(3*)   [some x: realistic-world(x) & non-piano-world(x)] Ingrid plays piano in x.

(Here a 'non-piano-world' is simply a world where Ingrid has no access to pianos.) (3*) is obviously false in this case, since Ingrid does not play piano in any non-piano worlds. In other contexts, however, the question might be whether Ingrid can play the piano, *in view of what she is like*. In other words, we might want to know whether Ingrid has the intrinsic features (both physical and mental) that are required for piano-playing. In that kind of context, (3) would express the following:

(3**)   [some x: realistic-world(x)] Ingrid plays piano in x.

This proposition is true, since there are some worlds in which Ingrid is intrinsically similar (and where the actual laws obtain), but where she has access to pianos.

Hence, there are some contexts in which (3) is clearly true and some in which it is clearly false. But there are also many cases in which it is unclear what kind of context one is in—for example, when the question comes out of nowhere in the middle of a book on time travel. This uncertainty is what generates ambivalence with respect to statements like (3).

1.2 Applications

Having clarified Lewis's framework, we can now apply it to the case of Tim and Grandfather.

---

[12] It is in this sense that the ape cannot speak Finnish—apes (we will assume) lack the physiological features required for pronouncing Finnish words.

[13] Austin (1956) discusses the case of a literate individual who wishes to read Jane Austin's *Emma*, but doesn't have a copy at hand. As he notes, there is a sense in which the individual can read *Emma* (since she has the skill) and a sense in which she cannot (since she lacks the opportunity). Or, as it is sometimes put, she has the "general" ability to read *Emma*, but not the "specific" ability to exercise that skill in this situation. For more on this distinction, see Honoré (1964), Mele (2002), and van Inwagen (1983: 13). For more on this distinction in the context of time travel, see Vihvelin (2011d).

In this example, the crucial claim is this:

(1)   Tim can kill Grandfather.

As Lewis notes, Tim's killing Grandfather is compatible with a fairly rich modal base that includes facts about Tim's intrinsic properties (both physical and mental) and his surroundings (including the fact that he has a gun and a clear shot at Grandfather).[14] These are the kinds of facts that are normally held fixed when making ability claims and, given these restrictions, (1) expresses a truth:

(1*)   [some x: realistic-world(x)] Tim kills Grandfather in x.

In other contexts, further restrictions are in place. For example, in some contexts we might hold fixed the fact that Grandfather wasn't actually killed. Relative to those contexts, (1) would express the following:

(1**)   [some x: realistic-world(x) & world-in-which-Grandfather-is-not-killed(x)] Tim kills Grandfather in x.

This statement is obviously false, since there is no world in which Grandfather is both killed and not.[15] But, as before, the crucial point is that there is no *single* context in which (1) would express *both* a truth and a falsehood. Hence, the possibility of time travel does not generate a contradiction.

Lewis's treatment of Tim's case also applies to other self-defeating cases. It also applies to the more general paradox of past-alteration. Recall again the first premise of that paradox:

(P1)   If backward time travel were possible, it would be possible to change the past.

In the last chapter, we motivated (P1) by focusing on a specific example: If time travel were possible, I could travel back to the time of Abraham Lincoln. And if I could travel back to the time of Abraham Lincoln, I could prevent his assassination. But if I could prevent his assassination, I could change the past. So, if backward time travel were possible, it would be possible to change the past.

On Lewis's account, this line of reasoning involves a subtle shift in context. The problem concerns the following pair of claims:

(2)   If I could travel back to the time of Abraham Lincoln, then I could prevent Lincoln's assassination.

(3)   If I could prevent Lincoln's assassination, then I could change the past.

These conditionals share the following component:

---

[14] Or at least it *seems* compatible. We will return to this issue in section 2.

[15] Here and in what follows we will assume that branching timelines and hypertime universes are metaphysically impossible, so that there are no worlds in which (for example) Grandfather is killed on one temporal branch and not on another.

(4)   I could prevent Lincoln's assassination.

This sentence is contextually shifty in exactly the way we would expect. In most ordinary contexts, it would express something like the following:

(4*)   [some x: realistic-world(x)] I prevent Lincoln's assassination in x.

On this reading, (4) is arguably true. For suppose that I can travel back to the time of Abraham Lincoln. To do that, I would have to have access to a time machine. And there are possible worlds in which (i) I have a time machine, (ii) my intrinsic properties and environment are roughly the same as they actually are, and (iii) I prevent Lincoln's assassination. So, given the ability to travel in time, I could prevent the murder. However, this does *not* mean that I have the ability to change the past. That is because the worlds in which I prevent the assassination are worlds in which it was always true that the assassination was prevented. In order for it to be the case that I can change the past, there would have to be some (relevant) worlds in which Lincoln's assassination was *not* prevented and yet I somehow manage to prevent it. Since there are no such worlds (setting aside the idea of branching timelines, etc.), it is not true that I can change the past. That is why (3) is false.

Of course, in discussing the time traveler's abilities, we sometimes keep additional facts fixed. This includes facts about the past (especially if those facts are known). Relative to those contexts, the modal base determines a more restrictive domain of worlds. For example, if we hold fixed the fact that Lincoln was actually assassinated, then (4) would express something like the following:

(4**)   [some x: realistic-world(x) & world-in-which-Lincoln's-assassination-was-not-prevented(x)] I prevent Lincoln's assassination in x.

(4**) is obviously false—there are no possible worlds in which Lincoln's assassination is both prevented and not (again, setting aside the idea of branching timelines, etc.). Given this, it is natural to think that (3) is trivially true, relative to this context.[16] However, Lewis would claim that (2) is false in this context. It *is* possible to travel back in time, and it *is* possible to prevent Lincoln's assassination on a less restrictive reading of "possible." But it is *not* possible to prevent an unprevented event, which is what the current reading requires. That is why (2) is false.

So, to sum up: The reasoning behind the first premise of the altered past paradox involves two conditional claims—(2) and (3). Relative to some contexts, (2) is true and (3) is false. Relative to others, (3) is true and (2) is false. But there is no context in which (2) and (3) are *both* true, so the argument for the first premise is invariably unsound. That is Lewis's solution to the paradox of past-alteration.

---

[16] Or, at least, that's the way most logicians would think about this statement. Here is an alternative way of thinking about (3): If I could—*per impossible*—prevent Lincoln's murder in a world where it was not prevented, then I could *also* change the past (since that is exactly what changing the past would require).

1.3 Reactions

There are many things to like about Lewis's account. It is *general* in the sense that it provides a uniform solution to all the paradoxes of freedom. It is *conservative* in the sense that it does not require a commitment to any controversial views about the nature of time. And it is *independently motivated* since it fits within a popular approach to the semantics of modal terms.[17] Perhaps most importantly, there is something undeniably *intuitive* about Lewis's account—it seems obvious that ordinary 'can'-claims function in something like the way Lewis describes, and it is natural to extend this account to talk about what time travelers can and cannot do.

Still, Lewis's account is not uncontroversial. Some object to Lewis's analysis of ability.[18] Others argue that, even if his analysis is correct, it does not do enough to solve the paradoxes of freedom.[19] Still others endorse Lewis's solution to the original paradoxes, but argue that there are other, closely related puzzles that resist his analysis.[20]

The remainder of this chapter is dedicated to addressing some of these concerns.

2. Killing Baby Suzy

The most famous objection to Lewis's solution is due to Kadri Vihvelin (1996, 2011a–d). Her objection focuses on the following kind of case:

Suppose that [a] time traveler, unhappy with her life, decides that it would have been better never to have lived it. She packs a gun and travels back through time, determined to kill her infant self. She picks a time when she knows that the baby will be alone. She checks carefully to make sure her gun is loaded. She fires. She misses. She fires again. This time the gun jams.

We don't need to go on with the story. We know that the time traveler's efforts will all fail. No matter how many times she tries, something will go wrong...   (1996: 315)

As Vihvelin notes, there is something about this story that seems deeply paradoxical:

We know that the time traveler's baby self will live—*must* live—for her survival is what makes possible the journey of the time traveler. So we know that the time traveler cannot kill her baby self...On the other hand, we can stipulate that our time traveler has the ability to shoot close-range targets and plenty of opportunity to shoot and kill the baby. By our ordinary

---

[17] As Lewis (1976) points out, it is also independently motivated by the fact that it provides a satisfying solution to the argument for logical fatalism. On fatalism, see Taylor (1962). On Lewis's response, see Carroll (2010). For more on fatalism and time travel, see Miller (2009), Tognazzini (2017), and Vihvelin (2013: 44–7).

[18] At least three different kinds of objections could be raised. First, one could object to the modal component of Lewis's analysis (i.e. the view that facts about ability are grounded, in some way, in facts about possibility). See, for example, Kenny (1976). Second, one could object to Lewis's analysis of possibility in terms of possible worlds. See, for example, Fine (1977). Finally, one could object to the contextualist element of Lewis's proposal (i.e. the view that which worlds are relevant will vary from context to context). See, for example, Feldman (2004). (Feldman's criticism is actually directed at Hawthorne (2001), but Hawthorne's theory is closely modeled on Lewis's.) It is also possible to read Smith (1985: 60), Stevenson (2005: 402), and Garrett (2016: 250–1) as objecting to the contextualist element of Lewis's view.

[19] See, for example, Vihvelin (1996, 2011b, 2011d, 2011e), Vranas (2009), and Spencer (2013).

[20] See, for example, Earman (1995), Horwich (1987: Chapter 7), and Riggs (1997: 52).

standards of what people can do, the time traveler can kill the baby who is her younger self. So if time travel is possible, it's true both that the time traveler can kill her baby self and false that she can do so. Therefore, time travel is not possible. (1996: 315)

Following Vihvelin, we will refer to her time traveler as 'Suzy' and we will formulate her argument as follows:

(P1)   If backward time travel were possible, then Suzy could kill Baby Suzy.

(P2)   Suzy cannot kill Baby Suzy.

(C)   Backward time travel is impossible.

This is an instance of what we have called the "retrosuicide paradox."

2.1 Vihvelin on retrosuicide

Vihvelin summarizes the "standard reply" to this argument as follows:

Of course the time traveler...will not kill the baby who is her younger self...But that doesn't mean she can't. We may be tempted to think she can't because we know that all her attempts to do so will fail. Since we know that Suzy in fact lived until 1995 (when she stepped into the time machine), we also know that any earlier attempts—by time-traveling Suzy or by anyone else—to kill Baby Suzy failed. But this is just a special case of our knowledge of the general truth that no one ever succeeds in killing anyone before the date of their actual death. It would be a mistake to conclude that no one can kill us before the day that we die. And it would be a mistake to conclude either that no one can kill Baby Suzy or that time traveling Suzy cannot do so. (1996: 315–16)

This response is a version of the standard Lewisian strategy. In this case, Lewis will grant that, if time travel were possible, Suzy could kill Baby Suzy *in the ordinary sense of 'can'*. That is, Suzy's killing Baby Suzy would be compatible with the kinds of facts we normally hold fixed in making 'can'-claims (e.g. that Suzy has a gun, that she is standing next to Baby Suzy, and so on). In this sense, (P1) is true and (P2) is false. Of course, there is another sense in which Suzy cannot kill Baby Suzy—for example if we hold fixed the (known) fact that Baby Suzy was not killed, then Suzy's killing her would no longer be compatible with *all* the relevant facts. But that is not the kind of fact we normally hold fixed when talking about what people can and cannot do. In any case, the main point is that there is no context in which (P1) and (P2) would both be true, so the argument is invariably unsound. That is the standard Lewisian response to the retrosuicide paradox.

Vihvelin rejects this response, since she denies that (P2) is false, given what we normally mean by 'can'. Her reasoning is based on the following kind of principle:

We should agree that someone can do something, in the relevant sense, only if it's true that if she tried to do it, she would or at least might succeed. And everyone should agree that if someone would fail to do something, no matter how hard or how many times she tried, then she cannot do it. (1996: 318)

Following Vihvelin (2011d), we will refer to this claim as the *Counterfactual Principle*:

> *Counterfactual Principle*: Necessarily, if someone would fail to do something, no matter how hard or how many times she tried, then she cannot do it.

Whether or not this principle is correct will depend, in part, on what is meant by 'can'. For example, we noted earlier that there's a sense in which an imprisoned pianist can still play a piano—she still has the skill, even though she lacks the opportunity. In the same way, there might be some contexts—even ordinary contexts—in which we would say that the pianist can run a mile, even if she is currently shackled to the wall. Clearly, that is not the sense of 'can' that Vihvelin has in mind.[21] Rather, she is thinking of the case in which we hold fixed certain facts about the environment, like the fact that the pianist is in prison. This is what she calls the "wide" reading of 'ability'.[22]

Thus understood, the Counterfactual Principle seems entirely plausible. For one thing, many examples seem to conform to this pattern.

> I can swim and ride a bicycle at least partly because it's true that I would succeed at both of these activities if I tried to do them... But I cannot walk on water or run faster than the speed of light because if I tried to do these things, I would fail, no matter how often or how hard I tried.   (Vihvelin 1996: 318)[23]

Moreover, this principle seems to underlie much of our practical reasoning:

> Think about how you deliberate when you decide what to do. You choose among possible course of actions [sic] that you believe are your options... But everyone agrees that a course of action is *an option for you* (something you have the *wide ability* to do) only if you would have some reasonable chance of doing it, if you tried, then and there, to do it. If the things you deliberate about are all things such that if you tried to do them, you would fail, you are wasting your time.
> (Vihvelin 2011d)

---

[21] Vihvelin makes this point clear in her original paper (1996: 318), but see Kiourti (2008: 345). For further discussion on this point, see Vihvelin (2011d).

[22] See Vihvelin (2011d). Roughly, one's narrow abilities are a function of one's intrinsic properties (plus the laws), whereas wide abilities take at least some environmental facts into consideration. This is equivalent to our earlier distinction between general and specific abilities. (See fn. 13.) Skow (unpublished) uses the same distinction to make a related criticism of Lewis's view. In the end, these distinctions may not matter much, since counterfactuals are context-sensitive in much the same way that 'can'-claims are. Take, for example, the case of the shackled pianist, and consider a context where narrow abilities are at issue. In that context, we hold fixed the agent's intrinsic features (plus the laws), but we do not hold fixed the presence of the cell walls or chains. If we keep the same facts fixed when we evaluate the relevant counterfactual ('If the pianist were to try to run a mile, she might succeed'), we will get a truth, since there are some worlds in which the pianist tries to run a mile (with her actual intrinsic properties) and succeeds. If 'can' and 'would' always shift together in this way, it does not matter what sense of 'can' is at issue in the Counterfactual Principle. (See 3.3 for further discussion on this point.)

[23] Here, Vihvelin seems to be suggesting a counterfactual analysis of abilities. She says, for example, that "I can swim and ride a bicycle *at least partly because* it's true that I would succeed at both of these activities if I tried to do them" (my emphasis). But one could just as well take the explanation to go in the opposite direction: It's true that Vihvelin would succeed at these activities, if she tried, *precisely because* she has the relevant abilities. Either way, the important point for Vihvelin's argument is just that the two things go together; the order of explanation is irrelevant.

The problem, of course, is that the Counterfactual Principle is inconsistent with the standard reply to the retrosuicide paradox. Given that Baby Suzy must live in order for Suzy to be present, we know that:

(1)   If Suzy were to try to kill Baby Suzy, she would fail (no matter how hard or how many times she tried).

Given the Counterfactual Principle, (1) implies the second premise of the retrosuicide paradox:

(P2)   Suzy cannot kill Baby Suzy.

More carefully, given that the Counterfactual Principle expresses a truth *relative to ordinary contexts*, (P2) will also express a truth relative to those contexts. Since this is inconsistent with what Lewis claims, Vihvelin concludes that his response is mistaken.[24]

In order to appreciate Vihvelin's view, it is important to be clear about what she does and does not say.

First, in disagreeing with Lewis about (P2), she does not say that the rest of his theory is mistaken. It is consistent with everything Vihvelin says to think that 'can'-claims are compossibility claims, for example, and to think that they are sensitive to context in the way that Lewis suggests. In fact, Vihvelin can even agree that there are some unusual contexts in which (P2) would be false.[25] The only disagreement between Lewis and Vihvelin is over whether Suzy's killing Baby Suzy is compatible with the kinds of facts we normally take as relevant in determining what someone can do.

Second, in disagreeing with Lewis about (P2), Vihvelin is not saying that the retrosuicide paradox is sound. In fact, she explicitly rejects this argument.[26] Her view is that the first premise of this argument is false. Time travel is possible (she says) but it does *not* give Suzy the ability to kill her younger self.

Third, in saying that time travelers cannot kill their younger selves (in the ordinary sense of 'can'), Vihvelin is not saying that retrosuicide is metaphysically impossible. In fact, she says the opposite. For example, Vihvelin allows that there are worlds in which Suzy travels back and kills Baby Suzy, only to see her younger self miraculously rise from the grave (in order to grow up, go back in time, and kill her younger self).[27]

---

[24] Vranas (2010) offers a related argument for the same conclusion. More recently, Rea (2015) provides a very different argument for an even stronger conclusion (namely, that no travelers to the past are free with respect to any of their actions as time travelers). For a discussion of Rea's argument, see Wasserman (forthcoming).

[25] Suppose, for example, that you are trying to explain the difference between logical and metaphysical possibility (from Chapter 1) and you take the resurrection of the dead to be metaphysically possible. In that case, you might say "Suzy can kill Baby Suzy, but she can't make contradictions true."

[26] Vihvelin (1996: 323).

[27] Vihvelin (1996: 317). Carroll (2016) suggests some other, very creative ways to commit retrosuicide.

Vihvelin's point is that such a world would require very different laws from our own, and is thus irrelevant to evaluating ordinary counterfactuals like (1).[28]

To understand this point, it may be helpful to go into a bit of detail on the standard semantics for counterfactual conditionals. The standard view, defended by Robert Stalnaker (1968) and David Lewis (1973), analyzes counterfactual truth in terms of comparative similarity of possible worlds.[29] According to Stalnaker, a counterfactual is (non-vacuously) true if and only if the closest world at which the antecedent is true is one at which the consequent is also true:

A > C is true at world w only if, and in that case because, the closest A-world to w is a C-world.[30]

(Here, '>' is the counterfactual connective, an *A-world* is a world at which the antecedent is true, and a *C-world* is a world at which the consequent is true.)

World closeness is then understood in terms of *comparative similarity*:

w_1 is closer to w_2 than w_3 only if, and in that case because, w_1 is overall more similar to w_2 than w_3.

Finally, comparative similarity is understood in terms of how well worlds match with respect to their laws and particular matters of fact. On Lewis's view, for example, overall similarity is determined by the following set of rules.

1. It is of the first importance to avoid big, widespread, diverse violations of law.
2. It is of the second importance to maximize the spatio-temporal region throughout which perfect match of particular fact prevails.
3. It is of the third importance to avoid even small, localized simple violations of law.
4. It is of little or no importance to secure approximate similarity of particular fact, even in matters that concern us greatly.   (Lewis 1986c: 47–8)

We will examine these rules in more detail in Chapter 5, when we discuss the counterfactual theory of causation. For now, we can illustrate the idea by considering the following three worlds:

w_1 = Suzy travels back in time with a gun, intending to kill her younger self. When she arrives at time t, she has a change of heart. Baby Suzy then goes on to live a full life, in which she eventually travels back in time with a gun, intending to kill her younger self.

---

[28] By analogy, there might be some possible worlds in which I walk on water, but those worlds are irrelevant to the question of whether I *would* walk on water, were I to try. So, according to the Counterfactual Principle, those worlds are irrelevant to the question of whether or not I can walk on water, in the ordinary sense of 'can'.

[29] For related suggestions, see Sprigge (1970) and Todd (1964).

[30] This way of stating the view assumes that there is always a unique closest antecedent world. Lewis rejects this assumption, but this will not matter for our discussion here.

w_2 = Suzy travels back in time with a gun, intending to kill Baby Suzy. When she arrives at time t, she aims and pulls the trigger. However, the gun jams, and the baby survives. Baby Suzy then goes on to live a full life, in which she eventually travels back in time with a gun, intending to kill her younger self.

w_3 = Suzy travels back in time with a gun, intending to kill her younger self. When she arrives at time t, she shoots and kills Baby Suzy. However, sometime later, Baby Suzy miraculously rises from the dead and goes on to live a full life, in which she eventually travels back in time with a gun, intending to kill her younger self.

Suppose that w_1 is deterministic, and that all three worlds are perfect duplicates up until t. In that case, w_2 and w_3 will each include at least one violation of w_1's laws when Suzy arrives. For example, a few extra neurons might fire in Suzy's brain, with the result that she tries to kill her younger self. This would be an example of what Lewis calls a "small miracle."[31] Moreover, w_2 will presumably include another event of this kind, since something prevents the gun from firing. For example, a little extra corrosion might miraculously appear in the firing mechanism at w_2. However, w_3 will include a much more obvious violation of the laws since it includes a human person being raised from the dead. This would presumably violate any number of w_1's laws, with the result that w_3 fails Lewis's very first rule. For this reason, w_3 counts as comparatively distant from w_1. That is why it is irrelevant to the evaluation of (1) at the world in question.

Finally, while Vihvelin disagrees with Lewis about the case of retrosuicide, she does not say the same thing about all cases of past-alteration. That is because Vihvelin takes there to be an important difference between self-undermining acts and other acts of past-alteration. To illustrate, suppose again that Suzy travels back in time with the intent to kill her younger self. And now consider the following pair of counterfactuals:

(2)   If Suzy were to try to kill Baby Suzy, she would fail.

(3)   If Suzy were to try to pinch Baby Suzy, she would fail.

Vihvelin argues that (2) is true, since worlds at which Suzy tries to kill her younger self and fails are closer than worlds at which she tries and succeeds. Crucially, this argument hinges on the fact that worlds in which Suzy successfully kills her younger

---

[31] Lewis (1986c: 44–5) says that an event in world w is *a miracle relative to world* w^* if and only if its occurrence, in its circumstances, would violate the laws of w^*. So, when we say that a miracle takes place in w_2, for example, we do not mean that w_2 contains an event that violates the laws of w_2. Rather, we mean that it contains an event whose occurrence would violate the laws of w_1 (the world at which we are evaluating the relevant counterfactual).

More terminology: Lewis (1986c: 55–6) says that a *small miracle* is a miracle that takes place in a small region and that a *big miracle* is a collection of many small miracles.

With this terminology in place, we can simplify Lewis's rules as follows:

Minimize big miracles.
Maximize exact match.
Minimize small miracles.
Maximize approximate match.

self include large-scale miracles (people rising from the dead, etc.). But that is not true of worlds in which Suzy successfully pinches herself. Suppose, for example, that Suzy does not try to pinch Baby Suzy at w_1. And consider the following pair of counterfactual worlds:

w_4 = Suzy travels back in time with a gun, intending to kill Baby Suzy. When she arrives, at time t, a small miracle occurs: She has a change of heart and decides to pinch the baby instead. Suzy reaches into the crib and successfully pinches the child. Baby Suzy then goes on to live a full life, in which she eventually travels back in time with a gun, intending to kill her younger self.

w_5 = Suzy travels back in time with a gun, intending to kill Baby Suzy. When she arrives, at time t, a small miracle occurs: She has a change of heart and decides to pinch the baby instead. But as she reaches into the crib, Suzy's arm miraculously undergoes temporary paralysis, and she fails to pinch the child. Baby Suzy then goes on to live a full life, in which she eventually travels back in time with a gun, intending to kill her younger self.

w_4 and w_5 both include a small miracle after Suzy arrives (extra neurons fire, leading to the unplanned pinching attempt). However, w_5 includes an additional miracle that prevents the baby from being pinched. For this reason, worlds like w_4 will count as closer to w_1. That is why Suzy would (or at least might) succeed if she were to try to pinch Baby Suzy. In other words, that is why (3), unlike (2), is false.[32]

If all of this is correct, Vihvelin's argument has a larger implication for how we think about the paradoxes of freedom. As we noted earlier, many philosophers have claimed that the grandfather paradox, the retrosuicide paradox, and other paradoxes of self-defeat are nothing more than "especially vivid" examples of past-alteration.[33] If Vihvelin is correct, this claim is mistaken. Self-defeating acts are paradoxical in a way that other past-altering acts are not.

2.2 Vranas on retrosuicide

We can summarize Vihvelin's argument against the standard solution as follows:

(P1)   Necessarily, if someone would fail to do something, no matter how hard or how many times she tried, then she cannot do it.

(P2)   If Suzy were to try to kill Baby Suzy, she would fail, no matter how hard or how many times she tried.

(C)   Suzy cannot kill Baby Suzy.

In this argument, (P1) is the Counterfactual Principle, (P2) is the main counterfactual from the previous section, and (C) is the second premise of the retrosuicide paradox.

---

[32] Of course if Lewis is correct, then there may be some contexts in which (3), like (2), would express a truth—for example a context in which we are holding fixed the future truth that Baby Suzy will not be pinched. But Vihvelin's point is that (2) and (3) will also come apart in ordinary contexts.

[33] See, again, Sider (2002: 115).

As before, the word 'can' (or 'cannot') should be understood in its ordinary sense (with the domain of quantification restricted to realistic worlds).

Vihvelin's argument has generated considerable debate in the literature. In what follows, we will consider several potential replies, beginning with a pair of objections from Peter Vranas (2010).

Vranas's first objection is to (P1). His objection is based on the following kind of example:

[S]uppose that if I tried to win the award for best singer I would become so nervous and I would sing so poorly that I would fail; but suppose further that in fact I sing without trying to win (I don't even know that I am being considered for the award), and thanks to my ability I sing so well that I do win.   (2010: 116)

In this example, the singer was clearly able to win the contest, since that is what he did.[34] Yet, if the singer had (consciously) tried to win, his nerves would have caused him to sing horribly. In other words, he would have failed to win the contest if he had tried. This result directly contradicts Vihvelin's Counterfactual Principle, so Vranas concludes that her first premise is mistaken.

Vranas anticipates the following response to his objection. The singer would not be successful if he *tried to win the contest*, but there is some other act—namely, *singing*—such that, if the singer tried to do *that*, he would win (again, suppose that the singer doesn't know that he is even being considered for an award, so nerves are not an issue).[35] This suggests that the Counterfactual Principle should be restated as follows:

(P1*)   Necessarily, if someone would fail to do something no matter what she did, then she cannot do it.[36]

As Vranas points out, this would avoid the problem of the nervous singer, but it would require us to replace (P2) with (P2*):

(P2*)   Suzy would fail to kill Baby Suzy, no matter what she did.

However, (P2*) seems incorrect—at least if we assume that retrosuicide is metaphysically possible.[37] For, in that case, there is something—namely, *killing Baby Suzy*—such that if Suzy were to do *it*, she would not fail to kill her younger self. In other words, it is not true that she would fail to kill Baby Suzy *no matter what she did*. The upshot is that the revised version of Vihvelin's argument turns out to be unsound.

Fortunately, there is a better response to Vranas's original objection. Rather than replacing (P1) with (P1*), we can instead use (P1**):

---

[34] This inference assumes that success implies ability: If A ϕs, then A can ϕ. This principle might seem plausible, but some philosophers have challenged it. (See e.g. Kenny (1976).) So, one option for Vihvelin would be to deny the claim that Vranas's singer *can* win the contest (without denying that he *did*).

[35] This counterfactual follows from the standard Lewis–Stalnaker semantics, given that Vranas actually sang and won.

[36] Vranas (2010: 117).

[37] Once again, this would be the case if the resurrection of the dead is metaphysically possible.

(P1**) Necessarily, if someone would fail to do something no matter what she *tried*, then she cannot do it.

Like (P1*), this premise avoids the problem of the nervous singer. After all, there is something (namely, *singing*) such that the singer would win the contest if he tried to do *it*. But it also avoids the previous worry, since the corresponding version of (P2) is much more plausible:

(P2**) Suzy would fail to kill Baby Suzy, no matter what she tried.

There might be some action (like *killing Baby Suzy*) such that, if Suzy *did* it, she would successfully kill her younger self. But there is no action such that, if Suzy *tried* to do it, she would kill Baby Suzy (e.g. if she *tried* to kill Baby Suzy, she would fail). That is the best way to put Vihvelin's point and, once we put it this way, we can avoid Vranas's objection.[38]

However, Vranas has a second objection to Vihvelin that would count against either version of her argument. This objection targets premise (P2):

To see why [P2] is false, consider a world—...say it is the actual world—at which Baby Suzy has an identical twin, Twin Baby Suzy, and at which Suzy sets off a bomb in a room where Baby Suzy and Twin Baby Suzy are asleep, intending to kill them both, but the bomb happens to kill only Twin Baby Suzy. Consider also a world *w* which is qualitatively identical to the actual world, but at which (i) the bomb happens to kill only Baby Suzy, and (ii) Suzy is a later stage of Twin Baby Suzy, not of Baby Suzy...Then *w* is a world at which Suzy tries to kill Baby Suzy and succeeds, and at which Suzy is a later stage of some baby-stage (namely Twin Baby Suzy) whose DNA matches the DNA of Baby Suzy *not* by some miracle or improbable coincidence, but rather because the two baby-stages are identical twins. Since *w* is qualitatively identical to the actual world, *w* is at least as close to the actual world as any world at which Suzy tries to kill Baby Suzy but fails.   (2010: 118–19)

There are several puzzling things about this case. For one thing, it is unclear why Vranas takes this to be a case of *Suzy* killing Baby Suzy. After all, the killer in this case is an extension of *Twin* Baby Suzy, so it is much more natural to think of this as a case in which *Twin* Suzy kills Baby Suzy.

Second, it is unclear what Vranas's case has to do with Vihvelin's argument.[39] After all, this is a case in which Suzy has a twin, and that was not a part of the original example—in Vihvelin's story, the only baby around is Baby Suzy. Since the entire question is about what Suzy can or cannot do in *that* situation, her abilities in Vranas's example are simply irrelevant.

---

[38] For a different response to Vranas, see Spencer (2013: 154).

[39] To be fair, Vranas's version of the argument does not exactly match our own. In particular, his second premise is that "A time traveler would always fail if she tried to kill her younger self" (116). Read as a universal generalization, this premise can be undermined by a single counterexample. But the problem is that this generalization does *not* appear in the official statement of Vihvelin's argument. (See Vihvelin (1996: 320).) In fact, all of her premises concern a particular individual—namely, Suzy. (See the claims labeled '(S)', '(F)', and '(C)' on page 320 of her text.)

Vranas anticipates this complaint, and says the following in response:

Vihvelin might…retreat to the weaker premise that a time traveler *who has no identical twin* would always fail if she tried to kill her baby self. I have two points in reply. First, this response seems ad hoc, intended to close a loophole. How can Vihvelin ensure that other loopholes in her defense of [P2] will not be found? Second, my argument against [P2] may work, mutatis mutandis, against the weaker premise as well: if Suzy at the actual world has no identical twin, then the world w…is not qualitatively almost identical to the actual world, but w…may be assumed to include no miracle or improbable coincidence and so may still count as at least as close to the actual world as any world at which Suzy tries to kill Baby Suzy but fails.   (2010: 120)

Let's take Vranas's two points in order.

First, suppose that Vihvelin's second premise said the following:

(P2***)   Every time traveler would fail to kill her younger self, no matter what she tried.

Restricting this generalization to *time travelers without twins* would indeed be ad hoc. But that is not Vihvelin's premise.[40] She is simply making a claim about a *particular* case, and there doesn't seem to be anything wrong with saying that there is no twin in that case. As a general rule, the ad hoc fallacy only occurs when defending a theoretical generalization. The objection, in those cases, is based on a commitment to the theoretical value of simplicity. Ad hoc maneuvers complicate a theory and to that extent detract from its overall plausibility. But that is not what Vihvelin is doing in her paper. She is simply telling a story, and she should be free to tell that story however she wants.

Turning to Vranas's second rebuttal, consider the following three worlds:

w_1 = Suzy travels back in time with a bomb, intending to kill Baby Suzy. When she arrives, she finds a twinless Baby Suzy alone in her room. But Suzy changes her mind and decides not to light the fuse. Baby Suzy then grows up to be Suzy, who eventually travels back in time with a bomb, intending to kill her younger self.

w_2 = Suzy travels back in time with a bomb, intending to kill Baby Suzy. When she arrives, she finds a twinless Baby Suzy alone in her room. A few extra neurons miraculously fire and Suzy lights the fuse on the bomb. However, the fuse miraculously fizzles out before the bomb detonates. Baby Suzy then grows up to be Suzy, who eventually travels back in time with a bomb, intending to kill her younger self.

w_3 = Suzy travels back in time with a bomb, intending to kill Baby Suzy. When she arrives, she finds Baby Suzy in her room with Twin Baby Suzy. A few extra neurons miraculously fire and Suzy lights the fuse on the bomb. The bomb explodes, killing Baby Suzy. Twin Baby Suzy then grows up to be Suzy, who eventually travels back in time with a bomb, intending to kill her younger self.

---

[40] See the previous footnote.

Vranas's claim is that w_3 "may be assumed to include no miracle or improbable coincidence and so may still count as at least as close to $[w_1]$." But this seems plainly wrong. Obviously, w_3 differs from w_1 in that it contains Twin Baby Suzy. Assuming the truth of determinism, there are only three possible explanations for how that baby got there: (i) w_3 *always* differed from w_1, in such a way that Twin Baby Suzy was eventually born without any miraculous intervention; (ii) w_3 exactly matched w_1 up until shortly after conception, at which time *a small miracle* produced Twin Baby Suzy from the existing embryo; or (iii) w_3 exactly matched w_1 up until Suzy's arrival, at which point *a large miracle* produced Twin Baby Suzy out of thin air. Case (iii) violates Lewis's first rule (avoid big miracles), case (i) dramatically violates the second (maximize exact match), and case (ii) involves two violations of the third (there is one small miracle when the embryo splits and another when the extra neurons fire in Suzy's brain). Of course, w_2 also includes a pair of small miracles (the firing of the neurons and the fizzling of the fuse), but it does a far better job than w_3 when it comes to maximizing exact match (since w_3 diverges from w_1 at the moment the embryo splits). So, w_3 is *not* among the closest worlds where Suzy tries to kill her infant self.

This result is intuitively correct—intuitively, it is *not* true that Baby Suzy might have had a twin, if Suzy had tried to go back in time and kill her younger self. What is true is that Baby Suzy would *not* have had a twin, *even if* Suzy had tried to do this. In other words, Vranas's objection to (P2**) fails.

2.3 Sider on retrosuicide

Like Vranas, Ted Sider (2002) challenges both premises of Vihvelin's argument. More carefully, Sider presents Vihvelin with a dilemma. First, he argues that (P1) is false. Second, he claims that the only response to his argument will require giving up on (P2). So, he concludes that—one way or another—Vihvelin's argument is unsound.

Sider's argument begins with a discussion of permanent bachelors—that is, men who never marry. As Sider notes, some permanent bachelors have no desire to get married, while others want to get married but never meet the right person. However, some permanent bachelors *do* find their true love and *do* attempt to get married. In these kinds of cases, we can expect some surprising results. After all, once one finds the right person and takes care of the relevant arrangements, the actual "getting married" part is not that hard. Yet we know that permanent bachelors will always fail at this task. We also know that, whenever someone fails at an easy task, there will be some sort of surprise. Putting these two points together, we have the following generalization:

(1)   For all x, if it had been the case that (x was a permanent bachelor who attempted to get married), it would have been the case that (x's partner had a last-minute change of heart, or x had a last-minute heart attack, or the minister fatally slipped on a banana peel, or ...).[41]

---

[41] This is what Sider calls a "counterfactual of coincidence."

(where the '…' includes all of the other things that might preempt a successful marriage ceremony).

Here, it is important to distinguish (1) from (2):

(2)   For all *x*, if *x* is a permanent bachelor, then (if *x* had attempted to get married, it would have been the case that *x*'s partner had a last-minute change of heart, or *x* had a last-minute heart attack, or the minister fatally slipped on a banana peel, or…).

In (1), the predicate 'permanent bachelor' falls within the scope of the counterfactual conditional. It concerns the closest possible worlds at which some men are permanent bachelors (whether or not they are *actually* married). (2), in contrast, concerns men who never actually marry. It says, in effect, that something strange would have happened if any of them had tried to get married. And this is plainly false. As Sider says, "Many of these permanent bachelors could have gotten married." It is simply the case that, "had they gotten married, they would no longer have counted as permanent bachelors" (2002: 125).

All of this is correct, but it may seem unclear what any of this has to do with time travel. First, note that (1) concerns the counterfactual failure of men *under a certain description*, whereas Vihvelin is concerned with counterfactual failure *absent any description*. To illustrate the point, recall the first premise of her argument:[42]

(P1)   Necessarily, if someone would fail to do something, no matter what she tried, then she cannot do it.

Now consider the case of a particular permanent bachelor—call him 'Bob'. Given the definition of 'permanent bachelor', we know that (3) is true:

(3)   Bob would fail to get married *while remaining a permanent bachelor*, no matter what he tried.

Moreover, (3) and (P1) would imply (4):

(4)   Bob cannot get married while remaining a permanent bachelor.

But this is no objection to (P1), since (4) is obviously true—Bob cannot get married *while remaining a permanent bachelor*.

Of course, if we drop the relevant description from (4), the resulting statement will no longer be true:

(5)   Bob cannot get married.

But in order to derive (5) from (P1), we would require the truth of the following counterfactual:

(6)   Bob would fail to get married, no matter what he tried.

---

[42]   This is the revised version of the premise from the previous subsection.

This claim is clearly false. Bob probably *would* have gotten married, if he had tried (he just wouldn't have been a permanent bachelor in that case). So—once again—we have no objection to Vihvelin's first premise.

Sider's response to this is to say that (6) *would* be true in certain contexts, owing to a non-standard similarity metric:

Imagine a similarity metric that holds constant a person's status with respect to permanent bachelorhood, and therefore counts possible worlds in which an actual permanent bachelor gets married as being very distant from the actual world. In that case [6] is true; nevertheless, actual permanent bachelors [like Bob] are still free to marry. (2002: 126)

Sider is at least half-right. Certainly there are possible contexts in which we hold fixed whether or not someone is a permanent bachelor and, relative to those contexts, (6) would be true. But in order for that to generate a counterexample to (P1), Bob would still have to count as "free" in those contexts. That is, (5) would have to be *false* in those contexts. And this seems wrong. If we hold fixed Bob's status as a permanent bachelor, it's natural to think that he *cannot* get married.[43]

Here is a second, more basic worry for Sider. Recall that Vihvelin's claim is that (P1) is true, *given what we ordinarily mean by 'can'*. But the context in which we hold fixed someone's status as a permanent bachelor is clearly not ordinary. That is why (5) and (6) normally strike us as false. But, in that case, the question of whether or not those statements are true *in Sider's imagined context* is not directly relevant to Vihvelin's argument.

The upshot is that Sider's argument against (P1) fails.[44] However, this response leads directly to the second horn of his dilemma.

Sider takes away the following moral from his discussion of permanent bachelors: "Vihvelin's principle seems to fail under similarity metrics that hold constant facts about agents that occur in the *future* of the actions in question" (2002: 130). For example, the standard similarity metric places little or no weight on whether or not a particular bachelor will get married at some point in the future.[45] That is why we normally take (5) and (6) to be false. And that is why Vihvelin says that the Counterfactual Principle is true, given what we normally mean by 'can'.

But now, Sider argues, we run into a problem in the case of retrosuicide. Suppose, once again, that Suzy travels back to shoot her infant self (in w_1), but has a last-minute change of heart. And consider two counterfactual worlds. In w_2, a small miracle takes place at t_2—a few extra neurons fire in Suzy's brain—and she decides to shoot her younger self. However, a second small miracle occurs at t_3—a little extra carbon buildup appears and prevents the gun from firing. Baby Suzy is spared and Adult Suzy goes on to die at t_5. (See Figure 4.1 on the next page.)

---

[43] See Carroll (2010: 89).

[44] Sider comes close to admitting this point: "Vihvelin's principle, for all we have said, may remain true when counterfactuals are *not* interpreted via these sorts of similarity metrics" (2002: 130).

[45] See the fourth condition in Lewis's standard similarity metric.

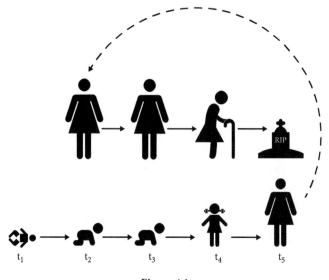

Figure 4.1

The second counterfactual world—w_3—is more unusual. In this world, Baby Suzy is born at t_1. At t_2, she miraculously undergoes bi-location and "splits" into two bodies, with the result that she is baby-like in one place, and adult-like in another. "Adult" Suzy then decides to shoot Baby Suzy, and no further miracles occur (in particular, no extra carbon buildup prevents the gun from firing). Baby Suzy is thus killed at t_3 and "Adult" Suzy goes on to die at t_5. (See Figure 4.2.)

One is tempted to say that w_3 is comparatively distant from w_1, since it seems to include a large (and strange) miracle at t_2. Sider disagrees. He admits this kind of world is "bizarre"

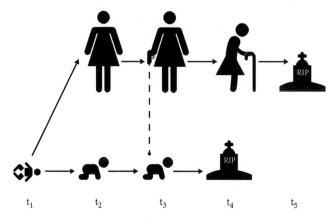

Figure 4.2

since it involves a person splitting in two for no reason whatsoever. Moreover, he admits that w_3 differs from both w_1 and w_2 in this way, since Suzy's bi-location has a causal explanation at those worlds (it is the result of time travel). However, Sider emphasizes that this explanation appeals to *facts about the future*—facts that are irrelevant to evaluating counterfactuals, under the standard similarity metric (i.e. the only metric that is relevant to evaluating Vihvelin's argument). If one *just* focuses on the times leading up to t_3, w_2 and w_3 are exactly alike. Moreover w_2, unlike w_3, includes an additional miracle at t_3 (the appearance of the carbon buildup). Hence, worlds like w_2—that is, worlds in which coincidences spare the life of Baby Suzy—turn out to be comparatively distant, *provided that we do not hold fixed facts about the future*. And Sider's point is that we *cannot* hold these facts fixed, since that would lead us back to the first horn of his dilemma. If we hold these facts fixed in ordinary contexts, it will turn out that Bachelor Bob would not get married, no matter how many times he tried (and this, together with Vihvelin's Principle would imply that Bob cannot get married, in the ordinary sense of 'can'). Hence, we must include w_3 among the closest trying-worlds to actuality. But w_3 is also a success-world. So, we will have to say that Suzy might have succeeded, had she tried to kill Baby Suzy. In other words, we must give up on the second premise of Vihvelin's argument:

(P2)   Suzy would have failed to kill Baby Suzy, no matter what she tried.

That is Sider's objection.

The problem with this objection is that it relies on a false dilemma. Sider's key assumption is that the only way to avoid the argument against (P1) is to rely upon a similarity metric that ignores future facts. This is what leads to the rejection of (P2). So, in order to avoid the dilemma, we must identify an alternative similarity metric. In particular, we must identify a reasonably "normal" metric on which (P2) comes out true, but statements like (6) come out false:

(6)   Bob would fail to get married, no matter what he tried.

There are various ways in which this might be done.[46] Vihvelin herself suggests what she calls a "sophisticated" causal theory of counterfactuals. On her view, the closest antecedent-worlds are worlds that:

(i) diverge from our world with respect to the *causal history leading up to the antecedent event* as far back as is required so that big miracles are avoided and a small miracle secures the divergence from actual causal history;

and

(ii) are exactly like our world with respect to all other facts *except* for those facts that are the causal upshots of the antecedent event. (2011d)[47]

---

[46]   See the discussion of "causal" theories of counterfactuals in Chapter 5, section 6.4.
[47]   Vihvelin also hints at this kind of account in her original article (1996: 327).

As Vihvelin notes, her account has many of the same features as Lewis's. For example, both are similarity-based accounts that call on us to preserve perfect match and avoid miraculous events. The crucial difference is that, when evaluating a counterfactual, Lewis tells us to hold fixed the *temporal history* leading up to the antecedent event. For example, if Bachelor Bob does not try to get married at t and we want to know what would have happened, if he had he tried to, we hold fixed the temporal past leading up to just before t, and then let a small miracle occur (so that Bob tries to marry). Vihvelin, in contrast, instructs us to hold fixed the *causal history* leading up to the (non-)event in question, and then allow a small miracle to do its thing. Of course, in the case of Bob, the two histories are the same. The important point is that Bob's failure to get married in the future is not a part of the temporal or causal past leading up to t. That's why we ignore that fact. And that is part of the explanation for why (6) is false.

In the case of time travel we get different results, since it is possible for one event to be in the causal history of another without being in its temporal history. For example, the fact that Baby Suzy is not killed at t_3 is a part of the causal explanation for how Suzy is in a position to try to kill her at t_2. So, according to Vihvelin's theory, we must hold this fact fixed when asking what would have happened, had Suzy tried to kill her. Here is how Vihvelin puts the point:

The theory tells you to causally (not necessarily temporally) backtrack as far as you need to go until you reach the earliest *small* miracle that allows the antecedent event to occur. In time travel cases, this small miracle can lie in the *external future*. When we search for the causally closest *small* miracle that permits the event that is the time traveler's *attempt* to kill the baby who is her younger self, we must causally backtrack through the time traveler's personal time in a way that ensures that she remains *in a position to make the attempt*, and the only way to do this while avoiding large miracles (popping into existence ex nihilo, resurrection from the dead, and so on) is by ensuring that she grows up from the child she once was, and the only small miracle that enables this is a jammed bullet or some other mundane event that prevents the time traveler's attempt from succeeding.   (2011d)

That is Vihvelin's explanation for why (P2) is true: If Suzy had tried to kill Baby Suzy, she would have failed (no matter how hard or how many times she tried).

If all of this is correct, we have a reasonably normal metric on which (P2) is true and (6) is false. In other words, we have an answer to Sider's dilemma.

We also have an answer to a residual puzzle about the grandfather paradox. Recall Lewis's earlier argument for the conclusion that Tim can kill Grandfather (from Chapter 3, section 1):

Suppose that down the street another sniper, Tom, lurks waiting for another victim, Grandfather's partner. Tom is not a time traveler, but otherwise he is just like Tim: same make of rifle, same murderous intent, same everything. We can even suppose that Tom, like Tim, believes himself to be a time traveler. Someone has gone to a lot of trouble to deceive Tom into thinking so. There's no doubt that Tom can kill his victim; and Tim has everything going for him that Tom does. [So] By any ordinary standards of ability, Tim can kill Grandfather.

(1976: 149)

The key premise in this argument is the claim that Tim "has everything going for him that Tom does." On Vihvelin's view, this is a mistake. Tim *does* have a lot in common with Tom. He has the same rifle, same intent, etc. But Tom also has one thing Tim lacks—namely, *a target whose continued existence is causally irrelevant to his being in a position to shoot.* Intuitively, this is an important difference between the two. Vihvelin's account helps to explain why this is so. Given the Counterfactual Principle, it is only true that Tim can kill Grandfather if he would have (or at least might have) succeeded, had he tried. Moreover, given the sophisticated causal theory, this counterfactual is only true if it is possible for Tim to kill his Grandfather without a large-scale miracle in his causal history. But, as in the case of Suzy, this is *not* possible. After all, if Tim were to kill his Grandfather, *he would have to be there to do the killing.* But, in order for Tim to be there, Father would have to have been born, in which case Grandfather would have to have met Grandmother, etc. The only way for these things to happen, given Tim's successful murder attempt, would be a large-scale miracle. Grandfather would have to have risen from the grave, or undergone bi-location, or experienced some other miraculous event. That, on Vihvelin's view, is why Tim cannot kill Grandfather. Crucially, the same thing is not true for Tom. It is possible for Tom to kill his target without a large-scale miracle because his target is not a part of his own causal history. That is the relevant difference between Tom and Tim.[48]

More generally, Vihvelin will say the same thing about the grandfather paradox that she does about the retrosuicide paradox: *Contra* Lewis, Tim cannot kill Grandfather by the "ordinary standards" of ability. But that is no objection to time travel, since time travel would not give Tim this power (for the reasons just given). Moreover, what goes for Suzy and Tim would go for any other time travelers who seek to undercut their own existence. In this way, Vihvelin provides a perfectly general solution to the paradoxes of self-defeat.

3. The Problem with Banana Peels

On Lewis's view, a time traveler *can* kill her younger self (in the ordinary sense of 'can'), but that is not an objection to time travel, since retrosuicide is compatible with the kinds of facts we normally hold fixed when talking about what someone can or cannot do. On Vihvelin's view, retrosuicide is *in*compatible with the kinds of facts we normally hold fixed when talking about what someone can or cannot do, but that is not an objection to time travel since time travel would *not* put one in a position to commit such an act (not, at least, in the ordinary sense of 'in a position to act'). Either way, both parties agree that the retrosuicide paradox fails to establish its conclusion. The same thing is true for all of the other paradoxes of freedom.

---

[48] For more on this point, see Wasserman (2017a).

Most philosophers are happy with this resolution, but for some there remains a lingering sense of puzzlement.[49] Consider, for example, Vihvelin's initial description of Suzy's suicidal mission:

She packs a gun and travels back through time, determined to kill her infant self. She picks a time when she knows that the baby will be alone. She checks carefully to make sure her gun is loaded. She fires. She misses. She fires again. This time the gun jams.

We don't need to go on with the story. We know that the time traveler's efforts will all fail. No matter how many times she tries, something will go wrong—her gun will jam, the bullet will be deflected, it will turn out to have been the wrong baby... [etc.].   (1996: 315)

There is obviously something strange about this imagined sequence of events. It is strange to think that there will be an unexpected jamming, followed by a miraculous deflection, followed by a careless misidentification, etc. As Ted Sider remarks, this would seem like a string of "coincidences" that "are guaranteed to happen" (2002: 117). In fact, Paul Horwich (1987: Chapter 7) claims that these kinds of coincidences give us good reason to doubt the reality of time travel. His argument is the subject of the following subsections.[50]

3.1 Horwich on coincidences

Horwich's argument begins with a claim about human nature—namely, that many of us would try to alter the past, were we given the opportunity:

[W]e have no reason to expect such a fortunate coincidence of time travel with disinterest in [changing the past]. Not only would such an uncaused correlation be an inexplicable coincidence—and highly improbable, given what we see of the world—but also there are facts about human capacities and inclinations that give us positive reason to expect no such correlation. Namely, we know that the ability to travel backward in time would engender attempts at self-defeating causal chains.   (1987: 120–1)

Three points of clarification are in order.

First, when Horwich speaks of "self-defeating causal chains," he has in mind self-defeating acts like Tim's killing of Grandfather and Suzy's killing of Baby Suzy. Horwich also refers to these acts as "bilking" attempts, where bilking involves "bringing about some past event that did not occur" (1987: 220). Here, he is thinking about cases in which someone knows that a particular event has not occurred and travels to the past to try to bring it about (where this attempt is motivated, in part, by the knowledge that the event did not occur). This kind of action would be self-defeating since, if it

---

[49] See Dainton (2001: 118), Earman (1995: 283), Fitzgerald (1974: 536), Lockwood (2005: 165–7), and Maudlin (1990: 304).

[50] We will follow tradition in focusing on Horwich's version of the argument. However, we will also note that Horwich was not the first person to raise this kind of worry. Similar points had already been made by Earman (1972: 307), Fitzgerald (1970: 427–8 and 1974: 534–6), and David Lewis (in his Princeton seminars in the early 1970s).

were successful, the relevant knowledge would be destroyed, and the corresponding attempt would be unmotivated.

Second, when Horwich speaks of "travel backward in time," he is thinking specifically of travel to the "local" (i.e. recent) past. The reason for this is presumably that our knowledge of the recent past is much more specific than our knowledge of the distant past. We should not expect travelers to the distant past to try to change the past, since they do not know much about those times (and thus do not know what would constitute a "change" in them).[51]

Third, Horwich does not say exactly what he has in mind when he mentions "human capacities and inclinations." But it is not hard to fill in the details. First, almost everyone has something about the past they would like to change (unkind words that were spoken, lucrative investments that were missed, grandfathers that were not murdered, etc.). Moreover, most of us have the general ability to talk to people, give money to stockbrokers, fire guns, etc. So, given these capacities and inclinations, we should expect there to be many bilking attempts if we gain the ability to travel into the local past.

The second premise of Horwich's argument is that, if we expect there to be many bilking attempts, we should also expect there to be many cases in which capable people fail at easy tasks. The reasoning behind this premise is based on two observations. First, bilking attempts will normally involve tasks that are generally easy to perform— tasks like talking, investing, shooting, etc.[52] These are the kinds of things that people normally succeed at, when they try. Second, bilking attempts will never succeed, since it is logically or metaphysically impossible to change the past.[53] Of course, one might try to challenge this claim by defending one of the models of past-alteration discussed in Chapter 3. But, setting those views aside, this claim seems uncontroversial.

The third premise of Horwich's argument is that, if we expect there to be many people failing at easy tasks, we should expect there to be many coincidences. The reasoning behind this premise is the same as the reasoning employed by Sider in the case of Bachelor Bob. Saying "I do" is an easy task. The same thing is true for talking, investing, shooting, etc. These are not difficult to do. So, whenever a capable person tries to perform these acts and fails, we should expect something unusual to have happened (a reliable gun jammed, or a healthy person died of a heart attack, or a sure-footed assassin

---

[51] It is unclear whether this restriction to local time travel is really required. Given current technology, our historical records will presumably last long into the future. So, even if it takes ten thousand years to develop time travel technology, one would still expect many time travelers to try to change current events.

[52] Of course, part of the reason these things seem easy is the generic descriptions being used. Is it easy to kill a baby? Yes. Is it easy to kill a baby who is your former self and whose continued existence is therefore required for you to be holding the gun in the first place? No. However, in the case of retrosuicide, 'the killing of the baby' and 'the committing of retrosuicide' would pick out the very same act. So, under one description at least, it does not seem as if time travel would result in people failing at "easy" tasks. However, this issue is not central to Horwich's argument. The key point is just that bilking attempts would give rise to a lot of banana peel slips, etc. That is all his argument requires.

[53] Recall from section 1 that this does not mean it is logically or metaphysically impossible to perform actions that were not actually performed. For example, it might be metaphysically possible for a time traveler to prevent Lincoln's assassination, even though the assassination was not actually prevented.

slipped on a banana peel, or . . .). Of course, not all unusual events are coincidences. It is unusual to win the lottery, for example, but we do not normally call a single lottery win a "coincidence." In order for something to be a coincidence, it seems as if it must be part of a *pattern*—the kind of pattern that would lead us to suspect a conspiracy of some sort. For example, if someone were to win the lottery *three times in a row*, we would normally suspect foul play. But that is *exactly* the kind of pattern we should expect if time travelers set out to change the past. Those efforts will be systematically thwarted in exactly the way one would expect if there was an elaborate conspiracy in place: "First, Suzy's gun jammed. Then her arm twitched. And *then* she slipped on a banana peel. And then..." This, as they say, would be "too much of a coincidence."

Horwich's final premise is that we should be skeptical of these kinds of happenings:

> [T]here is considerable strangeness in this—something ad hoc and unsatisfying about explaining the repeated failures in terms of changes of mind, guns misfiring, and so forth. Since it is implausible that such mishaps would occur so faithfully over and over again, we conclude . . . that time travel into the recent past will not take place on a regular basis.   (1987: 121)[54]

We can summarize this argument by adopting the following system of abbreviations:

T = the proposition that humans will gain the ability to travel into their local past
K = the relevant background knowledge about human nature
B = the proposition that there will be many bilking attempts
F = the proposition that capable people will repeatedly fail to complete easy tasks
S = the proposition that there will be a long string of coincidences

We can then formulate Horwich's argument as follows (where $P(x/y)$ is the conditional probability of x given y):

(P1) $P(B/(T\&K)) \approx 1$[55]
(P2) $P(F/B) = 1$

---

[54] This part of Horwich's argument was anticipated by Paul Fitzgerald, who appears to have been the first person to put the worry in print:

> [One] possibility is that there are no generally applicable empirical reasons for the malfunctioning of paradox machines; we simply have a fortuitous series of accidents which avert the embarrassment of self-contradiction every time. The first self-inhibitor fails to function because a screw comes loose; the second because an earthquake destroys it, the third because . . . To sustain the appeal, we would have to regard it as a lawlike regularity that unrelated accidents will always conspire [in this way]. We are not willing to accept such a principle as a law since it lacks direct empirical support, has no indirect support from nor organic interplay with accepted laws and theories, and doesn't even particularly resemble other things which we accept as lawlike regularities. So we surrender instead our belief in the empirical possibility of [time travel].   (1970: 427–8)

The "paradox machines" referred to in this passage were inspired by physicists' search for tachyons in the 1960s. For more on these machines, see Fitzgerald (1974: 534–5). For more on tachyons and their relevance to time travel, see Alvager and Kreisler (1968).

[55] Let's not worry too much about the exact value of $P(B/(T\&K))$. The point is just that it is very, very high, so that the value of $P(T)$ is very, very low.

(P3) $P(S/F) = 1$

(P4) $P(S) \approx 0$ [56]

(C) $P(T\&K) \approx 0$

Taking the relevant background knowledge (K) as given, it follows that the probability of T is close to 0. In other words, it is incredibly unlikely that we will ever gain the ability to travel into our local past. That is Horwich's argument. [57]

There is much to be said in favor of Horwich's argument, but it is clearly limited in scope. First, the argument does not show time travel to be impossible. At best, it shows time travel to be improbable. [58] Second, the argument does not teach us anything about forward time travel. At best, it shows us something about backward time travel (and then only to the local past). Third, the argument does not tell us anything about alien life forms, subatomic particles, or other potential time travelers that have no interest in changing the past. At best, it tells us something about *human beings as we currently are*. That is a much more limited conclusion than one might have hoped for.

Still, the conclusion has some important implications. After all, many contemporary physicists take time travel seriously. In fact, at least part of the interest in the Large Hadron Collider is the thought that it might be used to produce and control Higgs singlets. In particular, it might be used to send these theoretical particles into the (local) past, and thus communicate with earlier times. But, if Horwich is right, we know in advance that this research is almost certain to fail. Moreover, we know it is almost certain to fail *without knowing any of the relevant scientific details behind the research*. Our knowledge of human nature, together with some simple a priori reasoning, is

---

[56] How close is P(S) to 0? That depends. If time travel would engender millions of bilking attempts, then P(S) will be *very* close to 0. If time travel would only engender several *hundred* attempts, then P(S) will still be close to 0, but the probability will not be astronomically low. This is important for Horwich's argument since P(T) is presumably pretty low to begin with. So, if the number of expected bilking attempts is in the hundreds, rather than millions, Horwich's argument will have little or no effect.

Here is one reason to favor the lower estimate. If we eventually gain the ability to travel back in time, there will presumably be an initial spate of bilking attempts. But when word gets out that all of those attempts have failed, people will eventually realize that the past cannot be changed. At that point, the number of bilking attempts will presumably plummet. So, we should not expect an ongoing string of coincidences in the case of backward time travel.

[57] Horwich's argument is reminiscent of the "epistemic" arguments given by Clarke (1962), Fulmer (1980), Hawking (1994), and others (see Chapter 1, fn. 63). The main difference is that these other arguments focus on the actual lack of time travelers at the current time (or at recent historical events). For example, if we let T* be the proposition that humans will gain the ability to travel back to the early 1900s, and we let A be the proposition that many time travelers try to kill Adolf Hitler, we can argue as follows: $P(A/(T^*\&K)) \approx 1$, $P(A) \approx 0$, $\therefore P(T^*\&K) \approx 0$. In other words, it is extremely likely that many time travelers will try to kill the young Hitler, given what we know about human nature, and given that we will one day be able to travel back to the early 1900s. But it is almost certain that this will not happen, since there are no records of such attempts. So, taking our knowledge of human nature as given, it is almost certain that humans will never gain the ability to travel back to the early 1900s.

[58] This point is important to emphasize because Horwich goes back and forth between this conclusion and other, more controversial claims (like the claim that "spacetime does not permit time travel").

enough to show that we will never be able to send signals back in time. Something about this style of reasoning seems deeply paradoxical.

3.2 Smith on fallacious reasoning

There are many different things one might say about Horwich's argument. Here, we will focus on a pair of objections due to Nicholas J. J. Smith (1997).

Smith's first target is Horwich's first premise:[59]

(P1) $P(B/(T\&K)) \approx 1$

This premise says that the probability of bilking attempts, given that we will be able to travel to the local past (and given our background knowledge of human nature), is almost one.

As noted above, this premise seems initially plausible. After all, the ability to change the past is one of the most enticing aspects of time travel. This is evidenced by the fact that almost all time travel stories feature attempts to improve history (by killing Hitler, saving Doc, etc.). Surely, if time travel were to become a reality, then people would try to do these same kinds of things.

Smith states his objection to this premise as follows:

My reply will be to point out that backward time travel, *in itself*, does *not* entail slips on banana peels and other such coincidences. Rather, each argument which purports to derive such coincidences as output, given backward time travel as input, *also* uses as input...occurrences which are *themselves* as rare and apparently improbable as long strings of slips on banana peels. Hence, in order to derive a large number of output coincidences, the objections need to stipulate the occurrence of large numbers of input coincidences. This means that...the arguments in question cannot get started.   (1997: 381)

Smith's suggestion is that the probability of $(B/(T\&K))$ is actually low (or at least not high) and that the only way to arrive at a high probability for B is to conditionalize on T and K *together with the further assumption that certain coincidences will take place*. Let A be this assumption. Then Smith will grant that $P(B/(T\&K\&A)) \approx 1$. And from this premise, we can deduce that $P(T\&K\&A) \approx 0$. However, that conclusion does not tell us anything about the probability of T. Since A is the proposition that certain coincidences will take place, and since coincidences are unlikely, the prior probability of A is very low. Hence, the probability of $(T\&A)$ will also be very low, no matter what the likelihood of T. Thus, Horwich's argument teaches us nothing about the actual likelihood of time travel.

The crucial question concerns A: What kind of coincidences does Smith have in mind? And why does he think we need to assume these "input coincidences" in order to derive the relevant "outputs"?

Before answering these questions, let's begin with a distinction between *de dicto* and *de re* attempts. Someone tries to ϕ in the *de dicto* sense if and only if she believes that

---

[59]   Actually, this is Smith's second target, but we will address it first. See Smith (1997: 371–88).

she's trying to ϕ. And someone tries to ϕ in the *de re* sense if and only if the agent is trying to Ψ (in the *de dicto* sense) and Ψ-ing would, as a matter of fact, count as ϕ-ing (whether or not the agent is aware of this).[60] To use Smith's example, an agent might believe that her glass has milk in it, when in fact it is filled with white paint. In that case, she might try to drink white paint in the *de re* sense, without trying *de dicto*. Similarly, Suzy might travel back in time and try to kill a baby, without realizing that the baby is her infant self. In that case, she would be trying to commit retrosuicide in the *de re* sense only.

Given this distinction, we should ask: What kind of bilking attempts are at issue in premise (P1)?

Consider first the case of pure *de re* attempts. These are cases in which time travelers try to perform ordinary acts (in the *de dicto* sense) without realizing that those acts would involve past-alteration. As Smith notes, we should expect these cases to be fairly uncommon. Obviously, some time travelers will unwittingly try to do things that were not in fact done, just like some of us occasionally try to do things that won't in fact be done. But, on the pure *de re* reading, we should not expect failed attempts to change the past to be any more common than failed attempts to change the future. Of course, time travelers might turn out to be unusually unlucky, in which case *de re* bilking attempts would be more common. But Smith's point is that this correlation between time travel and bad luck would itself be a coincidence.

Now consider the case of *de dicto* bilking attempts. These are cases in which time travelers intentionally try to change the past. Smith argues these kinds of cases are also unlikely, even if time travel will one day become a reality. First, he claims that, in the *de dicto* sense, one cannot try to do the impossible. For example, if Suzy is absolutely convinced that the Pythagorean theorem is true, then she cannot honestly try to disprove it (*de dicto*).[61] Let's suppose that Smith is right about this. In that case, a *de dicto* bilking attempt would require a time traveler to think that past-alteration is possible. But past-alteration is obviously impossible. So in order to get a lot of *de dicto* bilking attempts, we would need a lot of stupid time travelers. But we shouldn't expect a lot of time travelers to be that stupid, so we shouldn't expect a lot of (*de dicto*) bilking attempts. Here is how Smith puts the point:

[I]f a high proportion of time travelers were to fall for the second-time-around fallacy, then local backward time travel would indeed entail a great many slips on banana peels and so on. But it seems very improbable that there should be a systematic correlation between time traveling intentions and fallacious reasoning. So ... only a few time travelers will try in the *de dicto* sense to kill their younger selves, and hence only a few banana-peel-slips and so on will occur—and we cannot baulk at that: it is not as if such slips never occur!   (1997: 382)

---

[60] See Smith (1997: 379).

[61] Smith says that this would be "incomprehensible" (1997: 379), which suggests that he takes the relevant principle to be a conceptual truth. Presumably, the thought is that intention requires the belief that one might succeed. So, if one is antecedently convinced of failure, one cannot genuinely intend the relevant outcome.

This line of reasoning is not entirely convincing. Four points should be made in response.

First, Smith says that we could predict a great number of banana-peel-slips if a "high proportion" of time travelers fell for the second-time-around fallacy. But in fact something weaker is true: In order to get a bunch of banana-peel-slips, we only need *a lot* of time travelers who fall for the second-time-around fallacy. It doesn't matter whether or not these time travelers constitute a high proportion of the time traveling population. For example, if there will be millions of time travelers and only 25 percent fall for the fallacy, then we should still expect a lot of coincidences.[62]

Second, the truth is many people *do* fall for the second-time-around fallacy.[63] After all, almost every popular time travel story involves this kind of thinking, and almost no one thinks twice about it. So perhaps we should expect a high proportion of time travelers to make the same mistake.

Third, one does *not* need to fall for the second-time-around fallacy in order to think that past-alteration is possible.[64] After all, a perfectly reasonable person might have non-zero credence in the branching timeline theory. That person would think that there's *some* chance of changing the past, in which case he would be free to try to do so (even in the *de dicto* sense).

Finally, suppose that all of the previous points are incorrect. In other words, suppose that the *only* reason we should expect a long string of coincidences is if we assume that there will be a systematic correlation between time traveling intentions and fallacious reasoning. Smith says that this correlation is "very improbable." But that just seems wrong. The number-one reason people want to travel to the past is to try to change it. So we should actually expect a high proportion of time travelers to think that past-alteration is possible—otherwise, most of them wouldn't bother to take the trip. And if only fallacious thinkers believe that bilking is possible then—*contra* Smith—we should expect a significant correlation between time traveling and fallacious reasoning.

For all these reasons, Smith's first objection is unsuccessful.[65]

3.3 Smith on tomato rolls

Smith's second objection targets Horwich's third premise:[66]

(P3) $P(S/F) = 1$

---

[62] This first worry is raised by Dowe (2003).

[63] Recall from Chapter 3 that the second-time-around fallacy is the mistake of thinking an event that a time traveler *experiences* twice actually *occurs* twice.

[64] This point is made by Goddu (2007).

[65] Smith's objection does leave us with some interesting questions about how to understand the mind of a time traveler who does *not* fall for the second-time-around fallacy. In particular, it raises the question of how to understand the mind of someone who knows with complete certainty what she is going to do before she even does it. For further discussion of this issue, see Rennick (2015), Smith (2005), and Zimmerman (2012).

[66] See Smith (1997: 368–71). Smith's second objection is endorsed by Dowe (2003), Goddu (2007), and Sider (2002: 119–20).

This premise says that a string of coincidences is certain, given that many people will fail at routine tasks. The reasoning behind this premise was as follows. In order for a capable person to fail at a routine task, he would have to experience equipment failure, or have a heart attack, or slip on a banana peel, etc. But a sequence of such events would constitute a string of coincidences. So, if there's going to be a string of unusual failures, there's going to be a string of unusual coincidences.

Smith's objection to this reasoning begins with the following story.

Parramatta Road is a road in Sydney that was once very quiet and is now very busy. Imagine someone attempting to roll ten tomatoes across Parramatta Road at two second intervals, starting at some randomly chosen time. In the olden days, it would have been a coincidence if even one of the tomatoes had failed to reach the other side. Nowadays, however, it would be no coincidence if all the tomatoes were squashed. Squashings are no longer coincidental because they are no longer improbable; they are no longer improbable because there are more cars on the road nowadays... Now suppose some old-timer once argued as follows. If the number of cars on Parramatta Road were to increase, persons with time on their hands and tomatoes in their pockets would make tomato-rolling attempts—and their attempts would entail long strings of coincidences (namely, many out of the set of ten tomatoes getting squashed, attempt after attempt). Hence, an increase in the number of cars on Parramatta Road entails arbitrarily long strings of coincidences. Long strings of coincidences are improbable. Hence an increase in the number of cars on Parramatta Road is improbable, and will very likely not occur.   (1997: 368–9)

As Smith notes, this would be a very bad argument for the "old-timer" to give. The problem is that the old-timer observes that a certain sequence of events (tomato rolls, followed by tomato squashings) is infrequent under one set of conditions (there being few cars around), and concludes that the same pattern will hold under a very different set of conditions (there being lots of cars around). In some cases, this kind of inference is perfectly fine—specifically, when the observed pattern is underwritten by a universal law. But the case of tomato squashing is not like that. The infrequency of squashings is partly due to the lack of traffic, so one should not expect that pattern to hold as cars become more common.

According to Smith, Horwich's argument is analogous to the old-timer's argument. Like the old-timer, Horwich observes that a certain sequence of events (e.g. infanticide attempts, followed by banana-peel-slips) is infrequent under one set of conditions (there being no time travelers around), and concludes that the same pattern will hold under very different conditions (there being many time travelers around). But this is a weak inference, given his other commitments. According to Horwich, time travel to the local past would lead to many banana-peel-slips and other related mishaps. Hence, the observed infrequency of these events is partly due to the current lack of time travelers. But time travel "traffic" will obviously pick up if we one day gain the ability to travel into our local past. So, we cannot appeal to the observed infrequencies in order to argue that this ability will never be gained. At best, we can conclude that it is extremely unlikely that we will develop time travel technology in the very near future.[67] But that, Smith says, is something we already knew.

To tie all of this back to premise (P3): If Smith is correct, the value of P(S/F) falls far short of 1. What *is* certain is that there will be a long string of failures if many capable people fail at very easy tasks. But if we one day develop time travel technology, then those failures will no longer be unlikely or surprising. In other words, those failures will no longer constitute a string of coincidences.

4. Paradox without Freedom?

To this point, we have focused on paradoxes of freedom that involve human beings. However, many people have argued that human freedom plays an inessential role in these puzzles—the exact same kind of worries can arise for automated devices and other inanimate objects.[68] If this is correct, one might worry that our focus in the past two chapters has been unjustifiably restricted, and that new solutions will have to be developed for the cases we have ignored.[69] In this section, we will argue that this is not the case.

Let's begin with a few examples involving inanimate objects. Here is one such case, suggested by John Earman:

[C]onsider a rocket ship which at some space-time point x can fire a probe into the past lobe of the null cone at x. Suppose that the rocket is programmed to fire the probe unless a safety switch is on and the safety switch is turned on if and only if the 'return' of the probe is detected by a sensing device with which the rocket is equipped.   (1972: 231–2)

This situation is depicted in Figure 4.3.

The problem with this case is clear. If the rocket launches the probe, that probe will travel back into the past and be detected by the rocket. In that case, the rocket's safety switch will be turned on and the probe will *not* launch. On the other hand, if the rocket doesn't launch the probe, no probe will be detected in the past. But, in that case, the safety switch will remain off and the probe will launch. Either way, we seem to have a contradiction.

Variations on Earman's rocket are easy to imagine. For example, C. J. S Clarke (1977: 102–3) describes a setup consisting of a box, a gun, a target, and a shutter.[70] The target and shutter are tied together so that the shutter will drop down and permanently block the opening to the box if and only if the target is struck. Imagine that this device (call it

---

[67] On a related point, see Arntzenius (2006: 609).

[68] See, for example, Deutsch and Lockwood (1994: 71), Earman (1995: 283), Horwich (1987: 121), Ismael (2003: 305), and Thorne (1995: 509), among others.

[69] Deutsch and Lockwood (1994) give a direct argument for this conclusion. For a critical analysis of their argument, see Sider (1997b).

[70] Clarke's case is inspired by the earlier work of Wheeler and Feynman (1949).

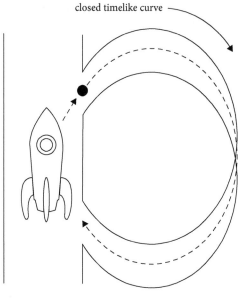

Figure 4.3

'Assassin') is sent back in time and positioned behind its earlier self ('Victim', as depicted in Figure 4.4).

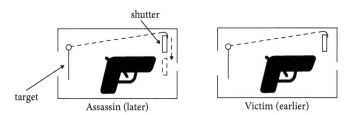

Figure 4.4

Here is the problem. If the gun fires with the shutter up, then the bullet will exit the box and strike Victim's target. In that case, Victim's shutter will (permanently) close. But if Victim's shutter closes, then Assassin's shutter should be closed as well. After all, Assassin is just a later version of Victim. So, suppose instead that Assassin's shutter is down. In that case, the bullet will be blocked from exiting the box. But then Victim's target will not be struck, in which case its shutter will remain open (let's suppose there's nothing else around to strike Victim's target). In that case, Victim's shutter should be open, which contradicts our initial assumption.

A third and final example is suggested by the physicist Joseph Polchinski. In 1988, Kip Thorne and his students (Michael Morris and Ulvi Yurtsever) published their seminal paper on wormholes and time machines.[71] Upon reading the paper, Polchinski wrote to Thorne about what he took to be an "unresolvable paradox":

Take a wormhole that has been made into a time machine, and place its two mouths at rest near each other, out in interplanetary space. Then, if a billiard ball is launched toward the right mouth from an appropriate initial location and with an appropriate initial velocity, the ball will enter the right mouth, travel backward in time, and fly out of the left mouth before it entered the right...and it will then hit its younger self, thereby preventing itself from ever entering the right mouth and hitting itself.[72]

Polchinski's example is illustrated in Figure 4.5, with the "younger version" of the ball in black and "older version" in grey.

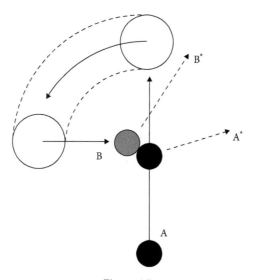

Figure 4.5

In this case, the billiard ball takes trajectory A into the right mouth of the wormhole. It then exits along trajectory B and collides with its earlier self. The result is that the earlier version of the ball is knocked onto trajectory A* and misses the wormhole entirely. This is clearly contradictory.

There are many other examples like this in the literature.[73] They are a lot of fun to think about. But what exactly do they show?

[71] Morris, Thorne, and Yurtsever (1988).
[72] As reported by Thorne (1995: 510).
[73] See, for example, Davies (1977), Everett (2004), and Fitzgerald (1974: 534–5).

Earman takes these cases to show that, among other things, the paradoxes of self-defeat "do not hinge on human agency" (1972: 231). After all, we can suppose that Earman's rocket is not built or programmed by human hands—it simply pops into existence in a galaxy far, far away. In that case, the example would not have anything to do with human beings. But it would still be paradoxical. So, it is possible to have a grandfather-style paradox without any human agency.[74]

This conclusion is correct, but it's unclear whether anyone has ever thought otherwise. After all, there doesn't seem to be any reason to think that every variation on the grandfather paradox must involve human beings.

Polchinski takes these cases to show something stronger—namely, that the paradoxes of self-defeat do not hinge on *any* kind of agency since they have "nothing to do with free will" (quoted in Overbye 2005).[75] Whether or not this is the case will depend, in part, on what one means by "agency."[76] But this much seems clear: Rockets, guns, and billiard balls do not have any will at all, let alone any *free* will. So, it is possible to have a grandfather-style paradox without any free will.

This conclusion is also correct, but it is not all that surprising. After all, we have been exploring the paradoxes of past-alteration and self-defeat for two whole chapters and the specific topic of free will has not come up once. Of course, we have said quite a bit about what time travelers can and cannot do. And presumably there is some sense of "can" that is closely related to the concept of freedom. That is why we've been referring to these puzzles as "paradoxes of freedom". But none of these arguments include any explicit talk of "freedom" or "free will." For example, our formulation of the retrosuicide paradox went like this:

(P1)   If backward time travel were possible, then Suzy could kill Baby Suzy.
(P2)   Suzy cannot kill Baby Suzy.
(C)   Backward time travel is impossible.

The rationale for (P1) was that, if time travel were possible, then Suzy would have the means and the opportunity to perform the relevant action. The rationale for (P2)

---

[74] In Earman's case, the non-detection is the "grandfather," the safety switch's being off is the "father," and the firing of the probe is the "son."

[75] The same conclusion is suggested by Deutsch and Lockwood (1994: 71) and Earman. In fact, Earman's reason for focusing on cases with inanimate objects is that "free will is a murky and controversial concept" (1995: 283).

[76] Some philosophers equate agency with personhood, and analyze personhood in terms of psychological features like consciousness, rationality, and the like. The rocket obviously lacks these properties, so there is no person-agent in the story. However, some philosophers simply take an agent to be something that acts. Of course, there are various views about what constitutes an act, and how acts are to be distinguished from other events, but there is obviously *some* sense in which the rocket "acts" since it *does lots of things*. For example, it runs programs, detects objects, and fires probes. So perhaps there is some sense in which the rocket counts as an agent.

was that the act of killing Baby Suzy would be self-defeating. Again, none of this reasoning appeals to any claims about free will. The paradox is simply about what Suzy can or cannot do.

The same thing is true for the "mechanical" paradoxes we have presented in this section. For example, we can formulate Earman's paradox as follows:

(P1*)   If backward time travel were possible, then Earman's rocket could fire a probe that would be detected at an earlier time.

(P2*)   Earman's rocket cannot fire a probe that would be detected at an earlier time.

(C*)   Backward time travel is impossible.

The rocket may not be an agent. It may not have free will. But there are obviously some things it can do, and other things it can't.[77] Suppose, for example, that the rocket's sensor does not detect an incoming probe, so that its "safety switch" is turned off. In that case, it seems obvious that it can fire its probe. After all, it has the requisite firing mechanism and, since the safety is off, nothing stands in its way. In short, the rocket—like Suzy—has both the means and the opportunity.[78] So if time travel were possible, it could fire the probe. That is the rationale for (P1*).

Of course, we know that the rocket will fail. Either the probe will not be fired or, if it *is* fired, it will not make it back to the earlier time (or if it *does* make it back to the earlier time, it will not be detected). One way or another, the rocket will not fire a *detected* probe for, if it did, the safety switch would be turned on and the rocket would not fire the probe. In other words, the firing of a detected probe would be self-defeating. That is the rationale behind (P2*).

What should we make of this argument? That depends on what we make of the retrosuicide paradox and the other paradoxes of freedom. We might postulate a branching timeline model, or we might side with Lewis or Vihvelin, or we might think that the original arguments against time travel were successful after all.[79] The

---

[77] Note that Earman himself describes the rocket in these terms. For example, he says that the rocket "*can* fire a probe into the past" (my emphasis) and that it is equipped with a sensing device that *can* detect incoming probes. Of course, one might argue that 'can' means something slightly different in this context than in a context where we are talking about what a person can and cannot do. But whatever features of 'can' that are relevant to the paradox (e.g. its context-sensitivity) are presumably going to be the same in both cases. (Thanks to Neal Tognazzini for discussion on this point.)

[78] We could also add that there are relevantly similar rockets that can successfully fire their probes. This would parallel Lewis's earlier argument about Tim and Tom.

[79] One further response is worth mentioning. Kip Thorne and his students famously replied to Polchinski's paradox by pointing out that, for any set of initial conditions, there is a consistent path that the billiard ball could take through the imagined wormhole. See Echeverria, Klinkhammer, and Thorne (1991). In Polchinski's scenario, the ball hits its earlier self straight on and thereby prevents it from entering the wormhole. But, given the same initial conditions and laws, it is also possible for the ball to barely hit the backside of its earlier self as it passes by. This would speed the younger version of the ball up a bit and change its trajectory slightly, but the ball would still enter the wormhole, travel back in time, and hit its earlier self.

point is that, whatever we say about the earlier paradoxes, we can (and should) say about the rocket case as well. And the same thing goes for all of the other examples discussed in this section.

Echeverria, Klinkhammer, and Thorne take this "glancing blow solution" to show that there will "never be unresolvable paradoxes for *any* inanimate object that passes through the wormhole" (1991: 509). But this seems too strong. For one thing, it is not clear that every case admits of a glancing blow solution (Maudlin 1990). More importantly, showing that there is a consistent continuation of Polchinski's story is very different from showing that there is no *in*consistent continuation of this story. For all Echeverria, Klinkhammer, and Thorne have said, the billiard ball could still prevent its earlier self from entering the wormhole (if backward time travel is possible). So, the problem for backward time travel remains. By analogy, pointing out that the laws of quantum mechanics allow for a banana peel to appear out of nowhere under Suzy's foot as she prepares to fire her gun is not enough to solve the retrosuicide paradox. After all, the laws also allow for the *absence* of a banana peel, in which case it would still seem possible for Suzy to kill her younger self.

5

Causal Paradoxes

And if before the past is through,
The future intervenes;
Then what's the use of anything;
Of cabbages or queens?

—W. H. Williams, "The Einstein and The Eddington"

In the early 1950s, the journal *Analysis* began a popular competition in which editors would pose philosophical puzzles and readers would send in proposed solutions. Winning essays were published in subsequent issues, along with a report from the editor. One of the most memorable entries in the series came from Jonathan Harrison, whose question concerned the following story:[1]

Jocasta Jones was walking in a secluded part of a local wood when she was attracted by the barking of her dog to a metal object which looked for all the world like an extremely old and rusty deep freeze. She opened it and found inside a man, alive, but frozen solid. With some help from [Jocasta] the man, who called himself Dum, thawed out. He handed [Jocasta] a book, which he said told one how to build a time machine and a deep freeze.

[Jocasta]...fell deeply in love with Dum, and married him. After a decent interval they produced a baby whom, because he was the spitten image of his father, they forenamed Dee.

When Dee reached maturity, he found the book, which had carefully been put away on a high shelf, out of the reach of children. Following the instructions in it, he built the machine and got inside, taking his father and the book with him, in case he should need some technical assistance on his journey. He pressed the starter button, and, though nothing unusual appeared to happen inside the machine, everything visible through its solitary porthole seemed to start moving in the opposite direction to what it had before, and much more rapidly. The sun rose in the West, and set in the East, backward day succeeded backward day, and reverse year followed upon reverse year. The journey was so long that Dee, who had underestimated the amount of food they would need, was reluctantly compelled to make use of his greater youth and strength in order to kill and eat Dum. Eventually Dee arrived at the date which was his preselected destination, and got out...

---

[1] The basic elements of Harrison's story can be found in many earlier works of science fiction, including Dee (1954), Gerrold (1973), and Heinlein (1959). Harrison's story would also go on to inspire other works of this kind, including the first (and only) piece of Doctor Who fan fiction to be published in an academic philosophy journal—see MacBeath (1982).

Dee, however, had not been happy in his new environment. The guilt he felt for what he...had done produced a mild attack of paranoia...which even changing his name to Dum could not eradicate...To escape he built the deep freeze, and got inside. He was prudent enough to take with him the book, in case he needed to build himself another time machine or deep freeze at an earlier or later date.

The next thing Dum remembered was being resuscitated by...Jocasta Jones, who had been exercising her dog in the neighbourhood...(1979: 65).[2]

Harrison's story raises a number of interesting issues,[3] but its most distinctive feature is its use of *causal loops*. These loops—and the paradoxes they engender—are the subject matter of this chapter.

1. Preliminaries

The causal paradoxes of time travel revolve around two related concepts: causal loops and backward causation. This section introduces these ideas in a preliminary way.

1.1 Causal loops

A causal loop is a sequence of events in which each member is a cause of its successor, and where the final member is a cause of the first.[4] More carefully:

A series of events, $<e_1, e_2, e_3 \ldots e_n>$, is a *causal loop* $=_{df}$ (i) e_1 is a cause of e_2, which is a cause of e_3, which is a cause of $\ldots e_n$ and (ii) e_n is a cause of e_1.[5]

For example, in Harrison's story (Figure 5.1), Dee's birth (①) is a cause of his trip (④), which leads to his encounter with Jocasta (⑤), which ultimately results in his birth (①). In the same way, his discovery of the book (②), leads to the creation of the time machine (③), which takes the book into the past (⑤) so it can be discovered by Dee (②).

---

[2] Students of Greek mythology will recall that Jocasta was both the mother and wife of Oedipus. 'Dee' and 'Dum' are presumably allusions to Tweedledee and Tweedledum.

[3] For discussion of these issues, see Denruyter (1980), Godfrey-Smith (1980), Harrison (1980), and Levin (1980). One of the most interesting worries raised by these replies concerns the DNA of Dee:

> Dee is the son of Dum and Jocasta. So Dee obtained half his genes from Dum and half from Jocasta. But Dum is diachronically identical with Dee, and is therefore genotypically identical with him (i.e. himself). That is, Dee is both genotypically identical with and distinct from Dum, which is absurd. (Godfrey-Smith 1980: 72)

Versions of this objection have been suggested by several different authors—see, for example, Nahin (1999: 320), Romero and Torres (2001), and Schulman (1971). But the objection is actually unsound. The problem is that it assumes Dee cannot be genotypically identical to Dum if he receives half of his genetic material from Jocasta. This is incorrect. Dee *can* be genotypically identical to Dum, provided that (i) Jocasta shares at least half of her genetic material with Dee and (ii) Jocasta and Dum contribute *exactly* the right halves to Dee. As Grey (1999: 67–8), Hanley (2004: 140), and Richmond (2001: 310) point out, this result would be extremely unlikely, but it would not be impossible.

[4] Other characterizations of causal loops are possible. See, for example, the comments in Ehring (1986).

[5] We will understand a *series* to be any ordered set of events, with no requirement for numerical distinctness. So, if self-causation is possible, and e is a self-caused event, then the ordered pair $<e, e>$ will count as a causal loop. We will return to this issue in section 3.

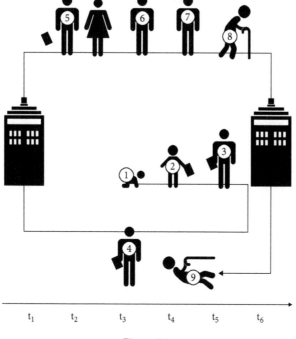

Figure 5.1

These kinds of loops are a popular plot device in many time travel stories.[6] But they have also created a great deal of confusion on the part of readers.[7] For this reason, it is best to begin with a few points of clarification.

First, it is sometimes said that causal loops are, in some sense, "cut off" from the outside world.[8] In the *Star Trek* series, for example, individuals caught in a causal loop are said to inhabit an "independent fragment of time."[9] It is unclear what to make of this claim, but the important point is that causal loops do not *require* any kind of separation. In Harrison's story, for example, Jocasta has many experiences before her encounter with Dee. Those experiences presumably play a role in their relationship, even though they were not part of the loop. In the same way, Dee's life will presumably have effects on the people and places around him, and those effects will carry on long after the loop is gone. So, there are many different ways in which the loop is "connected" to the outside world. The same thing will presumably be true for many other loops as well.

---

[6] For a survey of the literature, see Nahin (1999: 304–23).

[7] For a survey of these errors, see Hanley (2004).

[8] This is what Monton (2009: 54) would call a *closed* causal loop—namely a causal loop in which none of the events have any causes or effects outside of the series.

[9] The most famous example of this can be found in the classic episode "Cause and Effect" (*The Next Generation*, Season 5, Episode 18).

Second, it is sometimes said that causal loops involve the same events happening over and over again. Indeed, it is sometimes suggested that causal loops repeat *endlessly*, so that the same events will happen an infinite number of times. Consider, for example, Samuel Mines's story, "Find the Sculptor."[10] In that story, we are told of a scientist who travels five hundred years into the future and, upon arrival, finds a statue that commemorates his journey. The traveler takes the statue back with him to the past, where he tragically dies upon arrival. As a memorial, the statue is erected in his honor, right where he found it in the future. Mines's story then ends by looking ahead five hundred years...

Suddenly a strange machine will come out of the past and he will be here again—although he is dead and has been dead five hundred years. [He will take the statue] and go back to the past... to die. And once again that maddening cycle will begin, to go on and on forever as long as time spins its threads.   (1946: 120)

The last line of this passage is obviously the key. What does it mean to say that the maddening cycle will "go on forever"? If the claim is that the cycle will go on forever in *external* time, it is simply mistaken.[11] From the external perspective, the time traveler departs from the past, appears from the future, and dies; then, five hundred years later, he arrives from the past, collects the statue, and departs. That is all there is to the story, externally speaking, so the cycle does not go on forever in external time. Perhaps the claim is that the cycle repeats forever from the traveler's perspective? That too would be a mistake. From the perspective of the time traveler, he departs from the past, arrives in the future, and collects the statue; he then departs from the future, arrives in the past, and dies. Since the traveler is dead, his story is done. In other words, the cycle does not repeat in his personal time.[12]

But now consider the situation from the statue's perspective. If the statue were to recount its tale, the story would go like this:

I was discovered by a time traveler, taken back in time, and erected in his honor. Then, after five hundred years, I was discovered by a time traveler, taken back in time, and erected in his honor. Then, after five hundred years, I was discovered by a time traveler, taken back in time, and erected in his honor. Then, after five hundred years,...

Of course this way of putting things is a bit misleading, since it incorrectly suggests that there is a starting point to the story. But the important point is that there is no *end* to the story. From the statue's perspective, there will always be a next event in the

---

[10] For other examples from the science fiction literature, see Dick (1977), Fast (1959), and Piper (1983).

[11] Recall from Chapter 1 that "external time" refers to real time, whereas "personal time" refers to an ordering and metric of events that matches the relevant causal facts (in this case, the facts about how the relevant person-stages relate).

[12] Of course, some time travelers experience the same event twice over, but this will always be from different perspectives. In Harrison's story, for example, Dee experiences the same murder twice, but he plays a very different role on each occasion. For this reason, it would be misleading to say that these events "repeat" for the character.

series. In this sense, the loop will "go on forever." But, crucially, this is only the case relative to the statue's personal time. Since personal time is not *real* time, the series will not really go on forever. More generally, the events in a causal loop will not really. repeat themselves.

A different kind of confusion about causal loops concerns the relationship between causal loops and backward causation.[13] First, it is sometimes said that every case of backward time travel would result in the creation of a causal loop. For example, Hugh Mellor famously argues against backward time travel by trying to rule out "the causal…loops that cyclical time and backward time travel need" (1998: 131).[14] But this seems like a mistake. After all, it seems possible—at least *metaphysically* possible[15]— for an object to travel discontinuously into the past and to appear inside an impenetrable black box (a box which blocks all outward causal signals). This would give us a case of backward causation without creating any causal loops.[16]

Second, it is sometimes said that causal loops cannot occur without backward time travel—or at least not without backward causation. David Lewis, for example, says that causal loops require "some of the causal links [to be] normal in direction and others [to be] reversed" (1976: 148).[17] But this also seems like a mistake. In a curved spacetime, for example, it is possible for there to be causal loops in which each member of the series comes after its predecessor, and where the last member of the series comes before the first. However, it is arguable that this kind of loop would not involve backward causation.[18] Moreover, if simultaneous causation is possible, one could have a causal loop in which all of the events occurred at the very same time. In that case, none of the links would run in reverse.[19]

So, it seems possible for there to be backward causation without causal loops, and for there to be causal loops without backward causation. That being said, all of the loops in this chapter will involve backward causation, since all of them involve backward time

---

[13] We will take backward causation to involve an effect preceding its cause. An alternative definition would take backward causation to be a causal relationship that goes against the normal order of causation. As Weir (1988: 204–5) points out, these two conceptions can come apart in a closed time world (i.e. a world with "circular" time). In that kind of world, every effect would come before (as well as after) its cause, but none of the causal relationships would need to be abnormal (relative to the other relationships in that world).

[14] Mellor's thesis is (tentatively) endorsed by MacBeath (1982: 428). Faye (2010) endorses the related thesis that backward time travel entails causal loops (although Faye also claims that backward time travel does not require backward causation). We will examine Mellor's argument against casual loops in section 5 of this chapter.

[15] Whether or not this kind of case is physically possible is less clear. See Hanley (2004), Monton (2009), and Riggs (1991).

[16] Related points are made by Riggs (1991: 78–9) and Tooley (1997: 63–70).

[17] He is less committal about the converse: "Perhaps there must be loops if there is reversal: I am not sure."

[18] This point is made by Hanley (2004). Whether or not this counts as a case of backward causation will depend, in part, on whether or not causation is transitive. We will return to this issue in section 2.

[19] As Hanley (2004: 125) points out, this issue may be partly terminological. If Lewis, for example, is simply *defining* a causal loop as a closed causal chain *in which some links run in reverse*, then it will be trivially true that causal loops (in that sense) imply backward causation.

travel (and since backward time travel requires backward causation[20]). This, however, raises an immediate worry, since many philosophers have argued that backward causation is impossible.[21] Given the importance of this issue, some of these arguments should be addressed before moving on.

1.2 Backward causation

Many different arguments against backward causation have been given.[22] We cannot hope to address all of them, but we can comment on some of the most common.

One of the most common arguments against backward causation is based on a suggestion by David Hume.[23] Hume famously claimed that, "we may define a cause to be an object, followed by another... where all the objects similar to the first are followed by objects similar to the second" (1777/1975: 77). If this definition were correct, then every cause would have to precede its effect, in which case backward causation would be impossible.

The main problem with this argument is that Hume's definition is not very plausible.[24] As is well known, his definition suffers from a number of serious flaws, including the problems of irrelevant and imperfect regularities.[25] And even if we set those worries aside, it seems as if the defender of backward causation can simply run the above argument in reverse: Backward causation is possible, and backward causation is incompatible with Hume's definition, so Hume's definition is mistaken. Either way, the defender of backward causation should not be moved by the definitional objection.[26]

Another common argument against backward causation is based on the causal theory of time.[27] In its simplest form, the causal theory says that the direction of time is grounded in the potential for causation—for one event to precede another in time is for it to be a potential cause of the second. If this theory were correct, then backward causation would be immediately ruled out.

The problem with this argument is that it seems to beg the question against the possibility of backward causation. After all, it is widely known that the causal theory can be modified so as to allow for backward causation (by, for example, saying that the

---

[20] See the discussion of backward time travel in Chapter 1, section 2. Again, one could argue that backward time travel in a curved spacetime would not require "real" backward causation. (See fn. 18 and section 2.)

[21] In the scientific literature, this thesis—that causes must precede their effects—is sometimes referred to as "The Causality Principle". See, for example, Everett and Roman (2012: 84).

[22] The literature on this issue is voluminous. For a general overview of the debate, see Tooley (1997: Chapter 3).

[23] This argument is suggested by Flew (1956: 109) and Gale (1965: 209).

[24] It is unclear how seriously Hume took his own definition. Indeed, it is unclear how to interpret many of the things Hume says about causation. For an introduction to some of these issues, see Dauer (2008).

[25] See, for example, Lewis (1986b), Mackie (1974: Chapter 3), and Psillos (2009).

[26] In section 6, we will consider a different definitional objection based on the counterfactual theory of causation. This version is more interesting, since the counterfactual theory is more plausible.

[27] This argument is given, for example, by Mellor (1998: 126). On the causal theory of time, see Grünbaum (1963), Reichenbach (1956), and van Fraassen (1970).

direction of time is determined by the *typical* direction of causation).[28] So, the main motivation for sticking with the original causal theory would seem to be an antecedent opposition to backward causation.[29]

A third argument against backward causation is based on the immutability of the past. This argument goes as follows. Causation always involves bringing about some kind of change. For example, when one causes an object to move, one brings about a change in its position. But this means that backward causation would always involve bringing about a change in the past. Since it is impossible to change the past, it is impossible for there to be backward causation.[30]

The problem with this argument is that it conflates the distinction between *changing the past* and *bringing about a change* in *the past*.[31] In order to bring about a change *in* the past, one would simply have to bring about a past event. In other words, one would have to bring about a case of backward causation. In order to *change* the past, on the other hand, one would have to alter the truth-value of a past-tensed statement, either by bringing about an event that did *not* occur or by preventing one that *did*. It may be impossible to change the past in this sense, but that is not an objection to backward causation since backward causation does not require that kind of change.[32] In Harrison's story, for example, Dee successfully brings about a past event (his own birth) without changing the truth-value of any past-tensed statement (in Harrison's story, it was always the case that Dee was born at the relevant time). So, it is possible to bring about a past event—and thus bring about a case of backward causation—without changing the past.

A fourth argument against backward causation is related to the third. Even if backward causation does not *entail* changing the past, it does seem to *allow* for it. And the mere possibility of past-alteration is enough to get us in trouble. In Harrison's story, for example, it seems clear that Dum could kill the infant Dee (since he has both the means and the opportunity). But it also seems clear that he cannot (since Dee is his younger self). Since this combination of claims is contradictory, backward causation is proved impossible.

The problem with this argument is that it simply repeats the retrosuicide paradox from Chapter 4. Since it does not add anything new to the earlier argument, it does not create any new problems for backward causation.

A fifth argument—the "bilking" argument[33]—tries to improve upon the traditional paradox of self-defeat by introducing an epistemic twist. To begin, suppose that someone

---

[28] This is suggested by Lewis (1976: 148; and 1986c: especially 35 and 50–1). See also Frisch (2013), Mellor (1981: 157), and Roache (2009).

[29] It should also be noted that there are various theories of time's direction that have nothing to do with causation at all. For a survey of these accounts, see Frisch (2013).

[30] A version of this argument is given by Flew (1973: 366).

[31] This parallels the traditional distinction between *affecting* and *altering* the past. See Chapter 3, section 2.

[32] See, again, Chapter 3, section 2.

[33] Versions of this argument are given by Black (1956), Dummett (1964), Flew (1954, 1956), and Mellor (1981: Chapter 10). Note that the "bilking paradox" sometimes refers to any case of past-alteration. See Horwich (1987: 220).

claims that events of type L cause earlier events of type E. In that case, we would be in a position to test this hypothesis. First, we wait until we observe an event of type E. Then, we identify the time and place of the supposed future cause. Finally, we attempt to prevent the relevant L-type event. For example, Black (1956: 54–5) imagines a case of a supposed clairvoyant—"Houdini"—who claims that his present visions (and hence predictions) are caused by the outcomes of future events. Black claims that we could then test this claim by having Houdini predict a series of coin tosses. Having heard his predictions, we can then set out to falsify them (by, for example, using a two-headed coin, etc.). Suppose that we succeed in our attempt. In that case, we will have debunked the supposed clairvoyant by undermining the claim of backward causation. Suppose instead that our attempts are regularly frustrated, and that we end up observing a strong correlation between the predictions and the outcomes. In that case, the objector says, we will have evidence of a causal link between the two, but there is no reason to think that it is the outcomes that cause the predictions. Indeed, Black goes so far as to say that, "we shall have to say that Houdini's answer exerts a causal influence of an esoteric sort upon the subsequent toss of the coin" (1956: 54). This conclusion seems clearly overstated, but one might think that a more cautious conclusion is warranted: In the imagined scenario, we would have evidence of a causal link, but the hypothesis that the predictions somehow cause the outcomes is at least as plausible as the hypothesis that the outcomes cause the predictions. So, however the tests turn out, we will not have any reason to believe in backward causation.

One problem with this argument is that it does not show that backward causation is impossible. At best, it shows that we could never have a good reason to believe in backward causation. These are clearly two different things.[34] However, it is unclear whether the argument even establishes this weaker conclusion. The problem is that it is unclear why the hypothesis that E-events cause L-events should always be "at least as plausible" as the opposing hypothesis.[35] On one hand, it seems possible to have independent evidence that E-events do not cause L-events. On the other hand, it seems possible to have independent evidence that L-events *do* cause E-events. To take just one example: Suppose that Dee builds a time machine and conducts the following test. Every morning for a year, he gets into the machine, sets the controls for one minute in the future, and turns it on. Suppose that, on each occasion, Dee and his machine disappear and then, one minute later, reappear. Presumably, this would be evidence that the machine works—that is, that the settings on the machine when it is turned on are a cause of Dee's appearance at the corresponding time. Suppose now that Dee gets into his

---

[34] Unfortunately, these two things are often run together in the literature. Swinburne, for example, says that, "I shall argue that no change in the evidence could possibly substantiate the claim that someone had affected the past, and hence that affecting the past is not logically possible" (1966: 344). In fact, Swinburne says that we cannot even "give meaning" to the claim that someone has affected the past since we could never have evidence for this claim. Similar suggestions are made by Black (1956: 54–5), Mellor (1981: 138), and others.

[35] For discussion on this point, see Roache (2009).

machine, sets the controls for fifty years in the past, and turns it on. Suppose further that he disappears and that historical records confirm that a man resembling Dee (but going by the name 'Dum') appeared in the past at the specified place and time. Presumably, this would be evidence that the time machine has worked again. In other words, it would be evidence of backward causation.[36]

A sixth and final argument against backward causation is based on the idea that causes are "effective means" for bringing about their effects—very roughly, to say that one event causes another is to say that we can bring about an event of the second kind by bringing about an event of the first.[37] Now, suppose for the sake of argument that someone claims that events of an earlier kind, E, are caused by events of a later kind, L. Next, suppose that an event of type E has already occurred. In that case, bringing about an L-type event would not be an effective means of *bringing* about an E-type event, since the relevant event has already been *brought* about. Suppose instead that an event of kind E has *not* occurred in the past. In that case, bringing about an L-type event would not be an effective means of bringing about an E-type event (since we have already assumed that an E-type event did not occur). So, either way, there cannot be effective means of bringing about past events. In other words, there cannot be cases of backward causation.[38]

The problem with this argument is that both of its key premises can be challenged.[39] First, suppose an E-type event has already occurred in the past. Why think we can no longer do something to bring that event about? Of course, we cannot do anything to bring that event about *in the future*—that is, we cannot cause that event to occur at a later time, since it has already occurred in the past. But the question is whether we can do something in the future—namely, bring about an L-type event—that will have brought about the relevant past event. And that seems perfectly coherent. Suppose, for example, that we bring about an L-type event. And suppose that the relevant E-type event would not have occurred if we hadn't brought about the L-type event. In that case, it seems as if bringing about the later event was an effective means of bringing about the earlier one.

Second, suppose instead that an E-type event has not occurred in the past. In that case, we can suppose that it is physically impossible to bring about a corresponding L-type event now. (That is, it is physically impossible to bring about an L-type event at the current time without there being a corresponding E-type event in the past.) But why think it follows that L-type events are not effective means of bringing about E-type events? After all, it might still be the case that an E-type event *would have* occurred if an L-type event *had been* brought about. And, in that case, bringing about

---

[36] For further criticism and discussion of the bilking paradox, see Carroll et al. (2014: Chapters 1 and 2), Dwyer (1978: 29–30), Garrett (2014b, 2015), Price (1984), Rea (2014: Chapter 3), Riggs (1991), Roache (2009), and Scriven (1956).

[37] This is one way of stating a "manipulability" theory of causation. For an overview of this approach, see Woodward (2008).

[38] This kind of argument is suggested by Black (1956: 58), Dummett (1954: 27), and Flew (1954: 57–8). See also the discussion in Pears (1957).

[39] See Tooley (1997: 49–52). Some of the same points are made by Chisholm and Taylor (1960).

an *L*-type event would seem to be an effective means of bringing about an *E*-type event. In other words, it would seem to be an effective means of bringing about a case of backward causation.

If all of the foregoing is correct, we should not be moved by any of the traditional arguments against backward causation. More carefully, we should not be moved by any of the *direct* arguments against backward causation. However, backward causation also provides for the possibility of causal loops, and causal loops are often thought to create special kinds of problems. In this way, causal loops might be thought to raise an indirect argument against backward causation and, ultimately, backward time travel. Those arguments will be the focus of this chapter.

2. The Bootstrapping Paradox

One of the most striking features of causal loops is that they seem to allow for self-causation. For example, in Harrison's story, Dum is the father of Dee, but he is also identical to Dee. So, Dum is his own father.[40]

What goes for persons also goes for events. Consider, for example, the episode in *Harry Potter and the Prisoner of Azkaban* when Harry is attacked by a pack of dementors and saved at the last moment by a shadowy figure who casts a powerful Patronus charm. Later on in the story, Harry travels back in time and witnesses his earlier self being attacked by the same dementors. He soon realizes that *he* was the shadowy figure from his past, and this realization gives him the confidence to perform the difficult defensive spell. As Harry later explains, "I knew I could do it this time, because I'd already done it" (Rowling 1999: 412).[41] If this is correct, then it seems as if the casting of the spell is a cause of itself. More generally, it seems as if the possibility of causal loops would imply the possibility of self-causation.[42]

The problem is that many philosophers have claimed that self-causation is impossible.[43] Clement Dore, for example, claims that, "nothing can be the cause of its own existence" (1984: 51). Anthony O'Hear asserts that, "Self-causation is…nonsense" (1984: 122). And Morris and Menzel declare that, "self-causation…is almost universally characterized as absurd, incoherent, or worse" (1986: 359).

If these philosophers are correct, then we have a simple argument against the possibility of backward time travel:

(P1)   If backward time travel were possible, then backward causation would be possible.

(P2)   If backward causation were possible, then causal loops would be possible.

---

[40] He is also the father of his father, and the father of his father's father, and so on.

[41] "Does that make sense?," he asks Hermione.

[42] In the physics literature, self-caused objects like this are sometimes referred to as "jinn" after the Arabian spirits who are capable of appearing out of nowhere. See, for example, Lossev and Novikov (1992).

[43] This tradition goes back at least to Aquinas, who claimed that, "There is no case known (neither is it, indeed possible) in which a thing is found to be the efficient cause of itself" (*Summa Theologica* I q. 2 a. 3).

(P3)   If causal loops were possible, then self-causation would be possible.

(P4)   Self-causation is impossible.

(C)   Backward time travel is impossible.

Following Heinlein (1941), we will refer to this argument as *the bootstrapping paradox*.[44]

We have already granted the first premise of this paradox in giving our definition of (backward) time travel: In order for an arrival in the past to count as an arrival from the future, that arrival must be caused, in the right sort of way, by a future departure. In general, backward time travel requires reverse causal dependence. The second premise of the argument also seems reasonable. If a future event brings about a past event, then that second event could, in principle, cause the first. The most plausible targets in the argument are therefore (P3) and (P4).

Let's begin with (P3). One reason to think that this premise is true is the transitivity of causation.[45] Suppose that $<e_1, e_2>$ is a causal loop and that the following form of inference is valid:

x is a cause of y.

y is a cause of z.

So, x is a cause of z.

In that case, it will immediately follow that e_1 is a cause of e_1. So, if causal loops are possible, it is possible for there to be self-caused events.

One response to this argument would be to deny the transitivity of causation.[46] Many take this response to be independently motivated, since there are apparent counterexamples to that principle. Suppose, for example, that A and B each have a switch that can be flipped to the left or the right. If both switches are flipped in the same direction, a third person—C—will receive a shock. A sees that B's switch is currently flipped to the left and so (wanting to protect C) flips her switch to the right. B, however, sees this and (wanting to shock C) flips *her* switch to the right. As a result, C is shocked. Here is the problem. A's flip was a cause B's flip and B's flip was a cause of C's shock. So, by transitivity, A's flip was a cause of C's shock. But this seems wrong. After all, A's flip was intended to *prevent* C's shock.[47]

Obviously, there are many things one might say about this kind of case.[48] But we should note that (P3) might be plausible, even if transitivity fails. Take, for example, the case of Harry Potter and the Patronus charm. In that case, the success of Harry's

[44] The name comes from the title of Heinlein's novella, "By his Bootstraps." The term is also used in Faye (2010), Krasnikov (2002), and Visser (1995). For discussion of the bootstrapping paradox, see Airaksinen (1980: 116–17), Al-Khalili (1999: 180–4), Callender and Edney (2004: 70–5), Davies (2001: 102–5), Dummett (1986: 155–7), Fulmer (1980: 154–5), Gott (2001: 20–4), Hanley (1997: 218–23), Lewis (1976: 146), MacBeath (1982: 418–19, 427–8), Richmond (2001: 310–11), Riggs (1997: 58–64), and Romero and Torres (2001).

[45] This argument is mentioned by Berkovitz (2001: 2) and Nahin (1999: 189), among others.

[46] See Hall (2000), Hitchcock (1997), and McDermott (1995).

[47] This example is given by McDermott (1995).   [48] See, for example, Lewis (2000: section IX).

spell is largely due to the fact that Harry already saw it happen. Moreover, Harry already saw it happen because the spell was successful. So, one might think that the success of the spell is a cause of itself. And one might think that this is the case even if transitivity is false.

This brings us to (P4), and the claim that self-causation is impossible.

One might try to motivate this claim by appealing to a particular theory of causation. Consider, for example, the counterfactual theory defended by David Lewis:

(CT)   For any events c and e, c is a cause of e only if, and in that case because, (i) c and e are distinct events and (ii) there is a causal chain leading from c to e. (1973: 563)

(Here, a causal chain is a series of events in which each member would not have occurred without its predecessor. For example, <Dee's birth, Dee's discovery, Dee's birth> is a causal chain since Dee wouldn't have been born if he hadn't discovered the book, and he wouldn't have discovered the book if he hadn't been born.) We will discuss (CT) in more detail in section 6 of this chapter. For now, the important point is that this account directly rules out self-causation, since it explicitly requires c and e to be distinct events. In this way, the counterfactual theory could be used to support (P4).

The problem with this argument is that it is guilty of circularity. After all, the only reason for including a condition like (i) in the analysis is to rule out cases of self-causation.[49] But, in that case, one cannot turn around and use this principle to argue against the possibility of self-caused events.[50]

Of course, one might think that self-causation is intuitively implausible, even if one lacks an independent argument against it. However, it is important at this point to distinguish between *direct* and *indirect* causation. To say that c is an indirect cause of e is to say that there is some distinct event, d, such that c is a cause of d and d is a cause of e. A direct cause, in contrast, is simply a cause that is not indirect. Given this distinction, the defender of causal loops can say that there is *a sense* in which self-causation is impossible—it is impossible for any event to cause itself *directly*. That kind of self-causation *would* be strange, since it would be like the case of the man who tries to pick himself up, directly, by his own bootstraps. But there is no reason to think that this kind of causation is required by backward time travel.

In fact, the distinction between direct and indirect causation helps to bring out a certain irony in the name of the bootstrapping paradox. This name is obviously an allusion to the hypothetical "self-made man" who picks himself up by his own bootstraps. When one tries to imagine this scenario, one naturally pictures a man putting boots on his own feet, reaching directly down, and pulling up on the straps. This way

---

[49]   That, at least, seems to have been Lewis's motivation.

[50]   One might worry that, if condition (i) were dropped from (CT), every event would turn out to be a cause of itself. Fortunately, this is not the case. Lewis builds a requirement for distinctness into the definition of a causal chain by building it into the notion of causal dependence. As it turns out, this allows the counterfactual theorist to accept some kinds of self-causation—like in the cases of Dee and Harry Potter—without thinking that every event is a cause of itself.

of trying to pick yourself up is sure to fail. So, it is tempting to think that this task is impossible.

But this line of reasoning involves a failure of imagination. In order to picture a successful case of bootstrapping, one just has to imagine the following:

Step 1:   Build a time machine and travel back to the days of your youth.
Step 2:   Put your younger (and much lighter) self in a pair of boots.
Step 3:   Pull him or her up.

This kind of bootstrapping is not impossible. In fact, this kind of bootstrapping is almost *guaranteed* to work (provided that your younger self is willing to cooperate).

The important point is that literal bootstrapping only seems impossible when we ignore the option of time travel. The exact same thing is true in the case of figurative bootstrapping. When we try to imagine an event causing itself, we naturally try to picture a case of direct self-causation—that is, we try to picture an event that occurs and, at the same time, brings itself into existence. This is difficult to do. But that is not the right way to think about things. The right way to picture self-causation is to imagine a backward time travel scenario like the one involving Dee and Dum. And that kind of scenario is easy to imagine, since it involves a case of indirect causation.

To put the point the other way around: Self-causation only seems impossible if we ignore the option of time travel. But, in that case, the intuitive impossibility of self-causation cannot be used to rule out the possibility of time travel. This would be to argue in circles.[51]

3. The *Ex Nihilo* Paradox

In the 1980 film *Somewhere in Time*, a young man (played by Christopher Reeve) is approached by an older woman (played by Jane Seymour).[52] The mysterious woman gives the young man an antique watch, which he places in his pocket. Later, the young man travels back to 1912 (via self-hypnosis!) and gives the watch to a young woman with whom he has fallen in love.[53] Unfortunately, the young man is suddenly taken back to the future[54] and the young woman is left with nothing but the watch for a keepsake (a keepsake that she carries with her for many years until, one day, she sees a young man who looks exactly like her long-lost love...).

---

[51] For a related point, see Fulmer (1983: 32–3).

[52] The film is based on Richard Matheson's 1975 novel, *Bid Time Return*.

[53] Hypnosis is quite possibly the silliest method of time-travel ever suggested. Interestingly, one of the other leading candidates for this distinction also involves Christopher Reeve. In *Superman: The Movie*, Reeve turns back time by briefly reversing the direction of Earth's rotation.

[54] In the film, Reeve inadvertently pulls a 1979 penny out of his pocket, and sees the date. This breaks his (self-induced) hypnotic state, which throws him back into his own time.

The watch in this story is an example of *an object loop*.[55] If we think of an object as being composed of different stages at different times,[56] and we let the 'C-relation' name the special causal relation that makes for identity over time,[57] we can characterize an object loop as a series of object-stages in which each is C-related to its successor, and where the last stage is C-related to the first:

A series of stages, $<s_1, s_2, s_3 \ldots s_n>$, is an *object loop* $=_{df}$ (i) s_1 is C-related to s_2, which is C-related to s_3, which is C-related to $\ldots s_n$ and (ii) s_n is C-related to s_1.

These kinds of objects raise a number of difficult questions. The most obvious question is this: *Where do these objects come from?* In the case of the watch, for example, we can assume that the object is always in the hands of one of the characters—Seymour gives the watch to Reeve, who holds on to it until he gives it to Seymour, who holds on to it until she gives it to Reeve, etc. One naturally wants to ask: How did this whole process get started? Where did the watch come from?

There are actually several different questions here that need to be distinguished. First, there is the question of where the watch came from *most recently*. That question has a perfectly good answer at each point in the story. For example, if we ask Christopher Reeve (in 1980) where he got the watch, he can truthfully say that it was given to him by a mysterious old woman. And if we ask Jane Seymour (in 1912) where she got the watch, she can truthfully say that it was given to her by a mysterious young man. More generally, for each point in the story there is a local explanation for how the watch got to be where it is then.

Second, there is the question of where the watch came from *in the first place*. This way of putting the question is actually ambiguous, since "the first place" could mean "the first time the watch existed, according to external time" or "the first time the watch existed, according to its personal time." On the external reading, the question has a straightforward answer. The watch first shows up in 1912 when Christopher Reeve appears from the future, and the watch—like Reeve—*came from the future*. That's how it got to be there in the first place, externally speaking. On the personal reading, the question has no answer since it carries a false presupposition—namely, that *there is* a first time in the watch's personal history. There is no such time, so there is no question about how the watch got *there*.[58]

The same point applies to the question of who made the watch. We have assumed that the object is always in the hands of either Reeve or Seymour. Yet neither of these individuals creates the watch. So, this is a case of a watch with no watchmaker.[59]

---

[55] These kinds of loops are discussed by Hanley (2004), MacBeath (1982), and Nerlich (1981).

[56] See Chapter 2, section 2.   [57] See Chapter 1, section 1.

[58] In this respect, the watch is like the earlier example of the statue in "Find the Sculptor."

[59] Note that it is possible to tell a *Somewhere*-style tale in which the watch has a watchmaker. One way to do this would be to invoke the branching timeline model from Chapter 3. On the original branch (Branch no. 1), Seymour does not have a watch and is not visited by Reeve. Years later, Reeve buys a watch from a watchmaker and takes it back in time with him, thus ending up on an alternative branch. On that branch (Branch no. 2) Seymour receives the watch from Reeve, holds on to it until she sees him in the future,

What goes for object loops also goes for causal loops and the events of which they are made. Here it will help to focus on a simple example. Suppose there are two kinds of neurons, which can be represented as circles and squares (see Figure 5.2). Suppose also that neurons are connected by stimulatory axons, and that neuron-firings follow the arrows of axons in a perfectly law-like manner. Finally, suppose that the pattern of firings differs between the two kinds of neurons—circle-firings cause attached neurons to fire one unit later in time, whereas square-firings cause attached neurons to fire one unit *earlier* in time (in other words, square-neurons are backward causers). Now suppose that a circle-neuron and a square-neuron are interconnected, as in Figure 5.2.

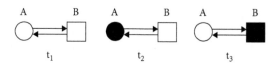

Figure 5.2

In this case A fires at t_2, which causes B to fire at t_3, which causes A to fire at t_2. Each event in the series has a cause, but what about the series itself?[60] Normally, we explain a causal series by explaining each member of the series. For example, we might explain why a series of dominoes tipped over by noting that the last domino (the one-hundredth, say) was knocked over by the ninety-ninth, which was knocked over by the ninety-eighth, which was…knocked over by the person who set up the dominoes in the first place. However, this kind of explanation inevitably appeals to something that lies outside the relevant series (e.g. the person who set up the series of dominoes). In the case of the neurons, this does not seem possible—the firing of A and the firing of B are both parts of the series to be explained, and there are no other firings to explain why that series of events takes place. So, we seem to have an example of a causal loop without a cause.

It is sometimes suggested that *all* causal loops lack causes in this way—that loops are, by their very nature, inexplicable.[61] But this seems too strong. Consider, for example, a variant on the neuron case in which a separate circle-neuron is connected to A, and fires at t_1. (See Figure 5.3 on the next page.)

In this case, the firing of A is causally overdetermined—it is caused by both the firing of B at t_3 and the firing of C at t_1. This latter fact allows us to explain the causal loop <A's firing, B's firing> in the exact same way that we explain a series of dominoes tipping over: The firing of B is caused by the firing of A, which is caused by the firing of C.

and then gives it back to him. He then takes it back with him into the past (ending up on Branch no. 3) and gives it to Seymour. And so on.

[60] Here, we can think of the "series" as a compound event: *the firing of both neurons.*

[61] Lewis (1976: 148–9) can be read as suggesting this, for example, although his official position is unclear.

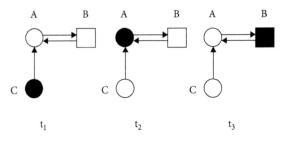

Figure 5.3

Since the firing of C is an antecedent event that lies outside the relevant series, we have a perfectly ordinary explanation of a peculiar causal loop.

Still, the fact is that many causal loops will lack this kind of explanation. This makes many people uneasy. David Lewis, for example, says that inexplicable loops are "Strange."[62] Franz Kiekeben (2008) deems them "disturbing." And William Grey (1999) calls them "queer customers." In fact, many philosophers have claimed that it is impossible for there to be uncaused entities of *any* kind, in which case there could not be uncaused causal loops.[63] If correct, this would suggest the following argument against backward time travel:

(P1)   If backward time travel were possible, then backward causation would be possible.

(P2)   If backward causation were possible, then causal loops would be possible.

(P3)   If causal loops were possible, then uncaused events would be possible.

(P4)   Uncaused events are impossible.

(C)   Backward time travel is impossible.

We will refer to this argument as *the* ex nihilo *paradox*, since the key premise—(P4)—rests upon the view that nothing comes from nothing (*ex nihilo, nihil fit*).[64]

The idea that everything must come from something has had many defenders throughout history. But it is not exactly clear what this idea amounts to. The most straightforward reading would be the following:

(P4*)   Necessarily, every event has a cause.

However, this way of putting the principle does *not* rule out loops like the one involving the neurons. The problem is that the loop in question has at least *some* causes, even if they are not the kinds of causes that we would normally cite. For example, if A and B

[62] "Strange!" he says, "But not impossible, and not too different from inexplicabilities we are already inured to" (1976: 149). See below for more on this point.

[63] For example, in discussing the idea that something could come from nothing, William Lane Craig (2002) complains that, "only academics could be so ridiculous. If made seriously outside the seminar room such claims would be evidence of clinical derangement."

[64] This thesis is sometimes referred to as the "Causal Principle" (Craig 1979) or the "Causal Law" (Warnock 1953). It is also closely related to the principle of sufficient reason, on at least some formulations of that principle. See Pruss (2010).

had not existed, or had not been connected by the stimulatory axons, then there would not have been any causation between them. So, it is natural to think that the existence of A and B, and the presence of the stimulatory axons, are causes of the loop.[65] But, in that case, the existence of the loop would be compatible with the principle in question.

Of course, even if the existence of A and B is a cause of the loop, that event (or state of affairs) is not *sufficient* for the series, since one could have both A and B, and all the stimulatory axons, without any neurons firing. In fact, one could have had the *entire* state of the world at t_1 *and* all the laws of nature, and *still* not have had the relevant loop.[66] Hence, this kind of loop could be excluded by strengthening (P4*) as follows:

(P4**)   Necessarily, every event has a sufficient cause.

(Where c is a sufficient cause of e if and only if (i) c is a cause of e and (ii) the fact that c occurred, together with a complete statement of the laws, entails that e occurred.) If this claim were correct, then causal loops without sufficient causes would clearly be impossible. And the neuron example would seem to be a case of this kind.

The problem is that most people today would reject (P4**). For one thing, it seems possible to have an infinitely long series of events that stretches back without beginning (e.g. the career of the universe) and it seems illegitimate to demand a sufficient cause for something that never came into existence. This would be like demanding a starter for something that never starts.[67] In fact, the *ex nihilo* principle originated with the pre-Socratic philosophers as a part of their effort to argue *for* the existence of eternal beings.[68] So, that principle was obviously not intended to rule out the existence of such things.

There is, however, a natural restriction to (P4**):

(P4***)   Necessarily, every event that has a beginning has a sufficient cause.

This claim would not rule out uncaused eternal events, but it would rule out uncaused causal loops, since those loops will always have an objective beginning.

Or will they? Here it's important to distinguish between *temporal* beginnings and *causal* beginnings. Event e is a temporal beginning for a series if and only if (i) e is a part of the series and (ii) e does not occur after any other part of the series.[69] Event e is a causal beginning, on contrast, if and only if (i) e is a part of the series and (ii) e is not caused by any other part of the series. Obviously, every causal loop will have a beginning in the first sense, but not the second. For example, the firing of A is the

---

[65] Actually, it is more natural to describe these things as causal *conditions*—that is, conditions that must be in place in order for a cause to bring about its effect. However, most theories of causation treat causal conditions as causes themselves. See, for example, Mackie (1965).

[66] Note that the causal loop only occurs if A fires, and A fires only if B fires. But B fires at t_3, and nothing that occurs at t_1 guarantees the occurrence of that event.

[67] This point is made by Levin (1980) in his response to Harrison's problem.

[68] See, for example, the arguments of Parmenides (as reported in Simplicius's *Commentary on the* Physics, 144.25–146.27).

[69] Here, we continue to think of a series as a complex event made out of other, simpler events (its parts). This is important since a series, in this sense, can lack a first "member." (That was not the case for our earlier characterization of series in terms of ordered sets.)

temporal beginning of the neuron-loop, but that series lacks a causal beginning since each of the constituent events is caused by the other. What's unclear is which sense of "beginning" we're supposed to be using in interpreting (P4***). Imagine a backward-running causal series that extends infinitely into the past—e_1 occurs today, which causes e_2 to occur yesterday, which causes e_3 to occur the day before, etc. It seems legitimate to ask for a causal explanation for such a series. More cautiously, it makes *more* sense to ask for a causal explanation in this case than in the case of the universe's career (under the assumption that the universe extends infinitely into the past).

This suggests that, when it comes to causal explanations, we care about causal beginnings, rather than temporal ones. And *that* suggests that (P4***) is to be interpreted as follows:

(P4****)   Necessarily, every event that has a causal beginning has a sufficient cause.

The problem, of course, is that this principle has no application to uncaused causal loops, since those loops do not meet the causal-beginning condition. In the neuron series, for example, the firing of A is a cause of the firing of B, which is a cause of the firing of A, so neither part of the loop counts as a causal beginning. So, (P4****) does not require that loop to have a sufficient cause.

To sum up: We have considered four different interpretations of the *ex nihilo* principle and we have seen that, on each interpretation, the principle is either false or irrelevant (to the case of causal loops). So, the key premise of the *ex nihilo* paradox appears to be unmotivated.

In closing, it is worth making one final, obvious, and very important observation: According to our best scientific theories, *uncaused events are everywhere*. More precisely, there are many events for which there is no sufficient cause. To take just one example:[70] The half-life of thorium-234 is 24.5 days. To say that the half-life of thorium-234 is 24.5 days is to say that the probability of any new atom of thorium-234 decaying in the next 24.5 days is 50 percent. So, suppose that an atom of uranium-238 decays on Monday, October 1, producing a new atom of thorium-234. And suppose that atom of thorium decays on October 25 (leaving an atom of protactinium-233). In that case, there would be various causes of the decay—for example, the existence of the atom, and the fact that it was produced when it was. But none of these causes are sufficient for the event occurring when it did. More generally, the state of the world before the decay, together with the relevant physical laws, did not guarantee the occurrence of the event at that time.

Perhaps it is the same for causal loops. There are various causes or conditions that must be in place for a loop to occur, but the laws (in time travel worlds) do not tell us whether or not there will be a loop, when those conditions obtain. In this respect, the occurrence of a causal loop would be no different from all the other indeterministic events that fill the world around us.[71]

---

[70] Other examples might include the big bang, quantum events, and libertarian free actions.

[71] This point has been made by many people, including Hanley (1997: 221–3), Lewis (1976: 149), and Meyer (2012).

4. The Restoration Paradox

To this point, we have discussed the worry that causal loops are inconsistent with general principles about causation (like the principle that every event must have a cause). But some have suggested that causal loop stories also suffer from *internal* inconsistencies. Paul Nahin, for example, invites us to

Consider once again...the watch in the central causal loop of the film *Somewhere in Time*. Assume that the watch received by the man in the present is bright and shiny. He then takes it back into the past and gives it to his love. It remains with her after his return to the present until, decades later, she gives it to him—bright and shiny. Why didn't it tarnish? Is there some peculiar anti-tarnish property to the watch? (1999: 315)

As Nahin notes, these questions are not as perplexing as they might first appear. Perhaps the watch *did* tarnish and Jane Seymour's character simply cleaned it up before returning it to Reeve. But Nahin claims that other loops are more problematic:

[R]eplace the watch with a crisp, new book. [Reeve] receives it, takes it back, leaves it with [Seymour], and gets it back years later—crisp and new! Why haven't the pages turned yellow and brittle and dark with decades of fingerprints?...This is all much harder to explain than is the shiny new watch. (1999: 315)

Murray MacBeath puts the general problem as follows:

If the book undergoes any change in the course of its particular time, say between point A and point B on its looped world-line, then that change must be reversed between point B and point A. For example...pages that have yellowed and turned brittle must whiten and become supple; tiny fragments of paper that have become detached must become reattached; every molecule must find itself back exactly where it was...Such things surely cannot happen of their own accord, or even be made to happen, in our universe. (1982: 417)

All of this suggests the following argument against backward time travel, which we will refer to as *the restoration paradox*:

(P1) If backward time travel were possible, then backward causation would be possible.

(P2) If backward causation were possible, then object loops would be possible.

(P3) If object loops were possible, then perfect restoration would be possible.

(P4) Perfect restoration is impossible.

(C) Backward time travel is impossible.

Nahin and MacBeath seem to take this paradox seriously, but it is hard to see why. The key premise is obviously the fourth, and that premise seems obviously mistaken. Just imagine an omnipotent Overseer of Time Travel whose job is to keep track of object loops, and to ensure that the relevant objects are restored before their loops are closed. Such a being is perfectly possible, so (P4) is clearly mistaken.

Of course, one might think that our world lacks this kind of supervision, in which case one could take (P4) to concern some sort of restricted possibility. This, in fact, is suggested by MacBeath's own wording. ("Such things surely cannot happen...*in our universe.*") But that reading seems no more plausible than the first. The atoms that make up a book could be scattered across the universe and then come back together again, in exactly the same arrangement, by perfectly random processes.[72] Of course, the odds of this would be astronomically low, so the chance of an object loop would be minuscule. But this is very different from saying that such loops are *impossible.*[73]

These observations should be enough to defuse any worries about the watch and book examples. However, Robin Le Poidevin offers a different kind of case, which he says raises a new kind of puzzle. Here is his story:

Peter and Jane, both 20 years old, are out for a walk one day in 1999 when suddenly a time machine appears in front of them. Out steps a strangely familiar character who tells Jane that he has an important mission for her. She must step into the machine and travel forward to the year 2019, taking with her a diary the stranger hands to her. In that diary she must make a record of her trip. Obligingly, she does as she is asked and, on arrival, meets Peter, now aged 40. She tells Peter to travel back to 1999, taking with him the diary she now hands him, and recording his trip in it. On arrival in 1999, he meets two 20-year-olds called Peter and Jane, out for a walk, and he tells Jane that he has an important mission for her.   (2003: 180–1)

Le Poidevin notes several strange features of this story, but he claims that the "really tricky" question is this:

[H]ow many entries are there in the diary when Jane first steps into the machine? We imagine it blank. But this is the very same diary as the one Jane hands to the 40-year-old Peter, which by then contains her entry. And by the time Peter arrives back in 1999, it will contain his entry too. But then, if the diary already contained two entries when Jane was handed the diary, then it would contain three entries when she handed it to Peter, who would then add another one, so the diary would have contained four entries when it was first handed to Jane, and so on. If the problem is not immediately apparent, this is because we imagine an indefinite number of trips, but in fact there are just two: Jane's trip to 2019 and Peter's trip to 1999. So there ought to be a consistent answer to the question, how many entries are there in the diary when it is handed to Jane? Yet, as we have seen, there does not appear to be a consistent answer.   (2003: 181)

Le Poidevin seems to be suggesting that this case presents a new kind of "consistency" paradox that goes beyond the original restoration puzzle.[74] But this seems clearly mistaken. In order for there to be a consistent answer to Le Poidevin's question, all we require is a possible world in which (i) Peter and Jane each make an entry in the diary and (ii) the diary undergoes perfect restoration before Peter hands the diary back to Jane. There are many such worlds, and thus many answers to Le Poidevin's question. Here is one way the story might go:

---

[72] For more details on what such a process might look like, see Lossev and Novikov (1992).

[73] Unless, of course, we are understanding "impossibility" to be the "impossibility of the astronomically improbable" (Nerlich 1994: 243).

[74] At least this is how Le Poidevin's critics interpret his example. See, for example, Carlson (2005).

Jane is handed a diary with exactly one entry, written by Peter.

Jane records her entry.

Peter's entry disappears without a trace.

Peter is handed a diary with exactly one entry, written by Jane.

Peter records his entry.

Jane's entry disappears without a trace.

Jane is handed a diary with exactly one entry, written by Peter...

On this version of the story, there is a straightforward answer to Le Poidevin's question: There is exactly *one* entry in the diary when Jane first steps into the time machine. Moreover, this story is perfectly consistent, since it logically possible for journal entries to suddenly disappear without a trace. In fact, on the standard interpretation of quantum mechanics, these kinds of disappearances do not even violate the actual laws of physics. The laws *do* say that such events are extremely unlikely, but—once again—this is very different from saying they are impossible. The upshot is that Le Poidevin's story presents no new challenges to causal loops or backward time travel.[75]

5. The Frequency Paradox

A different argument against causal loops is given by D. H. Mellor in his book *Real Time II*.[76] His argument is based on three assumptions about chance, causation, and frequencies.

Mellor's first assumption is that every effect has chances both with and without its causes (1998: 129). Suppose, for example, that a short circuit causes a fire. Let C and E be the facts that the short circuit and fire occurred, respectively. In that case, Mellor says, there must be some chances, p and p', such that $ch_C(E) = p$ and $ch_{\sim C}(E) = p'$[77] (where '$ch_C(E)$' is to be read as 'the chance that C gives to E').[78]

Mellor's second assumption is that facts about causation are logically independent of one another. More carefully, he assumes the chances that causes confer on their effects are logically independent of each other: If C causes E, then the chances of E with and without C are logically independent of the chances of C with and without its causes, and logically independent of the chances of E's effects with and without E.[79] Suppose, for example, that Jim died because he ran in the race and that the race was

---

[75] For more on Le Poidevin's case, see Carlson (2005) and Smith (2004).

[76] Mellor (1998: Chapter 12). My presentation of Mellor's argument is heavily indebted to Dowe (2001) and Berkovitz (2001).

[77] $ch_{\sim C}(E)$ can be thought of as the chance of there being a fire at the closest world where the short circuit did not occur.

[78] More carefully, Mellor assumes that every effect has chances given the relevant circumstances, both with and without its causes. Suppose, for example, that the fire occurs in the presence of oxygen and fuel. In that case, Mellor says, we can think of $ch_C(E)$ as a property of facts about those circumstances—it is a feature of those facts that the chance of a fire given the short circuit is p (1998: 130). In the interests of simplicity, we will ignore this qualification.

[79] Here we will follow Mellor in taking facts to stand in causal relations.

cancelled because Jim died. Let R be the fact that Jim ran, D be the fact that Jim died, and C be the fact that the race was cancelled. Given Mellor's first assumption, there must then be some chances, p, p', q, and q', such that $ch_R(D) = p$, $ch_{\sim R}(D) = p'$, $ch_D(C) = q$, and $ch_{\sim D}(C) = q'$. Mellor assumes that causes raise the probability of their effects, so he assumes that $p > p'$ and $q > q'$. But, beyond this, any combination of values (from 0 to 1 inclusive) is permitted. For example, it is logically possible that $p = 0.6$, $p' = 0.2$, $q = 0.9$, and $q' = 0.1$. But it is also possible that $p = 0.9$, $p' = 0.1$, $q = 0.6$, and $q' = 0.2$. In this sense, the conditional chances of effects, given their causes, are logically independent of each other.

Mellor's third assumption is that chances are connected to frequencies by the (weak) law of large numbers: Very roughly, if fact C obtains a great number of times, then the relative frequency with which fact E obtains should be close to the chance that C gives to E. That is, $f(E \mid C) \approx ch_C(E)$ (where '$f(E \mid C)$' is to be read as 'the frequency with which E obtains in cases where C obtains'). For example, if F is the fact that a fair coin is flipped, and H is the fact that the coin comes down heads, then $ch_F(H) = 0.5$. So, if there are a lot of coin flips, roughly half of them should be heads. Moreover, as more and more coins are flipped, it becomes more and more probable that close to half of them will have landed heads. That is, as the number of flips increases, the chances of $f(H \mid F)$ differing from 0.5 by any specified amount (no matter how small) will gradually approach 0. However, the chances will never actually *be* 0 (not, at least, in the finite case).

Mellor now argues that, given these assumptions, the possibility of causal loops can be reduced to absurdity. We can illustrate this argument with an example from Phil Dowe (2001). Suppose that a particular atom can both absorb and emit photons. Suppose also that this atom is placed near the mouth of a wormhole. At t_1, the atom absorbs a photon that emerges from the wormhole. Then, at t_2, it emits a photon back into the wormhole—a photon that travels back to t_1 where it is absorbed by the same atom. Let A be the fact that the atom absorbed a photon at the earlier time and let E be the fact that the atom emitted a photon at the later time.[80] Finally, suppose that A and E form a causal loop—the atom emits a photon at the later time because it absorbed a photon at the earlier time, and the atom absorbed a photon at the earlier time because it emitted one at the later time. Now, given Mellor's first assumption, we know that there are some chances, p and p', such that $ch_A(E) = p$ and $ch_{\sim A}(E) = p'$. Let's suppose that $p = 0.6$ and that $p' = 0.2$ (in other words, let's suppose that the chance the atom will emit a photon at the later time, given that it absorbs one at the earlier time is 0.6, and that the chance it will emit a photon at the later time given that it does *not* absorb one at the earlier time is 0.2).[81] Given Mellor's first assumption, we also know that that there

---

[80] The indefinite article is important in both cases. A, for example, is the fact that the atom absorbed *some photon or other* at the earlier time (not necessarily the same photon it will later emit). This is important because we will be assuming that there is some chance the atom would absorb a photon at the earlier time (from a different source) if it did not emit one at the later time. The same thing is true for E.

[81] Again, this would be a different photon from a different source. (See fn. 80.)

are some chances, q and q', such that $ch_E(A) = q$ and $ch_{\sim E}(A) = q'$. Moreover, given his second assumption, we know that p and p' are independent of q and q', so we can stipulate any values we want for the second pair of chances (provided that $q > q'$). So, let $q = 0.5$ and $q' = 0.25$. Now, given Mellor's third assumption, we know that the following approximations will hold in large samples:

$$f(E \mid A) \approx ch_A(E) = p$$
$$f(E \mid {\sim}A) \approx ch_{\sim A}(E) = p'$$
$$f(A \mid E) \approx ch_E(A) = q$$
$$f(A \mid {\sim}E) \approx ch_{\sim E}(A) = q'$$

Moreover, as Phil Dowe has shown (2001: Appendix 1), these principles allow us to approximate the relevant number of emissions $N(E)$ and absorptions $N(A)$ as follows:

$$N(E) \approx pN(A) + p'N({\sim}A)$$
$$N(A) \approx qN(E) + q'N({\sim}E)$$
$$N({\sim}E) \approx (1{-}p)N(A) + (1{-}p')N({\sim}A)$$
$$N({\sim}A) \approx (1{-}q)N(E) + (1{-}q')N({\sim}E)$$

So suppose, for example, that we repeat our experiment with the atom and the wormhole 20 million times. And suppose that, in half of these cases, the atom absorbs a photon at the earlier time (in the other half, it does not). Given the first and third principles above, we should expect there to be approximately 8m cases in which the atom emits a photon at the later time $((0.6 \times 10m) + (0.2 \times 10m))$ and 12m cases in which it does not $((0.4 \times 10m) + (0.8 \times 10m))$. But then, given the second and fourth principles above, we should expect there to be approximately 7m cases in which the atom absorbs a photon at the earlier time $((0.5 \times 8m) + (0.25 \times 12m))$ and 13m in which it does not $((0.5 \times 8m) + (0.75 \times 12m))$. This, however, contradicts our initial assumption that only half of the trials are ones in which the atom absorbs a photon at the earlier time. So, this loop is incompatible with Mellor's assumptions.

Of course, showing that one causal loop is incompatible with Mellor's assumptions does not show that *all* causal loops have this feature. In fact, it is easy to construct a loop that is compatible with all of Mellor's assumptions. Suppose, for example, that we keep everything in the preceding case the same, but reset the probabilities as follows: $p = 1$, $p' = 0$, $q = 1$, and $q' = 0$. In other words, suppose that in the relevant circumstances, a photon is emitted at the later time if and only if a photon is absorbed at the earlier time. In that case, we should expect $N(E)$, $N(A)$, $N({\sim}E)$, and $N({\sim}A)$ to all be approximately 10m $((0.5 \times 10m) + (0.5 \times 10m))$. This result would be perfectly consistent with our initial assumption that the atom absorbs a photon in half of the 20m trials. Call this kind of loop, in which the chances and frequencies conform to the law of large numbers, an 'ordinary loop'.

Now recall Mellor's independence assumption once more. That assumption says that the values of p and p' are logically independent of the values of q and q'—the only constraint on p and p' is that $p > p'$ (since causes raise the probability of their effects). So, if it is possible that $p = 1$, $p' = 0$, $q = 1$, and $q' = 0$, it is also possible that $p = 0.6$, $p' = 0.2$, $q = 1$, and $q' = 0$. In the same way, the independence assumption tells us that q and q' are logically independent of p and p' (where the only constraint on q and q' is that $q > q'$). So, if it is possible that $p = 0.6$, $p' = 0.2$, $q = 1$, and $q' = 0$, it is also possible that $p = 0.6$, $p' = 0.2$, $q = 0.5$, and $q' = 0.25$. In other words, if an ordinary loop like the one just described is possible, then so too is an 'anomalous loop' like the one described by Mellor (i.e. a loop in which the chances and frequencies do not conform to the law of large numbers). Since Mellor takes these kinds of loops to be impossible, he rejects all kinds of causal loops. And since he takes backward time travel to imply the possibility of causal loops, he concludes that backward time travel is impossible. We can summarize this "frequency paradox" as follows:

(P1)   If backward time travel were possible, then ordinary loops would be possible.

(P2)   If ordinary loops were possible, then anomalous loops would be possible.

(P3)   Anomalous loops are impossible.

(C)   Backward time travel is impossible.

Various replies to Mellor's argument are possible.[82] We will focus on just two points.

First, Mellor takes (P2) to follow from the assumption that the chances given by causes are independent of each other. As Phil Dowe (2001: S91–2) points out, this is incorrect. In our first example involving the atom and the wormhole, we began by assuming that $ch_A(E) = p = 0.6$ and $ch_{\sim A}(E) = p' = 0.2$ (in other words, the chance the atom will emit a photon at the later time, given that it absorbs one at the earlier time, is 0.6; and the chance it will emit a photon at the later time, given that it does *not* absorb one at the earlier time, is 0.2). Then, appealing to the independence assumption, we stipulated that $ch_E(A) = q = 0.5$ and $ch_{\sim E}(A) = q' = 0.25$ (in other words, the chance the atom will absorb a photon at the earlier time, given that it emits one at the later time, is 0.5; and the chance it will absorb a photon at the earlier time, given that it does *not* emit one at the later time, is 0.25). But this was not the only stipulation we made. We also assumed that the atom absorbs a photon in half of the 20m trials. Crucially, this assumption is not justified by the independence of causal chances—it requires the further assumption that initial frequencies are independent of the relevant chances. That is, any possible values for p, p', q, and q' are compatible with any possible values for $N(A)$ and $N(\sim A)$. Following Dowe (2001: S92), we will refer to this as the 'input-independence condition'.

In ordinary cases, this condition is entirely plausible. To return to an earlier example, let R be the fact that a man with a weak heart runs a race, D be the fact that the man dies while running the race, and C be the fact that the race is cancelled. Mellor's original independence assumption allows us to assign whatever values we want to $ch_R(D)$, $ch_{\sim R}(D)$, $ch_D(C)$, and $ch_{\sim D}(C)$.[83] Dowe's input-independence assumption then allows

---

[82] See, for example, the discussion in Berkovitz (2001).

[83] Provided, again, that $ch_R(D) > ch_{\sim R}(D)$ and $ch_D(C) > ch_{\sim D}(C)$.

us to stipulate whatever values we want for $N(R)$ and $N(\sim R)$. So, for example, we can assume that there are 20m men who are relevantly similar to Jim (from earlier) and who have the opportunity to run relevantly similar races in relevantly similar circumstances. Moreover, we can assume that half of those men run the race and that half do not ($N(R) = 10m$ and $N(\sim R) = 10m$). Alternatively, we can assume that there are 20 trials of this kind and that only 10 percent run the race ($N(R) = 2$ and $N(\sim R) = 18$). According to the input-independence condition, any combination of values is possible. And this seems right. The *outputs* of the trials obviously depend on the inputs, together with the relevant chances. But the inputs are naturally thought of as "independent variables"—in other words, the input-independence condition is naturally taken for granted.

However, this assumption is only plausible if we limit our attention to the linear case. In the case of causal loops, input-independence fails. In fact, as Berkovitz (2001: 14–15) and Dowe (2001: S91–2) point out, *both* the input and output frequencies in causal loops can be approximated on the basis of the relevant chances:

$$N(E)/N(\sim E) \approx (q'p + p' - q'p')/(1 - qp - p' + qp')$$
$$N(A)/N(\sim A) \approx (qp' + q' - q'p')/(1 - qp - q' + q'p)^{84}$$

For example, in the original wormhole scenario, we assumed that the chances were as follows: $p = 0.6$, $p' = 0.2$, $q = 0.5$, and $q' = 0.25$. Plugging these numbers into the above equations gives the result that $N(E)/N(\sim E) \approx N(A)/N(\sim A) \approx 0.5$. In other words, $f(E) = f(A) = \frac{1}{3}$.[85] So, it should come as no surprise if we run into trouble by assuming that $f(A) = \frac{1}{2}$ (that is, by assuming that half of the atoms absorb a photon at the earlier time).

More generally, it should not come as any surprise if there are additional constraints on input frequencies in cases of causal loops. After all, input frequencies, together with chances, help determine output frequencies. And, in the case of causal loops, output frequencies, together with chances, help determine input frequencies. So, the input frequencies are obviously not independent of the relevant chances. To put it another way: No one thinks that input and output frequencies are *both* independent of chances, in the sense that one can stipulate whatever inputs *and* outputs one wants without regard to the relevant chances. That would be ridiculous. But, in the case of causal loops, the input frequencies *are* output frequencies, since the causes are also effects. So, to vary the input frequencies independently of the output frequencies would be to vary things independently of themselves. That, of course, is impossible.

---

[84] Both of these formulas follow from our earlier formulas for calculating $N(E)$, $N(\sim E)$, $N(A)$, and $N(\sim A)$. See Dowe (2001: Appendix 2).

[85] To say the value of $N(A)/N(\sim A)$ is 0.5 (or $\frac{1}{2}$) is to say that, for every absorption, there are two non-absorptions. In other words, one out of every three trials involves an absorption. Thus, the expected frequency should be $\frac{1}{3}$.

The situation in this case is similar to the case of retrosuicide.[86] (Chapter 4, section 2.) When one imagines a case of attempted murder one is normally free to stipulate the initial conditions however one wants. One can suppose that the would-be murderer has a gun, that she has an unobstructed shot at the target, that the target is a helpless little baby, etc. Indeed, one is free to stipulate the initial conditions so as to ensure success (there is no miraculous carbon buildup to jam the gun, there are no banana peels to slip on, etc., etc.). But things are very different in the case of attempted retrosuicide. In that case, the would-be murderer is only present at the beginning because the murder attempt will fail in the end. In other words, the initial conditions are partly determined by the subsequent failure. So, it is no surprise that the initial conditions impose constraints on themselves. Once we stipulate that the would-be murderer is a later version of the would-be victim, we are no longer free to stipulate the rest of the initial conditions as we wish—in particular, we can no longer set up the initial conditions so as to ensure success. Banana peels will have to be built in.

The same thing is true in Mellor's case. Initial conditions impose additional constraints on themselves through the operation of causal loops. So, one is not free to stipulate initial conditions however one wants. In other words, we must reject the input-independence condition. But, once we do that, we are free to reject (P2) of Mellor's argument.

A second, and more direct response to Mellor's argument would be to reject (P3). That premise, again, says that it is impossible for there to be anomalous loops (i.e. loops in which the frequencies and chances do not conform to the law of large numbers). The justification for this premise was supposed to be the law of large numbers itself. But that justification does not seem adequate. The problem is that the law of large numbers is a law of *probability*. Accordingly, it can tell us that a certain sequence of events is improbable, but it cannot tell us that it is impossible. To return to an earlier example, the law of large numbers tells us that, as more and more coins are flipped, it becomes more and more probable that close to half of them will have landed heads. In other words, as the number of flips increases, the chances of $f(H \mid F)$ differing from 0.5 by any specified amount (no matter how small) will gradually approach 0. However, the chances will never actually *be* 0 (not, at least, in the finite case). A million heads in a row would be astronomically unlikely, but it would not be metaphysically impossible. The same thing is true for the relative frequency of photon absorptions in our earlier case. As more and more trials are run, it becomes more and more probable that close to a third of them will involve an absorption at the earlier time. Moreover, as the number of trials increases, the chances of this frequency differing from ⅓ by any specified amount (no matter how small) will gradually approach 0. However, the chances will never actually *be* 0 (not in the finite case). That is just to say that there is some possible world in which things are just as Mellor describes them. That world is anomalous, to be sure. But anomalous worlds are not the same thing as impossible worlds.

---

[86] Bourne (2006: 132) draws a similar analogy to the grandfather paradox.

6. The Counterfactual Paradox

A final argument against casual loops is based on the relation between counterfactuals and causation.[87] Typically, when one event causes another, the second event would not have occurred in the absence of the first. For example, if a lightning strike causes a forest fire, then there wouldn't have been a forest fire if the lightning hadn't struck. Moreover, counterfactual dependence is typically taken as evidence for causation. For example, if you are told that the fire would not have spread so far if there hadn't been so much wind, it is natural to conclude that the spread of the fire was caused by the force of the wind.

Given these links between causation and counterfactuals, it is natural to reason as follows: Backward time travel is only possible if backward causation is possible,[88] and backward causation is only possible if backward counterfactual dependence is possible.[89] So, backward time travel is only possible if counterfactual dependence can run in reverse. However, it has also been argued that one of the most popular accounts of counterfactuals—namely, that of David Lewis—turns out to be incompatible with these kinds of reversals.[90] That argument is the topic of this section.[91]

---

[87] Strictly speaking, the focus of the argument is on backward causation, rather than causal loops. However, the main example in the argument involves a causal loop, so it is not too much of a stretch to call it a "causal loop" paradox. See fn. 98.

[88] If one were to deny the transitivity of causation, one might argue that closed timelike curves allow backward time travel without any backward causation. We will not explore that worry here. (But see section 2 of this chapter and section 6 of Chapter 2 for relevant discussion.)

[89] To say that there could be backward counterfactual dependence is to say that there could be true counterfactuals in which the antecedent-time comes after the consequent-time—for example, "If Dee hadn't turned on the time machine at t_6, then he wouldn't have appeared at t_1." This kind of counterfactual should not be confused with what Lewis calls a "backtracking" counterfactual. That is:

> A counterfactual saying that the past would be different if the present were somehow different [and which] may come out true under the special resolution of its vagueness, but false under the standard resolution.   (1986c: 34)

Here, Lewis has in mind counterfactuals like those used in the following line of reasoning:

> Jim and Jack quarreled yesterday, and Jack is still hopping mad. We conclude that if Jim asked Jack for help today, Jack would not help him. But wait: Jim is a prideful fellow. He never would ask for help after such a quarrel; if Jim were to ask Jack for help today, there would have to have been no quarrel yesterday. In that case Jack would be his usual generous self. So if Jim asked Jack for help today, Jack would help him after all.   (1986c: 33)

As Lewis notes, backtrackers are distinguished by a "syntactic peculiarity":

> They are the ones in which the usual subjunctive conditional constructions are readily replaced by more complicated constructions: "If it were that…then it would have to be that…" or the like.   (1986c: 34–5)

The counterfactuals we are interested in differ from backtrackers in exactly these respects. For example, we do not require an alternative construction or a convoluted backstory in order to make sense of the claim that Dee wouldn't have appeared at t_1 if he hadn't turned on his time machine at t_6.

[90] If correct, this conclusion would be surprising, since Lewis repeatedly claimed that his views were compatible with both backward causation and backward counterfactual dependence. Indeed, he took this to be an important mark in favor of his views—see Lewis (1976: 148; 1986b: 170–1; and 1986c: 40–1).

[91] A different argument for this conclusion is given in Wasserman (2015).

6.1 Lewis's theory

Recall from Chapter 4 that Lewis analyzes counterfactual truth in terms of the comparative similarity of possible worlds. This analysis involved three steps. First, counterfactual truth is analyzed in terms of *world closeness*:

> $A > C$ is true at world w only if, and in that case because, the closest A-world to w is a C-world.

(Where '>' is the counterfactual connective, an *A-world* is a world at which the antecedent is true, and a *C-world* is a world at which the consequent is true.[92]) Second, world closeness is understood in terms of *comparative similarity*:

> w_1 is closer to w_2 than w_3 only if, and in that case because, w_1 is overall more similar to w_2 than w_3.

Finally, comparative similarity is understood in terms of how well worlds match with respect to their laws and particular matters of fact. More carefully, the standard similarity metric for worlds is given by the following set of rules:

Rule 1:   Minimize big miracles.
Rule 2:   Maximize exact match.
Rule 3:   Minimize small miracles.
Rule 4:   Maximize approximate match.[93]

These four rules will figure prominently in what follows, so it is important to understand their interpretation and application. To that end, it will be helpful to work through one famous example.[94]

On the morning of October 27, 1969, a squadron of B-52 bombers was dispatched over the Arctic Ocean, loaded down with nuclear weapons, and heading for the USSR.[95] The operation, codenamed *Giant Lance*, was the result of Kissinger and Nixon's "madman theory"—the theory that fake, finger-on-the-button aggression would help to overthrow the Soviet government. Let's suppose that, on that day in 1969, Nixon actually held his finger on the button. And let's suppose that all of the old fears about nuclear stockpiling were true—if Nixon had pushed the button, the bombs would have been dropped, in which case the retaliatory missiles would have been fired,

---

[92] This formulation simplifies Lewis's account by assuming that there is exactly one closest A-world. Dropping this assumption, Lewis's view is that $A > C$ is true in world w only if, and in that case because, there is some world such that (i) A and C are both true in that world and (ii) every A-world that is closer to w than that world is also a C-world.

[93] Recall that a *small miracle* is a miracle that takes place in a small region and that a *big miracle* is a collection of many small miracles.

[94] The example is given by Kit Fine (1975: 452) and discussed by Lewis (1986c). Similar cases are discussed in Bennett (1974), Jackson (1977), and Slote (1978).

[95] At least, that is the account given by Suri (2008).

in which case there would have been a nuclear holocaust. In other words, let's suppose that (1) is true:

(1)   If Nixon had pressed the button (at t), there would have been a nuclear holocaust.

Now, Lewis assumes (at least initially, for the sake of simplicity) that our world is deterministic. He therefore assumes that every button-pressing world will differ from the actual world ($w_@$) with respect to its past or laws (or both). There are many such worlds, but Lewis (1986c: 43–8) focuses on four in particular:

w_1 is a duplicate of $w_@$ until shortly before t, at which time the laws of $w_@$ are violated in a small way—a few extra neurons fire in Nixon's brain and, as a result, he presses the button. The signal races from the button, the bombers drop their bombs, and nuclear holocaust ensues. w_1 is then very different from $w_@$.

w_2 is a world in which there are no violations of the actual laws, and where Nixon presses the button at t. Given this difference, and assuming the truth of determinism, it follows that w_2 and $w_@$ have different histories leading up to t—the two worlds do not exactly match at any point in the past.

w_3 is a duplicate of $w_@$ until shortly before t, at which point a few extra neurons fire and Nixon presses the button. Shortly thereafter, another small miracle takes place—the fateful signal disappears on its way to the bombers, so that nuclear holocaust is averted. However, w_3 is no longer exactly like $w_@$, since it contains various traces of the button-pressing—Nixon's fingerprint is on the button, for example, and light waves from the event have raced out the window and on into space.

w_4 is a duplicate of $w_@$ until shortly before t, at which point a few extra neurons fire and Nixon presses the button. Shortly thereafter, a large miracle takes place—not only does the fateful signal disappear on its way to the bombers (so that nuclear holocaust is averted), but so do all traces of the button-pressing (the fingerprint vanishes, the light waves disappear, etc.). In this way, perfect match to $w_@$ is restored.

Initially, one might think that w_4 is most similar, overall, to $w_@$. After all, those two worlds are exact duplicates, with the exception of a few moments before and after t. But Lewis argues that this would be a mistake. w_4 *does* do better than all of the other competitors with respect to Rule 2 (maximize perfect match), but it does so only at the cost of including many small miracles (the various disappearances). These miracles add up to a big miracle and thus violate Rule 1. On the other end of the spectrum, w_2 scores better than all of the other competitors with respect to Rule 3 (minimize small miracles), but it only does so by completely ignoring the second (maximize perfect match). That leaves w_1 and w_3. Those worlds tie with respect to the first two rules since neither includes a large miracle, and both match $w_@$ perfectly up until shortly before t. But the first world scores better with respect to Rule 3, since it includes one small miracle rather than two. The upshot, Lewis says, is that w_1 turns

Table 5.1. Lewis's worlds

World	Rule 1	Rule 2	Rule 3
w_1	1st (tie)	2nd (tie)	2nd
w_2	1st (tie)	4th	1st
w_3	1st (tie)	2nd (tie)	3rd
w_4	4th	1st	4th

out to be the closest button-pressing world to $w_@$. (These points are summarized in Table 5.1, with each world being ranked according to how well it does with respect to Lewis's various rules.)

Since w_1 includes a nuclear war, Lewis's account delivers the right results: If Nixon had pressed the button, there would have been a nuclear holocaust.[96]

6.2 Tooley's argument

With a proper understanding of Lewis's theory in place, we are now in a position to consider an objection. The objection is due to Michael Tooley (2002), who argues that Lewis's theory of counterfactuals is incompatible with the possibility of backward time travel. His argument concerns the following kind of case:

Suppose that there is a time machine, M, at a certain location X on Earth at time t in the year 2100, and which is in a state such that if its blastoff switch were to be flipped, then, provided that its fuel has not been removed, either at an earlier time, or at the very moment when the switch is flipped, it would travel forward in time to the year 2101, to location Y on Mars, where it would, at time t^*, both immediately remove all the fuel from any time machines in its neighbourhood, and flip their blastoff switches. Suppose, further, that there is another time machine, N, in the immediate vicinity of location Y at time t^* in the year 2101, and which is in a state such that if its blastoff switch were to be flipped, then, provided that its fuel has not been removed then or earlier, it would travel backward in time to the year 2100, to the immediate vicinity of location X, where it would, at time t, remove all the fuel from any time machines in its neighbourhood, and flip their blastoff switches.   (2002: 193)[97]

In Tooley's world, we are to imagine that both machines (M and N) have fuel at their respective times (t and t^*), but that no switches are flipped.[98] Of course, if M's switch

[96] Wasserman (2006a) argues that this victory is short-lived, since Lewis's treatment turns on contingent facts about the ubiquity of traces. His account thus delivers the wrong results in deterministic worlds where traces can be contained.

[97] After describing this case, Tooley notes that it seems to open up the possibility of self-undercutting causal sequences (just imagine that machine M is reprogrammed so that it does not remove the rocket fuel from N before it flips N's switch—in that case, M would travel into the future if and only if it *doesn't* travel into the future). In order to avoid any worries about grandfather-style paradoxes, he refines his example so as to allow for backward causation, but no causal loops. (See section 3 of his article.) However, we will continue to focus on his first case since the second is more complicated and less intuitive. The same points will apply to both.

[98] Since the machines are not turned on, we do not have a normal causal loop. At best, we have a loop involving "negative" causation: M's switch not being flipped at t is a cause of N's switch not being flipped at t^*, and N's switch not being flipped at t^* is a cause of M's switch not being flipped at t.

had been flipped, then it would have wound up on Mars, where it would have removed N's fuel and then flipped its switch. That is, (A) is true at Tooley's world:

(A)   If M's switch had been flipped at t, then N's fuel would have been removed at t^*.

Similarly, if N's switch had been flipped, then it would have traveled into the past, removed M's fuel, and flipped that machine's switch. Hence, (B) is also true in Tooley's world:

(B)   If N's switch had been flipped at t^*, then M's fuel would have been removed at t.

"The upshot," says Tooley, is that

if backward time travel of the sort envisaged in this case is logically possible, then any similarity-across-possible-worlds account of counterfactuals cannot be correct unless the measure of similarity that is used makes it the case that the above two counterfactuals both turn out to be true.   (2002: 194)

Here, Tooley claims that we run into trouble. For consider two counterfactual scenarios. In w_1, machine M is full of fuel and has its switch flipped at t (so that it travels to the future, removes N's fuel, and flips its switch). In w_2, machine N is full of fuel and has its switch flipped at t^* (so that it travels to the past, removes M's fuel, and flips its switch). These worlds are summarized in Table 5.2, along with Tooley's original world (w_0).

Here is the problem. w_1 and w_2 are both worlds in which the antecedent of (A) is true, but w_1 is the only world in which the consequent of (A) is true (it is the only world in which N's fuel is removed at t^*). So, if that counterfactual holds at w_0—as we have assumed—then w_1 must be closer to w_0 than is w_2. In the same way, w_1 and w_2 are both worlds in which the antecedent of (B) is true, but w_2 is the only world in which the consequent of (B) is true (it is the only world in which M's fuel is removed at t). Since (B) is true at w_0, Lewis's account tells us that w_2 must be closer to w_0 than is w_1. Putting these two lines of reasoning together, we reach the conclusion that w_1 is closer to w_0 than is w_2 *and* that w_2 is closer to w_0 than is w_1. In other words, w_1 *both is and is not* closer to w_0 than is w_2.

Tooley takes this result to show that Lewis's theory of counterfactuals is incompatible with the possibility of backward time travel.[99] But we can easily turn this into an

Table 5.2. Tooley's worlds

World	@t	@t*
w_0	M has fuel	N has fuel
	M's switch is not flipped	N's switch is not flipped
w_1	M has fuel	N's fuel is removed
	M's switch is flipped	N's switch is flipped
w_2	M's fuel is removed	N has fuel
	M's switch is flipped	N's switch is flipped

[99]   Tooley (2002: 191).

argument against backward time travel by assuming that Lewis's theory of counterfactuals is correct:

(P1)   If backward time travel is possible, then w_0 is possible.

(P2)   If w_0 is possible, then (A) and (B) are both true there.

(P3)   If (A) is true at w_0, then w_1 is closer to w_0 than is w_2.

(P4)   If (B) is true at w_0, then w_2 is closer to w_0 than is w_1.

(P5)   It is impossible that (w_1 is closer to w_0 than is w_2 and w_2 is closer to w_0 than is w_1).

(C1) w_0 is impossible.

(C2)   Backward time travel is impossible.

(P3) and (P4) follow from Lewis's theory of counterfactuals, and the rest of the premises seem unobjectionable. So, one must either reject the similarity-based account of counterfactuals, or accept the conclusion that backward time travel is impossible. Either way, Lewis will have to relinquish one of his central commitments.

6.3 Tichý's hat and Morgenbesser's coin

Fortunately, Tooley's argument can be answered by making a small modification to Lewis's theory. In order to introduce this modification, it will be helpful to consider an old objection to Lewis's view.

Let's return to the case of Nixon and the bomb and let's suppose, once again, that the crucial neurons in Nixon's brain do not fire, that Nixon does not press the button, and that nuclear war does not take place. But now suppose that the actual world, $w_@$, is indeterministic. In particular, suppose that, leading up to time t (the moment of Nixon's decision), there was some non-zero chance that the relevant neurons in Nixon's brain would fire (in other words, the firing of the neurons was consistent with the past and the laws up until that point). Suppose further that the signal-sending button is part of an indeterministic system such that, if the button is pressed, there is some non-zero chance of the signal disappearing on its way to the bombers. Finally, suppose that the persistence of all traces is also an indeterministic matter so that, were the button pressed, there is some non-zero chance that all traces would disappear.

Now consider our original counterfactual once more:

(1)   If Nixon had pressed the button (at t), there would have been a nuclear holocaust.

In the deterministic case, (1) is clearly true. But in the indeterministic case, it is clearly false. After all, in the indeterministic case there is some chance that the signal would have disappeared on the way to the bombers. Hence, there is some chance that nuclear holocaust would have been avoided, even if Nixon had pressed the button. (1) should therefore be replaced with (2):

(2)   If Nixon had pressed the button (at t), there might have been a nuclear holocaust.[100]

---

[100] Depending on the probabilities involved, (1) could be replaced with something slightly stronger: If Nixon had pressed the button, there *probably* would have been a nuclear holocaust.

Lewis's original similarity metric was tailored to the deterministic case, so it should come as no surprise that it runs into difficulty in an indeterministic setting. The problem with the current example can be brought out by considering the following pair of worlds:

w_1 is a duplicate of $w_@$ until shortly before t, at which time an unlikely but lawful event takes place—a few extra neurons fire in Nixon's brain and, as a result, he presses the button. The signal races from the button, the bombers drop their bombs, and nuclear holocaust ensues. w_1 is then very different from $w_@$, at least insofar as the surface of the earth is concerned.

w_2 is a duplicate of $w_@$ until shortly before t, at which point a few extra neurons fire and Nixon presses the button. Shortly thereafter, an unlikely but lawful series of events take place. First, the fateful signal fizzles on its way to the bombers, so that nuclear holocaust is averted. Second, all traces of the button-pressing disappear, so that perfect match to $w_@$ is restored.

Here is the problem: w_2 does a far better job than w_1 with respect to exact match and—owing to the indeterministic nature of actuality—neither world contains any miracles. Hence, w_2 is closer to $w_@$ than is w_1. In fact, on Lewis's original metric, w_2 will come out closer to the actual world than *any* world in which there is a nuclear holocaust. So, there are no nuclear-holocaust worlds among the closest button-pressing worlds, in which case (2) will turn out false. What is true is that there would *not* have been a nuclear holocaust, even if Nixon had pressed the button. This is clearly mistaken.

Lewis's response to this objection is to modify his metric. He first introduces the notion of a *quasi-miracle*, which he defines as a pattern of events that is both unlikely and surprising (1986c: 60). He then suggests that quasi-miracles should be treated just like big miracles in the assessment of overall similarity:

What must be said, I think, is that for a quasi-miracle to accomplish perfect convergence, though it is entirely lawful, nevertheless detracts from similarity in much the same way that a convergence miracle does ... The quasi-miracle would be such a remarkable coincidence that it would be quite unlike the goings-on we take to be typical of our world. Like a big genuine miracle, it makes a tremendous difference from our world. Therefore it is not something that happens in the closest worlds to ours where Nixon pressed the button. (1986c: 60)

Hence, the proposal is that we modify Lewis's first rule so as to require the minimization of both big miracles and quasi-miracles. Since the indeterministic cover-up world (w_2) violates this rewritten rule, it will count as comparatively distant to $w_@$ and will therefore be irrelevant to the evaluation of (2).

Lewis's move might avoid the preceding problem,[101] but it also generates a new dilemma.[102] Paul Tichý (1976) invites us to imagine a man—"Jones"—who is disposed

---

[101] Or it might not. See Wasserman (2006a).

[102] It also does nothing to solve the problem of backward counterfactuals. In fact, the problem for Lewis is even more acute in the indeterministic setting. To return to an earlier example, suppose that Dee's time machine operates by indeterministic means—if the start button is pressed, there is a 50 percent chance the machine will work and a 50 percent chance it won't. Now suppose that Jocasta gets into Dee's

to wear his hat when the weather is bad, but is completely indifferent when the weather is good (on fine-weather days, he uses a randomizing device to decide whether or not to wear a hat). Now suppose that the weather is bad (so that Jones is wearing his hat) and consider the question of what would have happened, had the weather been fine. Intuitively, the answer is this:

(3)   If the weather had been fine (at t), Jones might have worn a hat and he might not.

However, this verdict is inconsistent with Lewis's view. For consider two fine-weather worlds that match the actual world up until just before t—in one, Jones wears his hat and, in the other, he does not. Given actual indeterminacy, neither of these worlds needs to contain any miracles (big, small, or quasi). Moreover, both worlds do an equally good job of preserving perfect match for the same amount of time (up until just before t). So, these worlds score equally well with respect to Lewis's first three rules. The crucial question concerns Rule 4. Here is the full statement of that principle:

It is of little or no importance to secure approximate similarity of particular fact, even in matters that concern us greatly.   (1986c: 48)

This rule is notoriously ambiguous—it can be read as saying that approximate match counts for *nothing* or that it counts for *something, but not much*. If we opt for the second reading, the fine-weather-and-hat world will count as comparatively close to the actual world, since it does a better job of preserving approximate match after time t (owing to the presence of the hat). But in that case, (3) will be false. What's true is that Jones would have worn his hat, even if the weather had been fine. That is the wrong result.

The obvious reply to this objection is to opt for the first reading of Lewis's rule. On that reading approximate match does not count for anything, so the fine-weather-and-hat world does not come any closer to actuality than the fine-weather-and-no-hat world. (3) will thus turn out true, as required.

Unfortunately, this reply leads directly to the second horn of the dilemma (due to Sidney Morgenbesser).[103] Suppose that a perfectly random coin is flipped and, while it's in the air, your friend bets that it will come down tails. You refuse the bet and the coin lands heads. Upset with yourself, you lament:

(4)   If I'd taken the bet, I would have won.

---

time machine, sets the controls for an earlier time, and...decides not to press the button. What would have happened if Jocasta had decided to do otherwise? According to Lewis, the answer is *nothing*, or at least nothing *interesting*. In particular, Jocasta would *not* have traveled back in time, since a world in which Jocasta appears in the past would break perfect match, whereas a world with a non-appearance would not. Furthermore, unlike the examples discussed in the previous section, this perfect match could be bought for free, since Jocasta's non-appearance in the past would not violate any of the indeterministic laws in the world in question. Hence, it is *not* true that Jocasta might have traveled in time, had she pressed the button. This is clearly the wrong result.

[103]   This case appears in Slote (1978: 27, fn. 33).

Intuitively, this counterfactual is true. (That's why you're so upset with yourself!) But this result is inconsistent with the current reading of Lewis's theory. For consider two alternative worlds that match actuality up until just before your decision—in one, you bet and it comes up heads; in the other, you bet and it comes up tails. Given the assumption of indeterminism, these worlds score equally well with respect to Lewis's first three rules. And given the current reading of Rule 4, these first three rules are the only ones that matter. The bet-and-heads world does a better job of preserving approximate match (after t) than the bet-and-tails world. But, on the current reading, this is irrelevant. Hence, the two worlds turn out to be equidistant to actuality and (4) turns out to be false. This seems clearly mistaken.[104]

6.4 A unified solution

The cases of Tichý's hat and Morgenbesser's coin constitute a serious dilemma for Lewis's theory of counterfactuals since they seem to require incompatible readings of his final rule. However, this dilemma can be avoided by making a small modification to his account.

Let's begin with the case of Morgenbessser's coin, and let's ask *why* the coin would still have come up heads if you had placed a bet with your friend. Intuitively, the answer is that the coin would still have come up heads because the outcome of the flip is *independent* of whether or not you take the bet.[105] This answer admits of several different interpretations,[106] but one natural idea is to read 'independent' as *causally* independent—the coin's coming up heads is independent of your not taking the bet in the sense that the latter is not a cause of the former.[107] That is why we hold the outcome fixed when we consider what would have happened, had you taken the bet.

There are various ways of working this informal idea into an account of counterfactuals,[108] but one particularly elegant idea—due to Jonathan Schaffer—is to build the requirement of causal independence into Lewis's second and fourth rules. The resulting system of weights and balances will look something like this:

(1C) It is of the first importance to avoid big miracles.
(2C) It is of the second importance to maximize the region of perfect match, *from those regions causally independent of whether or not the antecedent obtains.*
(3C) It is of the third importance to avoid small miracles.
(4C) It is of the fourth importance to maximize the spatiotemporal region of approximate match, *from those regions causally independent of whether or not the antecedent obtains.* (Schaffer 2004: 305)

---

[104] See Wasserman (2006a) for further discussion on this point.
[105] See, for example, Kvart (1986: 44).
[106] Compare, for example, Noordhof (2005) and Schaffer (2004).
[107] On this reading, see Hiddleston (2005), Kvart (1986), and Schaffer (2004).
[108] Recall, for example, Vihvelin's "sophisticated" causal theory from Chapter 4, section 2.3.

Here is how this system gives the right results in the case of Morgenbesser's coin. The bet-and-heads world does a better job than the bet-and-tails world when it comes to matching the post-t region occupied by the coin. Moreover, the coin's coming up heads is causally independent of whether or not you take the bet. Hence, the bet-and-heads world comes out closer than the bet-and-tails world. So, you would have won the wager if you had chosen to take the bet.

Turning to Tichý's hat: The fine-weather-and-hat world does a better job than the fine-weather-and-no-hat world when it comes to matching the post-t region occupied by Jones's hat. However, what goes on in that region (and, in particular, whether or not there is a hat there) is not causally independent of the weather (in the target world, the bad weather causes the hat-wearing). Hence, that match contributes nothing to overall similarity. As a result, the fine-weather-and-hat world and the fine-weather-and-no-hat world end up being equidistant from the target world. The upshot is that, if the weather had been better, Jones might have worn a hat, and he might not have.

Next, to Nixon's button: The problem in that case concerned the quasi-miraculous world in which Nixon presses the button, but where the signal immediately disappears, along with all traces of the button-pressing. That world does a fantastic job of maximizing perfect match with the actual world. However, the goings-on in the relevant regions (and, in particular, the presence or absence of button-pressing traces) obviously depend on whether or not Nixon presses the button. Hence, that match counts for nothing in determining overall similarity. So, the button-pressing-and-nuclear-holocaust world and the button-pressing-and-no-holocaust world are both among the closest to actuality. In other words, if Nixon had pressed the button, there might have been a nuclear holocaust and there might not.

We are now (finally!) in a position to return to Tooley's argument. Recall that we were to imagine three different worlds, as summarized in Table 5.2.

Table 5.2. Tooley's worlds

World	@t	@t*
w_0	M has fuel	N has fuel
	M's switch is not flipped	N's switch is not flipped
w_1	M has fuel	N's fuel is removed
	M's switch is flipped	N's switch is flipped
w_2	M's fuel is removed	N has fuel
	M's switch is flipped	N's switch is flipped

We were also to imagine that, in w_0, machine M is programmed to travel to t^*, empty the fuel from machine N, and then flip its switch. In the same way, N is programmed to travel back to t, to empty M's fuel, and to flip its switch. Given these facts, we were to conclude that both of the following counterfactuals are true (at w_0):

(A)   If M's switch had been flipped at t, then N's fuel would have been removed at t^*.
(B)   If N's switch had been flipped at t^*, then M's fuel would have been removed at t.

The problem was that this required Lewis to make incompatible judgments of comparative similarity: In order for (A) to be true, w_1 must be more similar to w_0 than is w_2, and for (B) to be true, the opposite must be the case. Since the opposites are incompatible, the view is inconsistent.

The problem with this argument is that it assumes that overall similarity is an absolute matter.[109] In particular, it assumes that w_1 is either more or less similar to w_0 *tout court*, and that the same thing is true for w_2. But on the current proposal, this is mistaken—comparative similarity is not absolute, but *antecedent-relative*. This relativity makes all the difference when it comes to evaluating (A) and (B).

To see why, begin with the antecedent of (A): 'If M's switch had been flipped at $t \ldots$'. Crucially, the fact that this antecedent does *not* obtain is part of the causal explanation for why N still has fuel in its tank at t^* (in w_0). In other words, the state of N's tank at t^* is *not* causally independent of whether or not the antecedent obtains. However, the state of M's fuel tank at t *is* causally independent of whether or not M's switch is flipped, since the presence of fuel in M's tank is not caused by the flipping or non-flipping of M's switch. Hence, only the latter match matters when evaluating (A). Since w_1 does a better job than w_2 when it comes to matching the state of M's tank at t, it counts as closest to w_0, *relative to (A)'s antecedent*. That is why (A) is true.

Now consider the antecedent of (B): 'If N's switch had been flipped at $t \ldots$'. The fact that this antecedent does not obtain is part of the explanation for why M had fuel at t. In other words, the state of M's tank at t is *not* causally independent of whether or not the antecedent obtains. However, the state of N's fuel tank at t^* *is* causally independent of whether or not N's switch is flipped, since the presence of fuel in N's tank is not caused by the flipping or non-flipping of N's switch. So, when evaluating (B), we only need to be concerned with the latter state when determining overall similarity. Since w_2 does a better job than w_1 when it comes to matching the state of N's tank at t, it counts as closest to w_0, *relative to (B)'s antecedent*. That is why (B) is true.

Thus, the right response to Tooley is to say that w_1 comes out closest to w_0 relative to the metric that is appropriate to evaluating (A) and that w_2 comes out closest to w_0 relative to the metric that is appropriate to evaluating (B). Since these metrics differ, there is no longer any contradiction. Hence, there is no longer any reason to think the similarity-based approach to counterfactuals rules out the possibility of backward time travel.[110]

That is the good news. Now for the bad.

At the beginning of this section, we noted that there is a close connection between counterfactuals and causation—typically, one event is a cause of another if and only if the second event wouldn't have occurred without the first. This observation has inspired many philosophers to pursue a counterfactual theory of causation, like the

---

[109] See Noordhof (2003).
[110] For more on antecedent-relativity, see Noordhof (2003). For a criticism of this approach, see Cross (2007).

one defended by David Lewis.[111] There is much to say in favor of this approach. The counterfactual theory avoids many of the problems facing traditional regularity-based approaches, it accounts for the intuitive link between causation and counterfactuals, and it is compatible—at least in principle—with the possibility of backward causation. Moreover, the counterfactual theory fits within a larger reductive project in which all nomological facts—including facts about causation, counterfactuals, and the laws of nature—reduce to facts about the arrangement of fundamental physical qualities. (This is what Lewis (1994) calls "the doctrine of Humean supervenience.") For many philosophers, this is a mark in its favor.

But if what we have said in this section is correct, the counterfactual theory must be mistaken. In order to make sense of backward time travel, we must move to a causal theory of counterfactuals and, once we have done that, we can no longer endorse a counterfactual theory of causation. This would be to go in circles.[112]

Of course, one might try to run the same argument in reverse: The counterfactual theory of causation is correct, and that theory is incompatible with the causal theory of counterfactuals. So, we should reject the causal theory of counterfactuals and, with it, the possibility of backward time travel. But the point to emphasize here is that the problem with the non-causal theory of counterfactuals is not just a problem about backward time travel. The cases of Tichý's hat and Morgenbesser's coin already demonstrate that Lewis's original theory is mistaken. Moreover, they strongly suggest that we have to invoke a notion of causal independence in order to provide an adequate account of counterfactuals. So, those cases provide us with independent evidence against the counterfactual theory of causation.[113] As a result, that theory does not give us a good reason to doubt the possibility of backward time travel.

---

[111] See (CT) in section 2 of this chapter.

[112] For a contrary view, see Schaffer (2004).

[113] There are many other problems for the counterfactual theory as well. For a helpful survey, see Menzies (2014).

6

Paradoxes of Identity

East is East, and West is West,
and never the twain shall meet

—Rudyard Kipling, "The Ballad of East and West"

In *Back to the Future II*, Doc Brown takes Marty McFly into the future to help avert a crisis involving Marty's children. Marty's girlfriend, Jennifer, is brought along for the ride. When they arrive in the future, Doc and Marty are caught up in a series of comic misadventures and, in the process, lose track of Jennifer. She is eventually found by the police and returned home, to the house of her future self. When Doc realizes what has happened, he is visibly distraught:

> DOC: No, no, no Marty, that could result in a...[gasp] Great Scott! Jennifer could conceivably encounter her future self! The consequences of that could be disastrous!
>
> MARTY: Doc, what do you mean?
>
> DOC: I foresee two possibilities. One: coming face to face with herself thirty years older would put her into shock and she'd simply pass out. Or two: the encounter could create a time paradox, the result of which could cause a chain reaction that would unravel the very fabric of the space-time continuum and *destroy* the entire universe! [pause] Granted, that's a worst-case scenario. The destruction might in fact be very localized, limited to merely our own galaxy.
>
> MARTY: Well, that's a relief.[1]

---

[1] From the script by Robert Zemeckis and Bob Gale. (Interestingly, the original script title for *Back to the Future II* was "Paradox.")

The idea that self-visitation is a Very Bad Thing is a familiar trope in time travel fiction.[2] It is also a popular topic in philosophy.[3] Among other things, it has been suggested that self-visitation creates problems for the perdurantist theory of persistence (Gilmore 2007), the endurantist view of persistence (Sider 2001: 101–9), and the principles of classical mereology (Effingham and Robson 2007). This chapter addresses these claims, and argues that self-visitation is not as problematic as it may at first appear.[4]

1. Two Puzzles about Sameness and Difference

Consider again the meeting of Young Jennifer (YJ) and Old Jennifer (OJ). YJ is young and, by hypothesis, YJ is the same person as OJ. But if YJ is OJ and YJ is young, then OJ must be young as well. However, OJ is not young, since OJ is old and what is old is not young. To put it another way: The properties of *being young* and *being old* are incompatible, in the sense that it is impossible for something to be both old and young. Self-visitation seems to make this impossibility possible, and is therefore paradoxical.

This paradox of identity rests on four assumptions about sameness and difference. We can make this paradox more precise by stating those assumptions more carefully.

The first assumption is that self-visitation involves numerical identity. When one visits one's former self, one visits *oneself*. That is, there is only one self, or one person, involved in the meeting.

The second assumption is that self-visitation always involves some variation in properties. For example, when Young Jennifer meets Old Jennifer, the "two" differ in height, weight, and hair color. Of course, not every case of self-visitation will involve

---

[2] The fictional explanations of this idea are often absurd. In the movie *Timecop*, for example, time travelers are cautioned not to come into contact with their earlier selves since "the same matter can't occupy the same space at the same time." This sort of warning appears in many time travel stories but, upon reflection, it makes little sense. First, coming into contact with your earlier self would involve occupying *adjacent* regions, not *identical* regions. Second, self-visitation would not normally involve *the same* matter coming into contact, since a person's matter is constantly changing. Finally, it is simply *false* that the same matter can't occupy the same place at the same time—in fact, *every* portion of matter occupies the same place it occupies, so the same matter *always* exists at the same place at the same time.

[3] See, for example, Benovsky (2009, 2011), Carroll (2011), Cotnoir and Bacon (2012), Devlin (2001: 42–3), Effingham (2011a, 2011b), Effingham and Robson (2007), Gilmore (2007), Hanley (1997: 215–18), Kleinschmidt (2011, 2015), Markosian (2004: 670–3), Miller (2006), Sider (2001: 101–9), Simon (2005), and Smith (2009). Of course, not everyone takes self-visitation to be a bad thing. For example, it has been argued that self-visitation provides a helpful model for the Christian doctrines of the Trinity (Leftow 2004, 2012), divine foreknowledge (Zimmerman 2012), and the Eucharist (Pickup 2015). (Who knew that time travel was so relevant to theology?)

[4] The problem of self-visitation is one of the oldest of time travel paradoxes, having first been raised by Israel Zangwill in his review of *The Time Machine* in 1895:

> Had [the Time Traveller] traveled backwards, he would have reproduced a Past in which...he would have had to exist in two forms simultaneously, of varying ages—a feat which even Sir Boyle Roche would have found difficult. (1895: 154)

(Sir Boyle Roche was an eighteenth-century politician who was famous for his use of mixed metaphors and malapropisms.)

observable differences of this kind, but they will all involve *some* variation in properties, if only of the historical sort (e.g. the visitor, but not the visitee, will have the property of *having just traveled in time*).

The third assumption is that the kind of variation involved in self-visitation requires incompatible properties. For example, the property of *weighing (exactly) 50 kg* is incompatible with the property of *weighing (exactly) 60 kg* since, necessarily, if something weighs 50 kg, it does not weigh 60 kg. So too, the property of *having just traveled in time* is incompatible with the property of *having not just traveled in time*, since possession of the former implies a lack of the latter.

The fourth and final piece of the paradox is *Leibniz's Law*: For any x and y, if x is numerically identical to y, then every property had by x is had by y and vice versa.

With all of these principles in place, we can now state the puzzle more carefully. Given the first assumption above, every case of self-visitation involves numerical identity. So, in Jennifer's case, it would follow that Young Jennifer (YJ) is numerically identical to Old Jennifer (OJ).

(P1)   If Jennifer self-visits, then YJ is OJ.

Since this is a case of self-visitation, our second assumption tells us that there must be some variation in properties. For example:

(P2)   YJ is 50 kg.
(P3)   OJ is 60 kg.

Our third assumption was that these properties are incompatible:

(P4)   For any x, if x is 60 kg, then it is not the case that x is 50 kg.

But now, from (P3) and (P4), we can deduce:

(C1)   OJ is not 50 kg.

When we combine (C1) and (P2), Leibniz's Law allows us to infer:

(C2)   YJ is not OJ.

Finally, from (C2) and (P1), we can conclude that this is not a case of self-visitation after all:

(C3)   Jennifer does not self-visit.

Moreover, since this argument does not rely on any particular facts about this case, we can universally generalize on our conclusion. Self-visitation, in general, is impossible.[5]

---

[5] The self-visitation paradox does not directly challenge the possibility of time travel, since one could still allow for time travel to times at which one does not exist. However, this kind of anti-visitation requirement would clearly be ad hoc. (Ad hoc, but not unheard of: In the *Superboy* comics, attempts to visit one's future self result in the time traveler and the future self "switching places" in time, so that the two never exist at the same moment. See, for example, *Superboy* Vol. 1, no. 53.)

Put this way, the paradox of self-visitation is reminiscent of the traditional problem of change.[6] That problem is an old one, going back to the Eleatic philosophers in the fifth century BCE. Melissus, for example, puts the problem this way:

> [W]hat is unique is always homogeneous with itself, and what is homogeneous can neither perish nor grow nor change its arrangement nor suffer pain nor suffer anguish. For if it underwent any of these things it would not be homogeneous. For anything that undergoes any change of whatever sort moves from one state into a different one. But nothing is different from what exists. Therefore it will not change.[7]

Change, according to Melissus, would require both uniqueness and diversity, since it would require a single thing to alternate between different states. However, Melissus takes this to be absurd, since nothing can differ from itself. He concludes that change is impossible.

Few today would accept this conclusion, but many still find change puzzling. To see why, suppose that a given leaf changes from green to red as it ages. If *the leaf* changes, then the young leaf (YL) must be the same leaf as the old one (OL):

(P1*)   If the leaf persists through change, then YL is OL.

But the young leaf must also be *different* from the old leaf, or else the leaf does not *change*:

(P2*)   YL is green.
(P3*)   OL is red.

However, the properties of *being red* and *being green* are incompatible, in the sense that nothing could be both red (all over) and green (all over):

(P4*)   For any x, if x is red, then it is not the case that x is green.

From (P4*) and (P3*), we can infer:

(C1*)   OL is not green.

And from (C1*) and (P2*), Leibniz's Law allows us to infer:

(C2*)   YL is not OL.

Finally, from (P1*) and (C2*), we can deduce:

(C3*)   The leaf does not persist through change.

Moreover, since the assumptions behind this argument apply to every case of purported change, we can conclude that change, in general, is impossible.[8]

---

[6] This point is made in many places, including Carroll (2011), Sider (2001: 101–9), and Simon (2005). For a more detailed introduction to the problem of change, see Wasserman (2006b).

[7] Simplicius, *Commentary on the* Physics, 103.13–104.15.

[8] Similar statements of the problem of change are provided by Haslanger (2003), Heller (1992), Hinchliff (1996), Merricks (1994), and Wasserman (2006b).

The parallels between the paradox of self-visitation and the problem of change are obvious. They might also be instructive, since we can consider various solutions to the problem of change and see whether there are parallel solutions available in the case of self-visitation. That will be our strategy in this chapter.[9]

2. Perdurantism and Self-Visitation

One of the challenges of self-visitation is to understand how a single object could be in two different places at the same time. This challenge has a temporal analogue: How could a single object exist at two different times? Put this way, the question doesn't seem all that challenging—an object exists at different times by persisting through time. But this answer is really a reformulation of the question. The question is: What is the nature of persistence? In this section, we consider the perdurantist's answer to this question (2.1), and its application to the problems of change and self-visitation (2.2). We then consider a pair of objections to this approach (2.3 and 2.4).

2.1 Perdurantism and persistence

According to the perdurantist (or "four-dimensionalist"), persistence through time is like extension through space.[10] A road, for example, stretches from one town to another by having different spatial parts at all of the places between. In the same way, a person who persists from one time to another does so by having different temporal parts at each of the intervening moments. More generally, all objects persist through time by having different temporal parts at different times.

In order to state this position more carefully, we will first need a few definitions. We begin with two primitives: 'x is a part of y at (or during) t' and 'x exists at (or during) t.'[11] The first primitive is a familiar part of ordinary speech (as well as formal mereology).[12,13]

---

[9] Not all replies to the problem of change will apply to the case of self-visitation. In Chapter 2, for example, we introduced the debate between the B-theorist (who takes tensed facts to be reducible to tense-less facts) and the A-theorist (who denies this claim). According to the A-theorist, the problem of change can be resolved by paying careful attention to tense. For example, (P2*) will only be true if the leaf is *now* green. But in that case (P3*) will be false—the leaf will be red when it is old, but it is not old now. Similarly, the A-theorist will claim that (P3*) is only true if the leaf is *now* red. But in that case (P2*) will be false—the leaf was green, but is not so any longer. The A-theorist will therefore conclude that there is no time at which (P2*) and (P3*) are both true, in which case the argument is always unsound. However, this response to the problem of change does not offer any help with the paradox of self-visitation. After all, if Young Jennifer meets with Old Jennifer, then Jennifer will be both 50 kg and 60 kg at the same time. So, the puzzle remains even if we focus on what is the case at a particular time.

[10] Prominent defenders of this view include Lewis (1983, 1986a: 202–4), Quine (1959), and Sider (1997a, 2001).

[11] Henceforth, the parenthetical parts will remain implicit.

[12] The extent to which the ordinary concept aligns with the formal concept is a matter of some debate. See, for example, Baker (2008).

[13] Classical mereology is built on a two-place parthood relation: x *is a part of* y. Many temporal parts theorists accept classical mereology, and would therefore be happy to rewrite my definitions without relativizing to times. However, many opponents of temporal parts take the predicate 'x is a part of y' to be

My arms are now part of me; my shoes are not. My baby teeth were a part of me during my childhood; they are not a part of me now. The second primitive leaves room for ambiguity, so we should say a bit about how we will be using the phrase.[14] Suppose that t is the temporal interval corresponding to the career of some persisting object o. Then we will say that o exists at all and only the intervals that overlap with t. So, for example, Descartes exists during the temporal interval that stretches from his birth (in 1596) to his death (in 1650). He also exists during the year 1599, and during the seventeenth century, but Descartes does not exist during the eighteenth century, since that period does not overlap with his life.

Next, we add the following pair of definitions:

(D1) t is the time span of $x =_{df}$ (i) x exists at t, (ii) x exists at every sub-interval of t, and (iii) x does not exist at any interval wholly distinct from t.

(D2) x overlaps y at $t =_{df}$ there is some z such that z is a part of x at t and z is a part of y at t.

With these definitions in place, we can characterize temporal parts as follows:

(D3) x is a temporal part of y at $t =_{df}$ (i) t is the time span of x, (ii) x is a part of y at t, and (iii) x overlaps at t everything that is a part of y at t.

(We can also say that x is a *proper* temporal part of y at t if and only if x is a temporal part of y at t and $x \neq y$.[15])

Condition (i) of (D3) guarantees that temporal parts have the right temporal extent. Condition (ii) guarantees that temporal parts are genuine *parts* of the objects that they compose. And condition (iii) guarantees that temporal parts are the right "size". For example, the northbound lanes of I-5 in Seattle are not the Seattle segment of I-5, since there is more to the road in that place. By analogy, the current temporal part of your heart is not *your* temporal part, since it does not overlap all the parts you have right now.

We now have a definition of temporal parts, but what exactly is the "temporal parts view"? Different philosophers formulate the view in different ways, but most people seem to agree that perdurantism is an *ontological* thesis, to the effect that persisting objects have temporal parts. Ted Sider, for example, equates perdurantism with the following principle:

Necessarily, for any object x, and for any non-empty, non-overlapping sets of times T_1 and T_2 whose union is the time span of x, there are two objects x_1 and x_2, such that (i) x_1 and x have the same parts at every time in T_1, (ii) x_2 and x have the same parts at every time in T_2, and (iii) the time span of $x_1 = T_1$, while the time span of $x_2 = T_2$.[16]

---

incomplete, on a par with 'x is between y and'. For our purposes, it is best to begin with the more neutral primitive. For more on this point, see Sider (2001: 57–8).

[14] For some possible interpretations of related primitives, see Parsons (2007).
[15] These definitions are based on the ones offered by Sider (2001: 59).
[16] Sider calls this the "Thesis of Temporal Locality" (1997a: 204).

This thesis implies that a persisting object has a temporal part for every interval within its career. Sider takes this to be the central claim of perdurantism. Similar accounts are offered by Heller (1984: 325–9), Hudson (2001: 59), Thomson (1983: 207–10), and others.

This characterization is popular, but it is also problematic. For one thing, the characterization is too strong, since it excludes many self-professed perdurantists. Some, like David Lewis, would reject Sider's principle because they take the connection between temporal parts and persistence to be a contingent matter.[17] Others would agree that persisting objects are necessarily composed of temporal parts, but would deny that there are temporal parts for *every* arbitrary way of dividing up an object's career.[18] Perhaps most importantly, the common characterization is *too weak*, since it leaves out an important element of our guiding analogy. We began with the observation that spatially extended objects exist in different places *by virtue* of having different parts at those places, and we extended this explanatory talk to temporal examples—we said, for example, that Descartes existed in different centuries *by virtue of* having different temporal parts in those centuries.[19] The standard formulation omits this element and is therefore incomplete. A theory of persistence should *explain* the facts of persistence, where this involves identifying the most general facts in virtue of which objects exist at different times. And the perdurantist explanation is simple: Objects persist through time by having different temporal parts at different times. In other words, facts about persistence through time are grounded in facts about temporal parts.[20]

2.2 Perdurantism, change, and self-visitation

Most philosophers who accept the perdurantist theory of persistence also endorse a related view of change.[21] Change, it is said, consists in having different properties at different times, where having different properties at different times is a matter of having different temporal parts with those properties.

Perdurantists who accept this view have two different ways of responding to the problem of change, depending on how we understand definite descriptions like 'the young leaf' and names like 'YL'.

First, we could think of these terms as denoting particular temporal parts or segments of the persisting leaf—'YL', for example, picks out a segment that exists when the leaf is young, whereas 'OL' refers to a segment that exists when the leaf is old. On that reading, the perdurantist will accept (P2*) and (P3*), but deny (P1*).

---

[17] See Lewis (1994: 374–5).

[18] For discussion on this point, see Hawley (2010: section 2), Mellor (1981: 132–4), and Wiggins (1980: 24–7). For the spatial analogue, see van Inwagen (1981).

[19] The objection to this characterization is tied to our discussion of philosophical methodology in Chapter 1.

[20] Of course, one could use the term 'perdurantism' for a purely ontological thesis, but that view would no longer be *a theory of persistence*. For more on this point, see Wasserman (2016).

[21] See, for example, Armstrong (1983: 79), Hawley (2001: 13), and Lewis (1986a: 204).

(P1*)   If the leaf persists through change, then YL is OL.

(P2*)   YL is green.

(P3*)   OL is red.

In other words, the perdurantist will say that one segment of the leaf is green and one segment is red, but that is not a problem since the first segment is not identical to the second. Moreover, he will insist that the non-identity of these segments does not show that *the leaf* does not persist through change (indeed, persistence through change *just is* having different temporal parts with different properties).

The other option is to understand the names 'YL' and 'OL' as referring to the whole of the leaf, rather than its proper temporal parts. In that case, the perdurantist will accept (P1*), but deny (P2*) and (P3*). Strictly speaking, the persisting leaf itself is neither green nor red. Rather, it is green relative to some times and red relative to others.

Of course, we could replace (P2*) and (P3*) with the following premises:

(P2**)   YL is green at t_1.

(P3**)   OL is red at t_2.

(Where t_1 is a time at which the leaf has a green temporal part and t_2 is a time at which it has a red temporal part.) We could also replace (P4*) with the following:

(P4**)   For any x, and for any time t, if x is red at t, then it is not the case that x is green at t.

(P3**) and (P4**) would then imply the following:

(C1**)   It is not the case that OL is green at t_2.

But this conclusion is unproblematic. In particular, (C1**), together with (P2**) and Leibniz's Law, does not imply that YL and OL are numerically distinct. So, it does not imply that the leaf cannot persist through change.[22]

Some perdurantists have pointed out that a parallel solution is available in the case of self-visitation.[23] To state this solution, it will be helpful to have a diagram of Jennifer's adventures in *Back to the Future II*. (See Figure 6.1 on the next page.)

This figure features five distinct "person parts". Prior to the time travel episode (at t_1) there is a young-looking person part (A) with good posture. Jennifer then travels to the future (to t_4), where there are two different person parts—one of which looks young (B) and one of which looks old (E). Jennifer then returns to the past (t_2), grows old (t_3), and is eventually visited by her younger self (t_4).

If we limit our attention to these person parts, there is nothing paradoxical about the story. D has a cane; A does not. C is straight; D is bent. B weighs 50 kg; E weighs 60 kg. None of this is problematic since all of these objects are distinct.

---

[22] For further discussions of the perdurantist solution, see Heller (1992), Lewis (1986a: 203–4), and Sider (2001: 92–8).

[23] See, for example, Hanley (1997: 216–7), Lewis (1976: 147), and Sider (2001: 101).

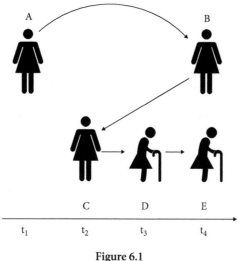

Figure 6.1

But to limit our attention in this way is to leave Jennifer out of the story. The question is: How does Jennifer relate to the person parts in this picture?

One natural suggestion is that each of the person parts is a temporal part of Jennifer, and that self-visitation therefore amounts to having two temporal parts at the same time.[24] Paradox can then be avoided by assigning incompatible properties to the different temporal parts of the same person.

More carefully, suppose that 'YJ' and 'OJ' refer, respectively, to person parts B and E. In that case, the perdurantist will accept (P2) and (P3), but deny (P1).

(P1)   If Jennifer self-visits, then YJ is OJ.
(P2)   YJ is 50 kg.
(P3)   OJ is 60 kg.

Suppose instead that 'YJ' and 'OJ' both refer to the persisting person—Jennifer—who is composed of the various person parts in the story. In that case, the perdurantist will accept (P1), but reject (P2) and (P3). In the case of change, we saw that persisting objects only have weights or other properties relative to certain times. In the case of self-visitation, it is natural to say that time travelers only have properties relative to certain times *and places*—or, better yet, relative to certain *spacetime regions*. On this way of thinking about our case, the perdurantist will reject (P2) and (P3) and replace them with the following:

(P2′)   YJ is 50 kg at r_B.
(P3′)   OJ is 60 kg at r_E.

[24] See Hanley (1997: 216–17) and Miller (2006: 310).

(Where r_B is the region occupied by B and r_E is the region occupied by E.) We can then say that *being 50 kg* is incompatible with *being 60 kg* in the sense that nothing could have both of those weights at the same region:

> (P4′)   For any x, and for any spatiotemporal region r, if x is 60 kg at r, then it is not the case that x is 50 kg at r.

Once again, the important point is that this set of premises does not generate a contradiction, since Young Jennifer and Old Jennifer do not have different weights at the same region. Region relativism therefore solves the original version of our paradox.

2.3 The problem with temporal parts

We will have more to say about region relativism in section 3.3. For now, we will focus on a more general worry about the temporal parts account.[25]

We have seen that the perdurantist theory of persistence suggests a natural account of self-visitation: Self-visitation involves a single object having two temporal parts at the same time. Unfortunately, this suggestion turns out to be inconsistent with the standard perdurantist definition of a temporal part.

Recall the standard definition:

> (D1) x is a temporal part of y at $t =_{df}$ (i) t is the time span of x, (ii) x is a part of y at t, and (iii) x overlaps at t everything that is a part of y at t.[26]

To see the problem raised by this definition, suppose again that B and E are both temporal parts of Jennifer at t_4 (B, again, is the younger version of Jennifer and E is the older). Given (D1)(ii), it follows that B and E are both parts of Jennifer at t_4. And given the standard axioms of mereology, the distinctness of B and E implies that neither is a part of the other (at t_4).[27] But then at least one of B and E will fail to include the other as a part. Hence, at least one of these objects will fail to meet condition (iii) of our definition (since at least one of B and E fails to overlap *all* of Jennifer's parts at t_4). So, the natural perdurantist description of self-visitation turns out to be inconsistent with the standard definition of temporal parts.

Of course, we could still call objects like B and E "person parts," if we wanted. And we could still say that (for people) self-visitation amounts to having more than one person part at a time. But we can no longer think of person parts as temporal parts.

Unfortunately, changing the description of the case does not avoid all the problems. Consider first the sum of Jennifer's person parts at t_4—B⊕E. Since B and E are each parts of Jennifer at t_4, the standard principles of mereology tell us that their sum is also a part of her at that time. Moreover, B⊕E exists only at t_4, and it overlaps everything that is a part of Jennifer at that time. B⊕E thus satisfies all three conditions of (D1) and therefore counts as Jennifer's temporal part at the time in question. Next, recall the

---

[25] This problem is noted by Effingham (2011b), Keller and Nelson (2001: 341), and Sider (2001: 101).
[26] See Sider (2001: 59).   [27] On the standard axioms of mereology, see Varzi (2014).

standard perdurantist account of change: Change consists in having different properties at different times, where having different properties at different times is a matter of having different temporal parts with those properties. This view about temporal predication is often summarized as follows:

(F@t)   For any object x, property F, and time t, x is F at t only if, and in that case because, x has a t-part that is F.[28]

This popular principle turns out to have some unpleasant results for Jennifer, in light of the preceding observation. For one thing, (F@t) implies that Jennifer doubles in size when she travels in time, since $B \oplus E$ is twice as big as A. She also undergoes a drastic change in appearance, since $B \oplus E$ has twice as many arms, legs, and eyes. Both of these claims seem wrong. In fact, given (D1) and (F@t), just about all of the things we would normally say about Jennifer at t_4 turn out to be mistaken—she is neither straight nor bent, neither short-haired nor long-haired, neither old-looking nor young-looking (though she does have proper parts at that time with all of these features). Perhaps most worrisome is that, given (D1) and (F@t), this no longer seems like a genuine case of self-visitation—B may meet E, but $B \oplus E$ does not meet itself, so we should not say that *Jennifer* meets herself at that time. Clearly, something has gone wrong.[29]

The perdurantist can respond to these worries by rejecting either (D1) or (F@t). As it turns out, there are independent reasons for taking the second option.

(F@t) is most plausible when restricted to "qualitative" properties like weight, shape, and color. Other kinds of properties prove problematic. Take, for example, the case of "sortal" properties, which divide objects into kinds. The leaf is a leaf whenever it exists, but many perdurantists would not say that the proper temporal parts of a leaf are themselves leaves.[30] Or consider the case of historical properties. My son is currently ten years old but his current temporal part is clearly not. These kinds of cases suggest that (F@t) is false.[31]

Of course, it would be nice for the perdurantist to have something to put in its place. Here is one suggestion. If we restrict our attention to persons and to qualitative properties, and if we focus on having properties at spatiotemporal regions, rather than times, we can revise (F@t) to read as follows:

(F@r)   For any person x, qualitative property F, and region r, x is F at r only if, and in that case because, r has a person part at r that is F.

(F@r) provides the correct results in all of the cases considered thus far. For example, it implies that Jennifer weighs 50 kg at r_B since the relevant person part—B—weighs 50 kg. It also implies that she weighs 60 kg at r_E in virtue of the fact that E weighs 60 kg.

---

[28] See Armstrong (1983: 79), Hawley (2001: 13), and Lewis (1986a: 204).
[29] The same objections apply to the endurantist who wishes to identify the time traveler with the sum of the "person-like" parts. See Sider (2001: 102).
[30] See, for example, Hudson (2001: Chapter 4).
[31] See Parsons (2005), Sider (2001: 57), and Wasserman (2005).

Moreover, (F@r) does not imply that Jennifer has four arms, four legs, and four eyes when she visits herself, since none of her person parts have those properties at that time. Finally, (F@r) allows us to say that Jennifer meets herself at t_4, since she has two person parts at that region that are appropriately related to each other.

(F@r) is a weaker principle than (F@t), given its restrictions. But note two things. First, although it is restricted to persons, (F@r) suggests parallel treatments for other kinds of objects. For example, we can say that a leaf has a qualitative property at a given time (or region) if and only if the relevant "leaf-part" has that property. Second, (F@r) is consistent with the general perdurantist program, despite its restriction to qualitative properties. The perdurantist claims that objects exist at different times, and have the properties that they do at different times, by virtue of their temporal parts. But the perdurantist does not need to say that all of the properties that I have right now are to be explained by reference to the properties of my *current* temporal part. Different temporal parts may figure into the explanation, depending on what kind of property is at issue. For example, the perdurantist might say that my son is currently ten years old in virtue of the fact that he has ten years' worth of temporal parts, leading up to and including his current temporal part. His current temporal part thus figures into the explanation of why he has the relevant property, but it is not the whole story. The perdurantist can also say that I am a person in virtue of what all my temporal parts are like, and how they are related to each other. If we add to this the plausible thesis that an object of kind K is a K at every time that it exists, we have an explanation of the fact that I am currently a person—an explanation that does not require us to say that my current temporal part is also a person.

To sum up: The perdurantist holds that the properties that objects have at times are determined, somehow, by the properties of their temporal parts. And this may very well be true, even if (F@t) is false.

2.4 The problem with person parts

At this point, we have replaced (F@t) with (F@r), and we have shown how the perdurantist can use the latter principle to give a satisfactory account of self-visitation. One last issue remains.

(F@r) replaces talk of temporal parts with talk of person parts, and we noted that, in the case of self-visitation, these two concepts come apart. That leaves us with the question: If person parts are not temporal parts, then just what are they?

One natural suggestion is made by Ted Sider, who identifies person parts with "person-like" parts of temporal parts.[32] The idea, presumably, is that we have a good idea of what people are typically like—in other words, we have a good idea of the kinds of qualities possessed by typical temporal parts of persons. For example, temporal parts of persons typically include only one head. That is why B and E are both person parts of Jennifer at the time of self-visitation, and why B⊕E is not—the individual parts

---

[32] See Sider (2001: 101). Sider uses the term "person stage" rather than "person part." See also Lewis (1976: 147–8).

resemble typical temporal parts, whereas the actual temporal part does not. This definition of 'person part' may be vague, but it does seem serviceable.

Unfortunately, vagueness is not the only problem with Sider's characterization. Imagine a world populated by very small people. These people move about and are held together, much like the subatomic particles of our own world. Sometimes, very many very small people come together to compose a larger person (just like many subatomic particles sometimes come together to compose a person at our world). This kind of case is depicted in Figure 6.2.

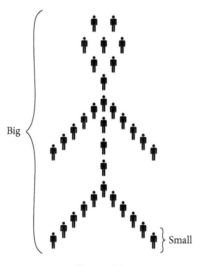

Figure 6.2

Call the designated small person 'Small' and the big person 'Big'. Suppose that Small is thinking about time travel at t. That should *not* imply that Big is thinking about time travel at t or at any other time or region. That is because the relation between Small and Big is fundamentally different from the relation between B and Jennifer in our earlier example. B is, in some sense, a *representative* of Jennifer at t_4—if you want to know what's going on with Jennifer at that time, you look at B (and also at E). Small is a part of Big at t, and he is person-like, but he is not a "person part" of Big in the relevant sense. The upshot is that there must be more to a person part than just being a person-like part.

In order to solve this problem, we will have to take a step back. According to the perdurantist, every person is composed of instantaneous objects. Whether or not a given collection of instantaneous objects will all be temporal parts of a single person will depend on various factors. Some of the factors concern what the individual temporal parts are like, in and of themselves. For example, in the typical, non-self-visitation case, each of the objects will have to be "person-like," in Sider's sense of the word. But those person-like objects must also be related to each other in the right kinds of ways. Different perdurantists have different views on what these "right kinds of ways" are, but, in the case of persons, most focus on the mental states of the person-like objects and the relations that hold between those states. Here, for example, is David Lewis:

> These successive states should be interconnected in two ways. First, by bonds of similarity. Change should be gradual rather than sudden, and (at least in some respects) there should not be too much change overall. Second, by bonds of lawful causal dependence. Such change as there is should conform, for the most part, to lawful regularities concerning the succession of mental states—regularities, moreover that are exemplified in everyday cases of survival. And this should be so not by accident... but rather because each succeeding mental state causally depends for its character on the states immediately before it.   (1983: 55–6)

For Lewis, a series of person-like objects composes a person because the mental states of those objects stand in the right relations of similarity and causal dependence to each other. Lewis refers to this complex relation as "the R-relation" and thus identifies a continuant person with "a maximal R-interrelated aggregate of person-stages" (1983: 60).

This identification can help us engineer an appropriate definition of 'person-part'. Here is the suggestion:

(D4) x is a person part of y at $r =_{df}$ (i) x is part of y at r, (ii) x is person-like, and (iii) x is a member of a set of R-related person-like objects that compose y.

Conditions (i) and (ii) come from Sider's earlier suggestion—a person part must be a part, and it must be person-like. Condition (iii) is added from Lewis, and it is this condition that helps to avoid the problem of Big and Small. Small's t-part is person-like, and it is a part of Big at the time in question. Moreover, that t-part *is* R-related to other person-like objects at other times. But those objects do *not* compose Big (they compose Small) so Small's t-part is not a person part of Big at t (or at any other region or time).[33]

(D4) also delivers the right results in the case of self-visitation. Looking back at our earlier diagram (Figure 6.1), Jennifer has exactly one person part at t_1 (A), one person part at t_2 (C), and one person part at t_3 (D). However, she has two person parts at t_4, since B and E are both person-like parts of her at that time and both are members of a set of R-related person-like objects that compose Jennifer.

To sum up: The perdurantist theory of persistence provides a simple solution to the traditional problem of change. Moreover, that solution suggests a closely related response to the paradox of self-visitation. Finally, the perdurantist is able to provide a natural account of self-visitation itself—for persons, self-visitation amounts to having more than one person part at a time, where 'person part' is defined in accordance with (D4).

---

[33] What if Small is himself a time traveler who repeatedly travels back in time until there is a gigantic gathering of R-related person parts who then compose Big? That's a good question. We will return to this kind of case in section 4.

3. Endurantism and Self-Visitation

The doctrine of perdurantism is commonly contrasted with *endurantism* (or "three-dimensionalism"). But it is not entirely clear what this alternative is supposed to be. This section examines what endurantism is (3.1) and what it says about the problems of change and self-visitation (3.2). We then consider a pair of problems for this approach (3.3 and 3.4).

3.1 Endurantism and persistence

The most common characterization of endurantism is due to David Lewis, who defines an enduring object as one that "persists by being wholly present at more than one time" (1986a: 202). Given this definition, we could say that endurantism is the view that all persisting objects are enduring objects—that is, all objects persist through time by being wholly present at different times. This is the standard formulation of endurantism.[34]

The standard formulation raises an immediate question: What does it mean for an object to be "wholly present" at a time?[35]

One natural thought is that being wholly present at a time is a matter of having all of your parts present at that time. That is:

(D1) x is wholly present at $t =_{df}$ every part of x exists at t.

However, many endurantists will reject this definition as incomplete, since many endurantists take the parthood relation to be a three-place relation that holds between two objects and a time.[36] In reading (D1), we must therefore ask: Every part of x *at what time*? There are at least two answers to this question, and thus two ways of understanding (D1):

(D2) x is wholly present at $t =_{df}$ everything that is a part of x at t exists at t.
(D3) x is wholly present at $t =_{df}$ everything that is a part of x at any time exists at t.

The problem is that neither of these definitions gives the endurantist what she wants. (D2) is too weak, since it would classify perduring objects as wholly present whenever they exist (since everything that is a part of a perduring object at a time will exist at that time). (D3), on the other hand, is too strong, since it implies that none of us is wholly present now (since all of us have had parts in the past which no longer exist).

One response to these problems is to restrict our attention to *temporal* parts. For example, we could say that being wholly present at a time is a matter of having all of your *temporal* parts present at that time:

---

[34] See Balashov (2000), Crisp and Smith (2005: 318), Hawley (2001: 14), Jackson (1994: 97), Kurtz (2006: 10), Merricks (1999: 421), Rea (1998: 225), Simons (1987: 175), and many others.

[35] This question is raised by many. See, for example, Markosian (1994), Merricks (1999), and Sider (2001: 63–8). For an overview of different definitions of 'wholly present', see Crisp and Smith (2005).

[36] This point is made by Markosian (1994), but attributed to Sider. See Sider (2001: 64).

(D4) x is wholly present at $t =_{df}$ everything that is a temporal part of x at any time exists at t.[37]

This definition may appear promising, since it is natural to think that an enduring object has only one temporal part—*itself*—and that that object exists whenever it exists. But this is too quick.[38] To see the potential problem, suppose that an ordinary lump of clay is created at t_1, formed into a statue at t_2, and then rolled up into a ball at t_3. According to many endurantists, this story involves at least two objects—a lump of clay and a statue.[39] The lump is not identical to the statue, since only the former exists at t_1. But the lump does coincide with the statue, since the two objects share all the same parts from t_2 to t_3. On this "co-location view" it is possible for two enduring objects to be in the same place at the same time and to share all the same parts. Here is the problem: If the statue and the lump share all of the same parts from t_2 until t_3 then, given the standard axioms of mereology, it will follow that the statue is a part of the lump during that period. But then, given the standard definition of 'temporal part', it will turn out that the statue is a temporal part of the lump from t_2 to t_3.[40] So, given (D4), it will turn out that the lump of clay is not wholly present from t_1 to t_2. That is inconsistent with what many endurantists want to say.

Here is a fifth and final idea. We have said that perduring objects exist at different times by having different temporal parts at those times. So one natural idea is to say that enduring objects are objects that exist at different times, but which do not exist at those times by having different temporal parts. This would suggest the following definition of 'wholly present':

(D5) x is wholly present at $t =_{df} x$ exists at t, but not by having a proper temporal part at t.

Several people have endorsed this definition,[41] and there are certainly some things to say in its favor. (D5) implies that enduring objects are wholly present at each moment they exist and that perduring objects are not wholly present at any moment they exist. Moreover, (D5) is consistent with what many endurantists want to say about the statue and the clay, since one can admit that the statue is a temporal part of the lump from t_2 to t_3, but deny that the lump exists at those times *by* having that temporal part.[42]

The only problem with this definition is that it would effectively undermine the standard formulation of endurantism. On the standard explanatory account, endurantism is the view that objects persist through time by being wholly present at different

---

[37]   This definition is suggested by Markosian (1994).   [38]   See Sider (2001: 64–5).

[39]   See, for example, Baker (2000), Fine (2003), and Wiggins (1980).

[40]   Since (i) that period corresponds to the time span of the statue, (ii) the statue is a part of the lump during that period, and (iii) the statue overlaps everything that is a part of the lump during that period.

[41]   See, for example, Carroll and Markosian (2010: 172), Markosian (1994), and McCall and Lowe (2009: 278).

[42]   If anything, the order of explanation would seem to go the other way around: The statue exists during that period because the lump exists during that time, and has the properties that it does.

times. Given (D5), this amounts to the view that objects persist through time by existing at different times, but not by having different temporal parts at those times. But *that* amounts to the view that objects exist at different times by existing at different times (just not by having different temporal parts). Since this view is circular, it does not provide an explanation. And since it does not provide an explanation, it does not constitute a theory.

Perhaps this is the right conclusion. Perhaps, that is, we should understand the endurantist as denying the perdurantist theory, rather than asserting a theory of her own.[43] In that case, we don't need to bother defining 'wholly present', and we shouldn't say that objects persist *by* being wholly present at different times. Rather, we should simply say that objects *don't* persist by having temporal parts. On this way of looking at things, the debate between endurantists and perdurantists is not a clash between rival theories of persistence. Rather, it is a debate over whether a single theory—the temporal parts theory—is correct.[44]

3.2 Endurantism, change, and self-visitation

Endurantists reject the perdurantist theory of persistence; they also deny the perdurantist account of change in terms of variation across temporal parts. But when it comes to the problem of change, the two opponents actually share some common ground.

Recall that the earlier argument against change assumed that the young leaf (YL) is green and the old leaf (OL) is red:

(P2*)   YL is green.
(P3*)   OL is red.

On the assumption that both premises are talking about the persisting leaf, the perdurantist rejected (P2*) and (P3*) and replaced them with the following:

(P2**)   YL is green at t_1.
(P3**)   OL is red at t_2.

(Where t_1 is a time at which the leaf is green, and t_2 is a time at which the leaf is red.)

Many endurantists make the same move.[45] On this way of thinking about things, the leaf does not have the simple properties of *being green* and *being red*. Rather, it has the "time-indexed" properties of *being green at t_1* and *being red at t_2*. For the endurantist, these time-indexed properties cannot be reduced to the non-indexed properties of the leaf's temporal parts. Rather, the leaf simply stands in the *green at* relation to t_1 and the *red at* relation to t_2. That is why (2**) and (3**) are true. The crucial point is that there is nothing paradoxical about this situation since there is nothing puzzling about a single object standing in different relations to different things.[46]

---

[43] This conclusion is not original. See, for example, the discussion in Sider (2001: 63–8).

[44] For more on this point, see Wasserman (2016).

[45] See, for example, Mellor (1981: 110–14).

[46] The relativization strategy is famously criticized by Lewis (1986a: 202–4). For replies to Lewis, see Eddon (2010), Haslanger (1989), Hawley (2001: 18), Lowe (1998), and Wasserman (2003b).

In section 2.2, we saw how this kind of relativization strategy could be extended to the case of self-visitation. (See Figure 6.1.)

The perdurantist took this diagram to depict five distinct person parts of a single person. For the endurantist, the diagram depicts a single person, present five times over—A = B = C = D = E. On this account, self-visitation does not consist in having two person parts at the same time. Rather, it consists in being "wholly present" in two places at the same time—that is, being present in two places at the same time, but not by virtue of having different person parts at those places.[47]

The perdurantist replied to the paradox of self-visitation by rejecting (P2) and (P3) and replacing them with the following:

(P2′)   YJ is 50 kg at r_B.
(P3′)   OJ is 60 kg at r_E.

(Where r_B is the region occupied by B and r_E is the region occupied by E.)

According to the perdurantist, (P2′) is true because Jennifer's person part at r_B weighs 50 kg and (P3′) is true because her person part at r_E weighs 60 kg. The endurantist cannot say exactly the same thing, but she can say something similar. First, the endurantist cannot identify regions r_B and r_E by referring to the different person parts that occupy those regions. Nor can she identify them as the regions occupied by persons B and E. For the endurantist, B *is* E, so every region occupied by the first is also occupied by the second. But the endurantist *can* identify the regions by referring to the different ways in which Jennifer relates to them. She can say, for example, that r_B is the region in which Jennifer is young, and that r_E is the region in which she is old. She can also appeal to these kinds of relations in accounting for the truth of (P2′) and (P3′). For example, the endurantist can say that (P2′) is true in virtue of the fact that Jennifer stands in the relation of *weighing 50 kg at* to r_B and that (P3′) is true because she stands in the relation of *weighing 60 kg at* to r_E. Once again, the endurantist will not say that these relations hold in virtue of the properties had by Jennifer's person parts at those regions.[48] But the main point here is the same point made earlier: There is nothing puzzling about a single object standing in different relations to different things. So, on the face of it, there is nothing paradoxical about self-visitation.[49]

3.3 From relativism to compatibilism

Upon further reflection, however, things are not so simple. The main problem with region relativism concerns the possibility of co-location.

---

[47] This characterization might be challenged—see Markosian (2004: 670–3). For worries about this approach, see Sider (2004) and section 2 of this chapter.

[48] That is not to say that the obtaining of these relations is inexplicable. The endurantist could say, for example, that Jennifer stands in the relation of *weighing 50 kg at* to r_B because (i) she is composed of some objects at r_B, (ii) each of those objects has a mass at that region, and (iii) those masses, taken together, total 50 kg.

[49] This response is noted by Sider (2001: 104) and endorsed by Miller (2006).

It is sometimes said that the standard model in physics allows for two bosons with the same energy to be in the same place at the same time. Whether or not this is the right description is a matter of some debate,[50] but many philosophers are willing to grant that co-location is at least metaphysically possible.[51] However, if self-visitation is also metaphysically possible, then it should be possible for a single object to co-locate with itself. This poses an obvious problem for the region relativist. Suppose, for example, that a particle p is moving along some path at t_1. At t_5, p is sent back in time and arrives at t_2 right above its earlier self, and moving in the opposite direction. At t_3 p passes through its earlier self and then continues on in the opposite direction. (See Figure 6.3.)

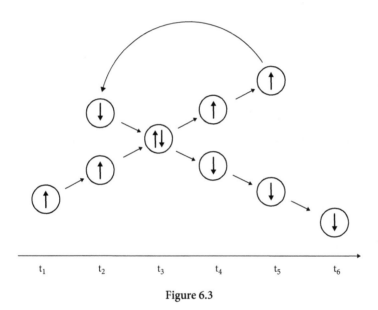

Figure 6.3

Call the region occupied by p during co-location 'r_p'. The region relativist will say that p has two different velocities at this region—say, 50 km/h in a northerly direction and 60 km/h in a southerly direction. But these velocities are no more compatible than the properties of *weighing 50 kg* and *weighing 60 kg*. So, region relativism does not avoid the paradox of self-visitation.[52]

The possibility of co-location also undermines our initial characterization of self-visitation. We said that, for the endurantist, self-visitation involves being in two different places at the same time. But if co-location is possible, then it is possible to

---

[50] See, for example, the exchange between Barnette (1978), Cortes (1976), Ginsberg (1981), and Teller (1983).

[51] See, for example, McDaniel (2007: 240), Saucedo (2011), Sider (2002: 133), Wasserman (2003a), and Zimmerman (2002: 604–5).

[52] Sider (2001: 105–6) raises a related objection involving objects without spatial location.

have the former without the latter, so there must be more to self-visitation than our original suggestion suggests.

One idea for avoiding both of these problems is to focus on moments of personal time, rather than regions of external spacetime.[53] In the case of the time traveling particle, for example, there are six moments of external time (t_1-t_6), but there are, in a sense, ten moments of personal time (pt_1-pt_{10}), since the particle experiences some times twice over. This suggests a natural account of self-visitation: Self-visitation occurs when multiple moments of personal time correspond to a single moment of external time.

The relativist could also appeal to moments of personal time in order to avoid the apparent contradiction. She could say, for example, that p has one velocity at pt_3 and another at pt_7. She could then point out that these "personal-time-indexed properties" are compatible with each another, since having those properties just amounts to standing in different relations to different things.

But this will not do.[54] The problem is that personal time is a derived notion—what is the case according to one's personal time is a function of what things are like at real times, and how one's states at those times relate to each other causally. So, for example, to say that p has different velocities at different moments of its "personal" time is to say the following: There are some times, x and y, such that (i) p has one velocity at x, (ii) p has a different velocity at y, and (iii) p's state at x is appropriately related to p's state at y. The problem is that, in the case of self-visitation, $x = y$. In our example, there is just one moment of time—t_3—which the particle experiences twice over. But then we are right back to our original problem—p has two different velocities at the same time.[55]

John Carroll (2011) considers (and rejects) a variant of the personal time proposal that he calls "age relativism".[56] He points out that we often relate the properties we had in the past to the ages at which we had them. For example, Jennifer might say that she had long hair when she was eighteen and short hair when she was forty-eight. The same thing is true when the eighteen-year-old Jennifer travels in time and meets the forty-eight-year-old Jennifer. We can say that Jennifer weighs 50 kg at eighteen years of age and that she weighs 60 kg at forty-eight years of age. Since these are different ages, there is no puzzle about how Jennifer could stand in different relations to the two.

---

[53] See Keller and Nelson (2001: 344). Sider considers the same idea (2001: 106). Paul Horwich makes a closely related suggestion, according to which properties are had relative to moments of *proper* time. See Horwich (1975: 433–5) and Horwich (1987: 114–15).

[54] Sider (2001: 106).   [55] For a different objection to this proposal, see Carroll (2011).

[56] Valaris and Michael also consider a variant of this idea, which they call the "causal network" view. On their view, properties are relativized to points in an object's "life history" (2015: 360). However, Valaris and Michael also allow for a single object to have seemingly incompatible properties relative to the same moment of external time, so it is probably best to understand their view as a version of property compatibilism (see p. 203).

However, it is not clear how to think about having a property *at* a certain age. Normally, when we say that *x* is *F* at the age of *n* years, we mean that there is a time, *t*, such that *x* is *n* years old at *t* and *x* is *F* at *t*. But that cannot be what Carroll has in mind, since Jennifer is eighteen years old and forty-eight years old at the same time (t_4).

The relativist seems to have run out of options. We cannot avoid incompatibility by relativizing to times or to places or to place-times or to personal times or to personal ages. Perhaps it is time for the endurantist to consider a different approach.

Recall that the drive to relativize came from the conviction that properties like *weighing 50 kg at t_4* and *weighing 60 kg at t_4* are incompatible. That was the thought behind the fourth premise of the self-visitation paradox:

(P4)   For any *x*, and for any time *t*, if *x* is 60 kg at *t*, then it is not the case that *x* is 50 kg at *t*.

It is easy to see why one might find this principle plausible. Just start putting things on scales! In every ordinary case, an object that weighs exactly 60 kg will weigh *only* 60 kg. But to generalize from the ordinary case is to overlook the extraordinary one, and that is exactly what we have in the case of time travel. Self-visitation is an unusual phenomenon and it allows an individual to do some unexpected things. You can have two locations at once, you can have two meals at once, and you can have two haircuts at once. Why should it be any different with weights? Why not just say that, in the case of self-visitation, one can have two different weights at the same time? In that case, one could weigh both 60 kg and 50 kg without any contradiction.

What goes for weight goes for other properties as well. One can say that the time traveling particle has two different velocities at the same time (and place) and that time traveling Jennifer has two different hairstyles, two different shapes, and two different ages at the same time. One can even say that, when YJ meets OJ, Jennifer has the property of *having just traveled in time* and the property of *having not just traveled in time* (this would just mean that having *not* just traveled in time does not imply that it's not the case that one *did* just travel in time). In short, the endurantist can avoid all of the objections by denying that the relevant properties are incompatible. This is the property-compatibilist response to the paradox of self-visitation.[57]

3.4 Endurantism and indiscernibility

The property-compatibilist response answers the original self-visitation argument, but it does not solve all of the endurantist's problems. In fact, Ted Sider (2001: 102–9) argues that there is an even deeper objection to the endurantist account.

Sider begins by imagining a case in which he travels back to visit his younger self:

[Suppose that] I am standing while my former self is sitting. But our roles might have been reversed—I might have sat where he sits while he stood where I actually stand. We have here

---

[57] This response is suggested by Sider (2001: 102) and endorsed by Carroll (2011). The same move is discussed with respect to the problem of change in Wasserman (2005).

what appear to be two distinct possibilities. When I meet my former self I think: "I am standing and he is sitting, but it could have been the case that I sat and he stood." The problem is that the three-dimensionalist cannot distinguish these possibilities. The *four*-dimensionalist can easily distinguish them. Each case involves two person stages, T_1 and T_2. In one case T_1 stands and T_2 sits, whereas in the other case T_2 stands and T_1 sits. But the three-dimensionalist can only speak of what properties *I* have at *t*. In the first possibility, I am standing at *t*, and also sitting at *t*. Exactly the same is true in the second possibility. (2001: 102–3)

The two worlds described by Sider are depicted in Figure 6.4.

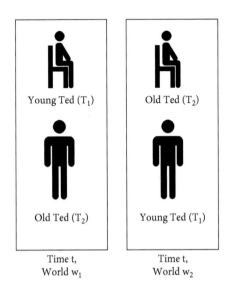

Figure 6.4

Once again, Sider's point is that the perdurantist (or four-dimensionalist) is able to distinguish between these two possibilities by saying that T_1 and T_2 are distinct stages that have different shapes in the two worlds. But the endurantist who identifies T_1 and T_2 cannot say the same, since she believes that both possibilities concern a single individual. Thus, the endurantist seems unable to distinguish between the two possibilities.

Sider mentions several ways in which the endurantist might respond to this worry. First, the endurantist might try to distinguish between w_1 and w_2 by appealing to differences at time *t*. Suppose, for example, that Old Ted is taller than Young Ted. In that case, there will be a point of space in w_2—a point just above Young Ted's head—that is occupied in w_1, but not in w_2. In order to get around this kind of worry, Sider stipulates that Young Ted in w_1 is an intrinsic duplicate of Old Ted in w_2 and that Young Ted in w_2 is an intrinsic duplicate of Old Ted in w_1.

A second way that the endurantist might try to distinguish between the possibilities is by appealing to differences at times other than *t*. Consider, for example, the moment just before *t*. In w_1, Young Ted would then be present in one place—call it 'p_1'—where we can imagine him preparing to sit down in his chair. There will also be an empty region—'p_2'—which will soon be occupied by Old Ted when he appears from the future. In w_2, the situation will be reversed. p_2 will be occupied at *t-*, whereas p_1 will be empty. (See Figure 6.5.)

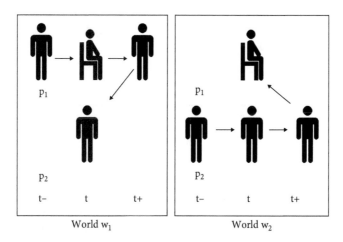

Figure 6.5

The arrows in these pictures indicate a second respect in which these cases seem to differ. In w_1, Ted's standing at *t* is causally dependent on his entering the time machine at *t+*. In w_2, it is not. So it seems as if the endurantist can distinguish between these worlds by appealing to causal differences.

Sider anticipates these replies and offers the following response:

I cannot get around this problem by stipulating that my emergence in the past is entirely causally unconnected to my entering the time machine since I accept that causation is a prerequisite of personal identity. What I need to do instead is, roughly, stipulate that my entry into the time machine causally determines that I emerge at the time of the meeting, but does not cause whether I am sitting or standing then. More carefully, I stipulate the following. First, in each case, I am standing when I enter the time machine. Second, in each case I am standing shortly before the time at which my former and later selves meet. Thirdly, the laws of nature in the two cases are identical, and are indeterministic. As applied to my entry into the time machine, they determine that I will emerge at a certain spatial location in the past, but they leave it open whether I am sitting or standing at that time. As applied to me immediately before the meeting of my former and later selves, the laws determine that I will remain in a certain spatial location, but leave it open whether I will be sitting or standing at that time.   (2001: 103–4)

These stipulations suggest a very different way of picturing world w_2—namely, the one presented in Figure 6.6 on the next page.

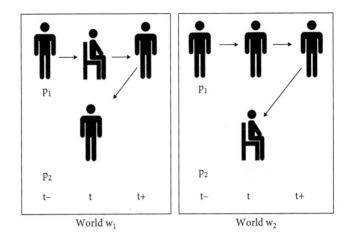

Figure 6.6

On this way of picturing things, w_2 matches w_1 perfectly at $t-$ and $t+$. Thus, on this way of understanding Sider, the endurantist cannot distinguish between his worlds by appealing to non-causal differences at times other than t. This is an advantage of the Figure 6.6 interpretation.

The problem with this interpretation is that the two possibilities no longer match at the moment of visitation. Take, for example, the region occupied by "Young" Ted's head in w_1 (the area right above the seated figure). That region is empty in w_1, but occupied in w_2. So, contrary to what Sider says, there is now a non-causal difference between the two worlds at the time of visitation.

Fortunately, we can avoid this problem by replacing Sider's properties with appropriate alternatives. For example, we can stipulate that, in w_1, Ted turns pale when he travels back in time (Figure 6.7). In w_2, he turns pale for a moment before getting into the machine and then goes back to his normal coloring.

The worlds depicted in Figure 6.7 do not differ when it comes to which points are occupied, but the endurantist could still try to distinguish between them by insisting that Ted stands in different relations to different regions in those worlds—for example, she could say that Ted is pale at p_2 in w_1 but not in w_2 and that he is pale at p_1 in w_2 but not in w_1.[58]

As in the previous section, we can block the appeal to region relativism by moving to a case of co-location. Suppose, for example, that Old Ted co-locates with Young Ted when he arrives in the past. Old Ted is pale and Young Ted is not, but the situation

---

[58] Sider complains that this response is ad hoc, since there is no independent motivation for the region relativist view (2001: 105). But it is unclear how much weight this worry carries. It is true that the original paradox of self-visitation did not support region relativism, but Sider takes himself to be raising a new problem of self-visitation, and new problems sometime require new solutions.

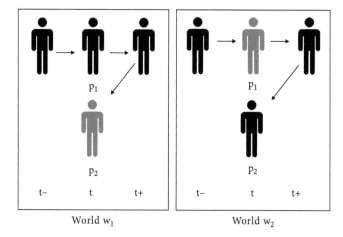

Figure 6.7

could have been reversed—it could have been that Ted was pale when he was young and normal looking when he was old. (See Figure 6.8.)

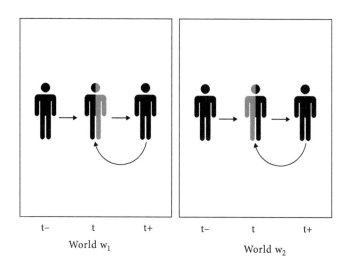

Figure 6.8

Here (finally!) we seem to have a clear case of two time travel possibilities with no non-causal differences. So we seem to have a genuine problem for the endurantist.

But now we must return to the issue of causal dependence. After all, it seems as if Ted's getting into the time machine at $t+$ is a direct cause of his being pale at t in w_1, but not in w_2. Intuitively, in w_2 Ted would have been pale at t, even if he hadn't gotten into the time machine at $t+$. In w_1, the situation is reversed—Ted's getting into the time machine is a direct cause of his being pale at t, but not a cause of his being normal looking (then).

Once again, Sider anticipates this objection:

Given [the previous] stipulations, it can be argued that the cases cannot be distinguished by causal means. Given stipulations one and two, the cases do not differ in non-causal ways at times other than the time of the meeting. And given three-dimensionalism, the two cases do not differ in non-causal ways at the time of the meeting (in each case I am [pale] at that time and [not pale] at that time). Given stipulation three, the laws of nature are common to the two cases but any differences in causation between the cases would need to be due to differences in the laws of nature or non-causal differences. Thus, the worlds do not differ causally.   (2001: 104)

Sider's key assumption is that causal facts supervene on non-causal facts, together with the laws of nature. This assumption can be challenged. Suppose, for example, that Merlin and Morgana both cast spells to turn the prince into a frog at midnight. Suppose further that spell-causation is unmediated and indeterministic—the laws of magic dictate that there is a 50 percent chance that the prince will turn into a frog, given Merlin's spell, and a (probabilistically independent) 50 percent chance that the prince will turn into a frog, given Morgana's spell. Here is what happens: The prince turns into a frog. Intuitively, there are three different ways in which this effect might have been produced—it could have been Merlin's spell that did it, it could have been Morgana's spell that did it, or it could have been both. The problem is that Sider's supervenience thesis would collapse all of these possibilities, since the "three" situations involve the exact same laws of nature and the same non-causal facts.

Of course, some philosophers are happy to bite the bullet in this case. Here, for example, is Jonathan Schaffer:

To my mind there is only the one possibility (the one in which Merlin and Morgana both cast their spells, and the prince transforms), confusingly described in [two] different ways...The philosopher who would uphold [the view that there are worlds that differ in causation without differing in history or laws] would presumably reply that the reason for accepting genuinely distinct possibilities here is *intuitive*, and that this shows that the alleged causal difference need not rest on *anything*—it is a brute and fundamental difference. But this seems a terrible metaphysical price for a relatively flimsy intuition...Our causal vocabulary allows us [two] different descriptions, and this leaves us prone to positing [two] different possibilities.   (2008: 89)

Perhaps this is the right thing to say about Merlin and Morgana. But, if it is, we should say the *exact* same thing about Sider's cases. In particular, we should say that the two pictures in Figure 6.8 are simply different ways of illustrating the same possibility. After all, the *only* reason we have for thinking that there are two different worlds in this case is if we think that there is some fact of the matter as to whether Ted's being pale at t is most directly caused by the events at $t-$ or $t+$ (i.e. which comes "first" according to his personal time). But we can assume that the laws in this case are just like the laws in the magic example—they dictate that there is a 50 percent chance that Ted will be pale at t, given his presence at $t-$, and a (probabilistically independent) 50 percent chance that

Ted will be pale at t, given that he enters into the time machine at $t+$. Given these stipulations, Sider should say that these two pictures correspond to a single possibility. But, in that case, the endurantist's inability to distinguish between those possibilities is no longer a mark against her view.

To sum up: The endurantist is free to accept or reject Sider's supervenience thesis about causation. If she accepts that view, she should identify his possibilities. If she rejects that view, she should distinguish between his possibilities by appealing to non-supervenient causal relations. Either way, she should say that Sider's case poses no new problems for her view.

4. Mereology and Multi-Visitation

To this point, we have focused on the relatively mundane case of one-time visitation, which produces two "versions" of the same thing. But we can also imagine a time traveler that makes repeated trips back to a single point and thus produces many versions of the same thing at the same time. These cases of multi-visitation lead to particularly puzzling scenarios.[59]

Let's start off with a relatively simple case. Suppose that, at time t_0, you buy an ordinary brick at the store. At t_1, you mark the brick with a '1', and lay it down in a spot marked 'A'. (See t_1 in Figure 6.9.)

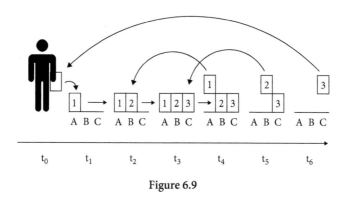

Figure 6.9

Next, suppose that you get into your time machine and travel to t_4, where you find what seem to be three different bricks sitting side-by-side. (See t_4 in Figure 6.9.) You

---

[59] This was actually pointed out long ago by H. G. Wells:

> [I]t is plain commonsense that a man might multiply himself indefinitely, pop a little way into the future and then come back. There would then be two of him. Repeat *da capo* and you have four, and so on, until the whole world would be full of this Time Travelling Individual's vain repetitions of himself. The plain-thinking mind apprehends this…and is naturally as revolted as I am by the insult to its intelligence. (Wells 1981: 114; originally published in 1945)

remove the brick marked '1', re-label it '2', and take it back to t_2, where you place it in the spot marked 'B'. In doing so, you put an older version of the brick next to its earlier self. (See t_2 in Figure 6.9.) Next, you travel forward to t_5 where two bricks remain in spots B and C. You take the brick marked '2', re-label it '3', and take it back to t_3, where you place it in the spot marked 'C'. In doing so, you put an older version of the brick next to *two* earlier versions of itself. (See t_3 in Figure 6.9.) Finally, you travel forward to t_6 where a single brick remains in spot C. You erase the '3' from the brick and take it back to t_0, just in time to sell it to your younger self. (See t_0 in Figure 6.9.)

This is a classic version of an "object loop," like those discussed in section 3 of Chapter 5. However, this is a loop with a twist: It results in a single object being located in three different places (A, B, and C) at the same time (t_3).

Nikk Effingham and Jon Robson (2007) imagine a more complicated version of this scenario in which a brick is taken back in time over and over again, with the result that it is located in a hundred different places at the same time. The one hundred "versions" of the brick are then arranged into the form of a wall. (As in Figure 6.10.)

91	92	93	94	95	96	97	98	99	100
81	82	83	84	85	86	87	88	89	90
71	72	73	74	75	76	77	78	79	80
61	62	63	64	65	66	67	68	69	70
51	52	53	54	55	56	57	58	59	60
41	42	43	44	45	46	47	48	49	50
31	32	33	34	35	36	37	38	39	40
21	22	23	24	25	26	27	28	29	30
11	12	13	14	15	16	17	18	19	20
1	2	3	4	5	6	7	8	9	10

Figure 6.10

(For future reference, let's suppose that the time traveler places the first version of the brick down at t_1, the second version down at t_2, etc., so that the wall is completed at t_{100}.)

Effingham and Robson now ask: What is the relationship between the brick and the wall in this picture?

Those who believe in temporal parts have a relatively straightforward answer to this question. For the perdurantist, our diagram depicts a single persisting brick that is composed of many momentary "brick-stages".[60] Since the brick is a self-visitor, there are times at which it has more than one brick-stage and, at some of those times, the various brick-stages compose a "wall-stage". The wall in the story can then be identified with the sum of the relevant wall-stages. Given our earlier definition of a 'temporal

---

[60] A brick-stage is a temporary brick-like part that is appropriately related to all the other brick-like parts that compose the persisting brick. (This is analogous to the characterization of a "person-stage" from section 2.4.) In our terminology, the brick has a hundred brick-stages at the time in question, but a single temporal part.

part' (from section 2.1) it will turn out that each of these wall-stages is a temporal part of both the wall and the brick. But it is also obvious that the brick has some temporal parts that the wall lacks—for example, only the brick exists prior to its time traveling adventures, so only the brick has a temporal part at that time. From these two observations, it follows that the wall is a proper temporal part of the brick. That, according to the perdurantist, is the relationship between the two.

For the endurantist, matters are less clear. There seem to be four potential ways of thinking about the relationships between the wall and the brick(s). First, we could say that the wall is *identical* to the brick(s). Second, we could say that the wall is *composed* of, but not identical to, the brick(s). Third, we could say that the wall exists, but is neither identical to nor composed of the brick(s). Finally, we could say that, despite appearances, there is no wall in the story. In that case, there would no longer be any question about how the wall relates to the brick(s).[61]

In what follows, we will consider each of these options in turn.

4.1 The identification account

The first option for the endurantist is to identify the wall with the brick. On this account, the time travel story features a single object. At some times (like t_1) that object is just a brick. At other times (like t_{100}) is it both a brick and a wall.[62] But the brick's coming to be a wall does not involve a new thing coming into existence—it simply involves an old thing taking on a new form of multi-location.[63]

Effingham and Robson raise three worries for this account. First, they complain that, "a brick is simply not the kind of thing that can be a wall" (2007: 637). However, the rationale for this complaint is unclear. After all, one can build a wall by stacking together many small bricks, but one can also build a wall by producing one very large brick. For that matter, even a normal-sized brick can serve as a wall for very small insects. So even if we set aside the case of time travel, it seems that a brick *is* the kind of thing that can be a wall.

Effingham and Robson try to press the point by imagining a case in which a single particle is repeatedly sent back in time and combined with its earlier selves so that we have what seems to be a human person. On the identification account, that person would be identical to the one time traveling particle. Effingham and Robson take this to be "exceedingly counterintuitive" (2007: 637), since a particle is not the kind of thing that can walk or talk or think like a human being.

Or is it? A person particle would certainly be stranger than a brick wall. But the fact is that time travel allows for some pretty strange things. Here it may be helpful to ask *why* the typical particle is unable to walk or talk or do the other kinds of things

---

[61] There is a fifth option that Effingham and Robson do not mention—namely, that there is a wall but no brick. We will discuss this option in 4.1.

[62] Keep in mind that t_1 is a time at which there is only one "version" of the brick and that t_{100} is a time at which there are a hundred versions of the brick stacked on top of each other.

[63] This answer is defended by Daniels (2014b).

that normal people do. The answer has to do with *structure*, or lack thereof. Walking, talking, and other person-related activities require having parts that are arranged in the right sorts of ways. Since particles are simple, they typically lack this kind of structure. But this possibility is *exactly* what self-visitation allows for. If a particle visits itself, it will be at some distance from itself, and thus instantiate a simple structural property. If it self-visits repeatedly, it can stand in more complex relations to itself. And once these relations are complex enough, they can give rise to walking or talking or any of the other things that human persons do.

Effingham and Robson's second objection is that the identification account is inconsistent with *sortal essentialism*—the view that an object's kind is an essential property of it. After all, the identifier says that the time traveling brick is a wall at some times and not others. Moreover, that object wouldn't have been a wall at all if it hadn't traveled in time. So the property of *being a wall* is accidental to the brick.

I suspect that this objection will have a limited audience. For one thing, not all endurantists accept sortal essentialism,[64] and those who do will either reject classical mereology[65] or reject the view that constitution is identity,[66] in which case they will presumably have a different view about the relationship between the wall and the brick(s) (see, in particular, sections 4.2 and 4.3). Or perhaps the essentialist will have their own answer to our question about the brick and the wall. To illustrate, consider a standard puzzle of material constitution. Suppose that an ordinary lump of clay is sculpted into a statue at t_2 and later squashed into a pancake at t_3. (See Figure 6.11.)

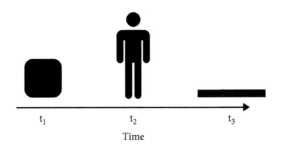

t_1 t_2 t_3

Time

Figure 6.11

Many of us would like to say that, in this kind of case, there is a single thing that changes from being a "mere" lump of clay into a statue. But that is not an option for the sortal essentialist. On that view, a statue would have to be a statue at every time it exists. So, there cannot be a single thing that is both a statue at t_2 and a non-statue at t_3 (after the statue has been destroyed).

---

[64] For example, it is possible to read Chisholm (1976: Chapter 3) as rejecting sortal essentialism (since he treats "substantial" sortals just like "phase" sortals).
[65] See van Inwagen (1981).   [66] See Baker (2000).

Michael Burke (himself a sortal essentialist) suggests an alternative account.[67] On Burke's view, when the artist molds the clay, one object (the lump) goes out of existence and a new one (the statue) comes into being. So too, when the statue is squashed (at t_3) it is destroyed and replaced with a numerically distinct object (a mere lump of clay). Presumably, the sortal essentialist who follows Burke will say something similar in the case of the brick and the wall—when the time traveler arranges the brick(s) into the wall, the brick goes out of existence and the wall comes into being. Then, at some point during disassembly, the wall goes out of existence and is replaced with a numerically distinct, multi-located brick. On this picture, there would no longer be any puzzle about how the wall and brick relate at t_{100}, since only one of those objects—the wall— exists at that time.[68]

The final objection to the identification account is that it generates mysterious weight gain. Here is what Effingham and Robson say:

The third, and strongest, response is that at t_{100} the brick that weighs one kilogram is now identical to a wall that weighs one hundred kilograms. The endurantist must explain why the brick has suddenly got heavier. It cannot be that it has time travelled, for intuitively objects can time travel without gaining mass...for instance, if Brick$_1$,..., Brick$_{100}$ were scattered about haphazardly...then there would be no wall, and the brick would not weigh one hundred kilograms. But it seems ridiculous that an object merely being located in one region rather than another can cause it to gain or lose mass. (2007: 638)

What we say about this objection depends on what we think about region relativism, and how we think about region occupancy. Begin with occupancy. Let $r_1@t_1$ be the region occupied by the brick at time t_1. Let $r_1@t_2$ and $r_2@t_2$ be the two brick-shaped regions occupied by the brick at t_2. And let $r_1@t_{100}$, $r_2@t_{100}$, etc. be the hundred brick-shaped regions occupied by the brick at t_{100}. Finally, let the union of $r_1@t_{100}$–$r_{100}@t_{100}$ be r_{wall} (the region that we would normally say is occupied by the wall at t_{100}). Question: Does the brick occupy r_{wall}? Obviously, the brick is not completely *absent* from this region, since it occupies each of the relevant subregions. But the question is whether the relation between the brick and $r_1@t_{100}$, for example, is the same relation that holds between the brick and r_{wall}. Here there is room for disagreement.[69] But one plausible view is that, in the fundamental sense, the brick only occupies each of the small regions at t_{100}. If the brick does occupy the larger region (r_{wall}) it does so in a derivative sense— the brick "occupies" r_{wall} in virtue of the fact that it occupies $r_1@t_{100}$, $r_2@t_{100}$, etc. The endurantist who endorses region relativism can say something analogous about weight. In the fundamental sense, the brick weighs 1 kg at $r_1@t_{100}$, 1 kg at $r_2@t_{100}$, etc. And in virtue of these facts, there is a derivative sense in which the brick "weighs"

[67] See Burke (1994a, 1994b).

[68] For more on this view as a solution to the puzzles of material constitution, see Wasserman (2009).

[69] See, for example, the exchange between Hudson (2005) and Parsons (2007, 2008). For further discussion of occupancy as it relates to the brick-wall example, see Daniels (2014b: section 3).

100 kg at r_{wall}.[70] Given all this, the endurantist can say that there is a clear sense in which the brick does *not* gain weight when it travels in time, since it always weighs 1 kg at each region that it occupies in the fundamental sense. Of course, there's also a sense—a derivative sense—in which it "gains" weight when it travels, but this sort of gain seems much less problematic.[71,72]

This ends our discussion of Effingham and Robson's objections to the identification account. But there is one more worry to consider.

Recall the case of the multi-visiting particle that purportedly becomes a person. Suppose that the various "versions" of this particle are gradually replaced by normal, non-time traveling particles. And suppose that each of the "versions" is destroyed upon removal. Presumably, the person will survive this process in the same way that a normal human survives the gradual recycling of his material parts. But the time traveling particle will no longer exist at that point. When the process is complete, we will have the person, but not the particle. Hence, the person cannot be identical to the particle, since they differ in their persistence conditions. Since this conflicts with the identification account, that account should be rejected.

4.2 The composition account

The second option for the endurantist is to think of Effingham and Robson's brick(s) as *composing* the wall, where 'compose' is defined as follows:

(D1) The xs compose $y =_{df}$ each of the xs is part of y and every part of y overlaps at least one of the xs.

'Overlap' in this definition is to be understood as follows:

(D2) x overlaps $y =_{df}$ there is some z such that z is a part of x and z is a part of y.

In both of these definitions, the term 'part' is taken as a primitive, but it is understood that everything is a part of itself (in the intended sense). In the case where $x = y$, we say that x is an *improper* part of y. And we say that x is a *proper* part of y if and only if x is a part of y, but not identical to it:

(D3) x is a proper part of $y =_{df}$ x is a part of y and $x \neq y$.

Normally, if one were to arrange one hundred bricks in the right way, they would compose a wall in the relevant sense—each of the bricks would be a (proper) part of the wall, and every part of the wall (like its left half or its right half) would have some parts

---

[70] The distinction between having a weight fundamentally vs. derivatively is related to McDaniel's (2003) distinction between having a shape *intrinsically* vs. *extrinsically*.

[71] Note that this kind of weight gain does not depend on the ways in which the brick relates to itself. If the various versions of the brick were scattered across the cosmos at t_{100}, then the brick would not be a wall at that time. But it would still "weigh" 100 kg at the sum of the regions it occupies.

[72] For a slightly different response to this objection, see Daniels (2014b: 98).

in common with the bricks. According to the composition account, the exact same thing is true in the unusual case of the time traveling brick.

Effingham and Robson object to this proposal on the grounds that it conflicts with the weak supplementation principle (WSP) of classical mereology:

(WSP) For all x and y, if x is a proper part of y, then there is some z such that z is a proper part of y and z does not overlap x.[73]

To simplify the argument, assume that the time traveling brick is a mereological simple (i.e. an object lacking proper parts). If the brick composes the wall, then it is a part of the wall (by (D1)). And if the brick is not identical to the wall, then it is a proper part of the wall (by (D3)). But if the brick is a proper part of the wall, then there must be some other object which is a proper part of the wall that does not overlap the brick (by (WSP)). The problem is that there is no such object. The wall has *itself* as an improper part and *the brick* as a proper part, but those are the only objects in the story, so there are no other proper parts. Hence, the brick does not compose the wall.

Of course, this argument is only as strong as its central premise, and this premise has surprisingly little support.[74] Effingham and Robson say that (WSP) is "eminently plausible" (2007: 635). Hud Hudson claims that it is "certainly true" (2001: 438). And Achille Varzi writes that, "This principle expresses a minimal requirement that any relation must satisfy... to qualify as parthood" (2008: 110–11). But none of these assertions is backed by an argument. The closest that Effingham and Robson come to offering an argument in support of (WSP) is by saying that it is "in accord with our intuitions" (2007: 635). But this is not obvious. It's certainly true that (WSP) accords with our intuitions in *ordinary* cases. My car has many proper parts, as do my couch and my cookie. The same thing goes for all of the other objects around me. Normally, an object can't have just one proper part. But again, time travel cases are not normal. And, in general, we should be very wary of the following recipe for doing philosophy:

Consider a bunch of boring cases.
Infer a general principle from those cases.
Use that principle to rule out all interesting cases.

This is not a recipe for success. If it were, we would have a very straightforward argument against self-visitation. After all, it's normally true that an object can't be on top of itself, or underneath itself, or to the left of itself. So, if we focus on normal cases, the following principle will seem obvious: *An object can't be to the left of itself*. In fact, this principle seems even *more* obvious than the principle that an object can't have only one proper part. The first principle is also more *powerful* than (WSP), since it would rule out even the most mundane cases of self-visitation.

---

[73] Note that every object overlaps itself, so if z does not overlap x, it is not identical to x.

[74] Perhaps the best argument is due to Simons, who suggests that (WSP) is needed to distinguish the parthood relation from other partial orderings (1987: 10–11). For a reply to this argument, see Donnelly (2011).

But, in that case, it is unclear whether (WSP) adds anything to the anti-endurantist argument.[75]

4.3 The constitution account

We have considered Effingham and Robson's objections to the identification and composition accounts. Surprisingly, they suggest that these are the only two ways of understanding the relationship between the wall and the brick(s).[76] But that is to omit an option that will appeal to many endurantists.

According to the constitution account, the relation between the brick and the wall at t_{100} is exactly the same as the relation between the lump of clay and the statue when the former constitutes the latter. (See Figure 6.11.) As noted earlier, many endurantists want to distinguish between the lump of clay and the statue. After all, the lump and the statue differ in their temporal properties, since only the former exists at t_1. The two also differ in their modal properties, since the lump, but not the statue, could survive being rolled into a ball. Moreover, the two differ in kind, since the lump is a lump and the statue is a statue.

But despite their distinctness, the statue and lump are intimately related. For one thing, the two objects occupy the same place whenever they both exist. The two also seem to share the same matter. And many of the properties had by the statue are determined by the features of the clay. For example, it is natural to say that the weight, shape, and coloring of the statue at t_2 are determined by what the lump is like at that time. When two enduring objects are related in this way, it is said that the one *constitutes* the other.[77]

Constitution, on this view, is to be distinguished from identity, since the statue is constituted by, but not identical to, the lump of clay from which it is made. Constitution is also distinguished from identity by its formal properties since identity, unlike constitution, is both reflexive and symmetric.

Constitution is also to be distinguished from composition. Composition can relate many different objects (the parts) to a single individual (the whole). Constitution, on the other hand, is always taken to relate one individual (the constitutor) to another (the constituted). Thus, the statue is composed of, but not constituted by, the many bits of clay from which it is made.[78]

In the case of multi-visitation, the constitution theorist will say that the time traveler who builds the wall is like the artist who molds a statue. When he does his work, he brings a new thing into existence, where the new object is constituted by the old. Given the distinction between constitution and identity, we can avoid the objections to the identity account. For example, we can say that the brick exists at times that the wall

---

[75] For more on the denial of (WSP) in this context, see Cotnoir and Bacon (2012).

[76] The only other options are to say that there is a brick but no wall (see section 4.4) or a wall but no brick (see the comments on sortal essentialism in 4.1) or that there is no wall and no brick.

[77] On the constitution view, see Baker (2000), Fine (2003), and Wiggins (1968). On the constitution relation, see Wasserman (2004b).

[78] See Wasserman (2004b).

does not, and that the brick and wall have different modal properties and persistence conditions. Moreover, given the distinction between constitution and composition, we can avoid the objections to the composition account. For example, we can avoid the question of whether or not the weak supplementation principle is correct.[79] The constitution account therefore represents a promising alternative to the theories discussed by Effingham and Robson.[80]

4.4 The elimination account

There is one final (very different) reaction to the story told by Effingham and Robson.

According to the *elimination* account, the story of the time traveling brick is just a story about a brick. In other words, *there is no wall in the story*. If that is the case, then there is no puzzle about the relation between *it* and the brick(s). Our original question can therefore be rejected, on the grounds that it carries a false presupposition.

Effingham and Robson reject this response since they think it leads to a nihilistic conclusion. They begin by asking us to imagine a hundred ordinary bricks—$Brick_{101}$–$Brick_{200}$—that match $Brick_1$–$Brick_{100}$ with respect to both qualitative properties and arrangement. So, for example, if $Brick_1$ weighs 1 kg, then $Brick_{101}$ weighs 1 kg. And if $Brick_1$ is 2 meters from $Brick_8$, then $Brick_{101}$ is 2 meters from $Brick_{108}$.

Effingham and Robson next suggest that causal facts and functional facts are both determined by the distribution of qualitative features. Since the distribution of qualitative features is the same in both cases, we will also have a match in these other respects. For example, if $Brick_{11}$ is exerting a force on $Brick_1$, then $Brick_{111}$ will be exerting a corresponding force on $Brick_{101}$. So too, if $Brick_1$–$Brick_{100}$ can provide shelter from the wind, then the same will be true of $Brick_{101}$–$Brick_{200}$.

Finally, Effingham and Robson claim that facts about composition supervene on facts about causation and function. So, if $Brick_1$–$Brick_{100}$ fail to compose a wall (as the eliminativist says) and there is the right kind of match between the time traveling brick(s) and the non-time traveling bricks (as Effingham and Robson say), then $Brick_{101}$–$Brick_{200}$ will also fail to compose a wall. Effingham and Robson conclude that "mereological nihilis[m] about walls made of time traveling bricks entails mereological nihilism about *all* walls" (2007: 633). Moreover, they point out that the same supervenience argument can be extended to every other purported case of composition, since we can always imagine a parallel case of self-visitation. Thus, "The Endurantist should not be a mereological nihilist about walls unless he wishes to be a mereological nihilist about everything" (2007: 637).

The eliminativist could accept this conclusion, but there are also less radical replies. We will mention three.

---

[79] Or, at least, we can avoid this issue if we claim that the lump of clay and the statue are not parts of each other.

[80] Of course, there are also objections to the constitution account. See, for example, Burke (1992), Heller (1990: 30–2), and Zimmerman (1995: 87–8).

First, the eliminativist could deny the initial claim that $Brick_1$–$Brick_{100}$ are qualitatively like $Brick_{101}$–$Brick_{200}$. Suppose, for example, that the wall-eliminativist is also a region relativist (see sections 2.2 and 3.2). In that case, she will say that $Brick_1$ is 1 kg at r_1, and also 1 kg at r_2 (where r_1 and r_2 are distinct regions occupied by the multi-located brick). But $Brick_1$'s counterpart—$Brick_{101}$—is only 1 kg relative to a single region. Hence, the pairing function does not preserve the relevant qualitative relations.

Second, the eliminativist could reject the claim that the arrangement of $Brick_1$–$Brick_{100}$ is the same as the arrangement of $Brick_{101}$–$Brick_{200}$. Effingham and Robson do not say exactly what they have in mind by "arrangement," but presumably $Brick_1$–$Brick_{100}$ are arranged in the same way as $Brick_{101}$–$Brick_{200}$ only if there is a mapping from the one set to the other that preserves spatial relations. That is not the case. For example, $Brick_1$ is 2 meters from $Brick_8$, but it is also 2 meters away from itself, since $Brick_1$ *is* $Brick_8$. The same thing is not true of $Brick_1$'s counterpart. $Brick_{101}$ is 2 meters away from $Brick_{108}$, but it is not 2 meters away from itself since it is not bi-located. The upshot is that the two cases seem to differ in how the relevant bricks are arranged.

Third and finally, the eliminativist could challenge the idea that facts about composition are ultimately determined by facts about causation or function or (ultimately) the arrangement of qualities. Ideally, what one would like to do is identify a *non*-qualitative difference that explains why composition occurs in one of the brick cases and not the other. And an obvious answer presents itself. In the case of time travel, there is only one brick present—$Brick_1 = Brick_2, \ldots = Brick_{100}$. In the non-time-travel case, there are many—$Brick_{101} \neq Brick_{102}, \ldots \neq Brick_{200}$. The eliminativist can then say that these differences in facts about identity explain the difference as to whether or not composition occurs. In fact, that is *exactly* what we should expect the endurantist to say if she has followed Effingham and Robson this far. For suppose that one has a complete qualitative description of objects a, b, and c, as well as a complete description of the spatial relations between a, b, and c. Do we then have enough information to determine whether or not a and b compose c? No! For suppose that $a \neq b \neq c$. In that case, a and b could very well compose c. Suppose instead that $a = b$ and $a \neq c$. In that case, (WSP) implies that a and b do *not* compose c. That is just to say that, given (WSP), identity facts are relevant to whether or not composition occurs. The endurantist who accepts (WSP) should therefore say that facts about composition are partly determined by non-qualitative facts, in which case the initial assumption of the anti-eliminativist argument is mistaken.

To sum up: Effingham and Robson's case raises many interesting questions about mereology and multi-location. But it does not do anything to challenge the endurantist view of persistence.

5. The Strange Tale of Adam the Atom

In the previous section we considered a case of multi-visitation that seemed to involve a brick and a wall. This case was taken to present a special problem for the endurantist, since the perdurantist had a natural account of how those objects were related. For the perdurantist, the sum of brick-stages at each time is a proper temporal part of the brick, and the brick is identified with the sum of those temporal parts. The wall, on the other hand, is identified with the sum of all the wall-stages, where this will include the temporal part of the brick at t_{100}, for example, but not the temporal parts at t_1 or t_2 (since the wall had not yet come into existence at those times). As a result, the wall turns out to be an extended temporal part (or segment) of the time traveling brick.

This account of the brick–wall case is very similar to the perdurantist's account of the lump–statue case. In that example, the perdurantist identifies the statue with the sum of statue-like temporal parts, and the lump of clay with the sum of lump-like temporal parts. Since the set of statue-like temporal parts is a proper subset of the set of lump-like temporal parts, the perdurantist says that the statue is an extended temporal part (or segment) of the persisting lump. That is the standard perdurantist solution to the puzzle of material constitution.

However, it is often pointed out that this solution turns on a contingent feature of the case—namely, that the lump of clay exists at times that the statue does not.[81] Consider a modified version of the statue-lump story in which a sorcerer creates a lump of clay *ex nihilo*. The sorcerer is also an artist, and creates his lump in the form of a certain famous Philistine. He names the lump 'Lumpl' and the statue 'Goliath'. Lumpl and Goliath persist for a period of time until the sorcerer waves his wand again and annihilates both objects simultaneously. In this case, the perdurantist will presumably want to identify Lumpl with the sum of lump-stages and Goliath with the sum of statue-stages. However, given the details of the case, the sum of lump-stages *is* the sum of statue-stages, so the perdurantist will have to say that Lumpl is identical to Goliath. This seems mistaken, however, since the statue and the lump differ with respect to their kind (only one is a statue), modal properties (only one could survive being squashed), and aesthetic features (only one is beautifully made). Hence, the perdurantist does not avoid the puzzle of material constitution.

The same is true for self-visitation, since we can alter the brick-and-wall story in the same way. For example, Cody Gilmore (2007) describes a simple case of self-visitation in which the brick and wall are replaced by an atom and a molecule. Suppose that a single hydrogen atom is created at t_2. This atom exists until t_4, at which point it is sent back in time to t_2, where it bonds with its earlier self to form a molecule of dihydrogen (H_2). The atom continues on until t_4, at which point it is annihilated. (See Figure 6.12 on the next page, where the numbers indicate the atom's personal history.)

Let 'Adam' name the atom and let 'Abel' name the molecule. Presumably, the perdurantist will want to say that Adam and Abel are one and the same. After all, Adam is composed of the atom-stages and Abel is composed of the molecule-stages. Since the molecule-stages are composed of the atom-stages, it follows that Adam and Abel are

---

[81] See Gibbard (1975).

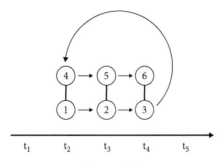

Figure 6.12

ultimately composed of the very same things. And, according to extensional mereology, objects with the same parts are always identical:

(EM)   For all x and y, if there is some z such that z is a proper part of x or y, then $x =$
y if and only if x and y have all the same proper parts.[82]

However, as Gilmore points out, there are several reasons for thinking that Adam and
Abel must be distinct. First, Adam is bi-located throughout its career, whereas Abel is
not. Second, Adam's career lasts for (say) two billion years, whereas Abel's lasts only
half that long. Finally, Adam and Abel seem to differ in their *mass histories*, where a
mass history is "a property that reflects the way in which the object's mass changes, or
stays constant, over the course of its career" (2007: 187). Gilmore offers the following
two examples, the first of which is instantiated by Adam and the second of which is
instantiated by Abel:

MH1 = *being an object that has a rest mass of 1 unit throughout its 2-billion-year career.*

MH2 = *being an object that has a rest mass of more than 1 unit throughout its
1-billion-year career.*

Gilmore then writes that:

MH1 and MH2 seem to be incompatible intrinsic properties. Each seems to be *intrinsic* in
the sense (roughly stated) that whether or not a thing has the property depends only on what the
thing is like in itself, and is independent of how that thing is related to anything else. They seem
to be *incompatible* in the sense that it's impossible for a single thing to have both of them.
Moreover, these properties seem to be purely physical, non-modal, and mind-independent.
The fact that Adam has MH1 and Abel has MH2 would, therefore, seem to provide a very firm
basis for the conclusion that Adam ≠ Abel.   (2007: 187–8)

---

[82] (EM) follows from the assumption that the parthood relation is a (strict) partial ordering, together
with the strong supplementation principle:

(SSP) For any x and y, if x is not a part of y, then there is some z such that z is a part of y and z does not
overlap x.

But if Adam ≠ Abel, then perdurantism is false in the case described. Gilmore assumes that perdurantism is necessarily true if true at all, so he concludes that perdurantism is (actually) false.[83]

There are a number of ways that the perdurantist might respond to Gilmore's challenge. We will mention three.

First, one could reject (EM) and say that Adam and Abel are distinct objects composed of the same atom-stages. However, as Gilmore points out, this move comes at a dialectical cost.[84] One of the primary arguments for temporal parts is that they provide the best overall solution to the puzzles of material constitution.[85] Perdurantists argue for the superiority of the temporal parts solution by attacking other accounts, like the constitution view. And one of the primary objections to the constitution view is that it violates (EM)—it says, for example, that Lumpl and Goliath are distinct objects that are composed of all the same parts. David Lewis famously complains that this "reeks of double-counting" and "manifest[s] a bad case of double vision" (1986a: 252). The perdurantist who gives up on (EM) will have to forgo this kind of complaint, and this goes some way toward weakening the case against endurantism.

A second option would be to treat either perdurantism or (EM) as a contingent thesis. One could then admit that the story of Adam and Abel is a genuine possibility, but insist that it's a world far from actuality. Perhaps (EM) or perdurantism fails there, but that failure tells us nothing about what things are like in the actual world.[86]

This response is difficult to maintain. Plausibly, a theory of persistence would identify a metaphysical law, and metaphysical laws determine what is possible, metaphysically speaking (Chapter 1). So, perdurantism must be metaphysically necessary if it is true at all.

Moreover, even if the contingency of perdurantism *could* be maintained, it would come at a cost. As Gilmore points out, many arguments against endurantism presuppose that the theory is necessarily true, if true at all.[87] Those who wish to press these arguments cannot endorse the contingency-reply to Gilmore's argument.

But perhaps there is a better option for the perdurantist.

Let's begin by going back to the case of Lumpl and Goliath. Here is a simple argument against the perdurantist who wishes to identify those objects:

(P1) Lumpl could survive being squashed.
(P2) It is not the case that Goliath could survive being squashed.
(C)   Lumpl ≠ Goliath.

The premises of this argument seem obvious and the conclusion follows by Leibniz's Law. Yet the conclusion is inconsistent with the standard perdurantist account.

---

[83] Gilmore (2007: 188).   [84] Gilmore (2007: 190).   [85] Sider (2001: Chapter 5).
[86] Lewis (1994: 475) suggests the same kind of response to a different problem for perdurantism.
[87] See, for example, the anti-endurantist argument given by Sider in section 3.4.

The most popular reply to this objection is due to David Lewis (1971, 1986a: Chapter 4) who defends a *counterpart theory* of *de re* modal ascriptions. According to this view, ordinary individuals like Goliath and Lumpl are *worldbound*—they exist in only one possible world—but they have *counterparts* in other possible worlds. These counterparts serve as the truth-makers for *de re* modal ascriptions. Roughly, to say that something is *essentially F* is to say that all of its counterparts are *F* and to say that something is *contingently F* is to say that one or more of its counterparts are not-*F*. The counterpart relation is a relation of *similarity*, rather than identity, and, as with all similarity talk, claims about counterparts are both vague and context-sensitive. The most important point in this connection is that names and other referring expressions are often associated with *kinds* that determine the appropriate counterpart relation for assessing *de re* modal claims involving those terms. In Gibbard's case, for example, we introduced the name 'Goliath' for *the statue* and the name 'Lumpl' for *the lump of clay*. Thus, claims that include the name 'Goliath' invoke a *statue*-counterpart relation, whereas claims that include the name 'Lumpl' invoke a *lump-of-clay*-counterpart relation. (P1), for example, attributes to Lumpl the property of *being such that at least one of its lump-counterparts survives squashing*, whereas (P2) denies Goliath the property of *being such that at least one of its statue-counterparts survives squashing*. Since the predicates in these premises express different properties, Leibniz's Law has no application.

It turns out that the perdurantist can say something very similar in response to Gilmore's argument. That argument goes like this:

(P1*)   Adam has MH1.
(P2*)   It is not the case that Abel has MH1.
(C*)   Adam ≠ Abel.

First, the perdurantist can emphasize that the two different names in this case are associated with two different kinds—the name 'Adam' is introduced for a hydrogen atom and the name 'Abel' is introduced for a dihydrogen molecule. Second, the perdurantist can point out that these two kinds are associated with two different ways of dividing up the relevant object—the first is associated with a partitioning into atom-stages, while the second is associated with a partitioning into molecule-stages. Finally, the perdurantist can suggest that how we describe the object will depend on which partitioning we are using. For example, on the atom-partitioning, the object in question has two stages at each time, and is thus bi-located throughout its career. (As Gilmore puts it, the object is bi-located "relative to the atomish way of being partitioned".) However, the object has only one molecule-stage at each time, so it is mono-located *under the molecule-partitioning*.

To tie these points back to (P1*) and (P2*): When we say that Adam has MH1, we are saying that the object in our story has MH1 relative to the atom-partitioning. In other words, if we divide the object up into atom-stages and then arrange those stages in causal order, we will find that (i) the career covers 2 billion years of personal time and (ii) each stage in the series has a rest mass of 1 unit. That is why (P1*) is true. However, when we assert that Abel does not have MH1, we are saying that the object does not have MH1 relative to the molecule-partitioning. That is also true. If we divide the object up into molecule-stages and arrange those stages in causal order, we will find that (i) the series is 1 billion years in length and (ii) each stage in the series has a rest mass of 2 units. That is why (P2*) is true. But—crucially—the move from (P1*) and (P2*) to (C*) will be invalid, since the second premise will no longer deny the same property attributed by the first.

Gilmore discusses a version of this response, but claims that it comes at a dialectical cost:

I concede that if the perdurantist applies some relativizing treatment of this sort to mass histories or the having of them, then he can resist my argument for the distinctness of Adam and Abel. It seems to me, however, that *if* the perdurantist makes this move, he will no longer be in a position to fault the endurantist who makes a parallel relativizing move in response to David Lewis's 'problem of temporary intrinsics'. (2007: 194)

Lewis's "problem of temporary intrinsics" is the problem of change, restricted to intrinsic properties. And the "relativizing move" is the endurantist response to the problem of change that was presented in section 3 of this chapter. Lewis summarizes that response as follows:

[C]ontrary to what we might think, shapes are not genuine intrinsic properties. They are disguised relations, which an enduring thing may bear to times. One and the same enduring thing may bear the bent-shape relation to some times, and the straight-shape relation to others... (1986a: 204)

Lewis complains this view is "simply incredible":

In this account nothing has a shape *simpliciter*. The temporary "intrinsic properties" of things, so understood, do not deserve the name...Intrinsic properties are genuine properties, and a thing can have them *simpliciter*, without regard to any relationships to anything else. (1999: 188)

Gilmore's point is that the perdurantist cannot consistently press this objection to the endurantist while also endorsing the relativizing response to his argument.

There are at least two things the perdurantist could say in response to Gilmore. First, he can point out that Lewis's objection to the relativist was never that strong in the first place.[88] So, giving up on that objection is not that great a cost.

Second, and more importantly, the perdurantist can claim that these two cases are importantly disanalogous. Recall that, for the endurantist, relations like *being straight at* and *being bent at* are not (or need not) be taken as fundamental. The endurantist can, for example, say that I am bent at the current time in virtue of the fact that I am currently composed of certain smaller objects, and those objects are currently arranged

---

[88] There are at least four different ways of understanding Lewis's objection, and none of those readings are particularly persuasive. See Wasserman (2003b).

in such-and-such a way. Thus, facts about the *bent at* relation are grounded in facts about the *composed at* relation and the *arranged at* relation. The more interesting case concerns the fundamental features of fundamental objects. Suppose, for example, that electrons lack proper parts and that charge is a fundamental feature of electrons. Now suppose that a particular electron is charged at the current time. That is, the electron stands in the *charged at* relation to the current time. For the perdurantist, this relation holds in virtue of the fact that the electron's current temporal part has the fundamental property of *being charged*. The relativizing endurantist, on the other hand, must take this relational fact as basic. Thus, the problem for the endurantist is not that some properties (like shapes) turn out to be relations. Rather, the problem (if it is a problem) is that *fundamental* properties turn out to be relations.

This, however, is *not* a problem for the perdurantist who gives the relativizing response to Gilmore's argument. Recall again Gilmore's example of a "mass history":

MH1 = *being an object that has a rest mass of 1 unit throughout its 2-billion-year career.*

According to the current response, the single object in Gilmore's story has this mass history relative to one partitioning and has a different mass history relative to another. Mass histories thus turn out to be a relational matter. But the key point is that these relational facts about the persisting object are grounded in the properties of that object's momentary parts. Once again, the object in Gilmore's story has MH1 under the atom partitioning in virtue of the fact that (i) the series of atom-stages is 2 billion years in length and (ii) each atom-stage in the series has a rest mass of 1 unit. Crucially, the momentary atom-stages do not have a rest mass of 1 unit *relative to* a time or a partitioning or anything else. Each stage just has a mass of 1 unit. Thus, the perdurantist can claim that the basic facts about the world are appropriately "monadic". The endurantist cannot say the same. That is the key difference between the two accounts.

The upshot is that Gilmore's case is like Effingham and Robson's: Both cases raise interesting questions about mereology and multi-location, but neither teaches us anything new about the debate over persistence.

References

Abbott, Edwin A. 1884. *Flatland: A Romance of Many Dimensions*. London: Seeley & Co.

Abbruzzese, John. 2001. On Using the Multiverse to Avoid the Paradoxes of Time Travel. *Analysis*, 61: 36–8.

Adams, Robert M. 1986. Time and Thisness. In P. A. French, T. E. Uehling, and H. K. Wettstein, eds., *Midwest Studies in Philosophy: Volume XI*. Minneapolis, MN: University of Minnesota Press.

Airaksinen, Timo. 1980. On Time Travel. *Dialectics and Humanism*, 1: 113–21.

Al-Khalili, Jim. 1999. *Black Holes, Wormholes & Time Machines*. Bristol and Philadelphia: Institute of Physics Publishing.

Alvager, T. and Kreisler, M. N. 1968. Quest for Faster-than-Light Particles. *Physical Review*, 171: 1357–61.

Anderson, Poul. 1981. *The Guardians of Time*. New York: Pinnacle.

Armstrong, D. M. 1980. Identity Through Time. In Peter van Inwagen, ed., *Time and Cause: Essays Presented to Richard Taylor*. Dordrecht: D. Reidel.

Armstrong, D. M. 1983. *What is a Law of Nature?* Cambridge: Cambridge University Press.

Arntzenius, Frank. 2006. Time Travel: Double Your Fun. *Philosophy Compass*, 1: 599–616.

Arntzenius, Frank and Maudlin, Tim. 2010. Time Travel and Modern Physics. In Edward N. Zalta, ed., *The Stanford Encyclopedia of Philosophy*. <https://plato.stanford.edu/>.

Asimov, Isaac. 1949. The Red Queen's Race. *Astounding Science Fiction*, 42: 65–86.

Austin, J. L. 1956. Ifs and Cans. *Proceedings of the British Academy*, 42: 107–32.

Baker, Lynn Rudder. 2000. *Persons and Bodies*. Cambridge: Cambridge University Press.

Baker, Lynn Rudder. 2008. A Metaphysics of Ordinary Things and Why We Need It. *Philosophy*, 83: 5–24.

Balashov, Yuri. 2000. Enduring and Perduring Objects in Minkowski Space-Time. *Philosophical Studies*, 99: 129–66.

Barnes, Elizabeth and Cameron, Ross. 2009. The Open Future: Bivalence, Determinism, and Ontology. *Philosophical Studies*, 146: 291–309.

Barnette, R. L. 1978. Does Quantum Mechanics Disprove the Principle of the Identity of Indiscernibles? *Philosophy of Science*, 45: 466–70.

Baron, Sam. 2017. Back to the Unchanging Past. *Pacific Philosophical Quarterly*, 98: 129–47.

Bars, Itzhak and Terning, Jon. 2010. *Extra Dimensions in Space and Time*. New York: Springer-Verlag.

Barwise, Jon and Perry, John. 1983. *Situations and Attitudes*. Cambridge, MA: MIT Press.

Bennett, Jonathan. 1974. Counterfactuals and Possible Worlds. *Canadian Journal of Philosophy*, 4: 381–402.

Bennett, Jonathan. 2003. *A Philosophical Guide to Conditionals*. Oxford: Oxford University Press.

Benovsky, Jiri. 2009. On (Not) Being in Two Places at the Same Time: An Argument Against Endurantism. *American Philosophical Quarterly*, 46: 239–48.

Benovsky, Jiri. 2011. Endurance and Time Travel. *Kriterion*, 24: 65–72.

Berkovitz, Joseph. 2001. On Chance in Causal Loops. *Mind*, 110: 1–23.

Berkovitz, Joseph. 2007. Action at a Distance in Quantum Mechanics. In Edward N. Zalta, ed., *The Stanford Encyclopedia of Philosophy*. <https://plato.stanford.edu/>.

Bernstein, Sara. 2015. Nowhere Man: Time Travel and Spatial Location. *Midwest Studies in Philosophy*, 39: 158–68.

Bernstein, Sara. 2017. Time Travel and the Movable Present. In J. Keller, ed., *Being, Freedom, and Method: Themes from the Philosophy of Peter van Inwagen*. Oxford: Oxford University Press.

Bigelow, John. 2001. Time Travel Fiction. In Gerhard Preyer and Frank Siebelt, eds., *Reality and Humean Supervenience: Essays on the Philosophy of David Lewis*. Lanham, MD: Rowman & Littlefield.

Black, Max. 1956. Why Cannot an Effect Precede its Cause? *Analysis*, 16: 49–58.

Bolton, Paul. 1931. The Time Hoaxers. *Amazing Stories*, 6: 428–35.

Booker, M. Keith and Thomas, Anne-Marie. 2009. *The Science Fiction Handbook*. Malden, MA: Wiley-Blackwell.

Borges, Jorge Luis. 1941. The Garden of Forking Paths. In *The Garden of Forking Paths (El Jardín de Senderos que se Bifurcan)*. Buenos-Aires: Editorial Sur.

Bourne, Craig. 2006. *A Future for Presentism*. Oxford: Oxford University Press.

Bradley, F. H. 1893. *Appearance and Reality*. New York: Macmillan.

Bridge, Frank J. 1931. Via the Time Accelerator. *Wonder Stories*, 5: 912–21.

Brier, Bob. 1973. Magicians, Alarm Clocks, and Backward Causation. *Southern Journal of Philosophy*, 11: 359–64.

Briggs, Rachael and Forbes, Graeme A. 2012. The Real Truth about the Unreal Future. In Karen Bennett and Dean Zimmerman, eds., *Oxford Studies in Metaphysics, Volume 7*. Oxford: Oxford University Press.

Broad, C. D. 1923. *Scientific Thought*. New York: Harcourt, Brace, and Company.

Broad, C. D. 1938. *An Examination of McTaggart's Philosophy*, Volume II, Part 1. Cambridge: Cambridge University Press.

Brogaard, Berit and Salerno, Joe. 2007. Counterfactuals and Context. *Analysis*, 68: 39–46.

Brown, Bryson. 1992. Defending Backwards Causation. *Canadian Journal of Philosophy*, 22: 429–43.

Burke, Michael. 1992. Copper Statues and Pieces of Copper: A Challenge to the Standard Account. *Analysis*, 52: 12–17.

Burke, Michael. 1994a. Dion and Theon: An Essentialist Solution to an Ancient Puzzle. *Journal of Philosophy*, 91: 129–39.

Burke, Michael. 1994b. Preserving the Principle of One Object to a Place: A Novel Account of the Relations among Objects, Sorts, Sortals and Persistence Conditions. *Philosophy and Phenomenological Research*, 54: 591–624.

Callender, Craig and Edney, Ralph. 2004. *Introducing Time*. London: Icon Books.

Calvert, Laurie. 2002. *A Teacher's Guide to the Signet Classic Edition of H. G. Wells's* The Time Machine. London: Penguin.

Cameron, Ross. 2008. Turtles all the Way Down: Regress, Priority, and Fundamentality. *Philosophical Quarterly*, 58: 1–14.

Carlson, Erik. 2005. A New Time Travel Paradox Resolved. *Philosophia*, 33: 263–73.

Carroll, John W., ed. 2008a. The Double-Occupancy Problem. *A Time Travel Website*. <http://timetravelphilosophy.net/>.

Carroll, John W., ed. 2008b. Relativity and Time Travel. *A Time Travel Website*. <http://timetravelphilosophy.net/>.

Carroll, John W. 2010. Context, Conditionals, Fatalism, Freedom and Time Travel. In Joseph Keim Campbell, Michael O'Rourke, and Harry S. Silverstein, eds., *Topics in Contemporary Philosophy, Volume 6*. Cambridge, MA: MIT Press.

Carroll, John W. 2011. Self Visitation, Traveler Time and Compatible Properties. *Canadian Journal of Philosophy*, 41: 359–70.

Carroll, John W. 2016. Ways to Commit Autoinfanticide. *Journal of the American Philosophical Association*, 2: 180–91.

Carroll, John W. and Markosian, Ned. 2010. *An Introduction to Metaphysics*. Cambridge: Cambridge University Press.

Carroll, John W. et al. 2014. *A Time Travel Dialogue*. Cambridge: Open Book Publishers.

Casati, Robert and Varzi, Achile C. 2001. That Useless Time Machine. *Philosophy*, 4: 581–3.

Chisholm, Roderick. 1976. *Person and Object: A Metaphysical Study*. Chicago: Open Court.

Chisholm, Roderick and Taylor, Richard. 1960. Making Things to Have Happened. *Analysis*, 20: 73–8.

Christensen, F. 1976. The Source of the River of Time. *Ratio*, 18: 131–44.

Clarke, Arthur C. 1962. *Profiles of the Future: An Inquiry into the Limits of the Possible*. New York: Harper.

Clarke, C. J. S. 1977. Time in General Relativity. In J. Earman, C. Glymour, and J. Stachel, eds., *Minnesota Studies in the Philosophy of Science, Volume 8*. Minneapolis: University of Minnesota Press.

Clegg, Brian. 2011. *How to Build a Time Machine: The Real Science of Time Travel*. New York: St. Martin's Griffin.

Cloukey, Charles. 1929. Paradox. *Amazing Stories Quarterly*, Summer Edition: 386–97.

Cohen, Yishai. 2015. Reasons-Responsiveness and Time Travel. *Journal of Ethics and Social Philosophy*, January: 1–7.

Cook, Monte. 1982. Tips for Time Travel. In N. D. Smith, ed., *Philosophers Look at Science Fiction*. Chicago: Nelson-Hall.

Correia, Fabrice. 2005. *Existential Dependence and Cognate Notions*. Munich: Philosophia Verlag.

Correia, Fabrice and Schnieder, Benjamin. 2012. *Metaphysical Grounding: Understanding the Structure of Reality*. Cambridge: Cambridge University Press.

Cortes, Alberto. 1976. Leibniz's Principle of the Identity of Indiscernibles: A False Principle. *Philosophy of Science*, 43: 491–505.

Cotnoir, Aaron J. and Bacon, Andrew. 2012. Non-Wellfounded Mereology. *Review of Symbolic Logic*, 5: 187–204.

Craig, William Lane. 1979. *The Kalam Cosmological Argument*. London: Macmillan.

Craig, William Lane. 1988. Tachyons, Time Travel, and Divine Omniscience. *Journal of Philosophy*, 85: 135–50.

Craig, William Lane. 2002. Atheism vs. Christianity. Presented at the Sydney Town Hall, August 27.

Crisp, Thomas and Smith, Donald. 2005. 'Wholly Present' Defined. *Philosophy and Phenomenological Research*, 71: 318–44.

Cross, Charles B. 2007. Antecedent-Relative Comparative World Similarity. *Journal of Philosophical Logic*, 37: 101–20.

Dainton, Barry. 2001. *Time and Space*. Montreal: McGill-Queen's University Press.

Daniels, David R. 1935. The Branches of Time. *Wonder Stories*, 7: 294–303.

Daniels, Paul R. 2012. Back to the Present: Defending Presentist Time Travel. *Disputatio*, 4: 469–84.

Daniels, Paul R. 2014a. Lewisian Time Travel in a Relativistic Setting. *Metaphysica*, 15: 329–45.

Daniels, Paul R. 2014b. Occupy Wall: A Mereological Puzzle and the Burdens of Endurantism. *Australasian Journal of Philosophy*, 92: 91–101.

Dauer, Francis Watanabe. 2008. Hume on the Relation of Cause and Effect. In Elizabeth S. Radcliffe, ed., *A Companion to Hume*. Malden, MA: Blackwell.

Davies, Paul. 1977. *Space and Time in the Modern Universe*. Cambridge: Cambridge University Press.

Davies, Paul. 2001. *How to Build a Time Machine*. New York: Penguin Putnam.

Davies, Richard. 2011. Lost in *Lost*'s Times. In Sharon Kaye, ed., *The Ultimate Lost and Philosophy: Think Together, Die Alone*. Hoboken, NJ: John Wiley & Sons.

Decker, Kevin S. 2013. *Who is Who? The Philosophy of Doctor Who*. London and New York: I. B. Tauris.

Dee, Roger. 1954. The Poundstone Paradox. *The Magazine of Fantasy and Science Fiction*, May.

Denruyter, Celine. 1980. Jocasta's Crime: A Science-Fiction Reply. *Analysis*, 40: 71.

Deutsch, David. 1991. Quantum Mechanics Near Closed Timelike Lines. *Physical Review D*, 44: 3197–217.

Deutsch, David. 1997. *The Fabric of Reality: The Science of Parallel Universes—and its Implications*. New York: Penguin.

Deutsch, David and Lockwood, Michael. 1994. The Quantum Physics of Time Travel. *Scientific American*, 270: 68–74.

Devlin, William J. 2001. Imaginary Peanut Butter: The Paradoxes of Time Travel in *Lost*. In Sharon Kaye, ed., *The Ultimate Lost and Philosophy: Think Together, Die Alone*. Hoboken, NJ: John Wiley & Sons.

Dick, Philip K. 1977. A Little Something for Us Tempunauts. In *The Best of Philip K. Dick*. New York: Del Rey.

Dickens, Charles. 1843/1908. *A Christmas Carol*. London: Blackie and Son.

Donnelly, Maureen. 2011. Using Mereological Principles to Support Metaphysics. *Philosophical Quarterly*, 61: 225–46.

Dore, Clement. 1984. *Theism*. Dordrecht: D. Reidel.

Dowden, Bradley. 2009. *The Metaphysics of Time: A Dialogue*. Lanham, MD: Rowman & Littlefield.

Dowe, Phil. 2000. The Case for Time Travel. *Philosophy*, 75: 441–51.

Dowe, Phil. 2001. Causal Loops and the Independence of Causal Facts. *Philosophy of Science*, 68: S89–S97.

Dowe, Phil. 2003. The Coincidences of Time Travel. *Philosophy of Science*, 70: 574–89.

Dretske, Fred. 1962. Moving Backward in Time. *Philosophical Review*, 71: 94–8.

Dummett, Michael. 1954. Can an Effect Precede its Cause? *Proceedings of the Aristotelian Society*, 28: 27–44.

Dummett, Michael. 1964. Bringing about the Past. *Philosophical Review*, 73: 338–59.

Dummett, Michael. 1986. Causal Loops. In Raymond Flood and Michael Lockwood, eds., *The Nature of Time*. Oxford: Blackwell.

Dwyer, Larry. 1975. Time Travel and Changing the Past. *Philosophical Studies*, 27: 341–50.

Dwyer, Larry. 1977. How to Affect, but not Change, the Past. *Southern Journal of Philosophy*, 15: 383–5.

Dwyer, Larry. 1978. Time Travel and Some Alleged Logical Asymmetries Between Past and Future. *Canadian Journal of Philosophy*, 8: 15–38.

Dyke, Heather. 2005. The Metaphysics and Epistemology of Time Travel. *Think*, 9: 43–52.

Earman, John. 1972. Implications of Causal Propagation Outside the Null Cone. *Australasian Journal of Philosophy*, 50: 222–37.

Earman, John. 1995. Recent Work on Time Travel. In Steven F. Savitt, ed., *Time's Arrows Today: Recent Physical and Philosophical Work on the Direction of Time*. New York: Cambridge University Press.

Earman, John, Smeenk, C., and Wüthrich, C. 2009. Do the Laws of Physics Forbid the Operation of Time Machines? *Synthese*, 169: 91–124.

Eaton, William. 2010. The Doctor on Reversed Causation and Closed Causal Chains. In Courtland Lewis and Paula Smithka, eds., *Dr. Who and Philosophy*. Chicago: Open Court Press.

Echeverria, F., Klinkhammer, G., and Thorne, K. S. 1991. Billiard Balls in Wormhole Spacetimes with Closed Timelike Curves: Classical Theory. *Physical Review D*, 44: 1077–99.

Eddon, Maya. 2010. Three Arguments from Temporary Intrinsics. *Philosophy and Phenomenological Research*, 81: 605–19.

Edwards, Anne M. 1995. Springing Forward and Falling Back: Traveling Through Time. *Contemporary Philosophy*, 17: 12–24.

Effingham, Nikk. 2011a. Mereological Explanation and Time Travel. *Australasian Journal of Philosophy*, 88: 333–45.

Effingham, Nikk. 2011b. Temporal Parts and Time Travel. *Erkenntnis*, 74: 225–40.

Effingham, Nikk. 2012. An Unwelcome Consequence of the Multiverse Thesis. *Synthese*, 184: 375–86.

Effingham, Nikk and Robson, Jon. 2007. Mereological Challenge to Endurantism. *Australasian Journal of Philosophy*, 85: 633–40.

Ehring, Douglas. 1986. Closed Causal Loops, Single Causes, and Asymmetry. *Analysis*, 46: 33–5.

Ehring, Douglas. 1987. Personal Identity and Time Travel. *Philosophical Studies*, 52: 427–33.

Eisenstein, Alex and Eisenstein, Phyllis. 1971. The Trouble with the Past. In Robert Silverberg, ed., *New Dimensions 1*. Garden City, NY: Doubleday.

Eldridge-Smith, Peter. 2007. Paradoxes and Hypodoxes of Time Travel. In J. Lloyd Jones, P. Campbell, and P. Wylie, eds., *Art and Time*. Melbourne: Australian Scholarly Publishing.

Evans, Gareth. 1978. Can there be Vague Objects? *Analysis*, 38: 208.

Everett, Allen. 2004. Time Travel Paradoxes, Path Integrals, and the Many Worlds Interpretation of Quantum Mechanics. *Physical Review D*, 69: 124023.

Everett, Allen and Roman, Thomas. 2012. *Time Travels and Warp Drives*. Chicago: University of Chicago Press.

Fast, H. 1959. Of Time and Cats. *Fantasy and Science Fiction*, 16: 54–63.

Faye, Jan. 2010. Backward Causation. In Edward N. Zalta, ed., *The Stanford Encyclopedia of Philosophy*. <https://plato.stanford.edu/>.

Feldman, Richard. 2004. Freedom and Contextualism. In Joseph Keim Campbell, Michael O'Rourke, and David Shier, eds., *Topics in Contemporary Philosophy, Volume II*. Cambridge, MA: MIT Press.

Feynman, Richard, Leighton, Robert, and Sands, Matthew. 1975. *The Feynman Lectures in Physics*. Reading, MA: Addison-Wesley.

Fine, Kit. 1975. Critical Notice of *Counterfactuals*. *Mind*, 84: 451–8.

Fine, Kit. 1977. Postscript. In A. N. Prior and K. Fine, *Worlds, Times, and Selves*. London: Duckworth.

Fine, Kit. 2002. The Varieties of Necessity. In Tamar Szabó Gendler and John Hawthorne, eds., *Conceivability and Possibility*. Oxford: Oxford University Press.

Fine, Kit. 2003. The Non-Identity of a Thing and its Matter. *Mind*, 112: 195–234.

Fitzgerald, Paul. 1970. Tachyons, Backwards Causation and Freedom. *PSA: Proceedings of the Biennial Meeting of the Philosophy of Science Association*: 415–36.

Fitzgerald, Paul. 1974. On Retrocausality. *Philosophia*, 4: 513–51.

Flew, Anthony. 1954. Can an Effect Precede its Cause? *Proceedings of the Aristotelian Society*, 28: 45–62.

Flew, Anthony. 1956. Effects Before their Causes? Addenda and Corrigenda. *Analysis*, 16: 104–10.

Flew, Anthony. 1973. Magicians, Alarm Clocks, and Backward Causation: A Comment. *Southern Journal of Philosophy*, 11: 365–6.

Forrest, Peter. 2005. General Facts, Physical Necessity and the Metaphysics of Time. In Dean Zimmerman, ed., *Oxford Studies in Metaphysics, Volume 2*. Oxford: Oxford University Press.

Forrest, Peter. 2010. Can a Soufflé Rise Twice? Van Inwagen's Irresponsible Time Travellers. Dean Zimmerman, ed., *Oxford Studies in Metaphysics, Volume 5*. Oxford: Oxford University Press.

Frisch, Mathias. 2013. Time and Causation. In Heather Dyke and Adrian Bardon, eds., *A Companion to the Philosophy of Time*. Malden, MA: Wiley-Blackwell.

Fulmer, Gilbert. 1980. Understanding Time Travel. *Southwestern Journal of Philosophy*, 11: 151–6.

Fulmer, Gilbert. 1983. Cosmological Implications of Time Travel. In R. E. Myers, ed., *The Intersection of Science Fiction and Philosophy*. Westport, CT: Greenwood.

Gale, Richard. 1965. Why a Cause Cannot be Later than its Effect. *Review of Metaphysics*, 19: 209–34.

Gale, Richard. 1968. *The Language of Time*. London: Routledge & Kegan Paul.

Gardner, Martin. 1987. *Time Travel and Other Mathematical Bewilderments*. New York: W. H. Freeman.

Garrett, Brian. 2014a. On the Epistemic Bilking Argument. *Thought*, 4: 139–40.

Garrett, Brian. 2014b. Black on Backwards Causation. *Thought*, 3: 230–3.

Garrett, Brian. 2015. Some Remarks on Backwards Causation. *Portuguese Review of Philosophy*, 71: 695–704.

Garrett, Brian. 2016. Tim, Tom, Time and Fate: Lewis on Time Travel. *Analytic Philosophy*, 57: 247–52.

Gaspar, Enrique. 1887/2012. *The Time Ship: A Chrononautical Journey*, trans. Yolanda Molina-Gavilán and Andrea Bell. Middletown, CT: Wesleyan University Press.

Gernsback, Hugo, ed. 1927. *Science Wonder Stories*, 2: 410–12.

Gerrold, David. 1973. *The Man Who Folded Himself*. New York: Random House.

Gibbard, Alan. 1975. Contingent Identity. *Journal of Philosophical Logic*, 4: 187–221.

Gilmore, Cody. 2007. Time Travel, Coinciding Objects, and Persistence. In Dean Zimmerman, ed., *Oxford Studies in Metaphysics, Volume 3*. Oxford: Oxford University Press.

Ginsberg, Allen. 1981. Quantum Theory and the Identity of Indiscernibles. *Philosophy of Science*, 48: 487–91.

Gleick, James. 2016. *Time Travel: A History*. New York: Pantheon Books.

Goddu, G. C. 2003. Time Travel and Changing the Past (Or How to Kill Yourself and Live to Tell the Tale). *Ratio*, 16: 16–32.

Goddu, G. C. 2007. Banana Peels and Time Travel. *Dialectica*, 61: 559–72.

Goddu, G. C. 2011. Avoiding or Changing the Past? *Pacific Philosophical Quarterly*, 92: 11–17.

Gödel, Kurt. 1949. An Example of a New Type of Cosmological Solution of Einstein's Field Equations of Gravitation. *Reviews of Modern Physics*, 21: 447–50.

Godfrey-Smith, William. 1980. Travelling in Time. *Analysis*, 40: 72–3.

Goff, Philip. 2010. Could the Daleks Stop the Pyramids being Built? In Courtland Lewis and Paula Smithka, eds., *Dr. Who and Philosophy*. Chicago: Open Court Press.

Gold, H. L. 1953. Perfect Murder. In G. Conklin, ed., *Science-Fiction Adventures in Dimension*. New York: Vanguard.

Goranko, Valentin and Galton, Antony. 2015. Temporal Logic. In Edward N. Zalta, ed., *The Stanford Encyclopedia of Philosophy*. <https://plato.stanford.edu/>.

Gorovitz, Samuel. 1964. Leaving the Past Alone. *Philosophical Review*, 73: 360–71.

Gott, J. R. 1991. Closed Timelike Curves Produced by Pairs of Moving Cosmic Strings: Exact Solutions. *Physical Review Letters*, 66: 1126–9.

Gott, J. R. 2001. *Time Travel in Einstein's Universe: The Physical Possibilities of Travel Through Time*. Boston: Houghton Mifflin.

Greene, Brian. 2004. *The Fabric of the Cosmos: Space, Time, and the Texture of Reality*. New York: Random House.

Grey, William. 1999. Troubles with Time Travel. *Philosophy*, 74: 55–70.

Grigoriev, Vladimir. 1968. Vanya. In M. Ginsburg, ed., *Last Door to Aiya*. New York: S. G. Phillips.

Grünbaum, Adolf. 1963. *Philosophical Problems of Space and Time*. New York: Knopf.

Hale, Edward Everett. 1895. *Hands Off*. Boston: J. S. Smith & Co.

Hales, Steven D. 2010. No Time Travel for Presentists. *Logos & Episteme*, 1: 353–60.

Hales, Steven D. 2011. Reply to Licon on Time Travel. *Logos & Episteme*, 4: 633–6.

Hall, Ned. 2000. Causation and the Price of Transitivity. *Journal of Philosophy*, 97: 198–222.

Hall, Thomas. 2014. In Defense of the Compossibility of Presentism and Time Travel. *Logos & Episteme*, 5: 141–59.

Hanley, Richard. 1997. *The Metaphysics of Star Trek*. New York: Basic Books.

Hanley, Richard. 2004. No End in Sight: Causal Loops in Physics, Philosophy, and Fiction. *Synthese*, 141: 123–52.

Harrison, Jonathan. 1971. Dr. Who and the Philosophers or Time Travel for Beginners. *Aristotelian Society Supplement*, 45: 1–24.

Harrison, Jonathan. 1979. Analysis 'Problem' No. 18. *Analysis*, 39: 65–6.

Harrison, Jonathan. 1980. Report on Analysis 'Problem' No. 18. *Analysis*, 40: 65–9.

Haslanger, Sally. 1989. Endurance and Temporary Intrinsics. *Analysis*, 49: 119–25.

Haslanger, Sally. 2003. Persistence Through Time. In Michael Loux and Dean Zimmerman, eds., *The Oxford Handbook of Metaphysics*. Oxford: Oxford University Press.

Hawking, Stephen. 1992. Chronology Protection Conjecture. *Physical Review D*, 46: 603–11.

Hawking, Stephen. 1994. The Future of the Universe. In *Black Holes and Baby Universes and Other Essays*. New York: Random House.

Hawley, Katherine. 2001. *How Things Persist*. Oxford: Clarendon Press.

Hawley, Katherine. 2006. Science as a Guide to Metaphysics? *Synthese*, 149: 451–70.

Hawley, Katherine. 2010. Temporal Parts. In Edward N. Zalta, ed., *The Stanford Encyclopedia of Philosophy*. <https://plato.stanford.edu/>.

Hawthorne, John. 2001. Freedom in Context. *Philosophical Studies*, 104: 63–79.

Heinlein, Robert A. 1941. By His Bootstraps. *Astounding Science Fiction*, 28: 9–47.

Heinlein, Robert A. 1959. All you Zombies—. *The Magazine of Fantasy and Science Fiction*, 16: 5–15.

Heller, Mark. 1984. Temporal Parts of Four Dimensional Objects. *Philosophical Studies*, 46: 323–34.

Heller, Mark. 1990. *The Ontology of Physical Objects: Four-Dimensional Hunks of Matter*. Cambridge: Cambridge University Press.

Heller, Mark. 1992. Things Change. *Philosophy and Phenomenological Research*, 52: 695–704.

Henderson, Lydia. 1983. *The Fourth Dimension and Non-Euclidean Geometry in Modern Art*. Princeton: Princeton University Press.

Hiddleston, Eric. 2005. A Causal Theory of Counterfactuals. *Noûs*, 39: 632–57.

Hinchliff, Mark. 1996. The Puzzle of Change. *Philosophical Perspectives*, 10: 119–36.

Hitchcock, Christopher. 1997. Probabilistic Causation. In Edward N. Zalta, ed., *The Stanford Encyclopedia of Philosophy*. <https://plato.stanford.edu/>.

Holt, D. C. 1981. Time Travel: The Time Discrepancy Paradox. *Philosophical Investigations*, 4: 1–16.

Honoré, A. M. 1964. Can and Can't. *Mind*, 73: 463–79.

Horacek, David. 2005. Time Travel in Indeterministic Worlds. *The Monist*, 88: 423–36.

Horwich, Paul. 1975. On Some Alleged Paradoxes of Time Travel. *Journal of Philosophy*, 72: 432–44.

Horwich, Paul. 1987. *Asymmetries in Time: Problems in the Philosophy of Science*. Cambridge, MA: MIT Press.

Hospers, John. 1967. *An Introduction to Philosophical Analysis*. London: Routledge & Kegan Paul.

Hudson, Hud. 2001. *A Materialist Metaphysics of the Human Person*. Ithaca: Cornell University Press.

Hudson, Hud. 2005. *The Metaphysics of Hyperspace*. Oxford: Oxford University Press.

Hudson, Hud and Wasserman, Ryan. 2010. Van Inwagen on Time Travel and Changing the Past. In Dean Zimmerman, ed., *Oxford Studies in Metaphysics, Volume 5*. Oxford: Oxford University Press.

Hume, David. 1777/1975. An Enquiry Concerning Human Understanding. In P. H. Nidditch, ed., *Enquiries Concerning Human Understanding and Concerning the Principles of Morals* (Third Edition). Oxford: Clarendon Press.

Hunter, Joel. 2004. Time Travel. *Internet Encyclopedia of Philosophy*. <http://www.iep.utm.edu/timetrav/>.

Hunter, Nick. 2016. *Is Time Travel Possible?* Chicago: Heinemann-Raintree.

Ismael, J. 2003. Closed Causal Loops and the Bilking Argument. *Synthese*, 136: 305–20.

Jackson, Frank. 1977. A Causal Theory of Counterfactuals. *Australasian Journal of Philosophy*, 55: 3–21.

Jackson, Frank. 1994. Metaphysics by Possible Cases. *The Monist*, 77: 93–110.

Jones, Matthew and Ormrod, Joan. 2015. Introduction. In *Time Travel in Popular Media: Essays on Film, Television, Literature and Video Games*. Jefferson, NC: McFarland & Company.

Kaku, Michio. 2009. *Physics of the Impossible: A Scientific Exploration into the World of Phasers, Force Fields, Teleportation, and Time Travel*. New York: Anchor Books.

Kaletsky, Milton. 1935. Time Travelling is Impossible. *Fantasy Magazine*, 32: 173–5.

Kaplan, David. 1989. Demonstratives. In Joseph Almog, John Perry, and Howard Wettstein, eds., *Themes from Kaplan*. Oxford: Oxford University Press.

Karcher, Carolyn L. 1985. Patriarchal Society and Matriarchal Family in Irvings's "Rip Van Winkle" and Child's "Hilda Silfverling." *Legacy*, 2: 31–44.

Keller, Simon and Nelson, Michael. 2001. Presentists Should Believe in Time Travel. *Australasian Journal of Philosophy*, 79: 333–45.

Kenny, Anthony. 1976. Human Abilities and Dynamic Modalities. In J. Manninen and R. Tuomela, eds., *Essays on Explanation and Understanding*. Dordrecht: D. Reidel.

Kiekeben, Franz. 2008. Three Time Travel Problems. In Ryan Nichols, Nicholas D. Smith, and Fred Miller, eds., *Philosophy Through Science Fiction*. New York: Routledge.

Kim, Jaegwon. 1976. Events as Property Exemplifications. In M. Brand and D. Walton, eds., *Action Theory*. Dordrecht: D. Reidel.

Kiourti, Ira. 2008. Killing Baby Suzy. *Philosophical Studies*, 139: 343–52.

Kleinschmidt, Shieva. 2011. Mereology and Location. *Philosophical Perspectives*, 25: 253–76.

Kleinschmidt, Shieva. 2015. Fundamentality and Time Travel. *Thought*, 4: 46–51.

Krasnikov, S. 2002. Time Travel Paradox. *Physical Review D*, 65: 1–8.

Kratzer, Angelika. 1977. What 'Must' and 'Can' Must and Can Mean. *Linguistics and Philosophy*, 1: 337–55.

Kratzer, Angelika. 2012. *Modals and Conditionals*. Oxford: Oxford University Press.

Kurtz, Roxanne Marie. 2006. Introduction to Persistence: What's the Problem? In S. Haslanger and R. M. Kurtz, eds., *Persistence: Contemporary Readings*. Cambridge: MIT Press.

Kutach, Douglas. 2013. Time Travel and Time Machines. In H. Dyke and A. Bardon, eds., *A Companion to the Philosophy of Time*. Chichester: John Wiley & Sons.

Kvart, I. 1986. *A Theory of Counterfactuals*. Indianapolis: Hackett.

Law, Stephen. 2008. The Time Machine. *Think*, 19: 47–8.

Le Poidevin, Robin. 2003. *Travels in Four Dimensions: The Enigmas of Space and Time*. Oxford: Oxford University Press.

Le Poidevin, Robin. 2005. The Cheshire Cat Problem and Other Spatial Obstacles to Backwards Time Travel. *The Monist*, 88: 336–52.

Leftow, Brian. 2004. A Latin Trinity. *Faith and Philosophy*, 21: 304–33.

Leftow, Brian. 2012. Time Travel and the Trinity. *Faith and Philosophy*, 29: 313–24.

Levin, Margarita R. 1980. Swords' Points. *Analysis*, 40: 69–70.

Lewis, David. 1971. Counterparts of Persons and their Bodies. *Journal of Philosophy*, 68: 203–11.

Lewis, David. 1973. *Counterfactuals*. Oxford: Blackwell.

Lewis, David. 1976. The Paradoxes of Time Travel. *American Philosophical Quarterly*, 13: 145–52.

Lewis, David. 1977. Letter to Bennett, March 29.

Lewis, David. 1979. Scorekeeping in a Language Game. *Journal of Philosophical Logic*, 8: 339–59.

Lewis, David. 1983. Survival and Identity. Reprinted with postscripts in *Philosophical Papers, Volume I*. New York: Oxford University Press.

Lewis, David. 1986a. *On the Plurality of Worlds*. Oxford: Blackwell.

Lewis, David. 1986b. Causation. Reprinted with postscripts in *Philosophical Papers, Volume II*. New York: Oxford University Press.

Lewis, David. 1986c. Counterfactual Dependence and Time's Arrow. Reprinted with postscripts in *Philosophical Papers, Volume II*. New York: Oxford University Press.

Lewis, David. 1992. Critical Notice of D. M. Armstrong, *A Combinatorial Theory of Possibility*. *Australasian Journal of Philosophy*, 70: 211–24.

Lewis, David. 1994. Humean Supervenience Debugged. *Mind*, 103: 473–90.

Lewis, David. 1999. Rearrangement of Particles: Reply to Lowe. Reprinted in *Papers in Metaphysics and Epistemology*. Cambridge: Cambridge University Press.

Lewis, David. 2000. Causation as Influence. *Journal of Philosophy*, 97: 182–97.

Licon, Jimmy. 2011. No Suicide for Presentists: A Response to Hales. *Logos & Episteme*, 2: 455–64.

Licon, Jimmy. 2012. Still No Suicide for Presentists: Why Hales' Response Fails. *Logos & Episteme*, 3: 145–51.

Licon, Jimmy. 2013. Dissecting the Suicide Machine Argument. *Logos & Episteme*, 4: 339–52.

Lockwood, Michael. 2005. *The Labyrinth of Time: Introducing the Universe*. Oxford: Oxford University Press.

Loss, Roberto. 2015. How to Change the Past in One-Dimensional Time. *Pacific Philosophical Quarterly*, 96: 1–11.

Lossev, Andrei and Novikov, Igor D. 1992. The Jinn of the Time Machine: Non-Trivial Self-Consistent Solutions. *Classical and Quantum Gravity*, 9: 2309–21.

Lowe, E. J. 1988. The Problems of Intrinsic Change: Rejoinder to Lewis. *Analysis*, 48: 72–7.

Lucas, John. 1999. A Century of Time. In Jeremy Butterfield, ed., *The Arguments of Time*. Oxford: Oxford University Press.

McArthur, Robert P. and Slattery, Michael P. 1974. Peter Damian and Undoing the Past. *Philosophical Studies*, 25: 137–41.

MacBeath, Murray. 1982. Who was Dr. Who's Father? *Synthese*, 51: 397–430.

MacBeath, Murray. 1993. Time's Square. In R. Le Poidevin, ed., *The Philosophy of Time*. Oxford: Oxford University Press.

McCall, Storrs. 1994. *A Model of the Universe*. Oxford: Clarendon Press.

McCall, Storrs and Lowe, E. J. 2009. The Definition of Endurance. *Analysis*, 69: 277–80.

McDaniel, Kris. 2003. No Paradox of Multi-Location. *Analysis*, 63: 309–11.

McDaniel, Kris. 2007. Brutal Simples. In Dean Zimmerman, ed., *Oxford Studies in Metaphysics, Volume 3*. Oxford: Oxford University Press.

McDermott, Michael. 1995. Redundant Causation. *British Journal for the Philosophy of Science*, 46: 423–44.

MacKaye, H. S. 1904. *The Panchronicon*. New York: Charles Scribner's Sons.

Mackie, J. L. 1965. Causes and Conditions. *American Philosophical Quarterly*, 2: 245–64.

Mackie, J. L. 1974. *The Cement of the Universe*. Oxford: Oxford University Press.

McTaggart, J. M. E. 1908. *The Nature of Existence, Volume I*. Cambridge: Cambridge University Press.

Madden, Samuel. 1733. *Memoirs of the Twentieth Century*. London: Osborn, Longman, et al.

Maier, John. 2010. Abilities. In Edward N. Zalta, ed., *The Stanford Encyclopedia of Philosophy*. <https://plato.stanford.edu/>.

Main, Michael. 2008. *storypilot.com*. Web. Accessed May 6, 2016.

Malament, David. 1984. "Time Travel" in the Gödel Universe. *PSA: Proceedings of the Philosophy of Science Association*, 2: 91–100.

Markosian, Ned. 1994. The 3D/4D Controversy and Non-Present Objects. *Philosophical Papers*, 23: 243–9.

Markosian, Ned. 2004. Two Arguments from Sider's *Four-Dimensionalism*. *Philosophy and Phenomenological Research*, 68: 665–73.

Martínez, Manolo. 2011. Travelling in Branching Timelines. *Disputatio*, 4: 59–75.

Matheson, Richard. 1975. *Bid Time Return*. New York: Viking.

Maudlin, Tim. 1990. Time-Travel and Topology. In A. Fine, M. Forbes, and L. Wessels, eds., *Proceedings of the 1990 Biennial Meeting of the Philosophy of Science Association*. East Lansing, MI: Philosophy of Science Association.

Maudlin, Tim. 2012. *Philosophy of Physics: Space and Time*. Princeton: Princeton University Press.

Meiland, J. W. 1974. A Two-Dimensional Passage Model of Time for Time Travel. *Philosophical Studies*, 26: 153–73.

Mele, Alfred. 2002. Agents' Abilities. *Noûs*, 37: 447–70.

Mellor, D. H. 1981. *Real Time*. Cambridge: Cambridge University Press.

Mellor, D. H. 1998. *Real Time II*. New York: Routledge.

Menzies, Peter. 2014. Counterfactual Theories of Causation. In Edward N. Zalta, ed., *The Stanford Encyclopedia of Philosophy*. <https://plato.stanford.edu/>.

Merricks, Trenton. 1994. Endurance and Indiscernibility. *Journal of Philosophy*, 91: 165–84.

Merricks, Trenton. 1999. Persistence, Parts and Presentism. *Noûs*, 33: 421–38.

Merricks, Trenton. 2006. Good-Bye Growing Block. In Dean Zimmerman, ed., *Oxford Studies in Metaphysics, Volume 2*. Oxford: Oxford University Press.

Meyer, Ulrich. 2012. Explaining Causal Loops. *Analysis*, 72: 259–64.

Miller, Kristie. 2005. Time Travel and the Open Future. *Disputatio*, 1: 223–32.

Miller, Kristie. 2006. Travelling in Time: How to Wholly Exist in Two Places at the Same Time. *Canadian Journal of Philosophy*, 36: 309–34.

Miller, Kristie. 2008. Backwards Causation, Time, and the Open Future. *Metaphysica*, 9: 173–91.

Miller, Kristie. 2009. Changing the Future: Fate and the Future. In R. Brown and K. Decker, eds., *Terminator and Philosophy: I'll be Back, Therefore I Am*. Hoboken, NJ: John Wiley & Sons.

Miller, P. S. 1951. Status Quondam. In R. J. Healy, ed., *New Tales of Space and Time*. New York: Henry Holt and Co.

Mines, Samuel. 1946. Find the Sculptor. *Thrilling Wonder Stories*, 28: 58–63.

Mitchell, Edward Page. 1881. The Clock that Went Backward. *The Sun*, September 18.

Monton, Bradley. 2003. Presentists can Believe in Closed Timelike Curves. *Analysis*, 63: 199–202.

Monton, Bradley. 2006. Presentism and Quantum Gravity. In Dennis Dieks, ed., *The Ontology of Spacetime*. Amsterdam: Elsevier.

Monton, Bradley. 2009. Time Travel without Causal Loops. *Philosophical Quarterly*, 59: 54–67.

Morris, M. S., Thorne, K. S., and Yurtsever, U. 1988. Wormholes, Time Machines, and the Weak Energy Condition. *Physical Review Letters*, 61: 1446–9.

Morris, Thomas V. and Menzel, Christopher. 1986. Absolute Creation. *American Philosophical Quarterly*, 23: 353–62.

Murray, Bridget. 2003. What Makes Mental Time Travel Possible? *Monitor on Psychology*, 34: 62.

Nahin, Paul J. 1999. *Time Machines: Time Travel in Physics, Metaphysics, and Science Fiction* (Second Edition). New York: Springer-Verlag.

Nahin, Paul J. 2011. *Time Travel: A Writer's Guide to the Real Science of Plausible Time Travel*. Baltimore: Johns Hopkins University Press.

Neale, Stephen. 1990. *Descriptions*. Cambridge, MA: MIT Press.

Nerlich, Graham. 1981. Can Time be Finite? *Pacific Philosophical Quarterly*, 62: 227–39.

Nerlich, Graham. 1994. *What Spacetime Explains: Metaphysical Essays on Space and Time*. New York: Cambridge University Press.

Ney, S. E. 2000. Are Grandfathers an Endangered Species? *Journal of Philosophical Research*, 25: 311–21.

Ni, Peimin. 1992. Changing the Past. *Noûs*, 26: 349–59.

Niven, Larry. 1971. The Theory and Practice of Time Travel. In *All the Myriad Ways*. New York: Del Rey.

Noordhof, Paul. 2003. Tooley on Backward Causation. *Analysis*, 63: 157–62.

Noordhof, Paul. 2005. Morgenbesser's Coin, Counterfactuals and Independence. *Analysis*, 65: 261–3.

O'Hear, Anthony. 1984. *Experience, Explanation, and Faith: An Introduction to the Philosophy of Religion*. London: Routledge & Kegan Paul.

Oliver, Chad. 1955. A Star Above It. In *Another Kind*. New York: Ballantine.

Overbye, Dennis. 2005. Remembrance of Things Future: The Mystery of Time. *New York Times*, June 28.

Parfit, Derek. 1971. Personal Identity. *Philosophical Review*, 80: 3–27.

Parsons, Josh. 2005. I am Not Now, Nor Have I Ever Been, a Turnip. *Australasian Journal of Philosophy*, 83: 1–14.

Parsons, Josh. 2007. Theories of Location. In Dean Zimmerman, ed., *Oxford Studies in Metaphysics, Volume 3*. Oxford: Oxford University Press.

Parsons, Josh. 2008. Hudson on Location. *Philosophy and Phenomenological Research*, 76: 427–35.

Pears, D. F. 1957. The Priority of Causes. *Analysis*, 17: 54–63.

Perry, John. 1976. The Importance of Being Identical. In Amélie Rorty, ed., *The Identities of Persons*. Berkeley: University of California Press.

Perszyk, Ken and Smith, Nicholas J. J. 2001. The Paradoxes of Time Travel. In Hamish Campbell, ed., *Maui and the White Rabbit: Maori and Pakeha Concepts of Time*. Te Papa: National Museum of New Zealand Press.

Pickover, Clifford A. 1998. *Time: A Traveler's Guide*. New York: Oxford University Press.

Pickup, Martin. 2015. Real Presence in the Eucharist and Time-Travel. *Religious Studies*, 51: 379–89.

Pierce, Jeremy. 2011. It Doesn't Matter What We Do: From Metaphysics to Ethics in *Lost*'s Time Travel. In Sharon Kaye, ed., *The Ultimate Lost and Philosophy: Think Together, Die Alone*. Hoboken, NJ: John Wiley & Sons.

Piper, H. B. 1983. Flight from Tomorrow. In J. F. Carr, ed., *The Worlds of H. Beam Piper*. New York: Ace.

Pitkin, Walter B. 1914. Time and Pure Activity. *Journal of Philosophy, Psychology and Scientific Methods*, 11: 521–6.

Price, Huw. 1984. The Philosophy and Physics of Affecting the Past. *Synthese*, 61: 299–323.

Prior, A. N. 1957. *Time and Modality*. Oxford: Clarendon Press.

Prior, A. N. 1967. *Past, Present, and Future*. Oxford: Clarendon Press.

Prior, A. N. 1968. Changes in Events and Changes in Things. In *Papers on Time and Tense*. Oxford: Oxford University Press.

Pruss, Alexander. 2010. *The Principle of Sufficient Reason: A Reassessment*. Cambridge: Cambridge University Press.

Psillos, Stathis. 2009. Regularity Theories of Causation. In Helen Beebee, Christopher Hitchcock, and Peter Menzies, eds., *The Oxford Handbook of Causation*. Oxford: Oxford University Press.

Putnam, Hilary. 1962. It Ain't Necessarily So. *Journal of Philosophy*, 59: 658–71.

Quine, W. V. O. 1950. Identity, Ostension and Hypostasis. In *From a Logical Point of View*. Cambridge, MA: Harvard University Press.

Rea, Michael. 1998. Temporal Parts Unmotivated. *Philosophical Review*, 107: 225–60.

Rea, Michael. 2014. *Metaphysics: The Basics*. New York: Routledge.

Rea, Michael. 2015. Time Travelers are not Free. *Journal of Philosophy*, 112: 266–79.

Read, Rupert. 2012. Why There Cannot be Any Such Thing as "Time Travel." *Philosophical Investigations*, 35: 138–53.

Reichenbach, Hans. 1956. *The Direction of Time*. Los Angeles: University of California Press.

Reinganum, Marc R. 1986. Is Time Travel Impossible? A Financial Proof. *Journal of Portfolio Management*, 13: 10–12.

Remnant, Peter. 1978. Peter Damian: Can God Change the Past? *Canadian Journal of Philosophy*, 8: 259–68.

Rennick, Stephanie. 2015. Things Mere Mortals Can Do, but Philosophers Can't. *Analysis*, 75: 22–6.

Rescher, N. and Urquhart, A. 1971. *Temporal Logic*. Berlin: Springer-Verlag.

Resnick, Robert. 1968. *Introduction to Special Relativity*. New York: John Wiley.

Reynolds, M. 2001. An Axiomatization of Full Computation Tree Logic. *Journal of Symbolic Logic*, 66: 1011–57.

Richmond, Alasdair. 2001. Time-Travel Fictions and Philosophy. *American Philosophical Quarterly*, 38: 305–18.

Richmond, Alasdair. 2003. Recent Work on Time Travel. *Philosophical Books*, 44: 297–309.

Richmond, Alasdair. 2008. Tom Baker: His Part in My Downfall. *Think*, 19: 35–46.

Richmond, Alasdair. 2010a. Time Travel, Parahistory and the Past Artefact Dilemma. *Philosophy*, 85: 369–73.

Richmond, Alasdair. 2010b. Time Travel Testimony and the 'John Titor' Fiasco. *Think*, 26: 7–20.

Richmond, Alasdair. 2013. Hilbert's Inferno: Time Travel for the Damned. *Ratio*, 26: 233–49.

Rickman, Gregg. 2004. The Philosophy of Time Travel: *Back to the Future* Again, or the Last Temptation of Donnie Darko. In G. Rickman, ed., *The Science Fiction Film Reader*. New York: Proscenium Publishers.

Riggs, Peter J. 1991. A Critique of Mellor's Argument Against 'Backwards' Causation. *British Journal for the Philosophy of Science*, 42: 75–86.

Riggs, Peter J. 1997. The Principal Paradox of Time Travel. *Ratio*, 10: 48–64.

Roache, Rebecca. 2009. Bilking the Bilking Argument. *Analysis*, 69: 605–11.

Roache, Rebecca. 2015. What is it Like to Affect the Past? *Topoi*, 34: 195–9.

Romero, G. E. and Torres, D. F. 2001. Self-Existing Objects and Auto-Generated Information in Chronology-Violating Space-Times: A Philosophical Discussion. *Modern Physics Letters A*, 16: 1213–22.

Rosen, Gideon. 2006. The Limits of Contingency. In Fraser MacBride, ed., *Identity and Modality*. Oxford: Oxford University Press.

Rosen, Gideon. 2010. Metaphysical Dependence: Grounding and Reduction. In R. Hale and A. Hoffman, eds., *Modality: Metaphysics, Logic, and Epistemology*. Oxford: Oxford University Press.

Rowling, J. K. 1999. *Harry Potter and the Prisoner of Azkaban*. New York: Scholastic.

Rucker, Rudy. 1984. *The Fourth Dimension: A Guided Tour of the Higher Universes*. Boston: Houghton Mifflin Company.

Russell, Bertrand. 1914. *Our Knowledge of the External World*. London: Allen & Unwin.

Salisbury, David. 2011. Large Hadron Collider could be World's First Time Machine. *Research News @Vanderbilt*. March 15, 2011.

Saucedo, Raul. 2011. Parthood and Location. In Dean Zimmerman and Karen Bennett, eds., *Oxford Studies in Metaphysics, Volume 6*. Oxford: Oxford University Press.

Schaffer, Jonathan. 2004. Counterfactuals, Causal Independence, and Conceptual Circularity. *Analysis*, 64: 299–309.

Schaffer, Jonathan. 2008. Causation and Laws of Nature: Reductionism. In John Hawthorne, Theodore Sider, and Dean Zimmerman, eds., *Contemporary Debates in Metaphysics*. Oxford: Blackwell.

Schaffer, Jonathan. 2009. On What Grounds What. In David Chalmers, David Manley, and Ryan Wasserman, eds., *Metametaphysics*. Oxford: Oxford University Press.

Schulman, L. S. 1971. Tachyon Paradoxes. *American Journal of Physics*, 39: 481–4.

Scriven, Michael. 1956. Randomness and the Causal Order. *Analysis*, 17: 5–9.

Shoemaker, Sydney and Swinburne, Richard. 1984. *Personal Identity*. Oxford: Basil Blackwell.

Sider, Theodore. 1997a. Four-Dimensionalism. *Philosophical Review*, 106: 197–231.

Sider, Theodore. 1997b. A New Grandfather Paradox? *Philosophy and Phenomenological Research*, 57: 139–44.

Sider, Theodore. 1999. Presentism and Ontological Commitment. *Journal of Philosophy*, 96: 325–47.

Sider, Theodore. 2001. *Four-Dimensionalism: An Ontology of Persistence and Time*. Oxford: Clarendon Press.

Sider, Theodore. 2002. Time Travel, Coincidences and Counterfactuals. *Philosophical Studies*, 110: 115–38.

Sider, Theodore. 2004. Replies to Gallois, Hirsch and Markosian. *Philosophy and Phenomenological Research*, 68: 674–87.

Sider, Theodore. 2005. Traveling in A- and B-Time. *The Monist*, 88: 329–35.

Simon, Jonathan. 2005. Is Time Travel a Problem for the Three-Dimensionalist? *The Monist*, 88: 353–61.

Simons, Peter. 1987. *Parts: A Study in Ontology*. Oxford: Clarendon Press.

Sklar, Lawrence. 1981. Time, Reality, and Relativity. In Richard Healey, ed., *Reduction, Time, and Reality*. Cambridge: Cambridge University Press.

Skow, Brad. Unpublished. Notes on the Grandfather Paradox.

Slater, Matthew H. 2005. The Necessity of Time Travel (on Pain of Indeterminacy). *The Monist*, 88: 362–9.

Slote, Michael. 1978. Time in Counterfactuals. *Philosophical Review*, 87: 3–27.

Smart, J. J. C. 1949. The River of Time. *Mind*, 58: 483–94.

Smart, J. J. C. 1963. Is Time Travel Possible? *Journal of Philosophy*, 60: 237–41.

Smeenk, Chris and Wüthrich, Christian. 2011. Time Travel and Time Machines. In Craig Callender, ed., *The Oxford Handbook of Philosophy of Time*. Oxford: Oxford University Press.

Smith, Donald. 2009. Mereology without Weak Supplementation. *Australasian Journal of Philosophy*, 87: 505–11.

Smith, J. W. 1985. Time Travel and Backward Causation. *Cogito*, 3: 57–67.

Smith, Nicholas J. J. 1997. Bananas Enough for Time Travel? *British Journal for the Philosophy of Science*, 48: 363–89.

Smith, Nicholas J. J. 1998. The Problems of Backward Time Travel. *Endeavour*, 22: 156–8.

Smith, Nicholas J. J. 2004. Review of Robin Le Poidevin, *Travels in Four Dimensions: The Enigmas of Space and Time*. *Australasian Journal of Philosophy*, 82: 527–30.

Smith, Nicholas J. J. 2005. Why Would Time Travelers Try to Kill Their Younger Selves? *The Monist*, 88: 388–95.

Smith, Nicholas J. J. 2013. Time Travel. In Edward N. Zalta, ed., *The Stanford Encyclopedia of Philosophy*. <https://plato.stanford.edu/>.

Smith, Nicholas J. J. 2015. Why Time Travellers (Still) Cannot Change the Past. *Portuguese Journal of Philosophy*, 71: 677–94.

Smith, Quentin. 1993. *Language and Time*. New York: Oxford University Press.

Sorenson, Roy. 1987. Time Travel, Parahistory, and Hume. *Philosophy*, 62: 227–36.

Spencer, Joshua. 2013. What Time Travelers Cannot *not* Do (but are Responsible for Anyway). *Philosophical Studies*, 166: 149–62.

Sprigge, Timothy L. S. 1970. *Facts, Worlds and Belief*. London: Routledge & Kegan Paul.

Stalnaker, Robert C. 1968. A Theory of Conditionals. In Nicholas Rescher, ed., *Studies in Logical Theory*. Oxford: Blackwell.

Stevenson, Gordon Park. 2005. Time Travel, Agency, and Nomic Constraint. *The Monist*, 88: 396–412.

Stocker, Kurt. 2012. The Time Machine in our Minds. *Cognitive Science*, 36: 385–420.

Stocker, Michael. 1971. 'Ought' and 'Can'. *Australasian Journal of Philosophy*, 49: 303–16.

Suddendorf, T. and Corballis, M. 1997. Mental Time Travel and the Evolution of the Human Mind. *Genetic, Social, and General Psychology Monographs*, 123: 133–67.

Suri, Jeremi. 2008. The Nukes of October: Richard Nixon's Secret Plan to Bring Peace to Vietnam. *Wired Magazine*, 16: 160.

Swinburne, Richard. 1966. Affecting the Past. *Philosophical Quarterly*, 16: 341–7.

Swinburne, Richard. 1968. *Space and Time*. London: Macmillan.

Taylor, Richard. 1962. Fatalism. *Philosophical Review*, 71: 56–66.

Teller, Paul. 1983. Quantum Physics, the Identity of Indiscernibles and Some Unanswered Questions. *Philosophy of Science*, 50: 309–19.

Thom, Paul. 1975. Time Travel and Non-Fatal Suicide. *Philosophical Studies*, 27: 211–16.

Thomson, Judith Jarvis. 1965. Time, Space, and Objects. *Mind*, 74: 1–27.

Thomson, Judith Jarvis. 1983. Parthood and Identity Across Time. *Journal of Philosophy*, 80: 201–20.

Thorne, K. S. 1995. *Black Holes and Time Warps: Einstein's Outrageous Legacy*. New York: W. W. Norton.

Tichý, Paul. 1976. A Counterexample to the Stalnaker–Lewis Analysis of Counterfactuals. *Philosophical Studies*, 29: 271–3.

Todd, Patrick. 2016. Future Contingents are all False! On Behalf of a Russellian Open Future. *Mind*, 125: 775–98.

Todd, William. 1964. Counterfactual Conditionals and the Presuppositions of Induction. *Philosophy of Science*, 31: 101–10.

Tognazzini, Neal. 2017. Free Will and Time Travel. In Meghan Griffith, Neil Levy, and Kevin Timpe, eds., *The Routledge Companion to Free Will*. New York: Routledge.

Tooley, Michael. 1997. *Time, Tense, and Causation*. Oxford: Oxford University Press.

Tooley, Michael. 2002. Backward Causation and the Stalnaker–Lewis Approach to Counterfactuals. *Analysis*, 62: 191–7.

Toomey, David. 2007. *The New Time Travelers: A Journey to the Frontiers of Physics*. New York: W. W. Norton.

Torre, Stephan. 2011. The Open Future. *Philosophy Compass*, 6: 360–73.

Valaris, Markos and Michael, Michaelis. 2015. Time Travel for Endurantists. *American Philosophical Quarterly*, 52: 357–63.

van Fraassen, Bas. 1970. *An Introduction to the Philosophy of Time and Space*. New York: Random House.

van Inwagen, Peter. 1981. The Doctrine of Arbitrary Undetached Parts. *Pacific Philosophical Quarterly*, 62: 123–37.

van Inwagen, Peter. 1983. *An Essay on Free Will*. Oxford: Oxford University Press.

van Inwagen, Peter. 2010. Changing the Past. In Dean Zimmerman, ed., *Oxford Studies in Metaphysics, Volume 5*. Oxford: Oxford University Press.

Varzi, Achille. 2008. The Extensionality of Parthood and Composition. *Philosophical Quarterly*, 58: 108–33.

Varzi, Achille. 2014. Mereology. In Edward N. Zalta, ed., *The Stanford Encyclopedia of Philosophy*. <https://plato.stanford.edu/>.

Vihvelin, Kadri. 1996. What Time Travelers Cannot Do. *Philosophical Studies*, 81: 315–30.

Vihvelin, Kadri. 2011a. Two Objections to the Possibility of Time Travel. *Vihvelin.com*.

Vihvelin, Kadri. 2011b. Fatalists and Hard Determinists Can Defend Time Travel. *Vihvelin.com*.

Vihvelin, Kadri. 2011c. Ability, 'Can', and Counterfactuals. *Vihvelin.com*.

Vihvelin, Kadri. 2011d. Counterfactuals, Indicatives and What Time Travelers Can't Do. *Vihvelin.com*.

Vihvelin, Kadri. 2011e. Time Travel: Horwich vs. Sider. *Vihvelin.com*.

Vihvelin, Kadri. 2013. *Causes, Laws, and Free Will: Why Determinism Doesn't Matter*. Oxford: Oxford University Press.

Visser, M. 1995. *Lorentzian Wormholes: From Einstein to Hawking*. New York: American Institute of Physics Press.

Vranas, Peter. 2005. Do Cry Over Spilt Milk: Possibly You Can Change the Past. *The Monist*, 88: 370–87.

Vranas, Peter. 2009. Can I Kill My Younger Self? Time Travel and the Retrosuicide Paradox. *Pacific Philosophical Quarterly*, 90: 520–34.

Vranas, Peter. 2010. What Time Travelers May be Able to Do. *Philosophical Studies*, 150: 115–21.

Warnock, G. J. 1953. Every Event Has a Cause. In Anthony Flew, ed., *Logic and Language*. Oxford: Basil Blackwell.

Wasserman, Ryan. 2003a. Hud Hudson's *A Materialist Metaphysics of the Human Person*. *Philo*, 6: 307–13.

Wasserman, Ryan. 2003b. The Argument from Temporary Intrinsics. *Australasian Journal of Philosophy*, 81: 413–19.

Wasserman, Ryan. 2004a. Framing the Debate over Persistence. *Metaphysica*, 5: 67–80.

Wasserman, Ryan. 2004b. The Constitution Question. *Noûs*, 38: 693–710.

Wasserman, Ryan. 2005. The Problem of Change. PhD Thesis, Rutgers University.

Wasserman, Ryan. 2006a. The Future Similarity Objection Revisited. *Synthese*, 150: 57–67.

Wasserman, Ryan. 2006b. The Problem of Change. *Philosophy Compass*, 1: 48–57.

Wasserman, Ryan. 2009. Material Constitution. In Edward N. Zalta, ed., *The Stanford Encyclopedia of Philosophy*. <https://plato.stanford.edu/>.

Wasserman, Ryan. 2011. Dispositions and Generics. *Philosophical Perspectives*, 25: 425–53.

Wasserman, Ryan. 2013. Personal Identity, Indeterminacy, and Obligation. In G. Gasser and M. Stefan, eds., *Personal Identity: Simple or Complex?* Cambridge: Cambridge University Press.

Wasserman, Ryan. 2015. Lewis on Backward Causation. *Thought*, 4: 141–51.

Wasserman, Ryan. 2016. Theories of Persistence. *Philosophical Studies*, 173: 243–50.

Wasserman, Ryan. 2017a. Time Travel, Ability, and Arguments by Analogy. *Thought*, 6: 17–23.

Wasserman, Ryan. 2017b. Vagueness and the Laws of Metaphysics. *Philosophy and Phenomenological Research*, 95: 66–89.

Wasserman, Ryan. Forthcoming. Freedom and Time Travel. In J. Campbell, ed., *A Companion to Free Will*. Hoboken, NJ: John Wiley & Sons.

Weingard, Robert. 1979. General Relativity and the Conceivability of Time Travel. *Philosophy of Science*, 46: 328–32.

Weir, Susan. 1988. Closed Time and Causal Loops: A Defence against Mellor. *Analysis*, 48: 203–9.

Weisinger, Mort. 1944. Thompson's Time Traveling Theory. *Amazing Stories*, 18: 118–23.

Wells, H. G. 1894. Time Travelling. Possibility or Paradox? *National Observer*, March 17.

Wells, H. G. 1981. A Complete Exposé of this Notorious Literary Humbug. In John R. Hammond, ed., *H. G. Wells: Interviews and Recollections*. Totowa, NJ: Barnes & Noble.

Wells, H. G. 2009. *The Time Machine*. New York: W. W. Norton.

Westerståhl, Dag. 2005. Generalized Quantifiers. In Edward N. Zalta, ed., *The Stanford Encyclopedia of Philosophy*. <https://plato.stanford.edu/>.

Wheeler, J. A. and Feynman, R. P. 1949. Classical Electrodynamics in Terms of Direct Interparticle Action. *Reviews of Modern Physics*, 21: 425–33.

Wiggins, David. 1968. On Being in the Same Place at the Same Time. *Philosophical Review*, 77: 90–5.

Wiggins, David. 1980. *Sameness and Substance*. Cambridge, MA: MIT Press.

Wilkerson, T. E. 1973. Time and Time Again. *Analysis*, 48: 173–7.

Wilkerson, T. E. 1979. More on Time and Time Again. *Philosophy*, 54: 110–12.

Williams, D. C. 1951. The Myth of Passage. *Journal of Philosophy*, 48: 457–72.

Williamson, Timothy. 1994. *Vagueness*. London: Routledge.

Wilsch, Tobias. 2015. The Nomological Account of Ground. *Philosophical Studies*, 172: 3293–312.

Woodward, James. 2008. Causation and Manipulation. In Edward N. Zalta, ed., *The Stanford Encyclopedia of Philosophy*. <https://plato.stanford.edu/>.

Wright, Crispin. 1983. Keeping Track of Nozick. *Analysis*, 43: 134–40.

Wright, Crispin. 1984. Comment on Lowe. *Analysis*, 44: 183–5.

Wright, John. 2006. Personal Identity, Fission and Time Travel. *Philosophia*, 34: 129–42.

Zangwill, Israel. 1895. Paradoxes of Time Travel. *Pall Mall Magazine*, 7: 153–5.

Zemach, E. M. 1968. Many Times. *Analysis*, 28: 145–51.

Zimmerman, Dean. 1995. Theories of Masses and Problems of Constitution. *Philosophical Review*, 104: 53–110.

Zimmerman, Dean. 1997. Immanent Causation. *Philosophical Perspectives*, 11: 433–71.

Zimmerman, Dean. 2002. Persons and Bodies: Constitution Without Mereology? *Philosophy and Phenomenological Research*, 64: 599–606.

Zimmerman, Dean. 2005. The A-Theory of Time, The B-Theory of Time, and 'Taking Tense Seriously'. *Dialectica*, 59: 401–57.

Zimmerman, Dean. 2011. Presentism and the Space-Time Manifold. In Craig Callender, ed., *The Oxford Handbook of Philosophy of Time*. Oxford: Oxford University Press.

Zimmerman, Dean. 2012. The Providential Usefulness of "Simple Foreknowledge." In K. J. Clark and M. Rea, eds., *Reason, Metaphysics, and Mind: New Essays on the Philosophy of Alvin Plantinga*. Oxford: Oxford University Press.

Index